Praise for *Reading, Wanting, and Broken Economics*

"This stimulating study of bookshops as 'insatiable' sites of openly participatory reading is an arresting departure from literary-critical perspectives, focusing instead on books as material, commodified, and contested objects of economic exchange. It is a compelling contribution to the contentious conceptualization of literature as a traded commodity, and one securely grounded in—and also provocatively reinterpreting and theoretically reconstructing—the rich historical resources of a globally-connected port city."

— James Raven FBA, author of *What is the History of the Book?*

"Simon Frost's study prompts book history to look both backwards and forwards. Its detailed study of the book trade in Southampton around 1900 recalls the Annales School, where fine-grained investigation of a single locale serves as a microcosm of a larger reality. But in its rethinking of the relationship between economics and literature, it pushes book history forwards—taking readers' desires seriously and asking how commerce and reading might be mutually constitutive. Impressively interdisciplinary, methodologically innovative, and engaged with the most recent critical theory, *Reading, Wanting, and Broken Economics* charts new ways to think about reading and its multiple payoffs."

— Simone Murray, Monash University

"*Reading, Wanting, and Broken Economics* provides a robust argument for fuller political economies of reading. In this impressive work, Simon Frost skillfully locates his case study within a richly nuanced historical, political, networked cultural, and economic landscape, which results in an intellectual—and, often entertaining—illustration of how we can study twenty-first-century readers within a commodity culture. This work is an exemplary illustration of the necessity to study historical and contemporary readers through an interdisciplinary lens. Our goal should be to do it as well as Frost does."

— DeNel Rehberg Sedo, Mount Saint Vincent University

READING, WANTING, AND BROKEN ECONOMICS

SUNY series in the History of Books, Publishing, and the Book Trades
———————
Ann R. Hawkins, Sean C. Grass, E. Leigh Bonds, editors

READING, WANTING, AND BROKEN ECONOMICS

A Twenty-First-Century Study
of Readers and Bookshops in
Southampton around 1900

SIMON R. FROST

Cover image: Gilbert's bookshop. Photographed by T.H. James, ca. 1895. Southhampton Museums, Cultural Services.

Published by State University of New York Press, Albany

© 2021 State University of New York

All rights reserved

Printed in the United States of America

No part of this book may be used or reproduced in any manner whatsoever without written permission. No part of this book may be stored in a retrieval system or transmitted in any form or by any means including electronic, electrostatic, magnetic tape, mechanical, photocopying, recording, or otherwise without the prior permission in writing of the publisher.

For information, contact State University of New York Press, Albany, NY
www.sunypress.edu

Library of Congress Cataloging-in-Publication Data

Names: Frost, Simon R., author.
Title: Reading, wanting, and broken economics : a twenty-first-century
   study of readers and bookshops in Southampton around 1900 / Simon Frost.
Description: Albany : State University of New York Press, [2021] | Series:
   SUNY series in the history of books, publishing, and the book trades |
   Includes bibliographical references and index.
Identifiers: LCCN 2020031594 | ISBN 9781438483511 (hardcover : alk. paper) |
   ISBN 9781438483528 (pbk. : alk. paper) | ISBN 9781438483535 (ebook)
Subjects: LCSH: Booksellers and bookselling—Economic aspects—England—
   Southampton—History—20th century. | Bookstores—England—
   Southampton—History—20th century. | Books and reading—England—
   Southampton—History—20th century. | Books and reading—Economic
   aspects—England—Southampton—History—20th century.
Classification: LCC Z330.6.S66 F76 2021 | DDC 381/.4500209422760904—dc23
LC record available at https://lccn.loc.gov/2020031594

10 9 8 7 6 5 4 3 2 1

To Louie, your relentless humanity insisted on this: save a seat for us, love—Kingsland 28/R, 702–3.

Contents

List of Illustrations   ix

Acknowledgments   xi

Introduction: Their or, Rather, Our Books   1

PART ONE
Theory, Methods, Tactics, and Politics

Chapter 1   Reading and Wanting: Commodity Culture Needs Readers   21

Chapter 2   Book Retail: A Test Bed for Sustainable Economics   35

Chapter 3   *Je Suis* the Unknown Public   57

Chapter 4   When Books Come to Town: International Aspirations, High Street-Bound   73

PART TWO
Southampton Stories

Chapter 5   What's Selling in Southampton: Commodity Culture, Dock Strikes, and Gas-and-Water Socialism   95

Chapter 6   The Daily Round   111

Chapter 7   High Street Southampton Bookshops   129

Chapter 8   Gilbert's: A Treetop in the Networked Forest   167

PART THREE
Factual Fictions

Chapter 9   Five Visits to Gilbert's   189

PART FOUR
Theory, Methods, Tactics, and Politics, 2.0

Chapter 10 Reading Entertainment and the Construction of
            Economic Reality   223

Chapter 11 Events, Frames, and History: Getting What We
            Want from a Book   245

Chapter 12 Whose Is the *Question Économique*?   267

Conclusion   285

Appendix: Biblioteca: Toward a Bibliography of Works
Published by H.M. Gilbert and Sons   295

Notes   301

Bibliography   347

Index   373

Illustrations and Tables

Figures

5.1	The site of Southampton's first public library, St. Mary's Hall, photographed before 1936.	104
6.1	Facsimile of a proposed window show card, from *The Successful Bookseller*, 1906.	113
7.1	Advertisement for bookseller Robert Batt, *Southampton Annual*, 1902.	146
7.2	Southampton High Street, Below Bar, showing on the left the bookshop of Robert Batt, after 1900.	147
7.3	Topographical Publishing Company, in Pembroke Square, 1899.	149
7.4	Advertisement for a range of services from George Buxey, 1895.	151
7.5	Thomas James's secondhand bookshop, photographed by his son, Thomas Hibberd James, after 1886.	153
7.6	View of Gilbert's bookshop, 26 1/2 High Street, Above Bar, photographed by T. H. James, ca. 1895.	154
7.7	The all-round book business of John Adams, 1899.	155
7.8	Advertisement for Lankester and Crook, selling everything from a circulating library service to ironmongery.	158
7.9	Lankester and Crook, County Supply Stores, Obelisk Road, Woolston, ca. 1896.	159

8.1	"Ye Olde Booke Shoppe," a carefully directed advertisement for bookseller Henry March Gilbert, 1896.	168
8.2	Typographic insistence: advertisement for Gilbert's, from Bernard Street days, in *Hampshire Advertiser*, 1873.	173
8.3	Henry March Gilbert, seated, left.	179
9.1	Gilbert's bookshop.	190

Maps

7.1	Southampton bookstores, 1876.	133
7.2	Southampton bookstores, 1887.	134
7.3	Southampton bookstores, 1897.	135
7.4	Southampton bookstores, 1900–1901.	136
7.5	Southampton bookstores, 1905–1907.	137

Tables

8.1	Gilbert's circulating library charges.	176
8.2	Gilbert's circulating library charges.	177
10.1	Four transactions and their following gains.	237
10.2	Four yeild-positions and their results.	237

Acknowledgments

This research was intended to be a modest investigation of book retail but was derailed—or, rather, developed in unforeseen ways—in 2014 by a grant from the Bournemouth University Fusion Fund, which enabled a nationwide UK survey of reader expectations. It also allowed me to undertake case-study research with the international bookselling chain John Smith's, part of the JS Group, to whose management, shop managers and employees I am extremely grateful for allowing me access to their operations. The combined experience of this and of the impact of relentless post-crash austerity throughout the 2010s called for a reframing of the entire project, and expansion of scope. Such re-framing has also meant that material in chapter 2, "*Je Suis* the Unknown Public," has been taken and reworked from an earlier publication, "Reconsidering the Unknown Public: A Puzzle of Literary Gains," in *Studies in Victorian and Modern Literature: A Tribute to John Sutherland*, edited by William Baker (Lanham, Maryland: Fairleigh Dickinson University Press, Rowman and Littlefield Publishing Group, 2015), 3–15, to whom I would like to express my gratitude for permission. For permissions, too, I would like to express thanks to the Southampton City Library, to Southampton City Archives and to Southampton Local and Maritime collections for use of several images, and to Joanne Smith in particular for invaluable assistance throughout; as well as thanks to the Bitterne Local History Society for providing such effective resources. For insights into retail book trade, thanks are due to Richard Gilbert, to the late and much-missed Emeritus Professor Iain Stevenson, and very much so to a dear friend, Sharon Murray, manager to several chain outlets, including Blackwells, Broad Street, Oxford, and Foyles, Charing Cross, London.

For invaluable criticism and for forcing me to think through various conceptual problems I could barely articulate, I would like to thank John Frow, and I would like to thank eminent economist Ha-Joon Chang for not reacting to my work as though it were a comedy. Of educators, scholars and editors who, despite my inability to stay proportionate, remained steadfast in their patient guidance, I would like to thank Simon Eliot, Leslie Howsam, Eva Hemmungs Wirten, Lars Ole Sauerberg, Henrik Kaare Nielsen, Frits Andersen, Lene Tortzen Bager, Lis Norup, Pat Shenstone and John Yeadon. As a node in a larger network, any work I might produce has only been possible because of the other nodes, so for our collective chatter to which this is one further utterance I remain completely indebted: and of us chatterboxes—many around the annual conferences of the Society for the History of Authorship, Reading and Publishing (SHARP)—special mention should go to Tabish Khair, Anders Bøggild Christensen, David Finkelstein, Sydney Shep, Simone Murray, Corinna Norrick-Rhül, Kate Macdonald, Alexis Weedon, Ian Gadd, Paula Rabinowitz, Claire Squires, Shafquat Towheed, Jonathan Rose, Robert Rix, Peter Simonsen, and Sebastien Doubinsky, and to my colleagues at Bournemouth University and in Denmark.

Lastly, as convention leaves personal acknowledgements to last, I would like to acknowledge the support and criticism of family and generous friends, either unawares or too-painfully aware, who have affected my work immeasurably; and of those closet of all, for the root and branch without which my work is a brittle stick and we are not a grove, my undying gratitude goes to Sussi, Amanda, Nige', Ilene and Howard, and to mighty, beautiful Louie Borges Frost (1997–2016), who achieved so much more than he'll ever be told.

Introduction

Their or, Rather, Our Books

People use valuable resources to access books. They spend time and money to get hold of books, to have them, to gift them, to think about and often read them. They have expectations from books deemed worth procuring, and institutions have developed to meet, encourage, and at times create those expectations; among these institutions are bookshops, both online and off. People go to bookshops and, accepting the risks and logic of commercial exchange, trust that their resources will provide them with satisfied desire. Such a contract enables bookshops, like any other retail operation, to take part in a human drive for satisfaction. Unfortunately, when it comes to books bearing fiction or even literature, the models we have for understanding such behavior emerge from late-nineteenth-century literature studies, based on a critical engagement with the text, validated, in many cases, solely on notions of literary judgment. Such models prevent us from understanding specific historical relationships between non-professional readers and their books.

An alternative would be to think about bookshop users and their fictions in terms of desire, and to examine the books' abilities to negotiate those desires as material objects in a system of economic exchange. The model could be appended to the various histories of printing, publishing, distribution, reading, and authorship that have built up in response to conceptions of the communication circuit, but would aim to account for the experience of books, both social and individual, based around the bookshop as a metonymic site for reading within commodity culture. The risk, however, is that the project could be confused with brute marketization. It might mistakenly be thought of as a surrender of those same literary values that the judgments of literary studies seek to maintain.

That marketization has already taken place. Like the capital-intensive early-modern book market, it pre-dates literary studies. The book is among the oldest of all commodities in the West, as John Frow observes in his study "Gift and Commodity," and its commercially mediated institutions already (re)issue the fiction-bearing objects that literary criticism elects to study.[1] By way of resistance, though, it should be noted that life in commodity culture has not been solely a depressing narrative of exploitation. The period establishing the regulation of desire through transnational market economies was also the period of late-nineteenth- and twentieth-century Anglo-American, European, Latin-American, Asian, and African leftism that pushed through every progressive labor-policy step that for many in the privileged West appears now to be such a given. Despite being colonized by the free market, people have taken opportunities for other welfare actions, and currently the breadth of people's experience is far wider than only a reductionist, neo-liberal history in a moment of late capitalism. Not despite but including the economic framing, therefore, the belief that a desire can be satisfied in a bookshop is not only deeply personal and irrational, but also social and political. It is active desire, in the system of economic exchange, that prevents the reader from becoming only a victim of what Adorno and Horkheimer insisted was the "mass deception" of the culture industry.[2]

By focusing on the bookshop, a distinction comes straightway into play between the academy-generated readings of literary professionals, in contrast to the readings of those living up to the requirements of commodity cultre. Leah Price described the two approaches separated by a "gulf," between the distinctive literary-critical reading and the prosaic readings scholars imagine people undertake far removed from the world of scholarship, more recently mapped "on to a division of labour between two disciplines, literary criticism and cultural history."[3] But academics are also driven by desires, from inculcating a love of fiction among students to strategic maneuvers in a career plan, and in the bookshop as a metonymic site academics cannot pretend they are not shopping. The literary is subsumed into a continuum, where Austen, Eliot, and Proust are in a bookcase next to Terry Pratchett and George R.R. Martin. Mohsin Hamid and Ngugi wa Thiong'o are along the corridor past Danielle Steel. The bookshop is insatiable. It subsumes all books and it takes in (both positively and negatively) all kinds of aspirations, including access to literary merit.

That there is a distinction in these two approaches to reading has long been recognized. In their refreshing analysis of literary and economic value, and of the history of its false dichotomy, Joshua Clover and Christopher Nealon conclude that the discourse in the humanities has been dominated by "a domain model of 'economics' and 'art' that endlessly worries over their degree of separation or inter-mixed-ness, [and] worries about the dominion of one over the other."[4] Its historians place the phenomenon back to at least the early nineteenth century, when "literary society isolated itself in an aura of indifference and rejection toward the buying and reading public" and from which site of production inspired readings attesting to the intelligibility of work could be generated, "while paradoxically excluding the public of non-producers from the entire business of attesting."[5] As Ika Willis confirms in her comprehensive history of reception, "The key forces in the modern construction of reading and the reader are, firstly, the privatisation of reading . . . and secondly, the division between 'good' and 'bad' forms of reading, and the way these map onto gender, class and race."[6] Part of literary studies' cartographical task, then, has been to address levels of inclusiveness while continuing, in an echo Alexander Pope's "horror of literary commodification," to 'Guard the Sure Barrier' against an ever-encroaching economic discourse.[7]

Conversely, on the far side, from where economics encroaches, what were once inalienable objects beyond the marketplace have increasingly become alienable market commodities, in a continual if uneven push "towards the commodification of everything."[8] There may be pushbacks—the sale of human bodies is no longer permitted, through anti-slavery laws—but the push has a habit of looking elsewhere: the sale of organs, blood, semen, and unfertilized eggs has become so, with evidence of accompanying kidney bazaars and cesarean sales.[9] Even emotional empathy has become affective labor to the care service industry. The push may have begun with late-medieval enclosures of common land to create more profit-extracting private space, but it continues with the planet's atmosphere, which, like ice caps and fish stock, also once belonged to communities, but which in free-market solutions to environmental degradation can now be parceled into commodity units for its "protection," with charges applied for the right to pollute it. The keenest encroachment comes from the ideological capture of economics by neoliberalism, which seeks to explain the entirety of life according to economic precepts. Gary Becker, Nobel economist and former president of the neoliberal Mont Pelerin Society, sought to apply economic thinking well beyond the realms of the economy. In the systematic calculation of how maximized ends can be met through scarce means, Becker and his acolytes deduced the notion of intra-household bargaining, where family relations were discovered to be nothing less than maximizations of personal utility, rather than, as Ha-Joon Chang observes, relations "between real-life family members, with their love, loathing, empathy, cruelty and commitments."[10] So pervasive is this application of economic thinking that popularizing volumes can regularly declare how the seeming altruism of parents is actually their "means of investing indirectly for their own old age."[11]

Certainly, any ideological pretense to the reified sanctity of literature has long been questioned by sociologies of literature and in literature sociology and by newer historicisms. Critical theory can involve much more besides commitment to literary aesthetic autonomy—the recent volume *The Literary and the Social*, for example, provides a review of such boundary-crossing research.[12] And even high-modernist formalism begins to be explained partly as a result of changes to the regimes of publishing, distribution, and reading.[13] But under extreme (often financial) pressure, literary study can be tempted to reclaim its allegiance to literary autonomy and lose sight of the strategic warning issued by Heather Love that "retrenchment around disciplinary commitments to the literary is not an effective response to the crisis in the humanities" when based on "humanist arguments that depend on assumptions about the singularity of literature or the ethical value of close reading."[14] Retrenchment leaves the ground open to other disciplines, only too keen to claim explanatory rights over the satisfaction of human desires. Such a take-over by economics has intensified over the past decades, forcing academics and educators to defend the humanities generally against ambitions to turn HEI (higher education institution) activities into tradable assets under metrics-based New Public Management. An appropriate term is *financialization*. *Marketization* is often used, and to effect, but the term obscures the market's long history and also that markets are social. Markets since their medieval regulation involve and have always involved people, knowledge, and goods. Financialization, on the other hand, as a term of neoliberalism, aims at reduction into assets. People, their knowledge, and what they identify as goods are reconfigured as assets that can be traded or used for speculation.

In defense of the humanities from this financializing onslaught, the argument often draws back to disinterested literary judgment and away from the money-tainted shop. A spat in the arts section of a liberal British newspaper serves by way of illustration. Following popular outpourings in obituaries to Terry Pratchett, an arts critic asserted somewhat forcefully that life was too short to read Pratchett: "A middlebrow cult of the popular is holding literature to ransom," he declared and, unlike the works of Günter Grass or Gabriel García Márquez, Pratchett's were not great books that could change your life, your beliefs, and your perceptions.[15] They were merely potboilers. The article brought an immediate response claiming Pratchett's books were the opposite of potboilers, and that his works brought with them moral complexity, emotional impact, careful plotting, and urgent humanity.[16] The initial writer later published a retraction, praising some elements of Pratchett's work but still insisting that it ought not to be considered literary fiction. What both commentators shared, and what was played out within the same arts section, was a common discourse centered on literary merit, and what both were at pains to escape was the territory of the potboiler. One assigned the author to the potboiler and denied him literary merit, while the other wanted to liberate him by asserting literary merit. Their assertions of merit were a matter of judgment based on their professional close readings. But what of the merits of potboilers, which are generated and gained from processes of moneyed exchange in the bookshop? "The literary" does not have a monopoly on merit, nor does it comprise the only constituting lens through which merit can be assessed. There are other merits worthy of attention for anyone interested in the human condition. And is not that condition itself the subject of fiction?

Rita Felski has identified the professionalized interrogation of texts as something distinct from other uses of literatures we might find on a city's main shopping street, known colloquially as the high street (though she does not present the distinction in the frame of economics). In contemporary Anglo-American, European literary-critical studies, she sees an entropic standardization, where an enthusiastic hermeneutics of suspicion and exquisitely self-conscious interrogation of the text has become *de rigueur*. Reconstructed as two groups, the entropy is classified by Felski into theological and ideological styles of reading.[17] Both forms seek to shore up the distinction between professional and non-professional reading.

The theological reading refers to literature's otherworldliness (secular rather than metaphysical); to its ability to resist concept-driven interpretation and signify what all else in the world cannot. It is found across a political spectrum from Bloom's romanticism, to Kristeva's avant-garde semiotics and Levinian criticism, and can be deemed to be politically transformative. The fissure Felski sees, which invites the deconstructive crowbar, is the task of explaining how such literatures arise from and move back into the world; of why in spite of their otherworldliness they can still infiltrate and inform our lives. The ideological reading points to social conceptions of literature, whereby text is either a function of or an author to ideology. As such, the text is secondary to the social, and the analyst's terms of interpretation are in the business of understanding what the text cannot. Felski's complaint is that the literary text is hauled in to confirm what the critic already knows,[18] and the work is denied the capacity to satisfy new desires by developing our (including the critics') beliefs and commitments.

Paradoxically for the critic, any recoiling from such theological or ideological theorizations is not an option, either, since theory lies in wait: as Felski puts it, "Harold Bloom's assertion that we read 'in order to strengthen the self and learn its authentic concerns' is a quintessential theoretical statement."[19]

All the while, bubbling beneath the critical discourse is the realization that people "often turn to books for knowledge or entertainment" and remain stubbornly unwilling to "read literature 'as literature.'"[20] These people and the uses they make of the books they purchase are the focus of this study: in all its glorious mundanity or, in Felski's terms, its "heterogeneous and complex microcosms, socially sculpted yet internally regulated complexes of belief and sentiments, of patterns of inertia and impulses towards innovation, of cultural commonalities interwoven with quirky dispositions."[21] Book purchases made here may accord to the spirit of modern consumerism, but the motives, as Colin Campbell would say, are

> anything but materialistic. The idea that contemporary consumers have an insatiable desire to acquire objects represents a serious misunderstanding of the mechanism, which impels people to want goods. Their basic motivation is the desire to experience in reality the pleasurable dramas which they have always enjoyed in imagination.[22]

In its simple sense, this study is an investigation of the everyday experience of shopped books, which suggests the interdiscipline known as book history, and rightly so. It sits alongside other historically attuned approaches to literature that Felski suggests are more a productive response than theological or ideological reading. But in attempting to recreate something of past understanding, historical readings run a severe risk of reducing "readers" to a homogenous research object and, in doing so, othering other readers.[23] Like theology and ideology, history ought not to become *our* alibi based on the unsophistication of past readers from whom we are distinct, so the glorious mundanity needs to remain ours.

In terms of politics and ethics, the distinction between readerships has been summarized by James Proctor and Bethan Benwell in a recent study of transnational reading groups and the reception of difference.[24] Their aim is to understand relations between disciplines of study in the university and the political domain. One cannot simply generate findings in the academy, they claim, and in the absence of determinable measures they insist they will affect the political domain, as anyone who has provided evidence of social impact from literary studies will know. Such an assumed transference is a political fantasy resorted to by contemporary literary study as a testament to its socially transformative power. The two realms of reading are bridged by neither political fantasy nor aspired-to (theological and ideological) reading practices. As a response, Proctor and Benwell argue that if literary studies are to retain an effective politics they must be self-reflexive about their core practice of reading. They acknowledge an analytical and cognitive approach to professional reading in the academy but then compare this to other motivations and to protocols and procedures undertaken, not by interpretive communities in the specialized cognitive analytical sense, but by "reading communities of practice."[25] By producing a transnational study of these other communities of practice, Proctor and Benwell reveal those communities' differing but equally valid and valuable reading protocols.

In his "The Ethical practice of Modernity: The Example of Reading," John Guillory further maps differences between professional and nonprofessional modes of reading. Professional reading requires *work* (compensated by salary) that follows *disciplinary* conventions and requires *vigilance*, which in Kantian terms might be translated as disinterestedness.[26] By contrast, lay reading is firstly a practice of leisure. Its motivation is primarily pleasure and the differences of its conventions are noted in differences of occasions and places of reading (in bed, or on tube trains, or "read" through headphones while commuting). These are two modes of reading, but to invalidate one by the value judgment of the other is to perform an ideological and theological act that should have no place in neutral *sciences humaines*.

The suspicion is that what truly divides and also what resolves the distinction in readerships is concerns about populism and, beneath that, perceptions about power and money. John Conrad described how his father, Joseph, after a day's writing would sit up at night reading John's *Boy's Own Paper*. John knew from the traces of cigarette ash he found between the pages in the mornings. He recalled, too, his father's more general borrowing of the family's reading materials, in between the serious business of writing novels. Andrew Glazzard, in whose work this vignette appears, uses the image to underline an exchange between the uncompromising, complex Conrad of early modernism and the Conrad of gripping adventure and espionage fiction.[27] Glazzard cites a list of studies that now add to Conrad-the-modernist an appreciation of how more popular forms wove into the authoring and reception of Conrad-for-the-people. Equivalent structures could be drawn for other canon authors: the elements of the comic novel in Joyce; or for George Eliot, whose formal epitome of literary realism *Middlemarch* she insisted be coordinated with the demands of the market, including its clothing in "Dickens' Green."[28] What Glazzard struggles against, though, is a "widely held orthodoxy that literary fiction and genre [popular] fiction are two separate categories . . . [and] its near ubiquity: across the political spectrum, from Richard Hoggart to Evelyn Waugh, from Theodore Adorno to Q.D. Leavis, cultural arbiters otherwise separated by the widest possible ideological gulfs have united in the view that popular literary culture is a contradiction in terms."[29] On the conservative right, the Arnoldian denigration of popular philistinism comes as no surprise, but on the intellectual left Glazzard traces the phenomenon, too: Frederic Jameson's *The Political Unconscious* (1981) names the populist elements in Conrad's *Lord Jim* as degraded cultural forms; Jeremy Hawthorn and Keith Carabine are cited, too, as finding the popular elements of Conrad to be mere stepping stones to a greater literary modernism. The height of intellectual Marxist hierarchy where popular is held low, Glazzard suggests, is found in the " 'Frankfurt school' of social and cultural theorists, [who] inevitably see popular fiction as a form of commercialised and capitalist (literary) production."[30] Across the political spectrum from left to right, the distinction comprises, on the one side, a professionalized exegesis of the literary text, and on the other, an undiscerning public unable to appreciate and, at worst, uninterested in reading great literature.

The struggle over terms is a power struggle in the Foucauldian sense, between reading practices and between ways of using fiction. It is fought throughout a matrix of terms, including "literature," "fiction," "book," "text," "work," "value," "commodity," "popular," "reading," "gatekeeping," "social transformation," and "cultural connoisseurship." Diffused throughout this struggle, I cannot help but believe, is the issue of economic exchange: the fear of it or at least a conviction of its corrupting power, lined against an everyday acceptance by people that economically framed exchange is an effective means of reciprocally obtaining what you need. Economic exchange is the element that both dogs and is evaded by the very category "professionalized literature." It is the element that will provide the resolution to this study of not specific literatures, but desire-negotiating agencies making best use of their bookshops. But it is also the element that will need to be redefined, because while the humanities worries about economics in the composition of the research objects its studies, institutionalized economics is increasingly accumulating explanatory territory, without ever acknowledging that political force has been a necessary component of both its history and of capital growth.

The study begins by asking what happens when we treat fiction primarily as a traded commodity. Its final answer is not solely inward-looking in defining a new taxonomy of lay reading, but, much to what would be Gary Becker's disapproval, it also finds the logical necessity of rethinking economics in the post-crash era, or at the least that section of the market that comprises symbolic goods, as a political economy.

This study of books and the wants that readers seek to satisfy through their reading sets its case in the early decades of commodity culture, first in Britain, through the end of the nineteenth century and the beginning of the twentieth, at the start of what Martin Lyons calls the golden age of the book. This was the period before radio and electronic mass media added a complexity whose suspected vulgarity persuaded scholarship to study those platforms as something distinct from the literature-carrying book. It was a period when the reading public acquired several new layers and books flowed toward the "lowest" and furthest audiences "desacralized, an everyday object of consumption like soap or potatoes."³¹ The study is situated in the UK port city of Southampton, which connected a globalized commercial network of cultural exchange through the mechanism of shipping. The new worlds of Argentina and Brazil, of Australia, New Zealand, and South Africa were connected by timetabled profit-generating oceanic trade with the old worlds of Hamburg and London. As cocreators of this network, Southampton people and their machines traded in goods and desires, and in books and dreams: "from carpenter's nails to chairs, paintings (or more often prints) and books—especially the ideas inside books—as well as people."³²

Onshore, Sotonians (the all-too-human inhabitants of Southampton) derived a percentage from helping create the network, and when not tending to the production side of this business, they spent their disposable income and leisure time on chasing the same possibilities that were the network's currency. They dreamed of relief from labor, of pleasure and sex, and of love and children; of power over disliked events, of revenge against enemies, and of justice that might err on the side of favoritism. Reviewing the Christmas holidays, when the network's desires had been resolutely chased, the 4 January 1899 issue of *The Southamptonian* held that "there has been less serious drunkenness than was ever known during the festive season"; that the "cry of bad trade and little money stirring has been proved utterly false by the crowds attending the places of amusement, the amount of railway travelling, and the clearance of the butchers and poulterers' shops"; that Sotonians were again looking forward to the weekend's favorite sports, justifying a full page of "football notes"; and that a major delight would be Southampton *World's Fair* at the St. Mary's Drill Hall (more prosaic than its cosmopolitan forebearers) offering "Hart and Rudd comedians, Sam Darling, eccentric character comedian, De Ora the Gymnast, Grand tug of war contest: contests, contests, contests . . . including . . . Grand onion eating contest, mouth organ contest, comic singing contest, lady or gentleman making the funniest face looking through a horse collar, 'climbing the pole,' and grand smoking competition; admission to the hall 1d."³³ That same edition of *The Southamptonian* offered chapter 1 of *The Ruby Ring*, in serial, by Ida Linn Gerard, author of *Caught* and other tales, about Paul Vere and his betrothed Judith, whose expectations on Paul's miserly grandfather do not go as they hope. Issue number 3 appended to *The Ruby Ring* a further fiction entitled *One of Life's Ordeals* by R. Silverman.³⁴ Sustained by and sustaining Sotonians, as well as doing both for the city's book trade—the popularity of *Ruby Ring* helped keep afloat fledgling publications such as *The Southamptonian*—fiction was as much imbricated in this complex of leisure-time desire as De Ora the Gymnast. Fiction promised a brief freedom from pain and the maximization of pleasure—exactly the terms on which the discipline of neoclassical economics is based, articulated by one of its earliest theorists, William Stanley Jevons: according to Jevons, the proper subject of economics is nothing less than a calculus of pleasure and pain.[35] Fiction for Sotonians formed part of a trade in desires and helped construct an economy not so very different from that which continues to touch the city's quays. And it is the nature of those differences or their lack that is the subject of the following chapters.

This Southampton-based study borrows partly from an aspect of cis-history that, to paraphrase David Armitage's definition, investigates a unique location within a world economy and seeks to define that uniqueness as the result of the interactions between local particularity and a wider web of connections.[36] Southampton's book retail may be uniquely local, but its particulars are formed *because* it is a node in a larger network of global trade. Such interconnectedness, Armitage suggests, can be most fruitfully applied to the very places most obviously transformed by their global connections: port towns and cities. From its boom period in the middle of the sixteenth century, when trade flourished with ports throughout the Baltic and Mediterranean, Southampton has developed its international reach to include the world, and, if we follow the logic of six degrees of separation, thus potentially to each of the world's book-reading households. Though the study remains ingloriously rooted in a grayed British city, it also knows that it is a boat ride away from New World plains and clear Nordic skies.

The current study does not claim to provide a history *per se*. For a historian, cis or otherwise, the work would begin with the historical material and derive from that whatever narrative it could. By contrast, the current narrative is a twenty-first century construction. The few histories available of Southampton and its book retail trade have been assembled and supplemented with original archival work, but the world it looks back to is seen through a postmodern perspective. More a historically informed cultural criticism, the study shows how book retail around 1900 might be understood if we were to implement a twenty-first-century understanding of theory. Thus, a version of Southampton of the past becomes a test for the robustness of the study's applied theory, and a historical justification for why in future we might begin to rethink the market for symbolic goods along new lines.

Therefore, taking its interdisciplinarity seriously, this study combines its historical research with quantitative surveys, critical theory, and practice-based research. The key research question the study asks is what happens when we treat books like commodities, as all shoppers do. The answer, with several intermediate steps, is that doing so reveals how neoliberalism's presentation of economics conceals the political and cultural constituents of market behavior. Were we to admit the cultural political dimension of market economics, especially in consumption studies of symbolic goods (books), we might be forced to embrace a conception of economics as it is, which is a political economy, and for consistency's sake abandon monetary and fiscal policies based on neoliberalism.

In reaching this conclusion, the study first enlists the historical Southampton High Street into the role of ahistorical metonymic site for life created by commodity culture. Instead of the institution of Art or *Ars Litterarum* constituting literature's frame, on the metonymic High Street commodity culture does the framing, in which reading becomes not a matter of finding meanings "in" texts, but of obtaining gains (through the market contract)—sometimes profound ones: remedies against loneliness, new identities, comforts, and pastimes. But to be more than a mere bridging exercise between the praxis of reading and the realm of the market, the study must then establish this commercially enabled material semiotics as a social praxis, and thus potentially a new kind of economy. This latter aim is achieved by conceiving the praxis as a specific actor network (based on the actor-network theory of Michel Callon, Bruno Latour, and others), continually (re)creating itself in real time, *a posteriori*. Thus, the politically economic High Street this study constructs has been consistently remade from historical events, including Southampton's retail High Street shops, trade-practice and legislation (such as the Net Book Agreement [NBA]), relationships between actants (those structured by scales of economy and those derived from friendship and love), and most importantly including the voices of the trade's unknown readers—all of which begins to reconstrue in cultural and political terms the demand side to this economy.

Divided into four parts, the study sets out in part 1 its understanding of the High Street, of the readings that take place there, and of the literary and economic theories and analytical methods that have enabled this understanding, along with the tactics and politics behind the study's aims. Part 2 provides a narrative specific to Southampton's book retail around 1900, in the early days of commodity culture, to provide a historical case that the study's conception of the High Street might measure. If that measure holds, then presumably there would be corroboratory evidence in remnants of readers' experience, which part 3 finds, contentiously, in historical fiction rather than in generalizable archival evidence that has eluded so many studies of reading history. Finally, if we are able to accept that the substantial "if" of parts 1 to 3 is plausible, then part 4 in its revisiting of part 1 can set out what could become a new understanding of reading and consumption, and grounds for a new form of culturally and socially based political economic modeling.

In part 1, chapter 1 develops the concept of reading for gains and introduces "efferent" reading, after the economist Deirdre McCloskey (from Latin *effero* "I take away"). In proposing that the chief gain of reading is identity formation, it brings the study in line with consumption studies, in that consuming significance becomes possible only through reading. Reading is therefore necessary for the consumption of all intangible value, thus explaining why commodity culture *needs* its readers. But unless a challenge can be mounted on the idea of identity formation (in consumption) as a purely individualist pursuit, such reasoning will remain stuck with its masculine Crusoe figure of *homo economicus*, isolated and doggedly pursuing rational self-interest. Conceptions of socially constituted identity, found in proposals such as self-discrepancy theory, are therefore introduced to show how the correlation between consumption and identity formation is impossible without a shared, collective domain that cannot be reduced to the free market's economic individualism.

Chapter 2 opens up the idea of varieties of capitalism and of economic pluralism, the need for which has become vital since the global economic crash of 2007–8, and the adoption of free-market neoliberalism that was both a root cause of the crash as well as its austere putative remedy. The suggestion is that so-called free markets, the antithesis of the cultural and political embeddedness articulated through cultural and literary studies, are themselves regulated political projects. As a test-bed for this proposition, a historical understanding of the retail booktrade is constructed following interactions between its two regimes of value: the market composed of purportedly indifferent financial structures, and the market as a social-political regime with its culturally motivated regulations and agreements—the former through various scales of economy affecting trade, and the latter through iconic regulatory controls such as the NBA. The suggestion is that presumed rational free markets in books are closer to civic markets with a sense of cultural value that is overt (and which by extension might apply equally to other areas of civic life such as health care, education, and transport).

Chapter 3 returns to the othering and gendering of the High Street shopper, in its reconsideration of the "unknown public." In parallel to William St. Clair's influential "Political Economy of Reading," the chapter examines levels of disposable income available to the unknown public, taking in tramping readers, workhouses, laborers, artisans, domestics, and the "young lady classes," as well as naming the writers who were "consumed" on the High Street. Chapter 4 follows these outlines in relation to Southampton, providing a history of leisure-time consumption, framed in surprising ways. Because while shopping defines the efferent practice of both men and women, in the negative it is valenced as something women do, duped into buying outputs that can only be commercial, while in the positive it becomes *the* condition that readers of masculinity must be seen to overcome, in works by Conrad, Kipling and the once-phenomenal but now-neglected Francis Marion Crawford.

In part 2, chapter 5 picks up the ambiguity of commodity culture as something both emancipatory and exploitative, but specifically played out between space, place, and time in Southampton. Economic history can often be presented as a linear narrative of unequal but nevertheless incremental improvement, guided by its invisible hand, whereas this study instead presumes a forked history of beneficiaries and casualties with each new development, where our assignment to one of those roles is a result of political decisions, which could and can always be decided in other ways—not an ineffable benign process, but an unforgiving divisioning created by us. This double-edged view of progress is exemplified in Henry George's *Progress and Poverty* (1879), which asked why, despite revolutionary labor-saving technologies, workers were and are still obliged to live in relative poverty. In this same dual pattern, the market that is Southampton book retail is then shown to be constantly poised between growth and collapse, as is the city's civic progress, caught between the advances of gas-and-water socialism and the turmoil of industrial conflict. The legacy of hunger and bayonets, in parallel with the progress of municipal socialism, libraries and affordable books, provides a composite frame to the efferent readings of bright and dark futures in technological fictions by H.G. Wells and George Griffith, and in emigratory calls of the New World in women settler narratives. "Progress" can mean progress or poverty depending on your position and gender in the network; and it is the exact same logic that makes credit out of debt, and debt out of credit, depending on whether you are lending or borrowing, and which turns economic growth into both a benefit and a cost.

Chapters 6, 7, and 8, the core of the study, apply the study's reasoning specifically to bookselling: providing firstly a historical narrative of book retail through the daily round of duties in a provincial bookshop; secondly in a detailed mapping and narrative of Southampton book retail from 1876 to 1907, comprising its up to twenty businesses located in or around the High Street; and thirdly a narrative of its longest-surviving business, that of Henry March Gilbert and Sons, from 1859 to 2002. Merely one segment of a new and second-hand trade in desires, books were read, robbed, and returned alongside stationery and leather goods, glasswear and dressing cases, with no more "singularity" than any other traded enablers. Outward facing, these businesses occasionally referred to themselves as bookshops, but sideways, upways, and downways they helped sustain a complex commercial, political, and cultural network consisting of newsagencies and printers, binders and publishers, and by trading in social improvements and civic careers, as much as tourism and local entertainments.

Part 3, chapter 9, comprises an exercise in practice-based research, in fictionalized but fact-based historical accounts of five visits to Gilbert's bookshop, drawing together the various forces that create each person's estimate of what books will best satisfy their desires. Far from a rational calculation to maximize utility, the consumption choices of these readers are the result of charged personal histories, shaped by factors of class, gender and race, otherwise written out of free-market methodologies based on universal (white) "man."

Part 4 expresses a new understanding of the consumption of books based on framed historical evidence, beginning with chapter 10, which considers how consumption of symbolic goods might be re-thought of as reading, and how, if reading is always inter-textual and social, it cannot be accounted for through the rational methodological individualism of neoclassical economics. With such a strategy, consumption becomes social reading, thereby rendering the key masculine figure of *homo economicus* much less useful than his market-active sister, *homo narrans*. From its survey of entertainment studies, the gains of reading for entertainment are then given greater depth beyond mere hedonic pleasure. Using a thick description of what happens when we entertain ourselves with literary texts, and empirical qualitative and quantitative studies of non-professional reading, I make a cautious proposal of what are the chief gains from reading: personal encouragement, relaxation, guidance, but also bibliotherapeutic remedies for boredom, loneliness, and pain, as well as very much the need for socialization and society building. If our society is an ongoing imaginative creation, then efferent readings are instrumental in the sustaining of it.

Chapter 11 addresses actor-network theory and the use of framing, examining how the value of symbolic goods, both in use and exchange, can be derived from relations within the social network, and how commodity culture provides those relations with a longevity sufficient to create a "market." Thus constituted, fiction becomes a networked event, comprising people, places, and bibliographic objects. A fiction becomes a Net Work, whose force is derived through social interactions rather than from any intrinsic meaning of the text. Through this application of network thinking, the chapter can therefore address the problem of recovering evidence of historic readers, whose thoughts are often no longer extant, but whose networks that were constructive of them are still active. In the same way that it is meaningful to talk of an Epsom Derby, as a node in the network of dreams for easy wealth by Southampton readers, it is meaningful to talk of a durable coincidence of leisure time, books, and disposable income that we designate in High Street bookshops. If that thesis can be accepted, it is then possible to understand the five visits to Gilbert's from part 3 as more detailed articulations of this chapter's surprising factual case studies of reading experience, of people reading Tennyson, Marx, and Patrick Hamilton's much-lesser-known *Hangover Square*, as evidence of not only against-the-grain efferent reading but of the power it has to intertwine with cultural and political forces.

Finally, it remains for chapter 12 to confront the disjuncture between the cultural network in which symbolic goods perform, and a regime of economic values that is purportedly apolitical—resolvable if we consider that the account of the market given by economics is inadequate when it omits the market's cultural composition. Working through the ever-mounting objections to the institutionalized neoclassical economics (inconstancies that neoliberalism exploits), the study calls for a new paradigm of economics that might begin with the study of consumption of symbolic goods epitomized in the history of the retail book trade.

In conclusion, it is proposed that the sure barrier that divides a regime of literary-critical distinction on the one hand and popular commodity values on the other is a false barrier based on prejudice around populism and on the misconceptions of economics. Furthermore, if the barrier is maintained by people struggling for ownership of the progressive qualities of book-borne fiction, then the struggle is a contradiction in terms. Far better would be a combined effort to provide a proper account of exchange in the rich network of books, places, and people in commodity culture that the truncated narrative of neoclassical economics has rightly called but inadequately understood as "the market." From that effort, we might be able to create a social description of human exchange and consumption, otherwise called a *political economy*, in which aggregated market behavior is replaced by consensus, and self-interest by whatever it is we, collectively, choose to be the most important of our desires. If this study were a B-movie, as some commentators may end up claiming, it would have a pithy strapline, voiced in gravelly baritone: the film poster would show a corporate edifice of glass and steel, beneath which a young girl holds a cheap paperback; the strap would run "When the book of the world is closed, ask a reader."

PART ONE
Theory, Methods, Tactics and Politics

Chapter 1

Reading and Wanting
Commodity Culture Needs Readers

In questioning what constitutes the demand side of the book market, this study of correlations between consumption and reading will focus on readerly gains and intangible values derived from symbolic goods—in this case, books. By considering how desire-negotiating readers may have used their published fiction in commercial contexts, it should be possible to open up some of the complexities involved when consuming symbolic goods. As Rosalind Williams says in her *ur*-study of mass consumption, it may be obvious how material commodities satisfy physical needs, but "less evident, but of overwhelming significance in understanding modern society, is how merchandise can fill needs of the imagination."[1] Indeed, in building her exposition of goods invested genuinely with our hopes and desires, Williams adopts Hannah Arendt's approach to consumption as something ambiguous that has the capacity not only to crudely sustain but also to give meaning to life; or, as Williams explains, based not only on *consumere*, to use up and destroy what has been produced, but on the more positive relationship between humans and their goods of *consummare*, to bring to fruition, to fulfill and to consummate.[2] What is required, therefore, is a theoretical approach and method that does not interfere with a sense of readers "consuming" published texts for progressive benefits they construe for themselves. If readers are not to be reduced to either subjects at the blunt end of market indifference or sovereigns impervious to market rhetoric, then we need terms that highlight desire and readers' choices that cover a spectrum from the most selfish to the most altruistic. The following section, then, will look at various goals of reading, suggesting "efferent" reading as a gain-oriented solution.

Current liberalist economic thinking is that we follow a path of individualized self-interest in the belief that Adam Smith's prescription may produce in the aggregate an overall benefit for society. It is a population of Robinson Crusoes, each *homo economicus* pursuing self-interest, which creates the social good. Leaving aside that not every economist has agreed that aggregated self-interest produces social good—"It is *not* a correct deduction from the Principles of Economics that enlightened self-interest always operates in the public interest" (Keynes's italics)[3]—it suffices to question how isolated is the economic model's isolated self. According to economic prescription, with a Robinson Crusoe–like figure, we only have to think of individual preferences and not where those preferences come from. But away from Crusoe's island, our preferences "are strongly formed by our social environment—family, neighbourhood, schooling, social class," and our consumption is not only *of* different things but *driven by* differences that are inescapably social: "this process of socialization means we cannot really treat individuals as atoms separable from each other."[4] The individual is created by society equally as much as society is created by its individuals.

Therefore, if gain-oriented behavior is to be considered collectively, reading needs to be anchored in social praxis, as our consumption is seen to be part of wider commodity-cultural behavior. Such collectivity is not only a requirement to talk about cultural formations, but also the endgame for economics in which methodological individualism is supposedly just a stepping stone to understanding something social.

Reading for gains might be thought of as ongoing socialization and as momentary coherences in a system of social differences between any numbers of consumer readers. When radiating beyond immediate local contexts, these coherences and differences might eventually be thought of as linked, contributing to what actor network theory calls a "collective," and to what economists perhaps might be led to call a market. To think beyond the self-interested individual to the collective, therefore, we need to find a reading goal that achives that shift, found paradoxically in identity formation, since one's interest in Self turns out to be remarkably social.

The New Critical Idiom volume *Reception* provides a good outline of its tripartite "reception study," "reception history," and "reception theory," which it understands as the decoding and interpretation of texts, the possible afterlives of that experience, and the modeling of those processes in a conceptualized framework. In this reorganization of the field, Ika Willis proceeds from a fundamental premise of texts only becoming meaningful when they are read, viewed, or listened to: "As the author and critic Ursula K. Le Guin puts it, 'The unread story is not a story; it is little black marks on wood pulp. The reader, reading it, makes it live: a live thing, a story.'"[5] Jerome McGann called those little black marks "black riders" and the print-culture precondition for literary fiction.[6] From an economics perspective, one might add that they are also the precondition to the exchange from which the social system known as a book market is created.

DeNel Rehberg Sedo provides a useful summary of theories of reading in "Reading Reception in the Digital Era," noting that they are many and without general agreement.[7] Citing a history of reader theorization beginning with I.A. Richards in the 1920s and developed by Louise Rosenblatt in the 1930s,[8] Sedo describes a heterogeneous twentieth-century reader-response criticism that nevertheless shares a rejection of the autonomous New Critical text in its premise that "the text cannot mean, or even exist apart from its readers."[9] In delineating the major trends, Sedo proposes the following inexhaustive sketch: theories of the reader can include, but are in no way limited to,

> the implied reader, whose responses are in part determined by the text itself and solidified by the reader filling in gaps;[10] the sign reader, who applies complex sign systems to interpret the text;[11] the model reader, who works with the author and the text to make sense of the story;[12] and, the resisting reader, who reacts to unbalanced power structures through the act of reading.[13]

For the twenty-first century, Sedo suggests that a number of approaches continue to see the reader and her text as complimentary, but further emphasize how reading has always been socially embedded. When analyzing a reader's individual reading practice, she recommends taking into account the "the social structures that bring a book into the hands of a reader, such as libraries, schools, family and friendship circles, and the publishing industry. In this way alone, reading is never an individual endeavour."[14]

If the social structure Sedo advises were commodity culture, the focus would need to fix on what is aimed at through exchange. Bortolussi and Dixon talk of a hierarchy of goals being relevant for any one reader at a given time, allowing for multiple goals to be held simultaneously.[15] These goals will also reorder themselves over time along with the reader's evolving history: books that were once read in the heat of adolescent challenge later on might be dismissed, revered, or affectionately satirized. Lowest in the hierarchy are basic goals of literary processing—recognizing that the text is indeed a narrative with specific plot(s), thematics and characterizations—while other goals might include appreciation of the language, evaluation of the mental states of the characters or relations between characters and institutions, evaluating the narrator, interpreting the supposed intentions of the implied author, or even (contestably) imputing an overall meaning to the text that Bortolussi and Dixon call the narrative's "message." In the academy, further goals might include the refinement of technical operations, cataloging textual and paratextual devices, or conducting maneuvers in sociological, aesthetic or cultural study.

Where Bortolussi and Dixon pull up, though, is at the boundary of cultural context, where processing stops and the remainder of a reader's life begins. What do readers hope to gain from their texts? Even assuming that readers hope to obtain an insight from the author sent in coded form, they must still interpret that message in personal terms, rendering it useful to themselves. Gains are modeled by institutional economics in terms of personal utility, and at the center of consumption lies an idea of benefits for the Self. So if the aim is to reconstitute and reconfigure, rather than reject economics thinking outright, it would make sense to focus on readings that have a primary aim in the acquisition of benefits to one's Self: no matter how erroneous the concept of an enduring homogenous self-identity might be. I shop therefore I am; I read therefore I am; I read because I hope to gain something from it.

Approaching reading from the side of economics, the renown economist Deirdre McCloskey has visited the conjunction between poetics and economics in "Metaphors Economists Live By." Using Lakoff and Johnson's work as a staging post, she draws attention to the foundations of economics, a mathematicized science, lying in its metaphors, such as competition and games, invisible hands, and markets.[16] The often-made argument McCloskey refers to, which she wishes to rebut, is that economics "is *not* poetry just to the degree that a piece of economics invites what the critic Louise Rosenblatt called an 'efferent' reading (from Latin *effero*, "I take away") as against an aesthetic reading."[17] In her rebuttal, McCloskey goes on to discuss the metaphorical structuring of much economic language, thus demonstrating the poetics of economics. But for the current purposes—of effecting a reverse maneuver to allow for a lay "economic" approach to poetry, if you will—the efferent reading should be embraced. Rather than reading as a purely aesthetic experience, exchange demands that the reader take something away. The *efferre* that Rosenblatt described was intended as a more emphatic counter-position to an aesthetic reading than the more accustomed term *instrumental*, since she suspected disinterested aesthetic experience might subsequently have an instrumental purpose.[18] Fortunately, *efferre* well describes the relationship between the reader and her fiction when poetry is approached as a source of gain. The interesting part is in finding out precisely what those gains might be.

Readers entering a bookshop (offline or on), choosing to remain there, browsing or targeting titles, deciding to buy or delay, purchasing, or surreptitiously consuming *in situ*, all represent attempts to secure personal gains. They are exercises in consumer and reader choice, and those choices say something about who the reader is, both to others and reflexively to the person. Psychological studies of economic behavior have long established that patterns of consumption are linked with the consumer (re)forming their identity. Reading, too, represents choice, and certain types of reading similarly say something about the person reading the text, both to others and to themselves. The choice to interpret this or that plot structure, theme, allusion, or irony in this or that way is in itself telling.

No one would want to claim that consumption is the same as reading, especially when reading refers to complex interpretation, but there may be a correlation. The correlation is not transitive—simply because someone consumes in one way, exercising certain patterns of consumer choice, does not mean that the patterning can be transferred directly onto reading. Patterns of consumption of goods do not directly match the patterns of meaning-making from any "text." But what if goods are symbolic goods, such as books? And what if the gaining from symbolic goods is what psychologists call identity formation? It might, instead, be helpful to think of an intransitive relationship. In gaining from symbolic goods, what identity formation can be to consumption, it can be to reading, too.

The conceptual artist Barbara Kruger, much of whose work politicizes our relationship to consumerism, articulates many of the findings of economics and cultural history. Her photographic silkscreen "I Shop

Therefore I Am" ties consumption inextricably with personal identity and articulates a major feature of commodity culture—a culture stretching back at least to the last third of the nineteenth century in many parts of the industrialized West. In *Modernity and Self-Identity*, Anthony Giddens writes of identity as an ongoing reflexive process sustained by, among other acts, the consumption of consumer goods.[19] As early as 1890, William James in his classic *Principles of Psychology* made the gendered observation that "a man's Self is the sum total of all that he can call his, not only his body and his psychic powers, but his clothes, his friends, his wife and children, his ancestors, his reputation and works, his lands and yacht and bank account."[20] Goods are valuable to "man" not only for their functional value. To put it more specifically, one of the functions of commodified goods is to provide the material, any material, that is necessary for the conveyance of intangible existential value. Such values are useful to individuals for processes such as identity formation. In the context of commodity culture, therefore, consumer choice is tightly linked to personal and, because cultural, collective identity.

Reading, too, and the interpretation that can result, also represents choice: the choice to read in one way and not another; to interpret in one way and not another. Simply by being context-bound, text is always available to more than one interpretation. That identity formation should be one of the functions of reading is also a matter of choice. Often, reading involves much else besides identity formation. Everything *but* the identity of the reader is important to forms of professional textual analysis assisted precisely through self-forgetfulness. After the hot emotive reading comes cool critical distance, with the final reading that procures judgment being a mutually informed resolution of the two. The primary goal of scholarly analysis is an understanding of, or a full cognitive "experiencing of," the text. Only secondarily does it aim to gain something, such an insight into the human condition or, more prosaically, a further career step as a perceptive close reader. Only in these secondary cases is analysis implicated quite naturally in private gain—a condition Rosenblatt acknowledges when she says that the aesthetic reading, like the efferent, can also be transactional.[21] The classroom, then, along with the analyst's display screen, is a possible but fraught place in which to look for self-interested efferent reading; the High Street is a much better.

By looking at reading undertaken squarely in commodity culture, we are obliged to focus on personal gain, since that concept is the driving force of the culture. The "rational choice" model of economics operates precisely along lines of gains and losses, of intentions to maximize pleasure and minimize pain. Reading in this context is precisely efferent—"to get something out of it," whether the deictic "something" points to pleasure, learning, amusement, or simply passing time.

Not all lay reading is directly bound to identity formation, and in *The Intellectual Life of the British Working Classes* Jonathan Rose makes clear the recurring pragmatism. A revealing example is of George Smith, a carpenter from Cornwall, who bought mathematics texts because of the slow pace they enforced: "a treatise on algebra or geometry, which cost but a very few shillings, afforded me matter for close study for a year," while Edwin Whitlock, a farmer from Salisbury low on reading matter, resorted to "a Post Office Directory for 1867, which volume I read from cover to cover."[22] Very many more of Rose's examples detail the identity-forming readings of underpriviledged people pulling themselves up by their bootstraps, but, to an extent, even Smith and Whitlock's struggles with boredom can be considered a pragmatic restatement of self-identities of steadfastness. An efferent reading may only require that its "taking away" not be disinterested, and a large portion of that self-interest is the interest in Self.

If the values of the bookshop's wares are dependent on their framing by commodity culture, what is meant by commodity culture? It is not an arbitrarily applicable term. Its prerequisites are surplus produce, disposable income, and a cultural system in which objects can become commodities—conditions that can be found as much among the native Gawa people of Australia exchanging kula shells as in nineteenth-century British docklands. In *The Commodity Culture of Victorian England*, Thomas Richards finds commodity culture arising out of the spectacle that was the Crystal Palace and filtering down to other groups when levels of leisure and disposable income allowed. His application of the term draws on the work of György Lukács and Guy Debord and is based on a specific understanding of capitalism in which capitalism's spectacular trick is in promising to make all possibly wanted goods exchangeable: to convince you that anything can be had for money. However, our bodies inhabit any number of systems at any one time, capitalism being only one of them, and other kinds of exchange are possible, which is one reason a certain reductionism can be seen in Richards's claim that the commodity is "the focal point of *all* representation, the dead centre of the modern world" (my italics).[23] Work on "gifts" has explored the possibilities of other such exchanges.[24]

Commodity culture has appeared in several studies: *Fictions of Commodity Culture* by Christoph Lindner; *Commodity Culture in Dickens's Household Words* by Catherine Waters; *Novels Behind Glass: Commodity Culture in Victorian Narrative* by Andrew Miller; and *Advertising and Commodity Culture in Joyce* by Garry Leonard; and it is a recurring theme in Jennifer Wicke's seminal *Advertising Fictions*. Excellent though these studies are, definitions of commodity culture are rarely tackled head-on: "By the mid-nineteenth century, the increasing influence of capitalism on everyday life generated in Britain what has come to be known as 'commodity culture.'"[25] Capitalism was increasingly influencing life in the final days of Tsarist St. Petersburg, but it did not generate commodity culture—other factors were involved that ought not be omitted from the definition—and Lindner's qualifier that commodity culture is a "culture organized around the production and exchange of material goods"[26] could still not differentiate exchange between actors in a subsistence economy on the one hand and circulations within an expansive consumer economy on the other.

If commodity culture among underprivileged classes is to be applicable on a large scale, then industrialization would be implied, providing a locus and time. Britain was the first to industrialize, yet the benefits derivable from leisure time and disposable income were not available for those under-resourced readers until the last third of the nineteenth century with the arrival of a full commodity economy, unilateral free-trade policy by a powerful steady-state economy encouraging emancipative consumption, the arrival of disposable income for the laboring classes, increased affordability throughout the food-staples chain derived from massive US wheat production at relatively low cost, the spread of Saturday half-day holidays in effect creating a concept of the weekend, and a major rise in the affordability of manufactured goods after significant increases in relative income.[27]

In 1907, University of Pennsylvania professor of political economy Simon Patten detailed *The New Basis for Civilization*, beginning with a somewhat sweeping claim that "All civilizations before the nineteenth century, like primitive societies of the Western World today and the backward despotisms of the East, were realms of pain and deficit." These societies, Patten argued, were being replaced by economies of pleasure and surplus, encouraging men of new "mental habits . . . chiefly governed by the new age of surplus in which they live. The economic revolution is here, but the intellectual revolution that will rouse men to its stupendous meaning has not yet done its work."[28]

A good indication of this surplus-driven intellectual revolution for the underpriviledged comes with the affordability of Saturday sports papers, since sports implies nonessential activities and Saturday publication implies weekend leisure. In general, sports publications saw a major increase in scale after the 1870s, but when the increase was in terms of book publication, it tended to be priced and worded for those interested in more prestigious country sports such as hunting and sailing—so while "working class money . . . drove much of the commercial expansion of Victorian and Edwardian sport," its treatment in literary-styled volumes was "fuelled from within a markedly different social world," exemplified in "sportsman's libraries" such as the Badminton Library of Sports and Pastimes, begun by Longman in 1885.[29] *The Athletic News*, on the other hand, rather than covering shooting and fishing as other sports magazines had done since the eighteenth century, focused instead on football, cycling, rugby, and athletics, and by 1887 it claimed a circulation of 180,000 per week.[30] That the Birmingham *Saturday Night* was made available by 7 p.m. each Saturday evening, at a price of a mere half penny, from 1882, demonstrates that large numbers of lower-income readers could afford textual nonessentials.

What I have proposed elsewhere is a definition of commodity culture based on a specific mode of private gain and a strategy for the satisfaction of human wants. Commodity culture would mean the culture of attempting to satisfy private wants not through collective action but through the private acquisition of commodities and the benefits they are perceived to convey. Alternative cultural formations might look to satisfy private wants through religious and collective political action. But for commodity culture, primary behavior would be in seeking satisfaction through objects that are, if only temporarily, commodified and which, in that phase of commodification, are perceived to bring with them the required tangible and intangible values.

The point about perceiving value in a commodity is that the operation requires some form of reading from an object. And if the benefit to be derived from an object is intangible, then it is only through reading that the benefit can be accessed. *Athletic News* may bring a functional benefit in its information about the form of a horse or ground conditions, but it may equally bring an intangible communicative benefit in its ability to say that the man with a copy tucked under his arm can afford to have a flutter. Goods or commodities take on significance because they signify, but in order to signify they must have a reader. As Tim Jackson puts it,

> Embedded within the idea that consumption and identity are linked, lies an even more important insight into our relationship to consumer goods. This is the claim that consumer goods play vital symbolic roles in our lives. . . . We value goods not just for what they can do, but for what they represent to us and to others.[31]

Whether by the intense social critique of Jean Baudrillard or the anthropology of Arjun Appadurai, there is agreement that material commodities "signify our lives, loves, desires, successes and failings, both to others and ourselves. . . . They derive their importance, in part at least, from their symbolic role in mediating and communicating personal, social and cultural meaning."[32] And if commodities are important for what they signify to ourselves and others, who carries out signification if not the reader? The important correlation between consumption and reading is that consuming significance is not possible without reading. Reading is a necessary component for the consumption of all non-material value, and thus commodity culture *needs* its readers.

As this study looks at readers' choices, we should question whether the inquiry is done a service by beginning with the individual as the point of departure, following what might be called methodological individualism that places causality for social phenomena with an aggregation of individual agency. Let us imagine for a moment that we are not created as individuals. Let us assume that our bodies are grown by, then pressed out from another female body that has "divided" itself to create us, and that we emerge into light as a object needy for the touch, milk, eye-contact, and love that prevents us from dying.[33] At first, we might continue to be an appendage of the "hopes, demands, love, neuroses, traumas, disappointments and unrealised lives" of those who care for us, and it is from this never fully escaped state of dependency that we gradually create a self-identity, as we grow, that again becomes enveloped in and sustained by our relations (or lack of them) with others.[34] As an experiment, it might be worth trying to explain human actions when the calculus of pleasure and pain is not calibrated only at the level of the individual.

For example, many of our actions are directly undertaken as part of a group activity. John Searle talks of group music-making or sports to illustrate collective intentionality, where the individual's actions can only be fully explained by reference to an "us" as part of an "our intention."

He uses the example of an assault in a street compared to a prize fight, the former being conceptually a conflict of individual interests, and the latter cooperative collective behavior.[35] Since an individual's choice of reading matter is similarly made possible by the collective actions of publishers, sellers, writers, distributors, programmers, advertisers, and so on, it might be wise to adopt a theory of readers' choice that is social. And there are some, Bourdieu's theory of cultural capital being a case in point. But to cope with Fetterley's resisting reader, or just the reader's downright capriciousness, the theory would have to be sensitive to the individual's constantly evolving self in relation to others. At the micro level, and unlike in Bourdieu, the theory would also have to be diachronic rather than synchronic, post-structural rather than structural. Choosing (a title from a bookshelf) takes place in a system of differences, but those differences are always on their way to becoming something else. In the selecting or rejecting of a book, change to the reader happens (even if that change is further entrenchment of her self-identity).

When considered through social identity theory, much of our behavior is seen as being guided by a need for solidarity within groups we adhere to, and for the capacity to acquire when faced with competition between groups. The social identity position, and its articulation since at least the first decades of the twentieth century by writers such as George Herbert Mead,[36] is summarized by Jackson, who states that "our concepts of self are (at best) socially constructed and (at worst) helplessly mired in a complex of 'social logic.' "[37] When changes in personal taste occur that are tied to our identity, not only from book to book but from page to page, they do not happen in social isolation. If only in the imagination, other people are involved.

None of the readers coming into a bookshop on a Southampton high street around the year 1900 know whether they will enjoy the title they select. They may enjoy the work and surprise themselves in identifying imaginatively with new kinds of people. They may acquire nothing but disdain for the work, again tilting the reader into a new counter-distinction of self in relation to others. They may encounter disruption, finding uncomfortable levels of self-discrepancy from mismatches between their own multiple perspectives on themselves and their perception of how other people perceive them. In finding a gap—that they enjoy what they ought not to enjoy or do not enjoy what they should—the purchaser is faced with a dilemma of self-acceptance. The acceptance will depend on how the reader believes others may react to that same enjoyment. When the gap is significant, then there is a strong motivation to understand the text in ways that lessen the gap, and to bring the reader to a closer cohesion among self-conceptions. At the very least, if on finishing the book a reader finds nothing but self-confirmation, then a process of re-evaluation has been undergone, with the reader refining their self-understanding—and providing us with an exemplification of self-discrepancy theory.

Proposed by Edward T. Higgins (1987) and applied in behavioral economics, self-discrepancy theory operates with an idea of self equally between self-perception and the perception of how others may see you. Furthermore, "there is a meaningful distinction between my actual self and my potential self—conceptions of how I am right now and how I might be or could potentially be in the future. And this potential self in its turn can be conceived either as an ideal self . . . [or] an ought self."[38] The three domains of "I" as I am, "I" as I ideally could be, and "I" as I ought to be are reflected in what we imagine are the perceptions of others. We incorporate what we believe to be others' perceptions of what we are, what we could be, and what we ought to be. The theory is left operating with "six distinct types of self-concept: actual-own, actual-other, ideal-own, ideal-other and ought-own, ought-other."[39] Lodged in any individual's self-concept are estimations of other peoples' attitudes toward oneself. When reading stories, if how readers read impinges in any way on self-identity, then that reading in a crucial sense has society as one of its preconditions.

Self-discrepancy is valuable in a further strategic way in respect of economics. The gap that discrepancy identifies is structurally the same demand gap inscribed long ago in the neoclassical model of economics as the aim to maximize pleasure. Discrepancy, if you cannot live with it, requires consumption. So to browse, select, and anticipate in a bookshop is to open up a gap of self-discrepancy that it is hoped the purchase will close. What is more, the closing is not done in isolation. Discrepancy brings in the social, propelled as it is by the perceived "actual," "ideal," and "ought" of others. All this browsing and efferent taking away is carried out in an imaginatively populated space—the same space imagined when people talk about marketing.

There are many goals in an efferent reading, but at the heart of its "taking away" is an interest in one's Self that paradoxically turns out to be highly social. The overall proposal, therefore, is that the taking away that efferent reading performs is primarily concerned with formation of the Self; secondly, in terms of an intransitive link, that what the discrepant identity is to reading it is to consumption, too; and lastly, that the consumption of symbolic goods, as with efferent reading, is itself a social practice. If we were lazy, this could be called aggregated "self-interest," but that is a false unpacking of the metaphor aganst which Deirdre McCloskey warns.[40]

These points mean the field cannot be scrutinized by methods based only on the individual's self-interest. Instead, imagining how readers navigate among the social conditions of consumption and reading, mapping plausible routes through readers' experiences of their texts, will tell a different story of how the retail book market, or any symbolic market came to be: as an effect of unequal social relationships, steeped in gender, race and class. If that is too much hyperbole, then there is more modest aim to this study, which is simply a dignified understanding of those unknown readers from whom commodity culture derives its force, along with their capacity to redefine it, and who with a few commendable exceptions remain unnecessarily and conspicuously below the radar of literary studies.

Chapter 2

Book Retail

A Test Bed for Sustainable Economics

If one were to ask proponents of free-market economics about public welfare and culture, they would almost certainly view those as costs. Free health care and financial supports for various social services, including the arts and humanities, would be seen as costs urged for political reasons, which could be sustained only if the economy were to deliver sufficient surplus in some profitable tomorrow—that in an age of austerity will hardly come. The relationship is one of separate spheres, between markets on the one hand and politics and culture on the other: such reasoning often underpinning the standoff in demands for free library services or tax breaks for cultural services such as books. As usual, in such apodictic structuring, one part is dominant. The market is first tasked with generating wealth that, if it trickles down in sufficient quantity, can *then* serve the needs of another sphere that is collective society. To even the most impeccably intentioned plan to support cultural activity, the question invariably raised is "Can we afford it?" Budgets have the final say and, without significant political support, culture is trumped.

However, we do not have to think only in terms of an opposition, in which culture invariably loses. In 2001, a group of political economists questioned this opposition between, on the one side, a monolithic conception of the market economy and, on the other, politics and culture.[1] They investigated instead the varieties of capitalism in advanced economies, and created from a continuum of change two nodes that were 1) liberal market economies, which operate according to competitive market arrangements, adjusting their supply and demand of goods and services in line with price signals, and 2) coordinated market economies, where industries cooperate more closely with state and other non-market institutions, in addition to cooperating collectively across the sector. The analysis then went on to identify, in both types of market economy, the legal and cultural institutions that such economies rely upon—hence the subtitle to Hall and Soskice's volume *Varieties of Capitalism: The Institutional Foundations of Comparative Advantage* (2001).

The need to reorganize the argument away from a crude opposition between "the market" and a system of socialized political values has become so pressing as to throw up a welter of both popularizing and scholarly new titles calling for an overhaul of economic theory, as well as give rise to economics organizations, in the UK alone, such as The Post-Crash Economics Society, the Cambridge Society for Economic Pluralism, and Positive Money, all in one way or another considering the possibility of a capitalized society with markets that is not necessarily market society.[2] The discussion is important for the book trade, too, since this also operates in the interface between economic and cultural capital. Believing that creative writing is socially important, and concerned that only 14% of UK authors can earn a full-time wage from writing (and that their average wage is 27% lower than the minimum wage for over-twenty-five year olds), the Westminster All Party Parliamentary Writers Group is looking for ways to intervene in the market to protect what they believe is socially valuable cultural production.[3] In a similar vein, academic publishing, which is the sector most concerned with delivering public and publicly funded goods, has experimented with models of open-access publishing that intervene in the free market, and can be seen applying new-economy thinking in proposals such as "A Journal is a Club: A New Economic Model for Scholarly Publishing."[4]

In the reorganized view, society's institutions and infrastructure are not a cost but a necessary precondition for a successful market. Roads and transport are needed to distribute goods and to move employees; health care to minimize periods of sickness; child care to free up labor time; domestic cleaning and housekeeping to enable people to be work-ready; policing to minimize crime; employment regulations to minimize labor disputes; state and trade regulations to agree on production standards; consumer information, safety regulations, and the protection of common pool resources such as water, air, and the rest of the environment, and, especially in an age of late capitalism, significant levels of education are needed, along with a well-regulated credit system to ensure the reliability of financial transactions. Without these and other social institutional arrangements, industry is unable to generate wealth.

The markets of advanced economies, including liberal market economies, are regulated by legal and institutional factors that are created for political and cultural reasons. As Ha-Joon Chang explains, there are strict rules governing the misleadingly termed "free market" but these are experienced so habitually as to become invisible.[5] First, there are restrictions on what can be traded: not only in the form of licenses for potentially harmful substances, but political and social restrictions, such as health and safety regulations, or labor and environmental standards. For example, you cannot trade in legal decisions, or electoral votes, or academic qualifications, or other humans—although the practice was legal in the UK two centuries ago. Second, participation in the market is restricted: children are banned from the labor market in advanced economies (a historically recent decision); professions that impact on human life require licenses (for example, doctors and dentists); patent rules restrict the use of certain intellectual properties; and only companies with adequate capital and a history of proven auditing may float shares. Third, there is a body of legislation governing exchange: regulating product reliability, failure in delivery, and loan default. Perhaps most important, there is price regulation, not merely in instances such as the minimum wage but directly through any number of non-tariff trade barriers, chief among which is immigration control that regulates the labor market, which would otherwise radically affect pricing in access to the world's near-unlimited cheap labor.[6]

In their analysis of market economies, Hall and Soskice insist that "Institutions, organizations and culture enter this analysis because of the support they provide for the relationships firms [industries] develop to resolve coordination problems."[7] In other words, institutions are created from and sustained by not only legal systems but cultural forces, too, and the informal "common" knowledge built up in the history and culture of a nation. The relationship is not one of an opposition between markets and culture but of cultural institutions in their broadest sense enabling a variety of markets.

The implication for the current study is not that books and reading culture are indirectly responsible for industries' ability to generate wealth (apart from the direct effect on the publishing and book retail industries) but that markets, all markets, are subject to regulations that are created, crucially, *for political and cultural reasons*. Those political and cultural reasons are instrumental in determining what the given market can most readily generate, whether that "output" is increased market share and investor dividends, or infrastructural social improvements such as health care and a thriving cultural sector. In this sense, culture is an institutional sustaining force for the market, and its cultural production is an output of the market *if* we choose the regulations to make it so.

For a development of the issues raised by Hall and Sockice as they relate to the interactions between cultural production and "free" and regulated markets, perhaps no better case can be examined than the book trade. Its organization has been both regulated and unregulated, and such "organisational arrangements . . . have a considerable impact on what books get published, publicized, purchased, and read."[8]

The trade's arrangements have been conditioned by its scale of economies, chief among which is the relationship between production cost and retail price. Although the industrialization of the trade that was in place first in Britain over the first three or so decades of the nineteenth century and accelerated thereafter was able to reduce production costs and raise volume to previously inconceivable levels, books remained relatively expensive items to produce compared to the retail prices that could be charged. This relationship has been defining for the trade and, thus, is crucial for any understanding of the text, the interpretation of which is consistently defined by its regime's frame, or, as Derrida puts, it the *parergon* as a constituting feature of the work done (*le fait/fait*).[9] But it is also crucial for our understanding of the economies in which bookselling operates, and of the opportunities or disadvantages that may be afforded through market regulation, which thus shapes the experience of books when they are part of the commodity regime.

Of the costs involved in production that include overheads spread through the supply chain, known collectively as factor costs, the most significant costs for much of the nineteenth and twentieth centuries have still remained paper and printing or, for luxury items such as gift books and in the less luxurious secondhand market where volumes require new covers, binding.[10] Books were expensive items for retailers to buy relative to the competitive price they needed to charge customers. The high factor cost relative to sales price has meant that profit margins on each item have been modest. The importance of this relationship can be explained in a hypothetical example.

As retail prices were not yet fixed, in the British case, it is reasonable to assert that just before 1900 a single-volume first-edition fiction in a standard publisher's cloth binding would have retailed for around six shillings.[11] The wholesale price for the retailer would depend on the deal they could achieve with the publisher, and depend largely on whether the retailer was a powerful national chain such as W.H. Smith or a small book shop relying on goodwill built up between the shop and the publisher's rep.

For ease of calculation, we could take a 10s volume—say, the Rev. S.P.H. Statham's *History of the Castle, Town and Port of Dover* published by Longmans, Green and Co. in 1899, which had a catalogue retail price of 10s 6d.[12] We can imagine that a Dover-located bookseller, responsive to local demand, procured a number of volumes from the Longman's representative, the price for each being 6s. The bookseller has already calculated on a sales discount of 1s 6d for cash since, as James Barnes notes with regards to discounting, "a provincial customer expected 10 percent discount from the retail price of a book in cash transactions, and a 15 percent reduction if he were a teacher or clergyman."[13] Subtracting the price to the retailer from the sale price, assumed to be 9s after discount, gives a retail markup of 3s, or a one-third (33.3%) profit margin for a single item (sale price − cost = sale price × profit margin: or profit margin = (sp − c) ÷ sp).

As a retail business, anyone operating with a business profit margin of around 33% is not exactly pressed, but neither is the margin over-generous. In the twenty-first century, successful retail companies such as department stores with cut-back centralized operations can operate effectively with a margin of less than 5%. Large industries such as pharma, tobacco, and biotechnology appear in various annual surveys of the most profitable industry, based on profit margin, with net margins around 25–30%.[14] The least profitable above-negative rates have margins in the 1–5% range. However, figures of 33% belie the true situation for smaller businesses, which have relatively much larger overhead costs and cannot take advantage of cost reduction through centralization. Added to this, there are historical shifts to take into account.

Around 1966, in the heyday of a well-regulated UK bookselling market, following a period of marked rising living standards in the 1950s, Dorothy Davis's study of shopping suggested a turnover level for the smallest independent shops: "Out of every twenty shops in Britain today, approximately three belong to the big organizations, another three to local firms with several branches, and the remaining fourteen are all independent small single shops (including no fewer than six with a vestigial turnover of less than £100 per week)."[15] With a cheaper paperback retailing at around 5s (say, Richard Collier, *The Indian Mutiny*, Fontana, 1966) and a color gift book retailing at around 15s (Kiaer and Eigil, *The Methuen Handbook of Roses*, Methuen, 1966), a small independent shop with a highly modest turnover of £100—which was 2000 shillings—would have the unenviable task of selling a minimum 100 of these books (proportional by price) over a five- or five-and-a-half day week, at roughly sixteen sales per day. It is essential for bookshops to sell relatively large numbers of their book stock—unless of course they sell more than books.

On an item-by-item basis, the picture is a little clearer. There are commodity items that offer very high margins between factor cost and retail price, such as bottled water or diamonds, with markups running sometimes to several hundred percent or more. Clothing and shoe markups in the twenty-first century in developed economies can reach up to several hundred percent.[16]

The situation for booksellers, however, has an added complication because, unlike secondhand cars or sofas, theirs is a trade relying on stocks of multiple copies of one title (in addition to its range of titles), meaning that the retailer must calculate profits derived from multiple sales of a single item. If the prescient Dover bookseller had secured three copies of Statham's *History* from the Longman's rep, at 6s each, for a total of 18s, he or she would still not yet be in profit on selling only two at 9s each. The third volume would need to be sold for the investment to go into profit.

One of the discounting practices offered to retailers in the late nineteenth century was to provide twenty-five books for the price of twenty-four, or thirteen for twelve, as a trade incentive.[17] If, again, the Dover bookseller had taken advantage of a "thirteen for the price of twelve" offer from the Longmans rep, let us imagine that, together with three of Stratham's volumes, the bookseller had also invested in ten other books of varying titles (at a discount). The retailer's prescience would then have to extend not just to guessing that Stratham's *History* would sell but that the others titles would sell, too, or else risk burning in with unsold stock. Market knowledge was at a premium, so keeping track of novel fiction alone meant that the bookseller would have to estimate which titles would sell among the approximately 500 new titles per year produced by 1901.[18]

For ease of calculation, let us assume that 6 of the 13 books cost the bookseller 3s and the remaining 6 cost 6s, totaling 54s (£2 14s). The thirteenth, also one of the more expensive books, was "free." The bookseller has calculated that for the shop to survive, a minimum profit margin of around 33.3% would be required (although a markup of about 50% would have been more sought after). If by good fortune all the cheaper volumes were sold at a 1s per item markup, and all but two of the more expensive volumes were sold on a 3s per item markup, the two unsold more expensive volumes would still threaten the overall profit.

The potential revenue on all thirteen volumes was 87s (£3 18s: 6 × 4s + 7 × 9s = 87s), meaning a profit of 33s (£1 13s). Instead the bookseller has a revenue of 69s (£3 9s: 6 × 4s + 5 × 9s = 69s), meaning a profit of only 15s. The two unsold volumes mean that the bookseller's potential profits have been cut from 33s to 15s—more than a half—and two unsold books are taking up valuable shelf space. Because outlay for stock is relatively large compared to margin, successful sale revenues continually need to be balanced by buying-in costs incurred, a relationship determined in turn by the publishers' production or factor costs and the markup that retailers can apply.

These relationships explain why for the bookseller the system of "sale or return" is invaluable, if not essential, to the retail book trade. The Dover seller would need to return his two unsold volumes to help return the business to full profitability. Practice throughout much of the twentieth century, however, was that booksellers had to pay the carriage on books returned, as well as bear the costs of thefts.

Overall then, the structuring relationship in the trade between relative high factor costs in production and low markup for retailers meant that book retail required large capital investment for modest returns, and that those capital investments were keenly vulnerable to factors such as the retailer's over-purchase. Locked in among the shop's assets was a high-value stock that could produce modest returns if sales were consistent, but the profits generated were slight compared with the risks to which those assets were exposed. Apart from sudden changes in taste, leading to a book dying on the shelf, or the bookseller failing to predict market exhaustion, retailers could be threatened by many other changes beyond their control: changes in business rates, rents, or services, or changes in tax rates or publisher's policy. The ratio of investment to return meant that the retail trade was extremely sensitive to outside pressure.

The contention is that such a structuring relationship characterized the retail book trade in the UK, at least, across the later nineteenth and much of the twentieth century before online retail. Consequently, the responses to this relationship oscillated between increasing trade regulation to protect the narrow margin, and opportunity-seeking reactions against it; between conservative consolidation and disruptive innovation; between regulative control and liberalization. Furthermore, it might be suspected that this oscillation has more often than not been debated, erroneously, as a discourse of cultural value, where the protection of perceived established values faces off against the positive and negative implications of commercial liberalization.

Clive Bloom's formative *Bestsellers: Popular Fiction since 1900* provides a case in point. Of the prewar introduction of Allen Lane's paperbacks that liberalized trade in bringing more books to an even wider range of readers than before, he remarks "The paperback revolution put publishing firmly within an industrial and commercial setting, yet 'serious' culture and 'serious' literature in particular were seen by many critics and publishers alike as antithetical . . . Thus the widening of the market was not merely a commercial but also a moral decision."[19] Discussing the later recovery of the booktrade in Britain after World War II, Bloom then notes that "rather than the content of books, it was their format in printed form that determined profitability"; then, around the 1960s in Britain, on sea-changes to young people's literature, he notes that literature was "[becoming] part of the growing popular *commercial* culture that included comic and cereal packet give-aways, cigarette and tea-packet cards" (original italics); and on yet newer sea-changes in the 1990s with the arrival of supermarkets to bookselling, Bloom remarks that "the bestseller on supermarket shelves ceased to be a piece of literature sold in a specialist shop (i.e., a bookshop) and instead became a product like any other."[20]

Bloom's narrative is one of commercializing innovations that create cultural loss in their wake, but it is also one in which tomorrow's cash nexus eventually becomes yesterday's period of stability. One is tempted to ask when was the preceding golden period when books were not commercial, nor sold on high streets or from colporteur's baskets in competition with other products? Since the industrialization of the book trade, the tactical use of format has helped determine profitability, and any revolutions in book production have been commercial revolutions, too. Profiting from popular cultural production has been commercialized for as long as vaudeville, if not long before.[21] If the history of the trade is a bipolar one between regulative control and liberalization, it should be remembered that fundamentally both modes are commercial strategies, and that the exchange is between two commercial systems rather than between commerciality and noncommercial moral choice.

This proposition can be tested by turning to the most important piece of bookselling-related regulation in the UK over the twentieth century, the Net Book Agreement (NBA), by which publishers set a minimum price at which a book could retail, backed by sanctions against retailers who sold at lower levels. Large market economies have legislation to prevent price fixing by industry, and if price fixing is undertaken at all, then most usually it is by governments. On the face of it, price fixing, or price agreements, seems a conspiracy to maintain high prices and increase profits, and flies in the face of free-market competition. The justification for the NBA was always that books are different and need protection, and in many ways books *are* different, but so is bread, and so is healthcare, which is increasingly being integrated into free-market pricing systems in the UK.[22] Perhaps they should not be, because in certain circumstances, as argued by the architects of the NBA, price fixing may be socially beneficial if it protects the longer-term sustainability of a practice. It depends on what outputs you require from a market.

The minimum price charged for a book under the NBA guaranteed rates of return, stabilized the market, and helped prevent what cooperating parties called "underselling," which in turn prevented the sector from cannibalizing itself, which would leave only the most rapacious (or hardy) businesses standing. For better or worse, the NBA was a measure taken to control the free market, but from the customer's point of view, it prevented access to cheaper books and prevented retailers with lower-income customers from providing for their market segment. This double edge to taking any totalizing ethical position on the NBA, and on market regulation in general, is highlighted in a contentious 1894 article on the decay of bookselling that the author found concurrent with a decay of literature.[23] What prevented the upwardly mobile "reading-man" from building up a "gentleman's library" was that he was frustrated by the concordance of monetary and cultural values from both above and below. He could not afford the aspired-to but overpriced thirty-plus-shilling editions, artificially hiked to that exorbitant price through trade consensus between publisher and the major circulating libraries, from which his freer-market Continental counterpart was exempt, but threatening from below, and perhaps more degrading to his collection, was the surfeit of cheap reprints and non-copyright books that he saw flooding the bookshops. The article contended that underselling was to blame for the cheapest books, provoked by excessive discounting by publishers, and, along with the general rise of periodical literature, the situation was threatening "the man who buys books for the sheer love of possessing and accumulating them."[24] The solution to the serious literary man's ambition, in the article's view, was the sale of books at "moderate prices," in the region of 6s, which logically led its author to support the adoption of net prices. For readers who could only afford the cheapest discounted prices, such a move would be one of exclusion. As with all kinds of social prescription, the question was not one of principle between regulation and non-regulation, but a political question of who will be included and who excluded by the proposed shift to existing boundaries.

Books, whether sold in a regulated market or the supposedly free market, are both taking part in a market. Indeed, all markets have some form of regulation, the limits of which are set through social, political decision-making. Even the most rampant neoliberal economies operate with stringent regulations: around immigration, for example, to protect the nation's labor market; against harm, in product labeling, refunding, or anti-pollution measures; or against market failure, as yet another example, in anti-monopolization measures. The choice is not between an ideal free market (which has never existed) and a market that is regulated in line with social or political will. The choice is between differing degrees of regulation that is socially and politically prescribed. The illusion of market objectivity breaks down once it is realized that some form of regulation is ubiquitous, as Cambridge economist Ha-Joon Chang explains:

> There is no scientifically defined boundary for the free market. If there is nothing sacred about any particular market boundaries that happen to exist, an attempt to change them is as legitimate as the attempt to defend them. Indeed the history of capitalism has been a constant struggle over the boundaries of the market.
>
> . . . Opposing a new regulation is saying that the status quo, however unjust . . . should be not be changed. Saying

that an existing regulation should be abolished is saying that the domain of the market should be expanded.[25]

Commentary falters when it argues that measures such as the NBA are somehow anti-market. Regulation such as the NBA is simply another line in the ongoing redrawing of market boundaries—in contrast to an unrealizable pure free market—and in no way is it a freedom from the market itself in its adoption of cultural, political values. A regulated book trade, instead, is very much a market operation, just with a specific configuration. It is another matter entirely to argue over which configuration of market might be sustainable, where free-market configurations are not, and whether regulated markets might distribute goods more equitably among participants compared to the free market's accumulation by dispossession. The mistake, however, is to replace the discussion of which market forms are most beneficial to most people with a discourse comprising exclusive moral, cultural values.

In terms of sustainable economics, in the book or any other trade, regulation is not always the bad and liberalization is not always the good, nor vice-versa, since as metaphors they are value-laden and misleading. Liberalization can free up restrictive, protectionist practices, as the optimistic version of the digitization of social communication claims; and regulation can place unwelcome power into censoring, restricting hands. But the reverse is also true. Regulation can prevent, for example, the (corporate) abuse of public communication away from the benefit of society; liberalization can make society vulnerable to corporate greed. The oscillation between regulation and liberalization in the book trade is not a mirror of the Arnoldian struggle between culture and anarchy.

With the exchange between regulation and liberalization viewed through the lens of political economy, our current history of bookselling becomes more resistant to pre-determination by well-meaning positions based on the preservation of cultural value. The literature on historical bookselling not simply as an aspect of publishing, but specifically on book retail from shops is relatively sparse. The main resource, commonly referred to simply as *Mumby*, is still the life work of *Times Literary Supplement* feature writer and epistolary historian Frank Mumby: *Publishing and Bookselling: A History from the Earliest Times to the Present Day* (1930). Several editions were edited by Mumby, a fourth survived him, edited by Max Kenyon from 1956, and a fifth was revised and updated by Ian Norrie from 1973 to cover the period 1870 to 1970. Mumby had earlier produced a trial run of his work entitled *The Romance of Book Selling* (1910). Both *Romance* and *Publishing and Bookselling* refer to a volume by *Times of India* editor Henry Curwen, *A History of Booksellers: The Old and the New* (1873), which is less about retail and more a history of eminent people and firms from the booktrade, despite useful chapters on remaindering, auctioneering, children's literature, W.H. Smith and Son, and provincial booksellers.[26] Mumby's 1910 work and the various editions of *Publishing and Bookselling* contain an increasingly updated bibliography originally compiled by William Peet, based on a catalog of multinational books from the library of the *Börsenverein der Deutschen Buchhändler* in Leipzig. From the inputs of successive editors, the mighty bibliography that emerged in Norrie's 1973 edition of *Publishing and Bookselling* contains still only a surprisingly few titles referring directly to retailing books from shops. Volume 3 (*1800–1900*) of *The Cambridge Bibliography of English Literature* has a list of some twenty-three titles on general retail bookselling, but with a predominance of writings concerned with issues of underselling and the NBA and a further fifteen titles on specific bookselling firms; while volume 4, covering 1900 to 1950, has a similar-sized general list and a list on specific London "booksellers."

More recent work on historical shop retail before the explosion of research prompted by online retail can be found scattered throughout articles in the journals *Book History* and *The Library*. If we leave aside the practice of larger circulating libraries such as Mudie's or Jesse Boot's retailing what was essentially library stock, then studies relevant to the turn of the century are found in Eileen Demarco, *Reading and Writing* (2006), which details the network of Hachette's rail-bookstores in nineteenth-century France; in Frost and Hall, "John Smith's: Historical Perspectives and Historical Precedence," which overlaps the period; and in references to, among other matters, W.H. Smith's railway bookstalls that can be found in Mary Hammond, *Reading, Publishing and the Formation of Literary Taste in England 1880–1914* (2006). Useful archive references can be found in the booksellers and stationers section of British Book Trade Archives 1830–1939 (or from portals such as Archives Hub) and from Giles Mandelbrote, *Out of Print and Into Profit* (2007); related, but covering slightly earlier periods, is work by Stephen Colclough, including "'Purifying the Sources of Amusement and Information'? The Railway Bookstalls of W.H. Smith & Son, 1855–1860."[27]

The main point of contention for book retail throughout much of the nineteenth century until the establishment of the NBA was what some commentators called the evils of underselling. Underselling derives from the entirely natural retail practice of encouraging sales by charging customers the least price for goods from which the retailer can maintain an overall profit. When in competition with other booksellers, however, this meant that any retailing firm having a strategic advantage could sustain lower prices and "undersell" competitors, driving prices down throughout the supply chain and, to the annoyance of publishers, chipping away at their potential revenues. Even after 1900, when the NBA had resolved the situation for better or for worse, there were persistent voices claiming the rights of book retailers to charge the prices they wished; these voices continued until the 1990s, when, again for better or for worse, the complainants won. From the underseller's point of view, the issue is put succinctly in an 1894 article, "The Decay of the Bookseller," for the Catholic Church's news journal *The Tablet*, wishing to bolster the provincial bookselling trade to increase readers' access to books:

> Among the many ingenious plans suggested by the surviving booksellers for the revival of their business, none seems so strikingly original as the proposal that there should be no such thing as a fixed price for a book. A pound of bacon or a yard of cotton is sold for one price in one town and at quite a different price elsewhere . . . does not the industrious housewife spend her days . . . in her perpetual quest for the cheapest? Why should the bookseller be in a worse position than the enterprising purveyor of sausages . . . why should not a bookseller in Cardiff ask five shillings for a new Kipling or Stevenson, although the same books in London are quoted at four shillings and sixpence? In other words, it is proposed that there should be no such thing as a "published price," but each man in the retail trade should be at liberty to fix his own price in accord with the expenses of his business and the amount of his turnover.[28]

The equating of books with other commodity goods such as sausages and the gendering of the purchaser will be dealt with in more detail later. For the present, however, what should be noted is that whether underselling is a service or disservice depends on your place in the communications circuit. Again, the question is one not of principle but of who any principle includes or excludes.

Centralized markets and the advantages of a large size as possible are exemplified in Stoneham's, a leading bookseller in the golden square mile of the City of London. In 1874, the industrious Edmund John Stoneham succeeded in opening an eighth branch of his firm at 4 Charlotte St., Mansion House. As a busy micromanager in such a homogenous site as the City mile, possibly the most concentrated center of affluence anywhere in the world at the time, Stoneham was able to gain an astute knowledge of his customers' tastes and the numbers of copies that would be reliably purchased. He is reputed to have been capable of ordering anything up to ten thousand copies of a book, and exploited his advantage to the annoyance of publishers, and certainly to the detriment of suburban and country booksellers from where Stoneham's customers may have commuted. On his death, alongside *The Times* obituary (10 April 1888), *The Bookseller* noted Stoneham none-too-kindly as "the well-known underselling bookseller of Cheapside and elsewhere."[29]

In contrast, arguing on behalf of small country booksellers, the *Tablet* similarly supported the rights of small shop owners to set their own prices, free of the price fixing imposed by London publishers, but it also decried an unregulated evil besetting the nation's small shops, which was the discounting system. Larger national and regional retailing chains were free to obtain significant discounts from book suppliers—both publishers and warehouse distributors—that were beyond the means of small independent traders. Mudie's especially could obtain stock at extremely "competitive" rates.

While on the one hand *The Tablet* decried the fixed price system, on the other hand it also believed that this discount system pressed "with great severity upon the smaller traders, and is fast handicapping them out of existence." The article argued for regulation in a reduction to book prices overall, imperatively with the eradication of the artificially high 31s 6d for a triple-decker that together would stimulate the buying of cheaper editions across the sector. The lines of competing interests, therefore, were not simply drawn between book suppliers and book retailers, or between regulation and liberalization, but were criss-crossed throughout the book-retail trade, between peripheral and central, as well as small-scale and large.

Early currents of the NBA can be traced to before the first major industrialization of the book trade but at a period when the various departments of book selling and publishing were only beginning to occupy separate spheres. A group of London booksellers tried to organize themselves into a formal association to prevent what for them were the disadvantages of underselling. The Associated Booksellers or, as they came to be known from the device of a beehive used in their books, the associated busy bees, formed in 1812 and lasted for an unknown period; they were revamped in 1828 but with no greater measure of success.[30] In 1834, the Glasgow Booksellers' Protection Association was formed for a similar purpose to agree prices but also collapsed, in part due to accusations that they were breaking trade law, voiced in a critical pamphlet "suggesting that membership of the association was a conspiracy rendering members liable to transportation for seven years."[31] Much of the debate was followed in the trade organ *The Bookseller* from 1858 onwards, while the *Cambridge Bibliography* lists evidence in earlier pamphlets such as "Bookseller's Monopoly: address to the trade and to the public" (1832) or "Ridge's Scheme for Promoting the Interests of the Country Booksellers and Publishers" (1855), although neither title is extant.[32]

In 1848, London booksellers and publishers made a further attempt to control prices. With publisher and trade figure Sampson Low as secretary to this new Booksellers' Association, a period arrived when "war was formally declared against all booksellers who did not abide by [the organization's] rules and regulations."[33] In response, the undersellers, or Free Traders as they were known, and buoyed by a section of public opinion, attracted the support of many authors, prompting the publication of *The Opinions of Certain Authors on the Bookselling Question* in 1852. Thomas Carlyle came out against the restrictions, as did Charles Dickens, who presided at a meeting in May 1852 held at John Chapman's bookshop, appealing to the sanctity of free enterprise. William Gladstone was so incensed by the restrictive practice that he made editions of several of his pamphlets available to nonconforming booksellers.

The wrangle around underselling continued until 1852, when a legal judgment was passed by Lord Campbell. The arguments were summarized with surprising impartiality in an *ex post facto* letter to Lord Campbell by Westminster bookseller James Bigg. Booksellers wished for restrictions to protect trade and ostensibly to maintain the supply of books—no one questioned the benefit to the public derived through bookselling—but disagreed with many publishers, authors, and some of their own retailing number on how best this could be achieved. Campbell came to the conclusion that any efforts to regulate the subsequent price at which a (retail) purchaser could resell a property (to a customer) was not only "unreasonable and inexpedient" but "contrary to the freedom which ought to prevail in commercial transactions . . . [and] derogates from the rights of ownership which, as purchaser, he has acquired."[34] Following Campbell's judgement, the Booksellers' Association disbanded.

Numerous smaller-scale attempts to regulate book pricing continued for the next four decades, until by 1889 in response to continued campaigning by *The Bookseller* "no less than 136 booksellers signed a 'memorial' to publishers calling upon them to discontinue supplying anyone who sold books at a greater discount than threepence in the shilling."[35] A number of issues within the book trade were resolved by the NBA, and underselling was curtailed, too, as a consequence of retailers agreeing to sell books at a set net price under penalty of losing the publishers' supply. The story of the Agreement has been covered in much detail elsewhere,[36] but a summary might be convenient.

Frederick Macmillan's famous letter to *The Bookseller* came in 1890. A reconstituted London Booksellers' Society was formed in the same year to accept net books from a limited number of publishers, led by Macmillan's; Macmillan's first title offered at a net price was (tellingly for this study) Alfred Marshall, *Principle of Economics* (1890), priced 12/6 Net. By 1897, the sixteen net books Macmillan produced in 1890 had risen to 136. (For Stoneham's failing to acquiesce, Macmillan is reputed to have cut off his supply of books to them.) By 1894, the London Bookseller's Society was encouraging regional collaboration, which resulted in the Associated Booksellers of Great Britain and Ireland being formed on 23 January 1895, determined to ensure the survival of the NBA. Rather than meeting directly with the booksellers' association, and mindful of Lord Campbell's earlier ruling, a group of major publishers—Longman's, John Murray's, Routledge, Heinemann's, Sampson Low, Bentley, Blackwood's and Smiths (Elder)—instead met informally at John Murray's house, out of which officially arose the Publishers' Association on 23 January 1896. The two associations, of publishers and booksellers, failed to agree until a meeting in 1897 when they proposed maintaining set prices for net books and limited discounts for titles not subject to the net agreement, on condition of approval from the newly formed Society of Authors (est. 1884), which was not forthcoming until 1899, when the three organizations finally reached an accord. Apart from a hiccup known as the Book War of 1905, prompted by The Times Book Club around the inclusion of book clubs in these "restrictive" pricing regimes, the NBA lasted unscathed, despite challenges, for over 90 years from its coming into force on 1 January 1900.

Important to the current study is the terms of the debate and their implications. In his 1852 letter to Campbell, Bigg presented two lists of notable figures, approving and disapproving of underselling. Both lists, however, came out strongly against regulation. Herbert Spencer Esq., who was for underselling, thought that a lack of regulation would allow book sales and hence authors' profits to increase, as well as enable the enlightening spread of books among the public. Conversely, John D. Coleridge, great-nephew of Samuel Taylor Coleridge and later Lord Chief Justice of England, disapproved of underselling but felt it was best tackled by allowing unrestricted trade that would "naturally" put the undersellers at a disadvantage. Underselling, and what it meant both for the survival of individual booksellers and for affordable literature, came a poor second to principles of free trade: "let there be entire freedom in the transactions between publisher and bookseller," Lord Campbell had decreed.[37] Much stronger than any regulatory commitment to achive a desired result was their overall faith in the "healing" invisible hand of laissez-faire.

Fifty years later, echoes of this faith were still in force. By 1905, at the time of the Book War, in paradoxical approval of underselling, left-leaning Bernard Shaw issued an edition of plays outside the auspices of his publishers restricted by the NBA, to be distributed via a book club. Thereafter, Shaw, Arthur Conan Doyle, and H.G. Wells drew up unrealized plans for a limited bookshops company that would circumvent the regulated bookselling system.[38] Oddly for us in an era of aggressive neoliberalism, when laissez-faire is on the side of exploitation of those with fewest resources, it can be seen that its progressive or regressive dimensions depend on the time, space, and place over which it operates. Not morally valanced, laissez-faire and regulation are two regulatory strategies, and, rather than being ideological points of adherence, their importance ought to lie in the outcomes they might deliver under specific conditions, to differently interested communities. Where you buy your book and what you pay for it matters, but what is meant by "you" matters too.

According to Bloom's *Bestsellers* narrative of trade developments from the middle toward the end of the twentieth century, commercialization has implied increasing cultural loss. But print culture has been commercialized since industrialization if not before. Masked in Bloom's comments is that the tension between liberalization and regulative control is primarily an issue of political economy, rather than one of culture versus commerce. The tension cannot be resolved by insisting on the overriding importance of cultural capital (never a winning argument when faced with what some might call "economic realities"). Resolution instead comes from discussing what we mean by socially useful business outcomes. The debate should be on what kinds of economic systems are sustainable and most desirable in the broadest sense for the largest numbers of people, rather than a standoff between money and soul.

Throughout cultural value criticism, the narrative of commercialized innovation and cultural loss is deployed and, as a simple story of entropy, it is too light. In the early twentieth century, this narrative was put to the US National Council of Teachers by an early Fabian, Percival Chubb. His concern was for the deleterious effect commercial print might have on the literary safety of the young. Literature needed to "regain its sway over the heart and its ministry in life," Chubb felt, because the print itself "is killing the sensuous beauty and emotional appeal of literature. It is extinguishing the old folk-culture and is substituting nothing for it. Instead of the ancient harmonies of song and speech . . . we now have the silences of print."[39] And attending "that monster, Print" was "advancing commercialisation over-seas also, and everywhere . . . with our over-commercialised life—commercialised drama and opera, commercialised book production and storymaking—[we] have carried farthest this strangling of the arts." With all respects to Walter Ong, the print culture that converged with orality brought with it others means of ensuring, risking and growing literature's "sway over the heart." The commercial structuring of print culture with its attendant exploitations matched the exploitations of the residual pre-print/oral culture but along different lines. Innovation and commercialization reconfigures ills and benefits evident from the previous formation; the real battle is a political one over how those ills and benefits are distributed.

Over the first seven decades of the twentieth century, John Feather claims, the aim of institutional structures of publishing and bookselling was to preserve rather than change, and that suspicion of innovation and innovators was an industry characteristic.[40] However, the exceptional developments of the golden period came from three innovative risk-taking giants of publishing: Stanley Unwin, Victor Gollancz, and Allen Lane, whose achievements include, respectively, publishing controversial writers such as Mahatma Gandhi, the substantial increase of leftist (and detective) fiction through more effective branded distribution, and increased access for resource-weak purchasers to quality books in paperbacks known as Penguins. Later in the century, their achievements become the normative, culturally valued practices from which further commercial liberalizations were seen as a corrupting departure. The trick is asking not whether liberalization aids or retards "progression," but asking who should have access to any progress that change brings.

In the late twentieth and early twenty-first centuries, with the arrival of corporate bookstore chains replacing independent bookstores, we again find the territory narrated in familiar oppositions. David Wright summarizes the historical development as follows:

> Book retail chains, in their offline or online variants, are able to dictate the terms of trade with publishers in a way unique in the history of the book trade. The effect of this is to shift the power dynamics in the field away from the publisher as arbiter of cultural value. Depending on your position this can be either towards the customer in a democratic republic of tastes or towards the powerful retailer homogenizing tastes for more profitable 'middlebrow' books.[41]

Wright's description dichotomizes culturally valued tradition and commercial liberalization for chain retail—positive or negative depending on interpretation—but from "your" point of view, when "you" are the customer, has not any homogenizing of taste already been pushed through by profit-hungry corporate publishing? The downward shift in power from publisher to retail chain, which Wright decries, might be, for the reader, no more than a hello to the new boss, same as the old.

In her milestone study of changes to bookselling in the US over the same tumultuous period, *Reluctant Capitalists*, Laura Miller details the arguments. She does not naively posit the independent booksellers as anti-capitalist per se but, since the issue is one of size, as "more anticorporate than anticapitalist."[42] The kinds of cultural capital accrued by independents in the US had changed over the latter twentieth century. Initially their capital was derived from the appreciation of aesthetic literary culture but by the late 1970s—when literary aestheticization could be seen as an elitism to which large bookselling chains were supposedly the egalitarian remedy—their capital drew on the role bookshops played as an asset to the local community.[43] Nevertheless, in both forms of cultural capital Miller recognizes among the independents and their supporters the adoption of a "moral high ground that stands *outside* the usual market criteria of efficiency and growth" (my italics).[44] The implication in public debate was that independent shops attained a higher cultural capital than corporate bricks-and-clicks chains (who in turn attained a higher cultural capital than the clicks-only Amazons). Although Miller is careful to remind us that, from the point of view of readers, it is uncertain whether the less-standardized variety of titles proffered by independents has not been countered by the combined concentration and unimaginably long tail of titles provided by corporate retail online.[45]

Understandably, given the Bourdieusian structures it adopts, Miller's study is underpinned by a dichotomizing of cultural capital against the capital of the market.[46] Trade is seen as a clash, or at least an inversely proportional relationship, between the two capital forms, one where negotiating the standoff between money and soul is registered as a reluctant compromise. But it is also a standoff that the final chapters move toward resolving.

The solution suggested by Miller is the citizen consumer, in direct contrast to the sovereign consumer constituted by the market. The citizen consumer shops with ethical consideration, knowing that consumption is tied to the common good. One is careful about where to shop and what to buy, and if we accept the model of market behavior proposed by institutionalized neoclassical economics, then the solution is a fair one. However, the proposal still works with an opposition or inverse proportion between markets and politics, in which ethics comes at a financial cost. The citizen consumer still needs to "weigh choices about when they are willing to make trade-offs and compromises in order to retain the benefits of the market."[47] Because the system is a "trade-off," the most radical suggestion can only be that "consumption can become an act of civic participation."[48]

But in sustaining the opposition, and in not insisting that markets, including "free" markets, are already the result of political cultural decisions, the argument is unable to ask instead whether the market economy can instead become civic. Miller's injunction that readers ought not act only according to economic self-interest prescribed by neo-classical economics, is difficult to sustain in periods of austerity. But what if, collectively, our economic interests were to include the goods and satisfaction of well-being, individual and social, as well as secure and well-paid employment, healthcare and education, modest (but stable) long-term returns to shareholders, and the benefits accrued from sustainable economic life. The neoliberal recommendation is for accumulation by dispossession, or the upward redistribution of wealth, which for many then busts.[49] Cultural value is only excluded—if indeed it can be excluded—from an absolute conception of the free market, which in its theorization admits *only* economic self-interest. But the free markets of western economies are regulated and indeed constituted by social political decision-making. Their interests are already politically and culturally construed. For all other than "free markets" as a pure metaphor, political decisions constitute the market's boundaries and thus their outcomes.

In the early 2000s, social scientists began talking about "market governance" as a way to indicate the network of actors beyond solely buyers and sellers that constitutes the market, including government (both as regulator and policy marker), NGOs, lobbyists, and consumer representatives.[50] For emerging markets where factors such as social responsibility are important elements of a given product's value (non-exploitative food or clothes production, for example), Melanie DuPuis uses the general term "civic markets," indicating those markets where social-democratized value is part of the value chain.[51]

If we choose to regard books as "different," then it is also possible to conceive, as indeed it has been possible to implement, a market in which other "different" services from health care and food security to education and transport can be conducted in sustainable ways. The NBA was not perfect and its procedures cannot be transposed. New criteria and procedures for other "different" services would better suit. Book retail never really was a civic market, although under the NBA it could have become one. The first step in the conception, however, is to recognize that cultural value need not be in opposition to but can be an outcome of an economic system. It depends purely on what market system you choose.

Chapter 3

Je suis the Unknown Public

A pitfall of bringing economics into the orbit of literature and fiction is that it invites a disruptive presupposition, namely the reciprocity between qualities of literature and levels of income—that a sliding scale of higher- to lower-income "classes" of reader equates directly with higher to lower classes of literature. While only an ideologue would deny that social standing, income, and literary quality separately display differentials, it is a nonsense to suppose these in any way are directly proportional. An increasing body of work, including studies by Jonathan Rose, Paul Rooney, and Chris Hilliard, reception histories of George Eliot and of middlebrow modernism, anthologies of print culture beyond the metropolis and database revelations in *What Middletown Read*, and much else besides—all in some way inspired by the seminal work of Janice Radway—show how variegated readers' choices could be, each reader encroaching and poaching across supposedly proscribed literary territories.[1]

Further evidence of varied reading lies in the dissemination of expensive works downward and outward via increasingly cheaper editions and especially cheaper colonial editions. One need merely to think of successive editions of Victorian and Edwardian science and canon literature that, as William St. Clair makes clear, was systematically sold in steadily cheaper editions, each tranche opening up the "same" work to successively larger audiences with lower disposable income.[2] Indeed, the exploitation of price elasticity, whereby the quantity of a given work's edition increases while the price decreases, paradoxically argues for the biggest appreciation at the widest, cheapest end of the market. Depending on who is doing the presupposing, many readers at the lower end of the market were clearly not reading what was expected of them.

That does not mean that levels of disposable income and the access it grants are a dispensible category. The consumption of intangible goods can be prompted and framed by ease of access, positively or negatively, while restricted access—as in the example of higher retail prices to maintain brand exclusivity among luxury goods—can similarly affect the efferent reader's evaluations. While we may refuse crude assumptions about social class and the types of literature read, and may be startlingly conscious of the many ways to access reading matter beyond purchase, it is still incumbent on us to sketch out some of the correspondences between income, access, and titles.

Relationships between purchasing power and products would most usually be covered under market history. Unfortunately for late nineteenth and early twentieth century book retail, beyond sales figures and lists of titles, we know relatively little about who was buying and why. Library lending records provide a parallel resource—factory and institute libraries; private libraries; semi-public and genuinely public libraries such as the rate-funded lending libraries in the UK later in the nineteenth century. But that libraries lend means those records are insufficient for detailing the retail market. Readers borrow what they have not (yet) bought, and it is precisely why readers sustain the opportunity costs of purchase that is of interest.

It may be that the historical retail market remains relatively unknown because of meager record, but it remains so, too, because business is based on risk. The book trade, like any other, thrives on market information only *sufficient* to take risk rather than complete information necessary for a predictive analytical model. By and large, the various *actants* in the market remain unknown to each other, as does their reasoning, a condition which industry specialists say persists even in the demand-driven post-Fordist universe.[3] The unknown element is a structural necessity expressed as business "risk," requisite for securing profit rather than mere exchange. Unlike the analyst's public, the business "public" *remains* unpredictable for the sake of capital accumulation. For book historians looking to establish concordances between audience and publication, the opportunities market struggles in exactly the opposite direction to the extent that every business venture is a gamble.

Prior to the audacious experiment in format for George Eliot's *Middlemarch* (1871–72) that by no means was assured success, a manager of Blackwood's publishing firm summarized their general anxiety: "But 'tis an incalculable animal the general reader!"[4] Eliot's *Middlemarch*—

four volumes of eight bimonthly parts retailing at 5s per part—indeed proved a success, but no one predicted the rocketing market created by the single-volume 1874 edition retailing at 7s 6d for the entire book: an unforeseen market of "lower-class" readers that Blackwood's catered to with their cheap single-volume reprints.[5] It is the incalculable animal, the by-no-means-assured gamble that the book historian attempts to explain, after the fact—not as an act of romantic heroism but as a barrier that will never entirely be crossed.

In an 1858 article for *Household Words*, Wilkie Collins claimed the existence of an alien Other that he termed the "unknown public."[6] The literary preferences of this unknown public, like his estimate of their social standing, Collins deemed to be poor, but he credited those readers with an emancipatory curiosity and predicted they would enlighten themselves along a path beginning, he suggested, with Scott's *Kenilworth* and ending with the "very best men among living English writers"—including, by implication, Wilkie Collins.[7] A later solution to who exactly was buying cheap penny literature, suggested by Thomas Wright in 1883,[8] would have come as a surprise to Collins, enmeshed as he was in specific conceptions of literary cultural capital. Since Collins shared the idea of a hierarchy of literatures, in which reading ought naturally to gravitate toward the "best," any attempt to understand the experience of the poorest literature would seem as perverse as any resistance to best. But from our perspective, the reading habits of the risk-filled unknown are exactly the goal.

Collins found his unknown public during his wanderings "more especially in the second and third rate neighbourhoods" of the city. Its outlets were the "small stationer's or small tobacconist's-shop." Its teeming publications were to be had in "the deserts of West Cornwall . . . a populous thoroughfare of Whitechapel . . . [and] a dreary little lost town at the north of Scotland."[9] This public numbered in the millions: three million was Collins's estimate although, towards the end of the century and based on the circulation of well-established penny magazines, Wright later put the figure closer to five million. The literature most eagerly consumed in this market was the fiction serialized in weekly penny journals, small quarto in size, consisting of a few unbound pages, each with a picture on the upper half of the front leaf, and a quantity of small print on the under half. According to Collins, the quality of this serial fiction, usually illustrated by the journal's only purpose-cut woodblock, lacked utterly any promise in style, characterization, or "arrangement of incident"—features, incidentally, that Collins had elsewhere perfected. He thought the stories remarkable only for their "extraordinary sameness," and so engrained was this public's literary taste for the formula that it would not be enticed even by the comparatively "low" literatures of Alexander Dumas or Eugene Sue. Collins's understanding, however, was that this public was in need of education and, with patience, he foresaw a progression in taste.[10]

What perturbed Collins, though, was that he could find no one among his extensive circle who was a subscriber to such penny journals. He could easily imagine the religious public with their own booksellers and literatures; the public who read for information, tackling biographies, histories and travel; the newspaper-reading public; and the public for amusements frequenting the circulating libraries and railway stalls. For Collins, the unknown public remained a blank that could be filled only by speculation, its intellectual capacity to be guessed at using criteria established within Collins's literary realm. But to his consternation, when republishing the article in 1863, Collins found no new evidence that the public's tastes had improved. "Patience! patience!" he counseled, but they seemed to remain impervious to better writing.[11]

That the public must exist was a matter of deduction on the part of Collins, since they were needed to explain the penny-journal sales, but Collins and critics like him had "never been able to discover a living specimen of the unknown public, and express themselves curious to know who and what manner of people the members of such a public can be."[12] Wright's 1883 reply initially followed lines of reason set up by Collins, but the bulk of his response came from the thick description of personal involvement, since "In my green and salad days . . . I belonged to the unknown public . . . and even now I do not feel the humiliation which I suppose I ought to experience in making this confession."[13]

The journal running Wright's 1883 article, *The Nineteenth Century*, was a British literary monthly established and edited from 1877 by Sir James Knowles, a thinker, critic, editor, and architect (works including the layout of London's Leicester Square and Aldworth House, the Gothic extravaganza that was Alfred Lord Tennyson's home on the Isle of Wight). Although Knowles was the proprietor, the journal was published in the sense of printed and distributed from London by Henry King, a successful up-by-the-bootstraps Victorian entrepreneur who had climbed vertically from his days as a Brighton bookseller.[14] The journal cost half a crown (2s 6d) in the 1880s, and its audience would not have been the unknown penny public of the article's title. Furthermore, like the current scholarly online provision of nineteenth-century material that enabled access to the journal, the article represents only a window onto an unknown public refracted through the dark glass of professional interest.[15] The author, Thomas Wright, was also a professional who produced copy to meet the journal's intellectual and moral standards, which may explain Wright's need to schematize his public and his unsurprising preoccupation with disreputability.

Wright's point was that Collins had metaphorically and mistakenly equated the style of penny-journal writing with class division—as the writing was "poorest," so too would be its audience and, linking stylistics to social standing, Collins thought to look among the very poor. A glance at contemporary surveys, however, shows us why Wright was right to suspect Collins was wrong.

At the very bottom of the socioeconomic ladder were "gentleman of the highway." In 1901, the *Bournemouth Daily Echo*, echoing an article in the *St. James's Gazette* only a day earlier, claimed to report on the reading interests of tramps. The information had almost certainly been gathered from an uncited publication by Josiah Flynt—his *Tramping with Tramps: Studies and Sketches* (1899), and possibly prompted by the recent release of Flynt's study of the criminal underground, *The World of Graft* (1901).[16] Though Flynt wrote about tramping in the US, some correlation might be supposed.

> Thackeray and Dickens, he [Flynt] reports, are the favourite novelists of the majority. Next in favour comes, Robert Louis Stevenson—a true open air man was he—who is particularly admired for what one of his patrons calls 'his big mouthfuls of words.' It is not surprising to hear that Henry George's 'Progress and Poverty' is the subject of lively discussion at the tramps 'hang outs' . . . Other authors who have a reputation at the lodging houses include the names of Shakespeare, Victor Hugo, Eugene Sue, Conan Doyle, Mark Twain, and Bret Harte. Contemporary periodical literature is not overlooked by travellers of this type, for Mr. Flynt has heard from some of them very intelligent criticisms of his own papers in the 'Century.'[17]

During his 1902 undercover slum explorations into London's East End docklands, recounted in *People of the Abyss* (1903), Jack London saw how scant and often nonexistent the disposable income was that might potentially be spent on reading, and how high were the competitive demands over its use. People could read or be read to and would when they had respite, but purchasing reading matter was another question. Looking at what else could be had for the price of a penny journal, we might start with London's inventory. The cigarettes they all smoked were often scavenged "kerb-butts" but, by the 1880s, Wild Woodbine had become one of the most popular cigarettes in the country and the price had dropped to as low as one penny for a packet of five, and rough tobacco could be had for less. In lodging houses, London budgeted gas for cooking at a penny, which was barely sufficient to cook a meal. For lunch, he ate in a coffee house: stewed mutton and peas, which cost him sixpence. When driven to a "doss-house," London paid five pence for his "cabin," which redeemed a space just large enough for a bed with a slot next to it in which to undress (each cabin formed by the interlocking of high partitions in the much larger hall). Most men in the doss-house were between twenty and forty, of working age. Older single men, less employable, were forced to make do with the workhouse.[18] Not mentioned in London's account, those hardest pressed at the workhouse could resort to the "two-penny hangover," when available, which was a rope stretched across the room or above a bench over which "occupants" could drape themselves, with the rope under the armpits, and gain whatever sleep they could for the price of two penny journals.[19]

Reading matter in the workhouse around 1890 was dependent on what books, magazines, and newspapers were donated by the public and by charitable organizations, almost certainly including material from the Society for the Promotion of Christian Knowledge (SPCK), who were actively involved in the workhouse movement.[20] Supplies would have been haphazard. The Bradford workhouse, with capacity for 300 men and 200 women, was unsupplied with either periodicals or newspapers; Derby, with capacity for 196 men and 162 women, was "fairly well supplied" with periodicals, and took in 30 newspapers per week, in addition to a stock of toys for its 156 children; while Dorchester's 95 inmates had access to "12 *Graphics* every fortnight" and daily to the previous day's newspaper.[21] Higginbotham describes collection boxes established after 1864 along the Lancashire and Yorkshire railways into which travelers could place discarded books and periodicals. By 1874, guardians of the

Haslingden workhouse who initiated the scheme were surprised to learn that one was full. After decisions made by the Local Government Board in 1891, charitable supplies were supplemented by acquisitions paid for from the poor rate, which included toys and illustrated books for children. These reading supplies were far from the deliberate acquisitions of desire-negotiating agents, or at least those of their end-using readers.

Staying in one of the better 5d "poor-man's hotels" in Whitechapel, London described the competing claims on the laborer's leisure time. After a day's work, a laborer could enjoy bread dipped in salt, washed down by a mug of tea. A piece of fish completed the meal. In the smoking room, driven up by nausea caused by smells from the kitchen, London more happily found "a couple of small billiard tables and several checkerboards were being used by young working men, who waited in relays for their turn at the games, while many men were sitting around, smoking, reading, and mending clothes."[22] Alcohol would not have been tolerated in such reforming houses, so it provided no financial competition to reading matter, though not outside the doss-house! Unlike smoking, the time spent mending was a necessity, as clothes were prone to rot.[23] Prior to the development of affordable water-resistant fabrics, people unable to stay indoors simply got wet and, if without drying facilities, their clothes rotted. Where would purchased reading material come on a list of priorities?

Henry Mayhew during the 1850s and Charles Booth during the 1880s proved (rather than supposed) the low level of wages among the urban London poor. An inexperienced bottle washer in a factory could earn 3s per week, working from 8:00 a.m. to 7:00 p.m.; a jam factory worker at the height of the fruit season might earn 7s per week, while the factory average was between 8s and 11s per week, though wages as high as 15s could be had from meat-packing factories.[24] London gives the example of a woman, a tie-maker, who for working a full week earned 5s (or eight and a half pence per day—and her husband had not worked for ten years). The 21s upon which London based his calculations of weekly expenditure for a family of five—rent 6s, bread 4s, meat 3s 6d, vegetables 2s 6d, coal and firewood 1s 4d, other necessities 46d (totalling 21/2)—meant that "the family cannot ride in busses or trams, cannot write letters, take outings, go to a tu'penny gaff' . . . join social or benefit clubs, nor can they buy sweetmeats, tobacco, books or newspapers."[25]

Although historical relative costs present a nightmare in calculation, we can still arrive at a non-numerical approximation of how much "cost" cost. An estimate from 1921, calculated over three periods from the nineteenth and early twentieth centuries, claimed that in 1880 a lower-income family consisting of man, woman, and three children, earning 17s per week would spend 69% of their income on food. The same family at a slightly higher income of 22s 6d would spend 16s on food, which is again just over 70%.[26] Maud Pember Reeve's classic survey, *Round About a Pound a Week*, conducted slightly later in 1913, found similar ratios of expenditure on food relative to accommodation.[27] Rents varied greatly from town to town and area to area but in general, unlike today, food and not rent took the lion's share of a lower wage, at very roughly a 7:3 ratio of food to shelter in income spent. From a single person's earnings of 16d per day, you would have to subtract about 11d to avoid starvation, and somewhere around 5d to avoid one of the smaller private doss houses that London described as a place of unmitigated horrors. You would have to think very carefully about spending 1d on a fiction-bearing news miscellany.

The area covered in the *Abyss* was the London equivalent of smaller but similar quarters to be found in any of the major ports or industrial cities throughout the UK. In Southampton, the workhouse for the city center was in the St. Mary's district, at 154 St. Mary's Road, which became the Southampton Technical College from 1952 and is now part of City College.[28] There were several areas of dilapidation, equivalent to London's Abyss, including an area known as the Ditches that endured until bombing during WWII, and in the medieval center around Upper Bugle Street, Simnel Street, and Back-of-the Walls before clearances after 1890. Indeed, it was a series of letters to the press that sparked the 1890s Southampton slum clearances, the first of which was headed "The Exceedingly Bitter Cry of Outcast Southampton," its title reflecting Andrew Mearne's "Bitter Cry of Outcast London" (1883).[29]

Southampton was unexceptional in its industrialized social conditions, which in turn would play out in reading choices. Other port hubs such as Hamburg—from where great lines like Hamburg-America, Hamburg-South America ("Dampfschifffahrts-Gesellschaft"), and North German Lloyd would dock carrying European emigrants on their way to the New Worlds—shared similar social conditions, but, because of later industrialization and late political union, according to different configurations.[30] The historic harbor-area slums of Hamburg, designated socially "sick," were not extensively cleared until after 1897, following a cholera epidemic in 1892, after which those uprooted by the clearances and newly attracted laborers from Schleswig-Holstein and elsewhere moved into industrial slum tenements built in Rothenburgsort and Hammerbrook.[31] And in the "City of Work," readers likewise made use of their fiction-bearing journals and cheap editions, as would industrial-port citizens of Antwerp, New York, Buenos Aires, Cape Town, Lisbon—all ports to where Southampton cargo, passenger, and mail services sailed.[32]

Overall in urban Britain, a frenetic micro-hierarchy at the lower-income levels of society could be found: from respectable semi-skilled laborers, artisans, and small sweatshop entrepreneurs at the higher end, to unskilled hand laborers, sweatshop employees, and costermongers at the low, and then the elderly and infirm at the very lowest levels. Some people, on some occasions, may have invested small sums in reading material but, with such tight margins, it would depend on which "third rate neighbourhood" of Britain, to use Wilkie Collins's phrase, you found yourself in and on what you were doing. A relatively prosperous period around the 1860s was replaced by the great depression in agriculture in Britain from the 1870s to the 1890s that, although increasing affordability of food staples derived from US wheat production, affected rural laborers, whose decamping to the cities further exacerbated the situation for those already in the city with least resources. Paradoxically, a series of education acts from 1880 requiring school attendance for children between the ages of 5 and 10 (increasing to 5–11 in 1893, and 5–12 in 1899), meant that the overall earning potential of the poorest families was further threatened. And by the 1890s the competition for urban jobs among hand workers was hiked yet again by European immigration fomented by pogroms in Russia and Poland.

In Britain, for many complex reasons, the situation for the poorest social groups did not improve notably until after these setbacks around the turn of the century and after, when commodity culture reached even these lowest levels. So such internationalized, impoverished urban settings were to be found in varying degrees throughout any industrializing country, wherever high ratios of population density to low income could be sustained and where the industrialization of print was promising but not yet providing a regular supply of affordable reading material.

If the market for Collins's five-million-strong avid public of penny journals was not to be found among the poorest classes, where should it be found? The objection that Wright's article raised was the assumption of one undiscriminating homogenous public who read—and only read—penny-journal novels. "That there may be individual members of the unknown public whose reading is confined to the penny journals I do not doubt," Wright contended, but penny novel readers did not lack discrimination. Rather, they were omnivorous and would devour everything from penny novels to Wilkie Collins. "I have seen the [penny] journals . . . lying on drawing room tables among the more permanent ornaments of which were—strange as the assertion may sound to those holding the hitherto prevailing views concerning the unknown public— such books as handsomely got up editions of Shakespeare's *Works*, the Doré edition of *Don Quixote*, and Farrar's *Life of Christ*."[33] Few adults from this public had not read in serialized form at least some of Dickens's novels, a few of Scott's, and many of Bulwer-Lytton's. The failure of Scott's *Kenilworth* in the penny weeklies, he claimed, was because its legion editions had already been available "from every second-hand bookseller's shelves or old book-hawker's barrow."[34]

Familiar titles among the unknown public were held to include *It's Never too Late to Mend* (Charles Reade 1856), *Hard Cash* (Charles Reade, serialized in *All the Year Round*, 28 March to 26 December 1863), *The Woman in White* (Wilkie Collins, serialized in *All the Year Round*, 26 November 1859 to 25 August 1860), *No Name* (Wilkie Collins, serialized in *All the Year Round*, 15 March 1862 to 17 January 1863), and "the earlier works in the Braddon series."[35] Indeed, Mary Elizabeth Braddon, author of the wildly bestselling *Lady Audley's Secret* (1862–63 in serial, 1862 in volume), shared the top three favorite slots among the unknown public along with the co-authored novels of Walter Besant and James Rice and the now wildly neglected James Payn, author of some forty-one novels, including the revealingly titled *For Cash Only* (1881–82), *What He Cost Her* (serialized in *All the Year Round*, 12 August 1876 to 2 June 1877), and *A Modern Dick Whittington* (1892). And among his own reading from his youth among the public, Wright had read "infinitely greater works" from an earlier age: *Pilgrim's Progress*, *Robinson Crusoe*, *Gulliver's Travels*, *Gil Blas*, the leatherstocking stories of James Fenimore Cooper, Sir Walter Scott, and several novels by Captain Marryat.[36]

Following the port-cities connection, Payn appeared in the international press, too: a Hamburg paper, *Hamburg Nachrichten*, 17 February 1882, ran a St. Georg district advertisement for the St. Georg Circulating Library, Steindamm 11, announcing volumes by Mite Kremnitz, A.J. Mordtmann, Erich Lilsen, and James Payn's *Die Diamanten der gnädigen Frau*, with low-cost subscription rates beneath.[37] A Dutch-language international trades paper *Locomotief: Nieuws, Handels en Advertentieblad*—also available by subscription throughout Europe and India, published by De Groot, Kolf and Co., a Dutch-Indonesian firm based in Semarang—ran Payn's 1877 three-volume novel *What He Cost Her* in feuilletton as *Wat Hij Haar Kostte*, from 2 November 1877 to 6 May 1878.[38]

The unknown public of the nineteenth and early twentieth centuries was prepared to read across genres and centuries. Unlike in the twenty-first century, where purchase price is relatively lower, their reading habits were driven as much by maximizing returns on financial outlay as by any serial fashion requiring the latest, or by avant-gardism (as prescriptive literary scholarship would have it) requiring the most advanced. The question remains, though, whether the unknown public regarded their penny novels as necessities, albeit in a tarnished format, or whether, like magpies, they picked around the book market for anything attractive.

Contrary to Collins's assumption, the consumers of UK penny novels were found among higher levels of disposable income. By 1861 over one and a half million domestic servants worked in Britain, topping at two million around 1914: "A general maid might get something between £10 and £16 per year, a footman £20 to £40 depending on experience."[39] Domestic servants, avoiding accommodation costs and receiving full board, would therefore have roughly 4s to 6 1/2s per week for personal items for a female maid and 8s to 15s for a male footman. For this group, penny journals were a thrifty alternative to the 3s or 6s novel, to the similarly priced single-volume reprints of a standard three-volume commercial-library novel at 5s to 6s, and to the extraordinarily high-priced library-accessed three-volume novel at 31s 6d that, well known to book historians, was artificially maintained at that level for much of the century until the system's collapse sometime after the Net Book Agreement of 1894.[40]

Nevertheless, Wright was reluctant to locate the unknown public only among domestic servants: "Thousands of servants are to be found among the millions of the unknown public; but they are comparatively outsiders and of little account."[41] For Wright, the penny public had a specific class and gender. They came from "several cuts above the domestic class. They belong to the Young Lady classes—the young ladies of the counters, of the more genteel female handicrafts generally and the dressmaking and millinery professions in particular." To these readers Wright also added a small army of unattached "real genteel" ladies, who lived comfortably on a limited family allowance, and, in what Wright considered a feminine aptitude for cooperation, "by a system of 'exchanges' . . . [they] manage to obtain a practically unlimited supply of this reading at an outlay of two to three pence per week."[42] The journals, witnessed in the houses of respected tradespeople, were purchased not only from small by-street shops or from newsboys selling by the armful, but also from the largest booksellers or newsagents of the high street. Being constant readers, Wright claimed, and averse to the enforced abstinence necessary for purchasing a novel in volume, the general alternative for the penny public was to be novel-less.

Carrying their tastes into married life, these ladies passed on their reading material to their clerk, shopkeeper, and artisan husbands, as well as to male and female siblings. "The men do not, as a rule, read the stories," and preferred the random columns of variety, views, news and answers to correspondents, but "there is no hesitation in thrusting them into the pockets of 'working clothes.' . . . Penny fiction journals are no uncommon sight in the workshop world, especially among hands who stay in the shop to their meals."[43] However, if "better" novels became available from beyond the penny journal, then opportunities were seized:

> Fathers, brothers, or lovers of the young ladies may be members of mechanics' or literary institutions, or work for firms having their own lending libraries, or be entitled to borrow books from free libraries. They may be haunters of second-hand bookstalls, or occasional buyers of new books.[44]

Such "better" books flowed readily into circulation along with penny literature. The unknown public were simply members of a broad-reading general public with an eye to thrift. By the 1890s, referring to this public's apparent preference for similarly cheap "snippets" associated with journals such as *Tit Bits*, one commentator could complain,

> The general public is now to be counted in millions, for it includes nearly all the mill-workers, tradesmen, domestic servants, errand-boys, and strikers. To these add the innumerable clerks of our great cities, and we have some notion of the public whom our novelists miss and Snippets catches.[45]

The unknown public ran from domestic classes to "several cuts above," from strikers to the clerks of great cities, or more simply they were a large swathe of the general reading public. The population of Britain in

1883 was around twenty-five million, whereof 35% were under fifteen.[46] Remembering Wright's figure of five million—the estimate's plausibility backed by Wright's position as a professional journalist working for the rags-to-riches publishing entrepreneur—it would seem that the circulation of penny journals reached 30% of the adult population over fifteen. A sizable chunk of Britain's readers at the turn of the century had access to cheap penny serials while less often, but no less significantly, to the better fiction of its and earlier ages, including Wilkie Collins.

The penny journal par excellence was the *London Journal*, from 1845 to 1912, specializing in working-class fiction. Edward Salmon, in an 1886 article less than supportive of progress and upward mobility, "What the Working Classes Read,"[47] complained that the *London Journal* had lost its earlier modicum of dignity and now published only trash—an odd claim, since the journal's first editor was that giant of labor agitation, republicanism, and entertainment George W.M. Reynolds, whose *Reynolds's Newspaper* (formerly *Reynolds's Miscellany*) was another outlet for penny fiction.[48] A representative list of penny journals would include *Lloyd's Weekly Newspaper*, an extremely popular one-penny Sunday paper for which Salmon claimed a circulation of three-quarters of a million weekly. Among other fictions, it serialized Conan Doyle's *The Parasite* (1894) and published Mrs. Linton's short story "My Charming Lodger" in 1895. The one-penny Saturday weekly *England: A Weekly Newspaper for All Classes*, which incorporated *The Primrose Chronicle* from 1886, was another serial fiction outlet and, according to Salmon, drew its popularity from publishing only facts that tended to discredit the Liberal Party. *The People: A Newspaper for All Classes*, a one-penny Sunday paper, included serializations of Wilkie Collins, Ouida, Mrs. Linton, Arthur Conan Doyle, Grant Allen, and Rider Haggard. The *Penny Illustrated Paper*, serializing Hall Caine, William Russell, Walter Besant, and Wilkie Collins, among others, sold "in its hundreds of thousands weekly" and secured "a well-merited popularity with every class"; it was itself a spin-off from the mighty six-penny *Illustrated London News*, which listed among its many contributors serializations by Joseph Conrad, Thomas Hardy, Henry James, George Gissing, Walter Besant, Wilkie Collins, and Rider Haggard.[49] Salmon particularly praised the one-penny *Family Herald* for serializing Florence Warden's *The House on the Marsh* (1883). *Rare Bits* and *Tit Bits*, along with *Cassell's Saturday Journal*, were popular with "readers among the poorer classes," as were *The Leisure Hour* and *Sunday at Home*. Not an outlet for fiction per se, but certainly of useful knowledge and high (though fragmented) cultural capital, was the magpie-like *Great Thoughts* that "culls from master works some of the choicest ideas ever given to the world."[50]

Rather than Collins's deduced necessity, the idea of an "unknown public" was an ideological accusation that concealed readers' wilfully undisciplined risk-filled behavior in a specific market, wherein popular authors such as M.E. Braddon and Ouida, canon writers such as Bunyan and Shakespeare, and writers now familiar on the nineteenth-century syllabus such as George Eliot and Wilkie Collins rubbed book jackets together with authors who now have little value: Caroline Cameron, Mary Albert, Grant Allen, Robert Francillon, and the man who Wright believed eclipsed Mary Braddon, James Payn, enticingly straddling high and low critical repute: "Mr Payn's novels, while favourites with polished and critical readers, are making more way with the many-headed than those of any contemporary writer."[51] Wright states how Payn compared well among the penny public, matching the humor of Walter Besant's *Ready-Money Mortiboy* (1872) published in the three-penny journal *Once a Week*.

John Sutherland credits Payn with a love of sensational plot and excessively melodramatic complication, but the same Cambridge-educated Payn also represents a confounding of "high" and "low" cultural value. Without apparent internal contradiction, Payn had been an editor of the *Chambers's Edinburgh Journal*, columnist for the *Illustrated London News*, a powerful literary broker, editor of the *Cornhill Magazine*, and author of around forty-one novels, including one based on Shakespeare forgeries from the eighteenth century and an 1896 mystery, *The Disappearance of George Driffell*, dedicated to Arthur Conan Doyle.[52]

At the fulcrum of this public's literary taste, too, was Ouida: "she is their literary prophet . . . Ouida's writing is essentially the acme of penny serial style. The novelists of penny prints toil after her in vain, but they do toil after her."[53] Of penny novelettes, Salmon notes that the editors are occasionally fortunate "to secure a story from such writers as Miss Florence Marryat [youngest child of Captain Frederick Marryat] and Miss Jean Middlemass."[54] Acknowledging that many penny writers were utterly obscure at the time, Wright does give more prominent examples, including William Harrison Ainsworth (39 novels), George Manville Fenn (33 novels; also editor of the three-penny *Once a Weeek*), Mary Cecil Hay (14 novels; also wrote under the pseudonyms Mark Hardcastle and Markham Howard), Mrs. Pender Cudlip (née Annie Thomas, 65 novels), and Francis Notley (16 novels), who published *Red Riding Hood* (1882) in the *Family Herald*, a penny weekly coming out on Saturdays. Wright also names no less a figure than George Augustus Sala, who contributed to the penny public in both formative and established years. Sala's early *The Baddington Peerage: Who Won, and Who Wore It: A Story of the Best and the Worst Society* came out in the weekly *The Illustrated Times* in 1857, while *Quite Alone* appeared in Dickens's *All the Year Round*, from February to December 1864, although both *The Seven Sons of Mammon* (1861) and *The Strange Adventures of Captain Dangerous* (1863) were serialized in the more pricey *Temple Bar*, a one-shilling monthly. His eponymous *Sala's Journal: A Weekly Magazine for All*, however, was a one-penny weekly that serialized the work of Mary Kennard, Edward Goodman, Rosa C. Pread, and the rags-to-riches playwright, novelist, and campaigner against anti-Semitism Benjamin Farjeon; it also serialized Sala's *Margaret Forster: A Dream within a Dream* from July to November 1893. For the two-penny public, Wright cites writers such as Charles Lever, Elizabeth Gaskell, Charles Reade, and Anthony Trollope.

For Wright, a particularly successful penny-fiction novelist was John Frederick Smith, who produced a number of serializations around mid-century, some of which were reissued in volume by Bradley and Co., London, from the late 1880s, including *Minnigrey* (1851–52, vol. 1897), *Stanfield Hall* (serial 1849, 3 vols. 1888–89), *Woman and Her Master* (1897), and *Will and the Way* (1888). Wright was particularly grateful to Smith for the habit of including an epigraph of verse with each chapter, "and there were two or three chapters in each weekly portion," some considerable in length and most of them "good bits" in themselves.[55] When finished with the chapters, Wright would reread and occasionally learn the epigraphs by heart, thus granting him his first liking for poetry, from writers such as Shakespeare and Thomas Gray.[56] Towards the end of the century, then, arising from a specific market configuration and an attitude to cost that was part of the current commodity culture, readers were just as likely to make personal gains from reading Cudlip, Payn, and Smith as they were Collins, Dickens, and Eliot, or Swift, Bunyan, and Shakespeare.

The implications of all these enmeshed efferent readings are revealing, both about readers' behavior *and* about crude assumptions concerning social class and types of literature being read. If we pretended that the unknown public was not a crude "phallogocentric" device for maintaining binary exclusivity, we could choose a linear interpretation, as Collins did, and imagine that these readers should progress to better works with increasing readerly sophistication—then damn them for their obstinacy in remaining unattracted to sophisticated literature. The evidence presented here, however, suggests not linearity but diversity, and the "unknown" exhibited is not the Other's secret demographic but the way people, and groups of people, arrange various types of literature into the overall composition of their lives. And like our developing self-discrepancy, those compositions are made of public, social materials.

Chapter 4

When Books Come to Town
International Aspirations, High Street-Bound

In an economically framed understanding of reading, we need to ask about the conditions of consumption for books, about the historic duration of those conditions, and about whether those conditions might be gendered. We need to ask what happens to an item of cultural production such as a text when it takes part in the leisure sector, in a port like Southampton, toward the end and turn of the nineteenth century. A rookie mistake would be to conceive this as a purely *cultural* object entering and buoyed up by the city's *economic* life. For Southampton, the city's culture is not a trade-enabled superstructure: the city's culture *is* trade, and so are its books.

Southampton has been recreating itself through trade for almost two millennia. It sits in the bowl of a Y-shape of land formed by the rivers Test and Itchen meeting in the Solent strait, with its advantageous double tide, and has attracted world trade since before the Roman conquest. The town decamped from its Saxon origins on the banks of the Itchen to its present Test-side center during the tenth century, and what is now its AI automated global container port is the heir to an international trade hub that has been active since at least the proclamation there of Knud of Denmark to King of England in 1014, later King Cnut of a Danish North Sea Empire.[1] In the twenty-first century, the port of Southampton brings in everything from game consoles to hybrid cars, from China and East Asia, while in the fifteenth century it brought in timber and furs from the western Baltic and Gdansk; wine, wax, and oils from the

French Atlantic coast, northern Spain and Portugal; more wine from Genoa; and silks, glass, and luxury goods from Venice and the Adriatic; mostly in return for exports of wool and cloth. Such trade in commodities has become the city's cultural landmark, visible across the oceans, bringing in wealth—but also disaster in the form of Vikings and then Frenchmen, early on, and later in the form of German national socialists. There have been large-scale squabbles with international merchant and finance organizations—Venetian or Genoese in fifteenth century, or the International Monetary Fund in the twenty-first; struggles always against would-be monopolies based in London, and then as now against neighboring ports such as Portsmouth and Plymouth, or European giants such as Rotterdam and Antwerp. Current competitive newcomers, such as global corporate finance institutions and franchises, provide a twist to an older narrative of market rivalry, at one time more likely pitching Southampton interests against Salisbury and Winchester—in 1450, men from the nearby hamlet of Romsey descended riotously on the town in a dispute about the city's trade with Lombardy.[2] This heritage of exchange-based conflict and growth *is* Southampton's culture.

Home to this vexatious market history has been the High Street, its pedigree as a purpose-built space established by at least the late middle ages, when institutional regulations stipulated what activities could be carried out there and what behaviors were acceptable.[3] In counter-distinction to French Street, which joined together the French-speaking areas of the town after the Norman Conquest, Southampton's High Street was initially called after its cultural signifier English Street. Colin Platt describes this "great street" of medieval Hamton as a broad thoroughfare, its direction dictated by the boundary of the waters to the west and south, and salt marshes to the east, and which functioned as the main artery of the town. Leading merchants lived on it or had property near it, and shops or open stalls spread along its length—smiths to the north end around All Saints, the butchers next to them in the St. Lawrence area.[4] The road extending north of the Bargate, called Above Bar Street ("bovebarrestreete"), was a continuation of English Street, gaining buildings and at least four inns by the early 1600s, by which time the entire road from Above Bar to Below Bar could be referred to as the High Street (from 1546 at the latest). Writing in 1801, Sir Henry Englefield claimed that "the most careless observer must necessarily be struck with the beauty of the High, anciently called English Street; which for breadth, width and cleanliness, can scarcely be equalled in England."[5] Dividing the High

Street is the Norman and medieval, then adaptively Georgian, Victorian, and restoratively twenty-first-century Bargate itself, which has witnessed a shift in business concentration from Below to Above Bar, accelerated in the twentieth century, and by new building in the 1950s enforced after the air-raid devastation on 30 November and 1 December 1940, two nights from a two-thousand-year history, and later by shopping-mall development at Bargate Centre (1989), West Quay (2000), and Westquay South (2016–17). And it is through this Bargate that so many companies of troops have marched, to fight Boers or interfere in the Suez, and more recently to return from Afghanistan and Iraq, in cultural wars that have never been unconnected to the interests of British trade.

Societies have always held markets. Privileges have granted the market special status as a bounded public space where, in its system of exchangeable commodities, taste and people could be re-designated as spices and slaves. Regulated from the outset, this public market was open to inspection, in distinction to private spaces (inns or domestic houses) that were sites of possible fraudulence. In the feudal regime, canonical and statutory law operated with the concept of the market's "just price" (*contra* fixed prices of bread and ale that were set by law) that was designed to prevent unfair pricing from "forestalling, engrossing and regrating: respectively the buying up of goods before they reach the market, the purchase and hoarding of large quantities of a commodity in order to push up prices, and the practice of buying wholesale to sell retail at a profit."[6] In effect, municipal legislation created this regulated market and stipulated who was to be included and to whom access was denied. In its medieval and current configurtations, the market was and is a legislatively controlled space very much for the benefit of invested men.

A point reiterated by Yanis Varoufakis, however, is that a society of markets is not market society, the form of capitalism that emerged in Britain across the eighteenth century and accelerated in the nineteenth, and which is subsequently spreading worldwide.[7] Market society extends the privileges of the bounded market space beyond the High Street into the everyday of labor and consumption, to become a mode of social organization. At market society's extreme, precious little is left outside of its domain. But at no time, however, has this organizational mode lost its cultural composition. Nowadays, the criteria measuring High Street behavior will admit to only economic rationality, but it runs as it always has done on people who think, and want, and feel. When economics presents itself as an exact science of calculation, Cambridge political economist John Rapley says it has "physics envy"—also meaning that the exactness masks an improbability, since, as American physicist Murray Gell-Mann said, "Think of how hard physics would be if the electrons could think."[8] Unlike in physics or chemistry, the smallest particles of the High Street have a mind of their own, resulting very much from the culture that created them. At Christmas, it is the thrill of outdoor drinking legitimized by "German" stalls that increases the High Street's gravitational pull, along with the nostalgia created from the computer-lit temporary ice rink. The High Street, then, is *the* locus of coordinating cultural and economic values—and is still important enough to warrant national protection for cultural reasons.[9]

The High Street's continuities and changes can be traced from nineteenth-century illustrations. Cunningham's street directory of 1811 includes professional services (clerks, solicitors, and bookkeepers) as well as the hairdressers, wig and umbrella makers, milliners, jewelers, grocers, drapers, and every other service one would expect in a sizable town.[10] In the same 1811 directory are a number of "Reading Rooms": Mr. Isaac Fletcher at 142 High Street; Mr. Thos. [Thomas] Skelton's reading room and circulating library; Mr. Thos. Seed's circulating library at 16 High Street; and, in an encouraging sign of gender parity, Mrs. M. Street's circulating library at 141 High Street. There is no suggestion of a cultural superstructure. The entire existence of the High Street, including its reading rooms, is predicated on trade.

At the height of Empire, Southampton's cultural commodification was hoggishly global. According to the directory of 1900, and no differently to Westquay South's 2017 Brazilian *churrascaria*, the city's popular restaurant for breakfasts, luncheons, dinners, and suppers was Suisse Café and Restaurant at 138–141 High Street (note the spelling), where a large Swiss flag was painted above the building front, and window notices made a point that it served Continental cookery. From Harry Crosby's at 64 High Street, the Anglo-Bavarian Brewing Company sold its ales, award winners for freedom from acidity at the Vienna Exhibition of 1873;[11] the "Hindoostan Tea company" operated from number 122; and the classified trades section of the directory has an entire list of shops acting as Berlin Wool and Fancy Repositories.[12] In the High Street's bookshops, you could browse for global exotica among histories and geographies, or in publications ranging from women's settler narratives, by writers such as Isabelle Aylmer and Ellen Ellis, to masculine writers of the colonial fringe like Rudyard Kipling and Joseph Conrad.[13] And it was along the High Street—where else—that a cortège carrying the embalmed body of David Livingstone made its way at local-authority expense after being landed at the Southampton Royal Pier on 15 April 1874, before transportation to London.[14]

The internationalism to High Street trade extended energetically beyond the borders of Empire. As Charles Emmerson notes of Argentina around 1910, from where fleets of ships carrying frozen meat, *frigorificos*, passed fleets carrying immigrant and seasonal labor from Liverpool, Southampton, Naples, Marseilles, Genoa, and Hamburg, "As in many other parts of the world, though Argentina was not formally part of the British Empire, the tentacles of British influence wrapped themselves around Buenos Aires' commercial life," such influence being underpinned by Britain's trade agreements with Argentina from 1825 onward.[15]

The High Street's retail and REST sector (Recreation, Entertainment, Sports, and Tourism) was a place where private dreams, Empire, global reach, and commodities came together and made sense. As much tools of social advancement as hobbies or pastimes, political guides and instruction books were recommended side by side with haberdasheries and fashions in the columns of local newspapers. In the *Southern Echo* gossip column "From All Quarters," Sotonians could read that jeweled combs, soft mantillas, and large coquettish fans of Spanish design were now all the rage due to the forthcoming Royal Spanish marriage (Alfonso XIII to Victoria Eugenie of Battenberg), before reading next that the British Queen Alexandra (of Denmark) was currently enthusiastic about a new book on improving children's diction—the column notes that "few people of any class . . . make the best use of their voices."[16] These aspirational tip-offs about what accoutrements and books were in vogue were immediately followed by a heads-up on how to pay for them, in that Argentina would soon compete with the colonies for British emigrants, and that London representatives of that republic had announced reception bureaus set up in Buenos Aires guaranteeing not only employment to British laborers but full cover for the costs of travel. The same newspaper printed notice that Sir Thomas Holdich would soon be leaving Southampton for Buenos Aires to delineate the new border between Argentina and Chile, then reported the death of Mrs. Duberly (Frances Isabella Locke), who was the author of two books recounting personal experiences in the Crimean War and the Indian Mutiny[17]—her books, like the column itself, becoming a "must" for those wishing to share in the heady sense of world affairs.

Locked into these global networks was a workforce that drew on populations from the surrounding Hampshire and Dorset countryside. The desires of that workforce also found expression in the same world spectacle, resonating to the lower of its socioeconomic layers. Expressed in a leisure activity such as local sports, a neighboring New Forest village had a football club named the Fordingbridge Turks (est. 1868), "its unusual though not unique title inspired by Turkish bravery in war"; their 1876–77 season match against Bournemouth Rovers (at Dean Park, drawing 1–1) was accompanied by an Italian band.[18] The Dell ground in the city (opened 1898), more usually the site for Southern League matches, hosted an international match in 1901 (England–Ireland), while in 1904 the city's Southampton St. Mary's team (the Saints) embarked on a tour of Argentina and Uruguay, as the first English side to do so, winning all matches and beating Liga Argentina by 5–3 in Buenos Aires on 10 July 1904.[19] Unlike the reception for Dr. Livingstone, the committee for the Saints' return comprised only the aptly named director of football, Mr. Bulpitt, and family and friends.[20]

For this retail and REST sector to function, a system was required in which the demands of work and leisure were made complementary. Leisure time is required in which purchased items can be enjoyed, which requires income, which requires work. In a capitalized "unity of opposites," leisure and work become entwined in commodity culture, each made necessary by the other. Taking football, again, as a leisure-related example, it was the early closing of shops and business on a weekday, throughout the country, that gave rise to clubs bearing the name Wednesday or Thursday as part of their name. The Hampshire village team of Pennington were known as the Moonlight Rangers for playing on the local common by moonlight, a situation dictated by the necessities of daytime work.[21] Stephen Colclough's early study of the reading of a Sheffield apprentice notes precisely that the lad's reading correlated with the rhythms of work and wages, augmenting in the summer and running to nothing during the winter evenings, when the cost of candles for reading light was prohibitive.[22] Remarking in 1939 on the state of reading in Britain, Queenie Leavis noted that "On the day of leisure even the poorest households take a newspaper," adding, however, that "it may be of a different type from that favored by the educated."[23] Leisure-time reading is a correlative of the purchasers' work, and as a meaning-making activity it is refracted by the economic dimension of the reader's working life.

To see how that correlative between reading and economics may have been acted out when fiction was read by turn-of-the-century working people, it is necessary to look no further than the bookshop examples of Rudyard Kipling and Joseph Conrad, on the High Street of international delights. The current reception of both writers is so heavily mortgaged to postcolonial studies and, in Conrad's case, to studies of early modernism that it is difficult to read them away from these disciplinary influences, as Southampton shoppers would have done before these approaches became known as postcolonialism and (post)modernism. The conspicuousness of the mortgage is precisely why they provide good examples, since it is remarkable to think of those authors being read in other ways. What we require is a third writer to supply a comparative against which to measure the writings of Conrad and Kipling afresh. Such a scale is provided in the prolific, wildly popular, but now neglected Francis Marion Crawford.[24] When proffered alongside Crawford, and alongside exotic teas and spices, writings by Kipling and Conrad become yet more items in the basket of mass-market cultural production, rather than examples of proto-modernism, in Conrad, or of approaches to colonialism in both (though later criticism develops important distinctions between them).[25]

According to Crawford, there was every reason for judging great fiction by the criteria of the mass market: "The Novel is a distinctly modern invention, satisfying a modern want."[26] Several essays were distilled into his one volume of criticism, *The Novel: What It Is* (1893), in which Crawford outlined a programme for the serious novel that is pointedly commercial.[27] "The novel is a marketable commodity, of the class termed 'luxuries,' as not contributing directly to the support of life or the maintenance of health. It is of the class 'artistic luxuries' because it does not appeal to any of the material senses—touch, taste, smell; and it is of the class 'intellectual artistic luxuries' because it is not judged by superior senses—sight and hearing."[28] This physiological economy of the novel, for Crawford, covered the novel's essential requirements that, beyond being "a story or romance," it should both "appeal to the intellect" and "satisfy the requirements of art."[29] That it could be "of no use to a man when he is at work" meant it was a luxury, but one that should "conduce to peace of mind" during leisure.[30] Crawford understood readers' gains as like those of Moonlight Rangers and Wednesday-playing footballers: not simply in access to a story, but because of work to a pursuit that brought value to leisure time. By pinpointing precisely why the opportunity costs were worth bearing, Crawford in effect provided the basis for a theory of literary art as a leisure resource.

Furthermore, the satisfactions Crawford's novels offered were not trivial. What he supplied was a political rhetoric of discipline, private integrity, and heroic but world-weary resolve. "Modern civilisation has created modern vices, modern crimes, modern virtues. . . . The crimes of today were not dreamed of a hundred years ago.'"[31] But "under the hand of genius [the novel] may purify the heart and fortify the mind."[32] What the novel should attempt, therefore, was an investigation "of the prime impulses of the heart [that] are, broadly speaking, the same in all ages and *almost* in all races" (emphasis added).[33] "Those deep waters the real novel must fathom, sounding the tide-stream of passion and bringing up such treasures as lie far below and out of sight . . . until the art of the story teller makes him [the reader] feel that they are or might be his."[34]

Crawford was aware of the wasteland. He knew the dangers that accompanied modernity, when "applied science is doing her best to eliminate distance as a factor from the equation of exchanges, financial and intellectual."[35] Offering a remedy to modernity (and modernism), Crawford instead asked readers to believe in a romanticized universal "tide-stream of passion" from where deep treasures might be had, which eventually for the reader "might be his." Profitable textual guidance could be gained from stories of the brave man's heart, the coward's heart, and that "men and women still suffer for love, and the old still warn youth and manhood against love's snares."[36] It was not a complicated, nor necessarily true, philosophy of life—the romanticized universal was remarkably middle-class and Caucasian—but on modernity's High Street, and because it was on the High Street, the antidote sold.

Crawford was something of a phenomena, publishing forty-four novels between 1882 and his death in 1909. His romantic far-from-modernist fiction overlapped with Conrad and Kipling chiefly in its use of the exotic and in its predilection for supernatural elements—mesmerism, spirits, ghosts, trance states, astral travels, and wicked eyes—that match the ghosts and horror of Kipling's tales and the tales of what Conrad called "unrest."

An Italian-American, Crawford was born in Italy of wealthy parents, in 1854, was fluent in several languages, and became expert in Sanskrit from studies at the University of Rome. Looking to capitalize on his skills, Crawford traveled to India, where he eventually contributed articles to the *Bombay Herald* and, from 1879, became editor of the *Indian*

Herald based in Allahabad. A journey to Simla—Kipling territory and the summer residence of the British administration in India—provided Crawford with material for his first novel, *Mr. Isaacs* (1882), published by Macmillan Company in New York and Macmillan & Co. in London, who published Crawford's novels almost exclusively, and who later took on Kipling.

With the same appetites as Southampton's leading Suisse restaurant and its "Hindoostan" tea, Crawford's novels flirted with many locations, including Germany, America, Turkey, India, Persia, and Arabia. Macmillan consolidated Crawford's success with his twenty Italian novels. Mostly, these followed a set pattern. A romantic conflict was played out in an Italian setting. Two courageous lovers, "uniformly individuals of high moral purpose,"[37] invariably have to preserve their love from idiocy, greed, or arranged marriages served up by lawyers, clerks, exhausted families, or even by their weaker selves. The inviolable condition, though, is that the lovers should not become uncoupled from their personal integrity.[38]

The settings of Crawford's novels could be historical or contemporary: often Rome, but also Umbria, Abruzzi, or Calabria. The Saracinesca family trilogy—*Sarascinesca* (1887), *Sant' Ilario* (1889), and *Don Orsino* (1892)—deals with Italian life in an earlier half of the nineteenth century, while *Pietro Ghisleri* (1893), *Taquisara* (1896), *Corleone* (1897), and *Casa Braccio* (1895) are stories of "modern" Italy: *Corleone*, set in Sicily (also featuring the Saracinesca family) is arguably the first "Mafia" novel ever.

What gave *Corleone* its distinction, though, was "Crawford's use of his extensive knowledge of Sicily and the Sicilian people . . . [particularly] the organisation, purpose, and operation of the Sicilian Mafia," which left the *Atlantic Monthly* finding *Corleone* "difficult to over praise."[39] The authenticity of Crawford's descriptions, from one who had explored such wild regions in detail, was one of his strongest selling points. On the High Street, like soft mantillas and jeweled combs, anything worth good money had to be convincingly real. In a letter about *The Roman Singer*, Crawford describes a heroine abducted to "Trevi, a place in Abruzzi . . . In that wild and desolate country I can introduce any romance I please. I know the scene very thoroughly, certainly better than any English living writer, for I have visited many places where no foreigner has ever set foot."[40] Like Melville, Pilkington suggests, Crawford lived most of his novels before writing them; and as Crawford corroboratively but impossibly wrote about this value of "authenticity," "I would almost say that to describe another's death [the novelist] must have died himself."[41]

In the period around 1900, Crawford, Kipling and, emergently, Conrad were authors held in high popular *and* critical esteem, and at the head by a country mile was Francis Marion. All three supplied adventures about forceful Anglophone males in far-off lands, often involving elements of the macabre, emphasized in "authentic" retrievals of the exotic Other. When Joseph Conrad's magazine-published short stories were being collected into *Tales of Unrest* (1898) for international release,[42] Kipling's path was already well recognized, his reputation established with reprintings of *Plain Tales from the Hills*, first published for Thacker Spink's Railway Library series, Calcutta (1888). Similarly mining Crawford's vein of authentic renditioning, Kipling consolidated the appeal of his 1891 collection of stories with the branding sub-title "stories of mine own people."[43] The distinction matches an early assumption about Conrad: Unwin's note to *Almayer's Folly* teasingly declared that the author was intimate with Borneo and its people, leading a *Bookman* reviewer to assume he was unmistakeably "a wanderer who has lived far from the atmosphere of European capitals."[44]

On the Saturday side of the working week, Fordingbridge Turks could sup original Bavarian ales, and ponder the universal "truth" of bravery, without ever having to leave Hampshire. They could buy a copy of Crawford (or Conrad) and contemplate the meanings of life, before life's real business of feeding and sheltering began on Monday. Excelling in this leisure-time provision, Crawford was believed by the New York edition of *The Bookman* to be superior even to "Balzac and Zola and Tolstoy, Thackeray and Meredith and Henry James," noting how comparatively limited was the latter novelists' response to the question "what have they really said? . . . [thus] forcing readers to exclaim 'How original, and how very true!'"—the one exception to this unfulfilled promise, the Bookman claimed, was "Mr. Marion Crawford."[45] In the grip of work-determined leisure, Crawford provided readers with a digestible antidote to modernity, and regardless of whether he and his coevals liked it (and often Conrad did not), these three writers took part, not in literature that regrettably entered the world of commerce, but in a lock-and-stock high-street trade.

Alongside the promise of authenticity in their descriptions of wild frontiers, Crawford, as well as Conrad and Kipling, provided the High Street with an adventurous masculinity. Novels in Britain throughout the nineteenth century were predominantly written by women, so the criteria for good and bad novels, like so much else, had to navigate the prejudice of gender, regardless of whether their writers were women or men.[46] Uncontentiously, frivolous romances could be bought on the High Street—this was the home of mass consumption, after all—but for literature that wished to be considered "serious," but which also needed to be bought, other strategies were required. Both men and women embarrassed at the thought of consuming "silly novels by lady novelists," to use George Eliot's phrase, would need to be seen to be reading something more muscular.

As the realm of the market widened from a society with markets to market society, women as they gradually became visible in the labor market and as legitimate consumers began to be incorporated into the market's expanding logic—though a proper accounting of the overlooked domestic labor women have always contributed to the economy remains far from realized. In a patriarchy, if that market society is valorized, whatever is deemed to be the lesser part will inevitably be feminine: in gendering those values underlying capitalism, 'earnings [are seen] as typically masculine, and, therefore, spending as typically feminine."[47] Furthermore, when focused on consumption, the good and bad aspects become similarly gendered: feminine when the consumer is the "seduced by advertising . . . a victim of fashion who is easily manipulated by the interests of production," and by contrast masculine when she is skeptical and judicious in the pursuit of self-interests—or, as Amy Koritz notes, "while the consumer as dupe is invariably feminine, the heroic consumer is, at least symbolically, masculine."[48] The importance of such gendered consumption lies not so much in making redundant claims that one sex is more prone to one form of consumption (both sexes are prone to both), but in its function as a category of judgement. When High Street consumption is good, shopping is male, but when it is a source of anxiety it must be female. If the aim was for a consumption that was unproblematic, therefore, any commercial literatures wishing to be considered "serious" needed to steer clear of overt "femininity."

In counter-distinction to feminine sensation and romance, therefore, though equally High Street–bound, were works by Crawford, Kipling and, emergently, Conrad whose masculinity was perhaps most directly expressed through their fascination with the sea. Crawford was an accomplished, even obsessive sailor, with a preference for escaping domestic responsibility and a failing marriage. In a hardly fecund message, he wrote in an 1894 letter, "The Sea is a nice place because there are no people in it. It would be nicer if the whole world were all sea, and if there were no one, not even one self, anywhere."⁴⁹ Apart from annual passenger-ship travel between the Americas and Italy, he extensively sailed the Mediterranean in the felucca *Margherita*, writing and collecting material for his novels on summer-long trips. Sea descriptions appear in nearly all his works, such as sailing by moonlight to Capri in *The Children of the King* (1893), and in his most reprinted ghost stories, "The Upper Berth" (1894 [1886]) and "Man Overboard!" (1903).

Crawford, like many of his heroes, was physically impressive, with a practiced unassuming air that filtered into his work. As the San Francisco *Chronicle* noted, Crawford was "cool, unimpassioned and deliberate. . . . His sentences are perfectly balanced, and there is not a single excrescence left unpolished. Yet he is never elocutionary."⁵⁰ Dutiful (rather than generous), with a strong individualism, and a faith in self-reliance (coupled to a surfeit of privilege), Crawford had no taste for revolutionary socialism and was nominally democratic, so long as political power remained with a privileged elite—a theme he explored in *An American Politician* (1885). And as Crawford's self-reliant Marlow-like first person narrator Paul Griggs explained in the first lines of *Mr. Isaacs*, "In spite of Jean-Jacques [Rousseau] and his school, men are not everywhere born free, any more than they are everywhere in chains, unless these be of individual making."⁵¹

Crawford's popularity throughout the 1880s and 1890s was astounding. Macmillan's strategy was to release a London edition (often in two or more volumes) with a simultaneous edition (or soon thereafter) in New York for the Macmillan Company. The multiple-volume London first printing was thereby followed by a single-volume second printing as a US first edition, doubling as a British second edition.⁵² Of Crawford's big Macmillan hit, *A Cigarette-Maker's Romance* (1890), more than 153,000 copies were printed for UK sales within several years of its appearance, while the US figures probably exceeded that number.⁵³ It was met with combined public enthusiasm and critical acclaim: according to Pilkington, the *Westminster Review* (May 1891) wrote "no other word than 'beautiful' in any degree fits it," while the *Athenaeum* (26 October 1890) believed it "a story of exquisitely pathetic interest"; "reviews from the *Spectator* (13 December 1890) and the *Critic* (27 December 1890) left little to be said in the way of extravagant endorsement."⁵⁴

For *A Tale of a Lonely Parish* (1886), Macmillan paid an impressive 31,250 lire for 25,000 copies and for *Saracinesca* (1887), serialized in *Blackwood's Magazine*, he received £1,350 for the serial rights and for a meager 1,500 volume copies, beyond which all copies would belong to Crawford for international publication. Crawford described his installation into the literary field after a visit to London in 1893: *gratis* business management from the editor of the *Fortnightly*, and "Henry James has got me in to the Athenaeum Club and is everything that is kind and friendly."[55]

So rewarding was Crawford that Macmillan provided him with an office at their 66 Fifth Avenue, New York premises, and they advanced him extensive funds to buy "Villa Crawford" in Sorrento. Sir Frederick Macmillan was said to have specially selected the artist Joseph Pennell, Slade School lecturer and friend of McNeill Whistler, to illustrate Crawford's *Salve Venetia* (1905), sending Pennell to Italy during the spring of 1901 and 1902, while no less a person than the actress Sarah Bernhardt at the peak of her career commissioned Crawford to write a play for her about the Guelf and Ghibelline struggles, emerging as *Franscesca da Rimini* (1902).[56]

In the provinces, circulating alongside Crawford were published items by Kipling and Conrad. In 1904, the *Tamworth Herald* ran a half-page ad and catalog for the Herald Lending Library, subscribing at 1d or 2d per volume. To "Lovers of Books," the ad quoted Francis Bacon's maxim on consumption that "Reading maketh a full man." and that by reading "your mind will acquire freedom and judgement," and recommended holiday customers to lay in a good supply of interesting books.[57] In the catalog, we find Crawford's *The Heart of Rome* and *Marietta: A Maid of Venice* alongside Kipling's *The Five Nations*, *The Light that Failed*, *Kim*, and *Stalky & Co.* By Joseph Conrad the catalog recommends *Typhoon* and his collaboration with Ford Madox Ford, *Romance*. Around the same time, in Warminster, Coates' Circulating Library offered Kipling's *The Five Nations* and *Traffics and Discoveries* as well as Crawford's *Whoever Shall Offend* and Conrad's *Nostromo*.[58] Next to an advertisement for Macmillan's illustrated edition of Kipling's *Puck of Pook's Hill* (1906), *The Manchester Courier* ran a "New Novels" review of Crawford's *Lady of Rome* (1906), another "story of Italian life."[59] Listing the most popular books for 1900, the London *Bookman* of January 1901 placed at number nine, preceded by Marie Corelli and James Barrie, Crawford's Madrid novel *In the Palace of the King* (1900). In its wake, among novels finding "a place more than once in the list of the six best-selling novels," was Conrad's *Lord Jim*, Kipling's *Stalky & Co.*, and Crawford's *Via Crucis*[60], with Kipling's *From Sea to Sea* taking fifth place under the section for

"History, Biography and Travel."[61] In its literature section, the *Manchester Courier and Lancashire General Advertiser* was keen to praise Kipling's best characteristics, "especially love of the sea and sympathy with England's soldiers, sailors and roving men," and noted that *The Four Feathers* still commanded favor, along with "'The Typhoon' by J. Conrad . . . and 'The Heart of Rome' by F. Marion Crawford," the latter being "one of the best three novels of the year."[62]

From the range of goods that Conrad and Kipling provided to the High Street, only some matched those that Crawford circulated in the market at the time: the advocacy of doggedness and of service, and a belief in the potential for overlooked men to learn and triumph—all qualities ready to take on a masculine inflection. In *The Outlook*, Conrad contributed "Tales of the Sea," his assessment of Cpt. Marryat and Fenimore Cooper, saying that Marryat's "pen serves his country"; "What sets him apart is his fidelity"; "in Marryat's novels we find . . . an insight into the spirit animating the crowd of obscure men who knew how to build for their country such a shining monument of memories"—this latent heroism of overlooked men also being found in Fenimore Cooper: "He has the knowledge of simple hearts."[63] Of both Marryat and Cooper, Conrad writes, "no two other authors of fiction had . . . given to so many the initial impulse towards a glorious or a useful career." In similar vein about Kipling's work ethic, another *Outlook* editorial said Kipling carved with his jackknife an oath into his desk as galley slaves did into their oars. He was "without the germ of self-conceit" and "believed in downright dogged hard work."[64]

For Conrad, Kipling, and Crawford, such heroic masculine integrity in the face of uncontrolled Otherness has a useful parallel in the judicious shopper resisting the hysteria of mass consumption. As played out through their colonizing men, such heroes could "invest" on the High Street without risk to self-interest, while irrational females turned the High Street into a place of unrestrained spending. It was a heroism that British men were supposed to exhibit among the potpourri colonial sites of production that supplied the High Street with its goods, as Crawford's narrator in *Mr. Isaacs* has it, "in the tropical kettles of Ceylon and Singapore . . . on the deck of the steamer in the Red Sea . . . in the crowded Swiss hotel, or the straggling Indian hill station."[65] Tales from Kipling's *Life's Handicap* picked effortlessly from the same inventory of settings, including Ireland, India, Russia, Africa, or East Asia, and, in Kipling's "The Mark of the Beast," a New Year's Eve has men "forgather from the uttermost ends of the Empire," whereupon "then some of us went away and annexed Burma, and some tried to open up the Sudan."⁶⁶ It is from the outposts of East Asian trade that Conrad's quiet heroes, like Captain Lingard in An *Outcast of the Islands* (1896), successfully resist temptations, which others such as avaricious Willems fail to do.

Such resistance to consuming appetite, to which Others fall prey, and the correlative between adventures of the plot and the High Street, is accentuated foremost in the short horrific fiction of all three writers, from the end of the 1800s, in enactments of what Tabish Khair identifies as a troika of Gothic, postcolonialism, and Otherness.⁶⁷ Reading stories from Conrad's *Tales of Unrest* and Kipling's *Life's Handicap*, for example, next to the supernatural elements in Crawford's Italian novels, and specifically Crawford's ghost stories "Man Overboard" and "Upper Berth," allows us to reconstruct from these tales of horror and unrest a distinct type of market narrative: of the perils of appetite and of white males in triumph over them.

Conrad's *Tales of Unrest* sail smoothly from a Malay archipelago to the Congo and London. To its British readers at the time, the encounter with exoticism was not a direct encounter—unexotically humdrum to East Asian and central African locals—but a mythologized encounter created out of leisure-time print. As the narrator to "Karain: A Memory" says, it was a work-leisure exotic that appeared in the "befogged respectability of their newspapers. . . . Sunshine gleams between the lines of those short paragraphs—sunshine and the glitter of the sea. A strange name wakes up memories; the printed words scent the smoky atmosphere of to-day faintly, with the subtle and penetrating perfume of land breezes breathing through the starlight of bygone nights.'"⁶⁸

When that exotic becomes horrific, its horror derives from the un-masculine behavior of Others toward each other, from failure to differentiate one's (white) self significantly from Otherness and, on occasion, from failing to behave in ways that serve to maintain the differentiated order. From a volume of Crawford's supernatural short stories published posthumously as *Wandering Ghosts* in New York and *Uncanny Tales* in London (1911), "The Screaming Skull" can be read as a retired sea captain's failure to rid himself a skull that torments him. Obsessed by why the skull should "scream," he commits the crime of inaction, and, failing to act resolvedly in the face of horrific Otherness, is implausibly bitten to death by the skull. Similarly, in "Man Overboard!" a sailor fails to uphold the duty of brotherhood above sexual desire by failing to save his twin brother from drowning so as to assume the twin's identity and marry the twin's fiancée. For his weakness, the surviving twin is haunted and finally drowned, tacitly judged by the narrating sea captain. In "The Upper Berth" the ghost of a drowned passenger haunts cabin 105. The transgression committed by the characters is that of failing to either steadfastly ignore the ghost or exorcise it, leaving an eerie juxtaposition between vivid descriptions of the ghost, "the dead white eyes ... the putrid odour of rank sea-water," and maritime procedure aboard an up-to-date ocean steam-liner.[69] The horror is expressed in the indecisive narrator's incredulity that in such modern contexts could be found a "creeping horror that began to take possession of me."[70]

Among very many examples from Kipling, the phantom rickshaw of that eponymous story drives "I," the narrator, toward madness and death because "I" failed, during the passage to Bombay, to control his psychosexual appetite. In Kipling's "The Strange Ride of Morrowbie Jukes" (1885), "I" falls into a land of the half-dead with only his British resolve to rely upon. While he plans his escape, he violently fends off "duplicitous" Indian cohabitants, who will compromise his plan. (There is no suggestion of a common front where everyone escapes together.) His slow descent into wretchedness is only halted when Dunnoo, his "dog-boy, who attended to my collies," tracks the narrator and throws him a lifeline, thus restoring the contract between master and faithful servant.[71] The most graphic example, however, comes from Kipling's "Mark of the Beast," wherein "I" and Strickland of the police use what might be called advanced interrogation techniques on "a leper"—the victimised man named either by his disease or called the Silver Man—who has put the social order out of kilter, they believe, by bewitching an unwise British compatriot. "I understood then how men and women and little children can endure to see a witch burnt alive."[72] The heroic "burden" Strickland and "I" take upon themselves is in committing this "necessary" horrific interrogation. But unlike the glittering seas that Conrad described gleaming from between lines of newsprint, the torture is too virulent to be recreated in print without compromising the required British virtue, and instead the narrator writes, "we got to work. This part is not to be printed," followed in the edition by a line space and five dots.[73]

Within the parameters of this leisure-time narrative market, where the High Street threatens to turn ghastly if unchecked, the stories of broken pledges, weak integrity, and killing that make up Conrad's *Tales* can be similarly read. "The Lagoon," first printed in the stately *Cornhill*

(1897), becomes a story of betrayal between Indonesian brothers. A weakness in otherwise fearless, half-naked Arsat has brought about his brother's death, caused by Arsat's too-great need to possess a woman; the story is presented to its initial *Cornhill* readers for approbation through the narrator, called simply "the white man."[74]

In the Congo-set "An Outpost of Progress" (1897), the Other's horrific behavior initially comes from Makola, who cherishes evil spirits that we learn are distinctly entrepreneurial in his trade of slaves for ivory. Makola is openly beyond the pale (also the title of a Kipling tale from 1888), so can be no real source of censure. The true crimes, however, are committed by Kayerts—un-Britishly Dutch—and suspiciously Francophone Carlier, a former non-commissioned officer "in an army guaranteed from harm by several European powers,"[75] who are both guilty of complicity and of failing to maintain discipline. Both die cruelly. Like the Dutchman Willems of *Outcast of the Islands*, who preceded them, they fail to master themselves or their conditions. Foreshadowing *Heart of Darkness*, "An Outpost" signals a criticism not so much of colonialism but of colonialism done badly. As William Atkinson has argued (2005), and as I have argued elsewhere, when considered as a specially commissioned short story for the anniversary, thousandth number of *Blackwood's Magazine*, whose advertising strapline once proclaimed itself to be "the empire in little," *Heart of Darkness* can be read on the British High Street not as a condemnation of colonialism but of Francophone colonialism that lacked the British ability to maintain the careful borders and self-discipline necessary for civilizing commerce.[76] No one but the British could navigate the Other's waters, whether by boat or in print.

It is with "Karain: a Memory," however, that this particular masculine market narrative is best revealed. To the crew aboard the narrator's schooner, the Malay prince called Karain is "incomparably dignified" (almost British, one is tempted to say): about him there is an "expectation of something heroic going to take place."[77] But Karain disappoints. He has murdered his brother to save a faithless woman or, rather, save her ghost that has transgressively become his spectral talisman. For this crime, Karain is haunted by the brother's spirit, so he seeks refuge aboard the schooner, where more powerful spirits of modernity reign. Recognizing Karain's mighty and obscure odyssey, the crew and narrator decide to help him by giving him an icon of their West. The material talisman they give Karain is a Jubilee sixpence—the smallest silver cog to British global commerce. Some years after, in London, along the

City's busy Strand, the narrator senses the animating spirit that turns the city's business wheels, recognizing it to be the spirit in the sixpence that had successfully overpowered the demons in Karain's primal forest.

In discussing the serious business of men compared to the *en masse* hysteria of Others, Andreas Huyssen has shown a discourse emerging in the mid-to-late nineteenth century that "consistently and obsessively gender[ed] mass culture and the masses as feminine, while high culture, whether traditional or modern, clearly remain[ed] the privileged realm of male activities."[78] The site of mass behavior in consumption was the High Street, but problematically the productions of high-cultural pretension also needed to find a home there. Therfore, if they were not to remain on the economic margins, "serious" market narratives like those by Conrad, Kipling, and Crawford had a gender issue that needed resolving. The distinction they applied, and still apply, and what justifies their High Street presence, is their masculinity. On the High Street, certain literatures face a problem from the "taint" of feminine consumption. The solution is to grasp consumption in a way that that is, symbolically at least, judiciously masculine, allowing those literatures a trading life on the High Street free of "devaluing" effeminacy. Only certain literatures face this problem, however—fashions and mantillas are relatively free—since only certain symbolic goods rely so heavily on masculine autonomy as part of their signifying value.

By patrolling gender borders, the High Street in the early nineteenth century resolved the problem of selling would-be "serious" literatures. In a Saturday column called "Literature of the Week," the *Hampshire Advertiser* provided its shopping list from selected national periodicals, in effect a 'best-buys' review, but couched in terms of masculine functionality.[79] For Saturday 6 August 1887, its recommendation to readers was that good political commentaries that week could be had from the *National Review* and *The Nineteenth Century*; it also recommended Blackwood's for "a good supply of solid intellectual reading." *Longman's Magazine* would be bringing Rider Haggard's *Allan Quatermain* to a conclusion and was commended to readers wanting "a series of wonderful incidents and narrow escapes. The battle pieces are very good, the author excelling in descriptions of hard fighting." The *English Illustrated Magazine* "sustains its credit for the excellence of its pictures"; the *Antiquary* "has once more an abundance of good reading for its votaries"; the *Cornhill*'s articles offered fine landscape descriptions—of Cornwall, Bavaria, and "a capital description of a district in Sweden"; the fifth installment of unpublished letters by Thackeray could be had from *Scribners Magazine*, with drawings (some humorous); Marion Crawford's *Paul Patoff* was to be found in *Atlantic Monthly*; and the "talents evinced by Mr Walter Pater, in his work 'Imaginary Portraits,' is the subject of a readable essay by Mr A. Seymour," available to readers in the monthly *Time*. Then, in a tip where the unruly feminine has threatened, the same column advises that "Blackwood's gives another lengthy instalment of Mrs. Oliphant's charming Scottish story, 'Joyce,'" but is able to reassure in-no-way-phobic readers that "the Colonel is not quite so weak and vacillating as he appeared to be in the earlier chapters."

The key to masculine market narratives lies not in any textual "content," revealed through textual hermeneutics, but in the reader relationships set up as these narratives take part in, or rather help create, that market. As John Frow said of any writing subject to a regime of value, our efforts should be directed at describing "relations rather than substances."[80] In this manner, works by Crawford, Kipling, and Conrad achieve cultural power when readers decode them as celebrations of personal integrity, duty, and hard work, thus enabling them to perform masculinity on the High Street's global stage. Furthermore, it should be stressed that these relationships are not singular. They are social, between all readers and the Empire's goods in a codified system of differences: coquettish fans, mantillas, and Ouida to one side, Bavarian ale, Argentinean beef, and Conrad to the other. Not as a meaning-bearing text, then, but as a market-society event, the success of High Street writers can be explained without recourse to a history of formalism or modernist aesthetics, nor to sub-fields of restricted and large-scale production. Theirs is a coordination where the "socio-technical apparatus, the structured articulation of a set of knowledge institutions . . . a more-or-less professionalised custodianship . . . [and] a designated set of proper social uses" combine to create a gendered production and a market made possible by the commodity regime.[81] And in the mutability of their values, created from how and where they are read, reading and economics thus become intimately bound.

PART TWO

Southampton Stories

Chapter 5

What's Selling in Southampton
Commodity Culture, Dock Strikes, and Gas-and-Water Socialism

Despite its genteel appearance, bookselling has always been a volatile profession, especially when unregulated by measures such as the NBA. The surviving record of provincial bookselling presents an image of start-ups and crashes, occasionally of successes often maintained as a family dynasty, but more often of businesses falling into bankruptcy, of conflagration, of being taken over by rivals or of passing in accession to former employees; the bankrupt then emerging some time later in a new start-up, or in a subordinate role for an established business. The picture is not one of stable growth, matching the acceleration of print production throughout the eighteenth and nineteenth centuries. Instead, the picture, in and around Southampton at least, is of hopefuls trying to trade off the back of a runaway industrial juggernaut, and only a very few staying a longer distance, like the mighty Gilbert's or the stationers Wiseman's. For those who stayed the distance, and for the new operators in the late nineteenth century when commodity culture took hold, trade with the unknown public was not only pushed from within by developments in book production but drawn from without by the emancipatory changes that expanded that reading public.

For new High Street readers, such socialized, contextualizing developments were both "good" and "bad." Every freedom gained is both a liberation *and* a loss of past security, however meager that security may have been. Industrial expansion can bring more jobs, but it can also push down wages and increase the size of the labor force at the bottom. Admittedly, there was a good deal of divergence along that bottom during the 1890s, which was more complicated than the neat three segments of laborers, intelligent artisans and educated working people that Victorians liked to refer to. But as Henry George asked in *Progress and Poverty* in 1879, despite continual improvements from the introduction of revolutionary labor-saving technologies, how come those bottom workers were still obliged to work exceedingly long hours and live in relative poverty?[1] On the individual plane, too, the ideas that lead to self-emancipation, also lead to both the pleasures of choice *and* the burdens of personal responsibility for failure. This dual condition of social progress as it contextualized the booktrade in Southampton is perhaps best captured in the two features that were gas-and-water socialism, and the Great Dock Strike of 1890.

Part of the push to trade was created by the remarkable increases in print production in the later eighteenth century that were superseded by even greater industrialized increases in the nineteenth; those being the product of, as well as an agency that helped produce a mechanized global empire.[2] On listing the "immense number of new applications and new arrangements" to later-nineteenth-century print worldwide, a *Blackwood's Magazine* article reminded its readers "that the railway, and the telegraph, and the penny postage, by bringing near to us a vast world beyond our own limited circles, and giving us a present interest in the transactions of the most distant regions, enormously increase the numbers of readers, and of themselves *create* a literature" (my italics).[3] Transactions in distant regions and the cultural forces behind nineteenth-century mass migration, for example, were the reason a local bookseller like Rayner published weekly information for passengers and visitors, along with a series of Southampton guides.[4] And it was part of the reason that, in addition to their rail station and High Street outlets, W.H. Smith eventually elected to have a dockside shop on Central Road inside the grounds of the city's Eastern Docks.[5] Such entwined cultural and production-level changes created a demand that necessitated the continual reinvention of newsstand-vending, library-lending, book-retailing points of access that many tried to provide but only a few accomplished successfully.

Rather than describing book-retail activity in a stable field, our narrative of desire satisfied through the delivery of print needs to be sensitive internationally and locally to cultural as well as industrial-technological conditions. For local disadvantaged communities, those changing conditions were never experienced as a straight line of improvement. The future dipped as much as it rose, which is why, in constructing a frame in which readers' desires can be narrated, it is important to include movements of both progressive optimism and regressive despair.

Bookselling in Southampton and its nearby south coast has a long heritage, although it required the lapse of the Licensing Act in 1695 before the area could have its own independent printers.[6] There is evidence of a printing press as early as 1710 in Gosport and Winchester, publishing for local use. The figure rose to three or four presses by mid-century, but by 1800, there were around twenty-five businesses operating in Hampshire County.[7] The *Hampshire Chronicle*, one of the oldest surviving newspapers produced in the UK, was first published in Southampton in 1772 as part of this growth, before moving to Winchester in 1778.

A good record of Southampton bookselling from the later eighteenth century survives.[8] It notes a rapid expansion in the town over the second half of the century, tallying with later findings on a national scale that the second half of the century was, indeed, a time of unprecedented growth in both titles and sizes of edition, despite the almost static condition of print technology since its Gutenberg introduction—an expansion that James Raven attributes to improvements in administration and auditing, along with improvements in the market knowledge and sheer confidence of booksellers in a period of general economic expansion.[9] Between 1740 and 1790, for example, there is evidence of a rise from around 400 booksellers and publishers in 200 towns outside London to around 1,000 establishments in 300 locations by 1790.[10]

A period of expansion, however, does not always imply stable growth. The business of James Linden, one of around eleven printer-booksellers operating toward the end of the eighteenth century, provides an illustration. From 1768, Linden's business was run from "opposite New Market House" on the High Street, including both printing and bookselling operations.[11] In 1774, Linden expanded and went into partnership with a London bookseller called John Wise, both men working out of the same Southampton shop. A mere two years later, in 1776, the partnership dissolved, whereupon Wise continued as a bookseller and Linden took up the job of printer of the *Hampshire Chronicle*—both men still working from the same Southampton High Street premises. But rather than follow the standard historical narrative of increased division of labor necessitated through (early) industrialization, Linden then allied himself with a bookseller from nearby Salisbury, Joseph Hodson, at the same time as the

Wise-Linden break up, establishing what must have been a competing bookselling business further along the High Street at number 130, also in 1776. This business lasted only a year, however: the Linden-Hodson partnership dissolved in 1777. By 1778 Linden was declared bankrupt, and Hodson disappears from the record. Wise continued at the initial High Street shop until 1779, five years after his arrival in Southampton, when he, too, gave up the ghost and sold his business to Thomas Ford. Ford is then recorded as buying a bookshop and circulating library, and ran Wise's bookselling business for a further two years until bankruptcy overtook him in September 1781.

Following his bankruptcy, Linden then resurfaced in nearby Portsmouth, and in 1780 set up as printer of the *Hampshire Chronicle; or, Portsmouth, Winchester and Southampton Gazette*. Whether or not Linden's Portsmouth paper was directly poaching on the territory of the like-named *Hampshire Chronicle* is unclear—Linden may have legitimately transferred the *Hampshire Chronicle* to Portsmouth and amended its title[12]—apart from the fact that at the same time in 1780 the *Hampshire Chronicle* was being produced from the High Street in Winchester by a printer named J. Wilkes, thereafter undergoing various iterations from the same Winchester address as the *Hampshire Chronicle; or the Portsmouth and Chichester Journal*, and the *Hampshire Chronicle; or the Southampton, Portsmouth and Chichester Journal*, printed first by Wilkes and then by a Mr. B. Long. It is uncertain whether any opportunism can be ascribed to Linden's choice of title—one can surmise that the ownership of the name *Hampshire Chronicle* was contested—but what can be observed is a degree of laxity in regard to intellectual property compared to the sheer determination to stay in business.[13] The last we see of Linden is in 1782, when he returned to Southampton, in partnership with a printer called Alexander Cunningham, until that partnership was dissolved in 1785.

Of the eleven booksellers and printers identified by Oldfield operating in Southampton at the time, five (including Linden) had businesses directly affected by Linden, another was James Linden Junior (operating from 1793 onward), and a further two, William Mills and Thomas Skelton, were both journeymen of the same Thomas Ford who had bought out Wise's bookshop and circulating library, and who became partners.[14] This leaves the remainders as Tomas Baker (printer and bookseller, in business 1767–1811), William Rooke (bookseller, in business 1798–?) and a W. Thompson (printer, in business throughout 1799). If the end of the 1700s in Southampton was an expansive period for the trade, it was also the period when agents in its provincial trade network crossed paths and fortunes and watched each other's successes—but more often watched each other crash and burn.

The mercantile expansion of the late eighteenth century was also one where books came increasingly to be regarded as commodities. Commodities have existed for as long as there have been goods exchanged in a market. The bookstalls of Ancient Rome, described by Martial, which were pretty much copy shops where the bookseller's corps of copyists would reproduce any of the scrolls displayed, were essentially running a commodified service.[15] In England toward the end of the 1700s, the degree of commodification had reached such a point that the integrated printing and bookselling trade, described in considerable detail by James Raven, was functioning as a mirroring affirmation of the country's empire-wide trade. The prosaic world of jobbing printing that underpinned the booktrade had not only become a substantial business sector in its own right, but was creating the means by which tradespeople could disseminate a national discourse about commerce and commercialism—hence the double meaning to the title of Raven's *Publishing Business in Eighteenth-Century England*. It would take a further hundred years before this national discourse could become a nationwide cultural formation, but its basis in print was formed here.

In terms of legal justification for this shift to book-as-commodity, Mark Rose describes the key role of copyright, covering the 1774 case of Donaldson vs. Beckett that, finding in favor of Donaldson, established the author as the owner of a work, and not the publisher-bookseller who argued for rights based on printing privilege, the latter conception inherited from the days of the Stationer's Company a century earlier.[16] Paradoxically, the recognition of the author as an owner meant that the work necessarily had to be a form of creative property over which ownership could be asserted. By bringing the author's work under the umbrella of property, rather than of printing privilege, it meant that the work as an immaterial product entered into what Maurizio Borghi calls the intellectual property paradigm: firstly, establishing the author as the proprietor of the work; and secondly, creating a legal framework where

> the creative work becomes an exchangeable good. It becomes, in the full economic sense of the word, a 'commodity.' The relationship between the writer and society thus takes the particular form of an 'exchange.' It is an exchange in which

the commodity exchanged is not just a product, but the *creative* product of an *author* who *freely* sells his *own* property.[17]

Conceptions of intellectual property were not comprehensively established on an international scale until the Berne Convention of 1886 and in its subsequent revisions. But in the run-up to the turn of the nineteenth-to-twentieth centuries, another set of conditions ought to be added to the narrative of bookselling. This is the emergence of commodity culture, wherein commodities are not only in operation but are seen as the primary means for sustaining that formation.

Analysts of literature and commodity culture who regard commodities as the structural center to all forms capitalism[18]—as sketched in chapter 1—will often refer back to "gaze" and "spectacle," taking a cue from Guy Debord's *Situationist Manifesto*, which ties the commodity intimately to the idea of "spectacle" that is the form of capitalist representation *par excellence*, and which seeks to reduce all things to fungible objects subject to the consumer's gaze.[19] With sufficient capitalized power, the mantra is that "if you can show it, it can be exchanged," and novels are especially good at showing all things immaterial—a point precisely picked up by Andrew Miller in *Novels Behind Glass* (1995).

It is entirely correct that such capitalist gazing is traceable to the early period in the late eighteenth and early nineteenth centuries. Johanna Schopenhauer, mother to Arthur, described a shopping trip to London in 1803, where she was dazzled by "the brilliant displays of precious silverware, the beautiful draperies of muslin . . . behind large plate-glass windows, the fairy tale glitter of the crystal shops."[20] James Lackington's extravagant "Temple of the Muses bookshop" of 1794 would be included in these spectacular displays,[21] as would Josiah Wedgewood's 1774 showrooms in Soho, London, displaying IKEA-like lifestyle interiors centered on dinner services set out as they were in royal or imperial homes (frequently changed to encourage repeat visits).[22] In Southampton, in 1799, there was a store named Glovers, which "was advertising 'Ware-Rooms' that were organized into separate departments with a range of stock that would have qualified it as a department store had the name existed."[23]

But without adequate levels of disposable income, the gaze remains unrequited for large sections of the population. An 1825 advertisement for Edward Shakell's Warerooms, 30 High Street Southampton, is improbably for the sale of an "Original Painting: *Two Angels Urging the Departure of Lot and his Family*, by Rubens" (possibly *The Departure of*

Lot and his Family from Sodom), which could be viewed at one shilling admission, the advertisement's respectful solicitation being made to "The Nobility and Gentry in the neighbourhood of Southampton."[24] Rather than basing an explanation solely on specific forms of representation, then, it is access to disposable income that sets the timer on when we can properly regard the general reader and her bookshops as networked actors in a commodity reading culture—and even modest rates of disposable income were not available to laboring classes in Britain until later in the nineteenth century.

What could have been a steady rise in income, or rather of wealth for the laboring classes in Britain from the middle of the century onward—detailed in William Hamish Fraser's classic *Coming of the Mass Market 1850–1914* (1981)—was interrupted by the Great Depression, renamed the Long Depression when outdone by the depression of the 1930s (and perhaps pushed into third place by that of 2008). Lasting for around twenty-two years after 1874, the Long Depression was exacerbated paradoxically by cheap food imports from North America and the southern hemisphere, derived from revolutionizing production methods applied in vast tracts of land opened up to agricultural development.[25] On the one hand there were very real setbacks for the most disadvantaged, compounded in urban centers by the arrival of those escaping depleted rural labour markets, and more genrally in England by refugees fleeing *An Gorta Beag*, the so-called "lesser" Irish Famine of 1879. On the other hand, Deirdre McCloskey has argued that the economy of the period was not a disaster overall, and was "growing as rapidly as permitted by the resources and the effective exploitation of the available technology."[26] Rather than a complete collapse of buyer's markets, therefore, it would be fairer to talk of incremental progress in purchasing power for some socioeconomic groups, but also of the widespread increase in wealth for the largest sections of the population being held back until the 1890s.

As national interests are frequently not the same as municipal interests, and neither is coextensive with the interests of the metropolitan center, any idea of commodity culture needs to account for local forces. It may have been in London's interests that Chatham docks expanded up to the mid-1880s, but not in Southampton's, which after 1876 expanded its Woolston docks when Thomas Oswald, to the dismay of workers on the Wear, ditched his operations in Sunderland and moved south. Oswald successfully built iron, then steel sailing ships (retrogressively, given the advent of steam) but, in a mirror of Southampton's disadvantage caused by Chatham, Oswald sold his ships to Liverpool ship owners to the disadvantage of Liverpool shipbuilders, and both developments were against the major national trend that was concentrating on the Cylde and Northern England.[27]

For Southampton, the period when the provincial bookshop became operative in commodity culture was marked by two general features, one progressive and one retrogressive, that in turn provide an interpretive framework for purchasing readers. Gas-and-water socialism and a series of industrial actions culminating in the Great Dock Strike of 1890 remain two monumental civic features that affected the lives of Southampton's citizens. These two are important not merely because they were formative local events, but because they represent twin movements in social change for resource-weakened groups: the optimism of aspirational opportunity, and the pessimism generated from disappointment and betrayal—a combined reflexive movement characterizing social "progress."

Municipal socialism, sometimes called gas-and-water socialism, describes a period over the last quarter of the nineteenth century nationally when civic authorities took over gas and water supply along with other amenities as part of an extension of the state—something that did not get underway in Southampton until the 1890s. Often this would go hand in hand with periods of slum clearance, which in the city also got underway in earnest around 1890, with a scheme known as the St. Michael's Improvements.[28]

Inverting twenty-first-century debates on the buying and selling of large civic assets, the municipal Southampton Corporation had tried to buy out a private gas company in 1875 for a purchase price of around £250,000, which rose to £300,000 from the need to remunerate the company's directors. However, it failed to push through the purchase because of doubts about whether the gas provided would be any cheaper and whether the Corporation was capable of achieving the estimated £800 per annum profit. It was not until 1898 that the Corporation had some success (and failure) in imposing a maximum gas tariff (charges made to customers) on the still-private gas company in certain borough areas.[29] A municipal supply of good-quality water in sufficient quantity was not secured until 1890, from just north of the town at Otterbourne village, which ended a history of surface collection and failed artesian wells from the city's open common (uncultivated public lands) as well as an impure supply from the city's River Itchen at Mansbridge.[30] Public baths then appeared in the city—unlike the more exclusive spa baths that had flourished during the eighteenth and earlier nineteenth centuries—with the development of an indoor public baths, wash-house, and outdoor lido (the equivalent of a modern-day water park) opened in 1892, and built by the company of Southampton son George Brinton, which also built large areas of workers' housing (in Newtown and St Mary's). The lido faced out to open water and fresh air along the Western Esplanade, and the entire complex represented a genuine improvement in civic sanitation.[31]

For improvements to the intellectual health of its citizens, the Corporation opened its first free public library in 1889. The right to set up such institutions had been available since the Public Libraries Act of 1855, and the idea had been floated before, after the bequeath to the town of a private library that was the collection of a Captain G.F. Pitt, dated by Richard Preston as 20 September 1831.[32] But pragmatically, a public library needed sufficient readerships before cities like Southampton felt compelled to act, which in turn required developments such as the passing of the Education Act of 1870 to produce enough readers and a strong movement in favor of a reading public.

Once it was decided that the Public Libraries Act should be adopted, the first public library was opened in St. Mary's Hall, on 15 January 1889 (see figure 5.1). Housed in two rooms above shops adjoining the Kingsland Tavern in the poorly resourced district servicing the city's eastern and southern docks, the library began with 5,000 volumes, loaned to 2,417 readers in its first year.[33]

The building had previously been the noisy St. Mary's *Palace of Varieties* music hall, which is telling, given that Kingsland had, and still has today, a reputation for being a rough-and-ready area. Part of the conditions for the lease was that the library landlords were to remove all stage fittings and to cease all communications with the next-door pub. We can only guess at the tensions in local attitudes to self-improvement, or toward those were seen to be demanding it, but it is a matter of record that the first librarian, Mr. Albert H. Davis, had occasionally to be escorted from the premises by police because of locals manhandling the library staff.

What ended the exceptional delay in setting up the city's first public library—only Hull among the larger towns in England was later[34]—was the initiative taken by the Hartley Institute, which was a privately funded institute sited on the High Street that hosted various concerts, public meetings, and debates. In the 1890s, and against earlier

Figure. 5.1. The site of Southampton's first public library, St. Mary's Hall, photographed before 1936. "Demand for Free Libraries," *Hampshire Advertiser*, April 18, 1936, fragment. *Source*: Southampton City Archives, D/NC/5.

intentions, it became a teaching college, or university college (later becoming the University of Southampton), offering evening classes on a term-by-term basis for "Technical and General Education . . . at reduced fees. For prospectus and particulars apply at the Institution."[35] Believed by some to be "ailing," the Hartley wished to reinvent itself as a city public library with a committee composed more or less of the Hartley Council, and the library's nucleus consisting of the Hartley's library. Indeed, the reference part of the public library would merely require a change of name at the High Street premises from Hartley-Reference to Town-Reference Library.[36] But marked differences in expectation between Hartley representatives and the town council meant that the grand plan became inauspiciously something else.

Conditions in the St. Mary's library were less than ideal. Directly above two shops (one a fried fish shop, for several months), its small rooms could only be reached by ascending a staircase, and to the rear there was a commercial stables for the Kingsland Tavern, complete with manure pit. Richard Preston estimated that in a poorly ventilated, gas-lit, and frequently overcrowded library, the stench would have been overwhelming, particularly in summer. In September 1893, the *Hampshire Independent* recalled the unsanitary building with "a feeling akin to horror" and compared it with the notorious conditions of the police courts in the Bargate.[37] Despite the drawbacks, public interest was so great that, from the start, there was standing room only in the reading rooms, and loans often reached a rate of 100 books per hour. New premises were sought almost immediately, secured and opened in 1893, but not without a "battle of the sites" waged between social reformers, philanthropists, municipal corporation careerists, and commercial developers, over which of the two preferred sites ostensibly satisfied the free library principles of educating, improving, and civilizing the working classes, and which was a profitable monument to civic achievement.

The up-market site on Southampton's London Road was eventually chosen, which meant that readers in the Kingsland area, where an opposing site had been proposed, and the nearby laboring district of Northam were disadvantaged. As compensation, a classroom in the local Kent Street Infants School in Northam was put at public disposal as a free evening reading room, but since it had no books it could only function as a newspaper reading room, and it closed in less than a year. One of the lobbyists to persuade the reluctant School Board to provide a classroom for readers was the leading High Street book retailer, Henry

March Gilbert. So it can be assumed that free public libraries were not seen as a threat in Southampton to retailed literature—and might quite possibly have been seen as a catalyst. Indeed, prior to the Hartley Institution and its library opening in 1862, Southampton had a public library of sorts, known as the Audit House Library, which had taken over the Pitt collection, but which was underused despite its semi-populist ambitions. When the Audit House collection was transferred to the Hartley—despite expectations that the Hartley would be "a place of thought unto the poorest free"—it was subsumed into a library charging a one guinea per year subscription, or 5s subscription for after 6 p.m. only, well beyond the reach of the lowest disposable incomes. Concessions for access by the poor were a farce; such applicants had to present a certificate of poverty, "together with a recommendation of character, and an assurance of their special capability to profit by the advantages of the institution signed by three members of the Town Council."[38] One of those to complain that a "public library" had been removed from the Audit House and that the public no longer had an opportunity to read books they formerly possessed was Thomas James, also the owner of a bookshop in Above Bar Street. Footfall at St. Mary's Hall library showed that demand existed and, if public initiatives were not up to meeting working-class needs in the way they should have (only partially achieved in 1889), then those people eventually would migrate to the commercial sector when enough disposable income was at hand.

As an image of how the laboring class's disposable income could be regressed, and hence of their ability to create a commodified reader's market, no more emphatic example can be had than the Great Dock Strike at Southampton of 1890, which grew out of a series of smaller actions in what turned out to be the build-up to the Great Depression. These included the engineers' bid for a nine-hour day in 1871–72; a larger seamen's bid for increased wages to cover rising food costs in May 1872 (involving employees of the Royal Mail, Union, South-Western and P&O companies); a tailors' action in 1873 to address stagnating wages in the face of a cost-of-living rise by 30%; shipwrights in 1874 asking for 34 shillings per week instead of the company's offered 32 shillings following a decrease from a ten-hour to a nine-hour day; and a dock laborers' strike in 1876.[39] Key negotiations in the Seamen's Union strike were held at the same Kingsland Tavern that was adjacent to Southampton's first free public library. As the national economy began to recover around 1887–91, so too did union expansion—the expansion being easiest when demand for labor was high and workers had more bargaining strength. Southampton—at times referred to as the Liverpool of the South[40]—was also hit by a spill-over from dock disputes in the north of the country and from the great London Dockers' strike of 1889, which incidentally also ushered in the period known as New Unionism, which saw union membership extended to the unskilled majority and sowed the seeds for the later formation of the Labour Party. At a meeting of the Southampton Operative Bricklayer's Society (typically supporters of New Unionism) in August 1890, it was suggested that a trade's council be formed consisting of local plumbers', painters and decorators', and carpenters and joiners' associations. Together with other town unionists such as the firemen, carters, and gasworkers, this new union council would join with a refreshed Dockers' Union that now included coal-porters, sweaters (stevedores), and cornrunners and bushellers (employees of corn merchants) to undertake one almighty Dock Strike that began at midnight on 7 September 1890. The strike continued until 15 September, defeated not by management or state pressure, but collapsing when London-based Dockers' Union executives arrived to inform the local men that they would receive no strike pay. Ben Tillet of the London-based Union executive was quoted in the *Daily News* as decrying irresponsible local agitators and that "the Southampton turnout was not only unauthorized, but was most clearly and emphatically forbidden"—the reason for the split perhaps being that Southampton had been one of the ports to accept work from London docks during the London strike of 1889.[41] Local papers described the ensuing collapse with men in tears and many tearing up their union cards.

Southampton's experience of the strike, however, had been one where train drivers had been pulled from their locomotives following news that "blacklegs" were being railed in, a major thoroughfare (Canute Road) had been occupied by strikers, rioting had taken place and the dock gates been blockaded, troops of the Yorkshire Light Infantry had been deployed with fixed bayonets, two gunboats had been dispatched by the Admiralty, the mayor had read the Riot Act and, despite a partial curfew being proposed by the mayor, crowds had gathered to console themselves at night with booing outside the houses of those they believed opposed them.

Socially, it can be imagined that the repercussions from the strike would have been immense, and the new kinds of social relations set up would have been lasting. The reaction would not have been unified, since there was no monolithic block of a laboring class to react in a unified way: slop-trade women producing garments in sweat shops would have been affected differently than domestic servants, as would skilled coach-makers to carpenters and joiners, or retailers like butchers and poulterers; and the effects of the strike would have filtered down the networked industries in differing ways. But in the manner that particularly painful events can reorganize accustomed binaries—grief, for example—there were effects that can be measured in the large scale. Certainly a measure of enmity between Southampton and neighboring Portsmouth can be traced to this period, when it is claimed that strike breakers were sourced from Portsmouth (no doubt with reverse claims made in connection to actions in Portsmouth).[42] One wonders whether former strikers would have been happy to travel down the coast to Colonel "Buffalo Bill" Cody's "vast show . . . [which] during this present week is exhibiting in Portsmouth . . . seats for 15.000 people," extolled in the *Southern Echo* on 6 October 1891 (recommending that the "antics of the Indians are of particular interest those who have never before witnessed the like").[43] The delights of Portsmouth may have been too galling and instead they might save their coin for something less diverting, like George W. Griffith's unironic and wildly popular *Angel of the Revolution: A Tale of the Coming Terror*. Released in illustrated volume October 1893, priced 6 shillings, Griffith's *Angel* described the ten-year-hence anarchist overthrow of all oligarchic tyranny—by which the narrative meant all contemporary government worldwide—by a group known as "The Terrorists," whose foot-soldiers were concealed in the ranks of trade unions. Bizarrely, or predictably—and a mollifying point that would not have been lost on Southampton dockers—the guardians of this new anarchist, egalitarian world order turn out to be white Anglo-Saxon men.

And what of Southampton women caught up in the strike? Apart from port services such as laundry and catering, large numbers of women working in the city were employed as unorganized domestic servants, earning rarely more than £8 per year (though saving on accommodation costs) and, despite the success of actions such as the Bryant and May match girls' strike, women did not have a prominent role in trade union life.[44] More lucrative options for Southampton women were found in local papers advertising for women of unimpeachable character to emigrate to the New World as "domestics." Might these women instead have been drawn to stories about their more liberated sisters such as the "American girl," drawn in Henry James's novella *Daisy Miller* (1878) from a retrieved copy of the *Cornhill Magazine*;[45] or might they have turned to less well-to-do first-hand accounts of the settlers' West, as in Mary MacLane's fiery confessional *The Story of Mary MacLane* (1902), set in the mining town of Butte, Montana.[46] So unburdened was MacLane that she openly declared her bisexuality, as well as writing and starring in the silent film *Men Who Have Made Love to Me* from 1918. In anticipation, might not Southampton women have been attracted to a trip to Portsmouth for the "Buffalo Billeries," as the *Southampton Echo* called them, since the paper also recommended the spectacle of the American women sharpshooters?

The forces that governed how Southampton people experienced their lives were the same forces that compelled their reading, and what joined life to efferent reading was desire for another life that could be dreamed of or the old one to be escaped. Gas-and-water socialism and the Great Strike are two examples of formative framing and priming, each in their way representing optimism for a bright future and pessimism at its ever being achievable. By way of an emerging methodology, therefore, with such positive and negative axial framing, it is then possible to begin to estimate what sorts of desires the book trade needed to meet in a designated place, at a particular time—an argument that will be picked up in chapter 9, in the narrative nonfictions of five individuals' shopping trips to a bookseller. But it also suggests that not only modes of interpretation were shaped by those contextualizing cultural forces but likewise the values people placed on their symbolic goods. With such a proposition, the value of symbolic goods therefore becomes something nigh on impossible to describe solely in brute economic terms.

Chapter 6

The Daily Round

The NBA introduced a note of stability to running a bookshop, and we have a fairly good record of how the smaller independent bookshop was run in the middle and later period of the NBA's effective functioning. For the turn of the century, however, the few guides to running a bookshop in the UK are scattered across various trade periodicals (many of which merely publish publication lists), in reminiscences of individual booksellers, and in a good deal of polemic around the NBA; most sources are included in Frederick Bateson's *Cambridge Bibliography of English Literature*, vol. 3, 1800–1900 (1969).[1] But perhaps the most relevant and under-researched guide for England, around 1900, is *The Successful Bookseller: A Complete Guide to Success to All Engaged in a Retail Bookselling, Stationery, and Fancy Goods Business* (1906), its title sheet claiming advice culled from over twenty years' business experience.

Volatility was a condition of the retail book trade throughout the nineteenth century, but it persisted well into the early days of the NBA. As the subtitle of *The Successful Bookseller* suggests, the general rule, especially for businesses without large metropolitan customer bases, was that a trade model built on books alone was not viable. A serviceable example of the range of goods, services, and values those regional retailers proffered is found in A.H. Coates of Market Place, Warminster, who in 1899 advertised the following:

> A.H. Coates, General and educational bookseller and stationer . . . respectfully solicits orders for books of all kinds

and stationery. Most of the new and popular books kept in stock, in cloth and many in bindings for presents. Books not in stock procured from London immediately. Two pence in the shilling allowed off all new books for cash, except those published at net prices. A large stock of Bibles, prayer books, hymn and devotional books, in good and expensive bindings. Special attention devoted to educational books and stationery. And all school requisites supplied promptly. Note paper and envelopes, and other stationery supplied at lowest remunerative prices, being directly procured from mills and manufacturers. Packets of notepaper at 4 1/2d, 6d, 6 1/2d, 9d, and 1s, and envelopes at the same price. . . . Address cards and note paper printed from plates. Note paper and envelopes stamped from dies in coloured and plain, and dies engraved. An extensive show of ladies and gentleman's bags, albums, purses, inkstands, frames, and writing cases, and a large selection of the newest fancy goods and games. Practical bookbinders on the premises. Subscription and circulating library.[2]

William Corp of the Bookseller's Association, as an unequivocal supporter of the NBA, bemoaned the turn-of-the-century condition where bookselling was "entirely dependent on, and subsidiary to, the sale of postcards, toys, and bric-à-brac."[3] David Stott, in his polemic on the difficulties faced by the reading man in building up a gentleman's library in *The Nineteenth Century*, was dismayed to find the bookseller who "fills his shelves with stationery and other articles which yield a more remunerative return," and found the genuine country bookseller "compelled to eke out a livelihood by becoming a general dealer in all kinds of knick knacks."[4] Indeed, the allied goods *The Successful Bookseller* details even had their own monthly journal, the *Stationery World and Fancy Good Review*, published from 1892 onward; and occasionally one wonders whether, like flights at certain airports, the most visible goods or services offered (books) were not merely a device to enable other forms of revenue generation—in the case of airports, from parking and shopping.[5]

The *Successful Bookseller* spent much of its energy advising how to trade successfully in leather goods, and recommends the healthy margins available in activities such as binding, a fountain pen hospital, and in some cases in afternoon teas (see figure 6.1).

> **FOUNTAIN PEN HOSPITAL.**
>
> All kinds of Fountain Pens and Stylographs carefully and expeditiously repaired by experienced workmen.

Figure 6.1. Facsimile of a proposed window show card, from *The Successful Bookseller*, 1906. Source: Author's copy.

The situation in the twenty-first century, too, can be similar. In the early 2000s, large high-street chain bookstores consciously provided many of the coffee-and-sofa features of the environmentally restorative "third place."[6] And around the middle of the first decade, when the practices of online bookselling giants had accelerated the liberalization of the trade, the infrastructure of academic on-campus bookselling deteriorated to the breaking point. Preferring generic textbooks bought more cheaply online, students no longer bought tutor-recommend titles bulk-purchased by the campus bookshop, and a campus chain such as John Smith's found stationery and, ironically, cigarettes becoming life-saving lines. In an interview, John Smith's CEO, Peter Gray, estimated that for the period 2006 to 2008 around 60% of the company's sales at the University of the West of Scotland were no longer related to books.[7]

Despite the degree of interchangeability between main and secondary lines, however, there were core features of the book retail business at the turn of the nineteenth century that continued throughout much of the twentieth century, until the digital upheavals of the 1990s. By a comparative treatment, and by referring back to those extant documents from the period, we can still gain some idea of what running a provincial bookselling business may have entailed around 1900.

Much of the daily round for the bookseller was predictable in four major areas of buying, selling, staff, and advertising. Buying in took place through wholesales or from publishers, either directly or via the publishers' "rep." For smaller or start-up businesses, the wholesaler was often preferred, since a wide range of stock could be sourced from that one supplier, easing the administrative and delivery burden, and concentrating the buyer's bargaining power. *The Successful Bookseller* advised one wholesaler for books, one for leather goods, another for stationery, and so on, recommending Simpkin for books, and Sutton's, Foster's, and the Global Express Co. for conveyance. Its recommendation of Simpkin Marshal, to use the company's full title, was spot on: they were also a publishing house, and acted as agents for small provincial publishers, but their outstanding service was the centralized book-supply system that flourished until the misery of the blitz in 1940. It was Simpkin Marshall, too, who were among the early supporters of Frederick Macmillan's net book proposal.[8] Recommended by the guide, too, was an interview with the wholesaler's "head men," indicating the importance of the interpersonal network to secure credit and trade references.[9]

By focusing on levels of discount, and by avoiding overstocking that was preventable through meticulous monthly accounting, it was claimed that "the money saved per annum by obtaining the best discounts is more than equivalent to the rent of the premises."[10] With larger businesses, the wholesaler would remain useful for emergency and single orders and, particularly in the era before print-on-demand, for when the publisher but not the wholesaler was out of stock.

In sourcing directly from the publisher and therefore circumventing the wholesalers' margin, the book shop could get a better deal. But calculations would still be needed to decide on whether half a dozen orders of single titles from different publishers would be less economical than collecting the volumes, or having them dispatched from one wholesaling source, even at a slightly poorer discount, since few publishers, if any, would give the bookseller a better discount than the wholesaler for single copies.[11]

For multiple copies of new titles and for replenishing general stock—stock defined as books ordered for the mutual benefit of publisher and bookseller but without any immediate prospect of sale—the bookseller gained the best discounts from the publisher's representative. As the business grew, the bookseller was advised to stay on good terms with the rep, since this source of supply could eventually outstrip all others. Visits from reps could be frequent in the publishing metropolis, perhaps once per week, but in the provinces the frequency could be as little as four times or even twice per year. Large and, again, large metropolitan businesses could stipulate hours for appointments, at inconvenience to the rep, who risked unprofitable waiting times, whereas "the bookseller, especially in the provinces, is at the mercy of the representatives."¹² So it was up to the provincial bookseller to cultivate relationships with the rep and to suggest to publishers whose reps were not in contact that they should be.

An anecdote supporting the idea of networked *acteurs* is of a book business near-ruined through hasty treatment of a rep. On discovering that a rep was seemingly selling outside the legitimate bounds of the booktrade to a draper's firm, one bookseller is said to have berated the rep so badly that the rep threatened to have the seller's account with the publisher cancelled. The rep contended that the books sold to the drapers were intended for that firm's international export but the bookseller, not believing the publisher would close his lucrative account, continued his accusations. The bookseller was then surprised that the publishers upheld the rep's closing of his account and that the rep also carried out his threat to encourage the drapers to enter the book business in earnest, so that "now the drapery house has the largest book business in the district."¹³ Indeed, of draper's shops generally—in which H.G. Wells worked thirteen-hour days as a youth apprentice—there are examples of the two types of *textus* being sold, suggesting the practice was far-from unusual.¹⁴ The American twenty-five-cent household-library publisher Frank Lovell set up in London with a view to selling cloth-bound shilling books through draper's shops, and Lynn Knight writes of a widespread practice in haberdashery departments prior to World War I in England, where instead of the "inconvenient" farthings and ha'pennies being returned to customers as small change, papers of pins were returned in lieu, or in smaller draper's stores farthing novelettes, while the department store Morley's "gave out 'Wonderful Books' and 'Citizen Books' instead."¹⁵

Unless the book business could afford to pay an experienced buyer, the task of meeting the rep and going through the list of titles was considered a job for the manager. However, help from sales staff was advised when business size meant the manager no longer had particulars of the shops' departments at his or her fingertips. Business size would dictate whether the shop's assistants had acquired specialized knowledge that might inform discussions with the rep: how well a certain author sold; how well the shop was covering and selling titles for any given subject; whether price was restricting sales of some titles for certain sections of the shop's customer base; whether the success of a local factory's library or mechanics institute was already meeting readers' needs for other subjects;

or whether investment in the rep's new title, no matter how glossy or attractive, and no matter how warm the rep's recommendation, would take away from similar books already in stock and thus contribute to what Langdon-Davies called the nightmare of overstocking. Such decisions were best informed by an intimate knowledge of the stock and its sales patterns, often possessed by the sales assistant, but they also needed the input of someone with an overview of the business's access to capital, often the owner, and of his or her commitments "to his turnover, the extent of his credit with the publisher, the general balance of one kind of stock with another, the state of mind of the public in regard to particular subjects and any other general points which may determine his order for a particular book."[16] The crux was that knowledge of the day-to-day movement of stock *and* of the business's overall financial health was not necessarily held by the same person.

Someone able to produce the forms of knowledge needed would ideally have experience both of bookselling and of the buying public, the latter in a catholic sense as an interest in "the activities and characteristics of the greatest possible variety of his fellow human beings."[17] Langdon-Davies defined the "essence" of the trade in books as the transference of the thought of one person to (in a revealing demand-sided phrase) the "needs and aspirations of many" and, therefore, that the more a bookseller is concerned with "the social life of man in its myriad aspects" the better.[18] It can be imagined what decision-making might come from a shop owner prone to private serial enthusiasms, or whose view of the world was so personal as to be out of step with the majority of customers. And it can be seen how important to the bookseller would be astute staff who understood the customer, too.

Having a shop assistant—perhaps in the position of apprentice—who understood a wide range of business functions would facilitate buying decisions, but it would also have been a form of insurance for times when the bookseller was absent. On the other hand, reliance on an assistant for buying revealed where the bookseller was vulnerable. Growth beyond the point where the bookseller could commit all aspects of the business to memory was predicated on the good judgment of the shop's assistant, but their interests were not always mutual, and neither the bookseller nor the assistant's interests aligned completely with those of the rep.

For example, from the point of view of the assistant, the primary task was to sell books, and so an alternative title to offer the customer would be seen as a benefit. From that point of view, the rep's new title would be an advantage. From the point of view of the shop-owning bookseller, on the other hand, who paid for the stock and whose primary task was to maximize revenue by selling it, having many variants of essentially the same product would be a cost, against which the assistant ought to convince the customer that the title the shop holds is equally good if not better. Alternatively, the rep's highly recommended but superfluous new title actually might present the bookseller with an opportunity to piggyback on the incoming book's popularity to move otherwise languishing volumes—assuming the shop's salespeople were skillful enough, or, alternatively, that the customer could see the advantage.

To deal with that mismatch of interests within the shop, what business studies call conflicting stakeholder objectives, the guidebooks suggest that a remedy to the non-concordance could be found in trust. In the successful bookshop, the guide's advice is to cultivate an environment where "management and staff are in the true sense colleagues, for the amount to be learnt is infinite and each one needs the co-operation of the others."[19] Expressed more analytically, this meant that despite conflicting interests every *acteur* needed to imagine they were creating a single heterogenous network of bookselling, and that it was this network that brought sustainable benefits. Furthermore, as a challenge to twenty-first-century competitive New Public Management strategies founded on metric-based measurement of outputs, as the network's complexity became unknowable, trust was proposed as a remedy for something fundamentally immeasurable.

On arrival, the quantity and titles of new stock would need to be checked against the wholesaler's or publisher's invoice, noting the cost price and selling price. The recommendation of *The Successful Bookseller* is for a mark-up of 50% on the cost price as a legitimate profit, but it is unclear whether that estimate refers to books or lines "such as a fancy clock, a line of vases, fern pots or purses."[20] The guide recognizes the practice of buying by the dozen (and receiving thirteen), and of discounts of a third from book suppliers for smaller numbers of books, and half-price net for larger quantities, representing mark-ups of around 30–50% for books.

When not going into stock, sales items would be consigned either to shelving or to display cases and tables. If finances permitted, shelving with glazed easily operable doors was recommended to preserve books from soil and dust, while for Bibles, Prayer Books, and all leather-bound volumes, glazed doors were considered essential. Glass counters were recommended for fancy goods, with movable trays beneath, while wooden counters were considered suitable for books, on condition that they were large enough to display several titles at once. By contrast, the desk for entering orders and for housing the till was to be inconspicuous, although little novelties could be placed there to encourage the impulse purchase.

Attractive arrangements of special window-display lines were advised, the passing public supposedly unable to deny themselves a genuine bargain. Once customers were inside the shop, the ability of the salesperson was called upon to ensure they left with considerably more than the window item that brought them in. Recommendations for such window lines included the latest titles and, especially, with less-than-literary criteria, "special purchases of six shilling novels [that] may sometimes be made when publishers are clearing their stocks, at from 8d. to 9d. per volume, and these, if good titles are secured, will sell readily for 1s 4 1/2d. or 1s 6d. per volume . . . establish[ing] your business in the mind of the public as being a shop where goods are sold at very reasonable prices."[21]

Assuming that a double-fronted shop has been secured, the guide recommended the large window front for stationery and the smaller one for books. A sealed boxed partition was advised, to prevent condensation on the glass, at a depth of at least three feet from front to back. Mirrors ought to line the back of this box, with side mirrors at each end facing slightly toward the window shopper, away from 90 degrees, to create the illusion of additional volume. Window shelving should be plate glass, preferably to a height of four rows, and best with a graceful curve to overcome the shopfront's flatness. Dark or plush cloth should be placed in the base of the enclosure, but not fitted to allow for cleaning. Small projecting bracket shelves would hold special items, and an attractive display of books was recommended for the entrance lobby, together with whatever window tickets and announcements the shop chose to include.

Echoing the importance of what would now be called epitextual point-of-sale materials,[22] window dressing was identified as absolutely necessary, as opposed to merely exposing goods for sale. Governing the window display was the rule of heterogeneity, demanding that different "departments" of the shop not be crowded into a "mixed" window: "a little selection of stationery jammed against a row of purses . . . [should not] jostle a pile of the latest novel by 'Marie Corelli.'"[23] A page of window ticket designs was provided in the guide, including elongated tickets for placing inside a book, denoting a special price for cash, and it was suggested the shop's best retail price might be written beside a favorable estimate of what the item might otherwise cost elsewhere.

Dressing from the top down, to avoid damage if items should fall, the window should aim for depth from front to back, composed in the manner of stage *coulisses*, with a suggestion that small items such as knives could be fastened to the shop window using adhesive paper or suction hooks. To provide a hint of luxury, leather-bound books were proposed, but paper-covered series such as Temple Classics and The New Century Classics were also recommended, "pleasingly" stacked in neat piles, along with "the little bijou volumes issued on India paper by the Oxford Press."[24] In a parable of old and new booksellers, the guide described two shops each with six dozen copies of a popular novel. In the first shop, three copies of the novel are crowded in among other books, all ticketed in an identical way, while in the second shop two shelves are properly dressed with an array of copies, and a single large ticket is placed, legible from across the street. The reorders necessary for the progressive second shop were then compared to the first shop, whose excess copies had to be passed back to the rep for sale (at a commission) to country shops further afield.

As much care was required for displays inside the shop as in the front window. The customer of the successful shop was encouraged to stroll around and examine goods at leisure, rather than being forced to wait at a counter. An 1889 announcement by newly opened Rydill's Book Shop in Bristol extolled, among many other virtues, the firm's invitation to the public extended in the shop's circular "to walk in and inspect for themselves whether they purchase or no, in fact, to use it as a free public library."[25] The announcers predicted a great flourishing business for Mr. Rydill. The downside to all this free access was to be mitigated by mirrors attached to shelving, as a defense against theft. If at all possible, electric was the lighting of choice, unexcelled for cleanliness and absence from risk of fire. Hanging lamps with mantles were considered vastly attractive and, overall, the bookseller was advised to aim for a brilliantly lighted shop, which was considered an unparalleled medium of advertising in itself: light and what it signifies as the advertised good.

Locked into this shopping spectacle were books and a range of other goods and services, and between them *The Successful Bookseller* saw no incongruity. The guide's alphabetical list of stock was as precise as it was exhaustive; a small sample includes Acceptance cards, Address (and "where is it?") books, Adhesive labels, Bands (elastic), Bezique playing cards, Black bordered cards (complimentary, correspondence, and visiting), Carbon paper, Carpenter's pencils, Compasses, Confetti, Cribbage pegs, Dance invite cards, Dish papers, Drawing Pins, Ebony rulers, and so on, and so on. Among soufflé cups and sealing wax are pie-dish collars and pens: Brandauer, Esterbrook, Gillot, Macniven and Cameron, Mitchell, Relief, Stylo, Waverley and, surprisingly, Quill. Dummies of the famous Swan pens for window display were to be had from Messrs. Mabie, Todd and Bard.

Orders for copper-plate engraving could be outsourced to external partners (Messrs. H.S. Croker and Co., or Messrs. F.W. Bristol and Co.). One useful trade-bringing innovation was to offer 50 engraved cards for 2s 6d complete, including "At Home" cards, and other invitations. A personalized die stamp service might also be offered, to individualize a customer's writing paper or cards, but the recommendation of *The Successful Bookseller* was that the die stamp remain the property of the retailer, to secure repeat orders: "the margin of net profit is small on the first order . . . [but] a customer has been obtained who may be relied on for a continuance of orders."[26]

The guide devoted half a chapter to selling writing paper—preferably octavo or Albert in size (full octavo for commercial customers)—while leather and fancy goods took a chapter each. Books were dealt with in a single chapter. In much the same way as the guide detailed varieties of black-bordered card, and with a caveat accounting for regional variation to literary taste, it advised a book business built around the following reliably selling authors: Rudyard Kipling, Sir A. Conan Doyle, A.E.W. Mason, Sir Gilbert Parker, Anthony Hope, H.S. Merriman, Mrs. Braddon, H. Rider Haggard, Guy Boothby, S.R. Crockett, Mrs. Humphry Ward, Miss Cholmondley, Miss Gertrude Atherton, Miss Kate Douglas Wiggin, Maurice Hewlett, Max Pemberton, our old acquaintance F. Marion Crawford, and of course Marie Corelli and Ouida. From the classic authors, its recommendation was for George Eliot, the Brontës, Thackeray, Dickens, and Scott. The stock of religious and devotional books would depend on the shop's class of customer. Nowhere did the guide mention critical categories recognizable to students of literature, such as realism, romanticism, or fin-de-siècle modernism.

Worth stocking, too, according to the guide, were juvenile and reward books, the latter being books produced during the second half of the nineteenth and early twentieth centuries and given by schools or religious organizations to children who attended the given institution.

Designed not to please but to "improve," these books would have usefully bound the child to the organization awarding the prize.[27] From a research perspective, however, the idea of reward books is revealing. As the guide stated, the conservative trader whom the guide uses to exemplify bad practice conceives merely of the customer's functional *requirements*, whereas the guide's insistence above all was that "it is desirable to satisfy customer's *wants*" (original italics).[28] In the case of reward books, the book is given by an agency other than the user, and the want that is satisfied is the pleasure of receiving a reward. But what if the giving agent were the user herself? All objects in the bookshop then become rewards, made so by the user's desire. Books, along with cribbage pegs and playing cards, become private rewards for pains taken and competing opportunities passed over—because the reader "is worth it," as the slogan says—possession itself being what is efferently gained. Following on, the organization to which the rewarded reader is then bound is the bookselling network of producers, distributors and, above all, other readers who made the publication of the title possible. No wonder, then, that it was the bookseller's enthusiasm for society's interests in general, rather than the seller's private interests per se, which formed Langdon-Davies's prescription for what makes the best bookseller.

The objective of the bookseller, according to the guide, was not simply to obtain but to *retain* customers, and it was toward this latter purpose that efforts by the shop's owner and the assistants were to be directed. If the former business objective could be achieved by providing a well-priced book, the latter required entering into a field of interpersonal relationships—and if we translate the latter goal into business terms, then we get a very different idea of what intangible goods and services were on offer. By advocating respectfulness "without being servile, not cringing to those who appear wealthy, and overbearing to those whose garb proclaims them to be less blest with the world's goods," the guide effectively suggested dignified affirmation as a primary service. Not for philanthropy but for sustainable profit, "as much pains [should be] taken with a small purchaser as with those who have the power of spending large sums," as well as being afforded to the difficult class of customer "euphemistically described as 'tabs.'"[29] The guide's author claimed to have secured a long-term and, as it predictably turns out, highly profitable customer, by overspending 6d to procure a book for Christmas that rival department stores claimed could not be done. And indeed, this personal-care approach can be seen repeated in an offer by Pollet's Advertising

Agency to provide booksellers with seemingly personal business circulars in the form of private letters, from between 25 for 2s to 3000 for 39s.[30] For current purposes, what the bookseller provides in these approaches is an affirmation: the good of a relationship in which the customer is demonstrably proved to be someone worth "taking pains" over. Alongside books, or perhaps in the same manner as books, the shop sold a valuable coded performance of affirmation.

Still in the very early part of the twentieth century, a further means for the shop to generate revenue from its stock beyond direct sales was to set up a circulating library. Since "the abolition of the cumbersome three-volume novel and the introduction of the six shilling edition," *The Successful Bookseller* claimed the whole system of the circulating library had been revolutionized.[31] No longer waiting on the pleasure of the library wholesaler, which could mean delays of months, the bookseller could now afford to buy a six-shilling edition outright and have the most up-to-date stock possible. Purchase also meant the bookseller eventually owned the stock, rather than having to return it to the wholesaler at the end of the year; and the entire cost of purchase was comparable to the subscription price charged by the wholesaler. With a library of between 300 and 3,000 books, the guide promised a satisfactory income to supplement ordinary business, without having to devote any additional special knowledge or time to it. What is more, the library would attract business to other departments of the shop, and it was exactly this retail and library combination that was practiced at the longest-running bookshop in Southampton, Gilbert's, until at least November 1905.[32]

The library was to be set furthest from the entrance, the customer thus having to run the fullest "gauntlet of temptations." A four-page monthly folder was advised, showing the most recent additions, posted or delivered to customers. Two card catalogues were suggested, too, arranged alphabetically under author name and again under title, so that customers "can almost serve themselves."[33] Most importantly, a registration system would be needed to cover loans and borrowers (the latter in two categories: subscribers and casual readers); an example of such a registration system was made available to booksellers by the Successful Bookseller Company in foolscap folio, at 500 pages, for 10s and 6d.

In 1906, the authors recommended for library purposes were Alan St Alban, J.M. Barrie, Robert Barr, Miss Braddon, Walter Bessant, Guy Boothby, Hall Caine, Rosa N. Carey, Marie Corelli, Marion Crawford, Dick Donovan, Conan Doyle, Ch. Garvice, Sarah Grand, H. Rider Haggard,

Joseph Hocking, Anthony Hope, Fergus Hume, Rudyard Kipling, Edna Lyall, Lucas Malet, Mona Maclean, Seton Merriman, Frankfort Moore, L.T. Meade, Phillips Oppenheim, Max Pemberton, Gilbert Parker, William le Queux, Stanley Weyman, and Curtis Yorke—and not a Henry James or Joseph Conrad in sight. But of utmost importance was keeping pace with the latest publications, and making sure that the publication dates of forthcoming titles were included in the shop's information to subscribers. In a 1964 article on the closing of one of the last surviving commercial circulating libraries in Birmingham, the business's librarian, Mrs. Beatrice Hill, was said to have known her "older generation" customers so well that they often received a new book by their favorite author before they heard of its being published.[34] A conclusion that might be induced is that emphasis on latest publications meant the circulating libraries in their late period sold *access to the newest* fiction as a primary gain rather than the given work of fiction *per se*; since post-three-decker, the cost of purchase was no longer beyond the customer's reach. But for that newest access to function in a business model, the price needed to be well pitched, because combined with the anticipatory excitement of the latest was the possible disappointment of the latest, and although the book's attractions for readers might lay in its newness, outright purchase still represented a risk if the balance weighed for the latter. With a modest library subscription—Gilbert's charges in 1905 ranged from 1s 6d for one volume to 7s for six volumes per month, for the latest season's publications—buying the thrill of the new became for readers a reasonable investment rather than an unjustifiable risk.

Unlike the major department stores, small shops were unable to operate without offering credit. This meant that a major task for shops was chasing up customer payments. As an incentive—given that the standard cash discount was not allowed on books sold on account—it was suggested by *The Successful Bookseller* that the sales bill might be stamped with a comparable discount if the payment were made within fourteen days. As a general rule, accounts were to be sent promptly at the turn of the month, rather than on haphazard days, which suggests either a lax attitude among customers generally toward payment or monthly salary. Monthly payments were preferred to quarterly and, despite the threefold clerical workload, it was felt that the third reminder represented a psychological watershed for payment. If quarterly accounts were kept, a damaging nine months would elapse before the customer received the third reminder for purchased books.

It was advised that credit only be extended on receipt of satisfactory references, which again highlights the interpersonal, social nature of the trade—and anyone excluded from local networks of social approval on grounds of class or race was to be held to cash only. In cases of default, the guide suggested carefully drafted letters, escalated in cases of further default, with each draft peeling back layers of deference to the customer. The initial "Dear Sir, I venture to call your attention to the enclosed account that I feel sure has escaped your attention," and the regret that rules of the business do not allow for extended credit, segues into a notice that the shop is receiving its auditor on the 31st of the month and therefore that it would be kindly favored with a remittance of the outstanding amount. If that failed then "We regret that we have not yet been favoured with a reply to our letter" should morph implacably into "We very much regret . . . [and] should be sorry to be compelled to take any actions of a harsh nature . . ." and then to "(Final Notice) . . . it is with much regret that . . . unless a settlement be made within seven days from date, proceedings will be taken to enforce payment without further notice."[35]

As to the proceedings that would force payment, the guide acknowledged that most traders would write off the amount as bad debt. The shop had little more recourse than to appeal to good faith, or apply wider social censure where it could. If it were to hand the debt over to a solicitor and be unsuccessful, then the solicitor would have to look for the shop for the legal fees. There were two forms of summons that the shop could pursue through the County Court—"default" and "ordinary"—but, again, neither would secure an immediate payment, as the guide suggested each would be flouted by the defendant, whose primary aim was to gain time. If a payment were ever forthcoming, it would be made far into whatever legal recourse was adopted, just before the court hearing and in sufficient time for the defendant "to prevent his name appearing in Court Lists." In the retail environment of the turn of the century, then, we can conclude that public reputation operated as a sometimes compelling sanction that located power in the public sphere. Such a system of public self-regulation would necessarily be both positive and negative: positive where social regulation represented democratic inclusion; negative when it represented democratically held prejudice; and, in parallel to the public shame of failing twenty-first-century creditworthiness ratings, this shift of power to the public sphere also risk passing power to those institutions claiming to represent the public interest. What it does confirm, however, is that the core of the book retail business was located in a social network.

Toward the end of the 1800s, advertising was continuing its shift from being a mere giving notice of items for sale, with its exaggeration of qualities sometimes known as "puffery." Slowly, it was becoming an institutionalized (and international) semiotic system offering private access to those intangible values created out of the advertisement's narrative around the goods and services for sale.[36] A figure known to *The Successful Bookseller* as "last century man" felt advertising unnecessary, while his twentieth-century counterpart knew it to be an invaluable means of increasing the desirability and value of the stock. If so, it is noteworthy that advertisements for book shops so rarely foreground specific titles. Browsing the nation's periodicals of the period, it is striking that commercial book advertising focus on generic goods, which is not the case for other retail sectors. Advertising for commercial libraries might foreground prices, rates and availability, on occasion drawing attention to genres—travel, history, biography, "novels"—while advertisements for booksellers highlight the shop itself, and the services it had to offer. Gilbert's ran regular advertisements in local Hampshire papers along these lines, advertising the shop's buying and selling policies for new and secondhand, and the availability of postal and circulating library facilities. Only rarely would bookshops announce a particular title or author name, that being the natural territory of "Books and Bookmen" and literature review columns.

In discussing the direct advertising of publishers, Langdon-Davies argued that, compared to the attractions of the book's subject matter, the "little-reading" public were less interested in the author's name, and utterly uninterested in that of the publisher, shocking though that might be to both. The rose-grower would want books on roses, footballers on football, would-be travelers on travel, and gossipers on scandal. For this general public, advertising in high-class daily papers or in an intellectual weekly was also deemed a waste of time, and instead cheaper notices were recommended in local papers, or journals dealing with the trades, hobbies, and sports in which these customers took an interest. Trade union journals were recommended along with "obscure weeklies of all kinds of which most publishers have never even heard."[37]

Once the shop's book department was running smoothly, *The Successful Bookseller* recommended that a form of advertising available only to that department in the form of a trade list of "publications of the month" be sent to the shop's customers. The list—obtainable from trade journals or from wholesalers such as Simpkins, and stamped with the name and address of the bookshop—could be sent out in the expectation that readers would keep the sheet for reference and thus routinely be reminded of the shop over the ensuing month. Catalogues were also suggested, and bookshop ads in British periodicals of the time very often drew attention to catalogues sent free on application. As Ian Mitchell notes, "general booksellers who sold both new and second-hand books from town centre shops and who regularly issued sales catalogues were common in provincial towns from at least the early eighteenth century,"[38] and, still in the 1920s, a Rochester bookshop owner claimed that provincial booksellers lived by matching the right books to the shop's customers "and then offering them to contacts or issuing catalogues."[39]

The recommendation of *The Successful Bookseller* was for the catalogues of Messrs. Barnicott and Pearce, who could also supply theological and devotional catalogues, *The Country Gentleman's Reference Catalogue* and, most rewardingly, *The Successful Bookseller's* own annual catalog of around 150 pages in crown 8vo, at £5 for 500 copies, suitably stamped with the shop's name. This catalog included a copious index, "by no means the least important feature of the publication."[40] The joys of such catalogues are illustrated in a 1905 editorial piece, in the *Southampton Daily Echo*, "Books and Catalogues," which claimed "The book lover is often a poor man. . . . He may not have a library but he has the second hand bookshops, where he can spend hours diving into treasures that he can never hope to own. Then too he has the catalogues to study. . . . There is no need to see the works themselves. The titles conjure up dreams of other days, and recall scraps of history and romance. Truly, the book lover has many real compensations for his lack of the necessary cash."[41] And the joys of catalogue browsing must be persistent, too, since a blog post by author Debbie Young on children's reading during World Book Day 2017 recalled the pleasures of "laying on my stomach on our living room carpet reading and re-reading the toy section in my mum's mail order catalogue."[42] Distanced from the risks of actual purchase but safe with the pleasures of potentiality, Alison Clarke describes catalogues as a portable shop window (her case study was the British catalogue retailer Argos), in which a degree of extra control passes to the browser without detaching from the identity-creating activity of shopping.[43] Not as unique titles secured by the shop, but as the culmination of the entire book trade, the book catalog advertised reader-choice and the potential of self-empowerment from a common body of bibliographic goods.

Overall, the daily round of a bookshop at the turn of the century represented a series of negotiations undertaken as part of a wider retail network, one node of which was the bookshop. In this sense, the shop constitutes an ongoing intervention in and creation of bibliographic activity, happening outside and inside the shop, borne by the imaginations of customers, retailers and publishers. As a generator of value for symbolic goods, it is not production but relationships in this actor network that provides specific objects with much of their value, and it is that which creates the network's common wealth, in a way that institutionalized economics would have difficulty describing.

Chapter 7

High Street Southampton Bookshops

Ascertaining the number and nature of book shops operating in the city center in the late nineteenth and early twentieth centuries is not a straightforward matter.[1] Bookshops were often known as stationers and, as has been shown, stationers were often bookshops. In the 1876 Southampton classified trades directory, for example, the entry for "stationers" merely states "see booksellers." Furthermore, businesses selling leisure-time print that included fiction and other genres available to the bookshop could well include newsagents. Various local street directories provide a start, but these are commercial directories and not empirical studies, and cannot be relied upon for a comprehensive picture. In the classified sections, for example, not all operative business are listed, which might be explained by charges for inclusion applied by the directories (Chaplin and Weeks is a notable absence) and, understandably for visibility, some businesses may have wanted to appear under as many headings as possible, whether or not the activity was genuinely representative. Advertisements in the local press are an important indicator, but in the nature of advertising they can conceal as much as they reveal: a sudden promotion of one line may mean that residual, unrepresentative stock is being moved before that line is closed.

Unfortunately, the Southampton City Archives suffered considerably during the Blitz, and a great deal of the business records held there were destroyed. Cross references have been made in the few local histories available, including their reissue online in the excellent Sotonopedia, and additional material has been recovered through wider searches unavailable to the pioneering local historians who compiled the first records.[2]

The most substantial data available is on the bookshop known locally as Gilbert's, though its records were also destroyed in the bombings of 1940 and available information is still meager, necessitating again the extant published descriptions being substantially supported from local archive and newspaper records as well as by material from a series of interviews held with the last owner of the family shop, Richard Gilbert, in 2017–18.

On the five address point maps below (7.1–7.5), the town's main booksellers are indicated. Ideally, the periods of their operation would have been recorded precisely at decade intervals, but the limited extent of archive detail and the need to capture a representative picture has disrupted the uniformity of the periods and intervals. Unless otherwise stated, businesses appearing within a date range were in operation throughout the period.

Only those bookselling businesses are included that are or would have been considered to be central, a conception that has altered with changes to flows of passage along Southampton's High Street, most notably in a shift from Below Bar to Above Bar, and in a transfer of relative importance from the Terminus to Central railway stations. Details of selected businesses in nearby districts are provided below each map. It should also be noted that road names and building numbers could change and occasionally disappear—for example, while at the same premises, Gilbert's changed building number from 26 1/2 to 24.[3]

Each business has been selected because of evidence of retail bookselling operations, in one way or another, that provides reasonable grounds for considering them to be booksellers. A few chose to emphasize specializations in binding, printing, and publishing, or in providing a circulating library; there is additional notation included for these, but care needs to be taken over what these specializations imply. John Adams, for example, advertised as a bookseller but also published: George Buxey's varyingly called their business a bookseller, a stationer, and a publisher, and would advertise in all of those classified trade columns in the same directory; and there are many cases of publishers selling books and materials printed from their own press. Many businesses ran circulating libraries and, in principle, the circulating library was simply one highly common form of retail practice among several, which may or may not have been worth emphasizing.

A greater number of printing businesses have been omitted from the maps, despite the increase in their numbers nationally. A study of unionized labor from 1897 recognized that the printing trade, "once concentrated in half a dozen towns, has today crept into every village" but it also notes that "the vast majority of printing offices [are] tiny enterprises of small working masters,"[4] and many Southampton print businesses would have been jobbing printers, removed from the business of books.

Regrettably, the town's newsagents have proven too numerous to include. Relatively less capital-intensive than bookshops, newsagents would have been the preferred business of those with limited investment capacity. Newsagents were found throughout the town, including its laboring-class districts such as St. Mary's and Northam, and in the poorer areas. Following a section of the eastern line of the old medieval walls, or rather along its moats, was Canal Walk, a short street (about 300 meters) of tumble-down shops known as the "Ditches": two newsagents operating there were John Grayson at number 58 and Isaac George at number 74 (1897 and 1907, respectively).[5] Since newsagents provided a cheaper source of fiction to those with less resources, in fiction-bearing periodicals, the decision to exclude newsagents is regrettable, but doubly so since other businesses that chose to be listed as newsagents—W.H. Smith's, for example, or again Buxey's—were clearly booksellers.

Lastly, there was a more-or-less immeasurable book trade at the very bottom of the market, which perforce this study must ignore. Evidence of vagrants selling writing paper in Southampton suggests that even the smallest fractions of book trade may have been able to provide an income for the poorest sections of the community.[6] John Thomson and Adolphe Smith produced a volume of thirty-seven photographs in 1877, *Street Life in London*, one of which shows a secondhand shop, known as a "broker's," where cheap and often near-to-ruined furniture could be bought, and from which a few volumes can be seen jumbled onto a table on the street.[7] The dimensions of this kind of informal booktrade is unknown, as is the measure of its importance to people with no other means of access to books.

As a final piece of contextualizing data, population figures should be provided to give an idea of density of book shop per adult resident. In the early 1890s the population of the city, then called a town, was effectively around 90,000, if we include the populations of several nearby districts that provided the city with its workforce, many of which were incorporated into a borough extension by 1895 (Shirley, Freemantle, Millbrook, and the Bitterne Park estate); just after 1900 it had topped 105,000, and by 1911 it was 119,000.[8] The Office for National Statistics calculates that life expectancy in 1901 was 48.5 years for women and

52.4 years for men (averaging at 50).⁹ Given that figures are skewed from high rates of infant mortality, we can still propose a working estimate for Southampton of people aged fifteen and over who may have had access to disposable income of some kind at 70,000. (The Elementary Education, School Attendance Act of 1893 raised the school leaving age from ten to thirteen, thus placing those over thirteen in work.) This of course says nothing about literacy rates, or whether Southampton citizens favored buying print over so much else.

With a good deal of caution, and with the caveats already noted, it can be suggested that in Southampton city center over a thirty-year period from the mid-1870s to the middle of the first decade of the 1900s, there were at any one time between twelve and seventeen businesses involved substantially in the selling of books, while smaller bookselling businesses dotted around the city brought the total to approximately twenty. From the center alone, the ratio of shops to potential readers over fifteen years old sustaining the city's network of bookselling businesses was between 1:4,200 and 1:5,800. Overwhelmingly, Southampton's book dealers were also stationers, printers, and binders, and often had interests in publishing, or at least in the publication of anything that might capitalize on local needs.

For each map legend, the following abbreviations have been used: Prt, Portland Street; Abv, High Street, Above Bar; HS, High Street, Below Bar; Pm, Pembroke Square (no longer extant); Hnv, Hanover Buildings; Wst, West Street; StM, St. Michael's Square; Brg, Bridge Street (no longer extant); Bnd, Bernard Street; Oxf, Oxford Street; StMry, St. Mary's Street. Although all businesses listed identified themselves as booksellers, several chose to emphasize other activities, denoted by the following: †, stationery; †† publishing and printing; ††† bookbinding. A * denotes precise status unknown. (See maps 7.1–7.5.)

What is noticeable from the map data of booksellers is the way in which agents in the network cross paths and combine interests, some to disappear in suspicious circumstances and others to successfully remain, such as Gilbert's—the presence of the latter spreading throughout the network, and seeming at times to specialize in mopping up where others have gone to ground. Book businesses expand and then perhaps fragment into the hands of family relations, or pass to former managers and employees. Organizations on the edges of what should strictly be referred to as the retail book trade, such as religious societies and newspapers, play key roles in bookselling and publishing, as do wealthy entrepreneurs

○ 1: Harle, Mrs. 6 Prt   ● 6: Gilbert, H.M. 103 HS   ● 12: Broadbere, Kelita. 5 Pm †††
● 2: Rayner, John F. 25 Abv   ● 7: Domony, C. 116 HS   ○ 13: Cawte, G. 9 StM †††
● 3: James, T. 26½ Abv   ● 8: Randle, Alfred. 139-140 HS   ○ 15: Rayner, Mrs. 21 Brg
○ 14: Clark, Mrs. 14 StM ††   ○ 9: Gutch and Cox. 150 HS   ● 16: Adams, John. 49 Oxf
● 4: Phillips, G. 12 HS †   ○ 10: Knight, Edward. 178 HS   ○ 17: Budden, W. 41 StMry
● 5: Virtue and Co. J.S. 23 HS †† ○ 11: Rayner, John, F.180 HS

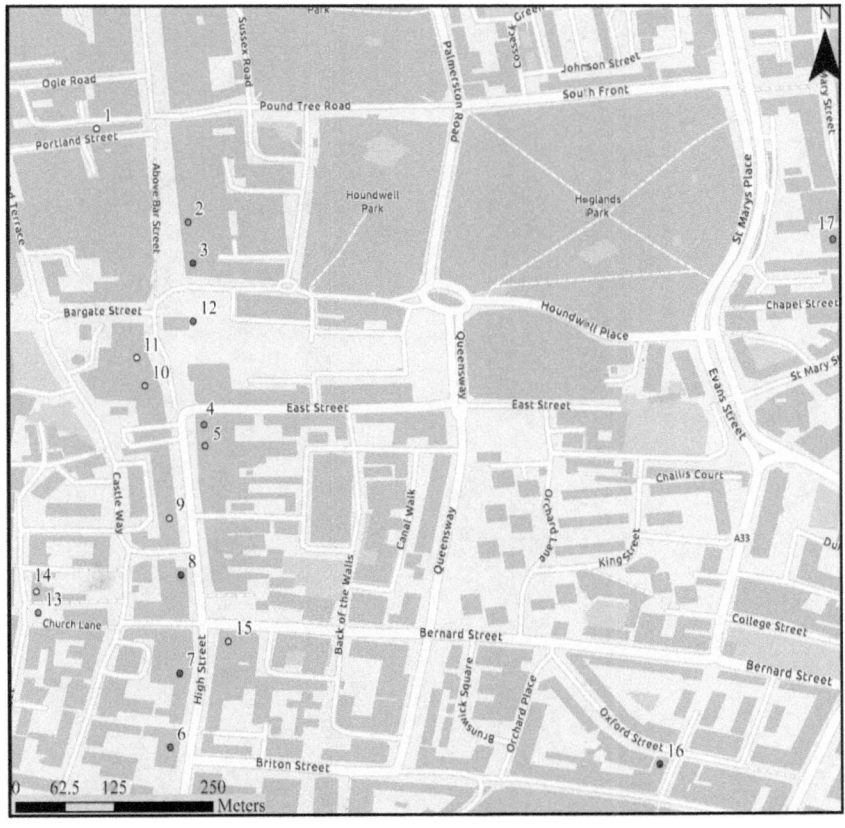

Map 7.1. Southampton bookstores, 1876. Bridge Street once comprised the western end of Bernard Street and derived its name from the town ditches that it once bridged. Pembroke Square was a small *cul de sac* on the east of the Bargate, demolished to make way for the Bargate circus. From 1871 through to 1878, bookseller Robert Harris operated from 24 Orchard Street (not to be confused with Orchard Place or Orchard Lane, adjacent to Bernard Street). Orchard Street ran west from Above Bar Street to Western Shore Road but is no longer found in street directories by 1884. Gutch and Cox later became Cox and Sharland. Mrs. Rayner operated from premises announced as offices for the *Southampton Observer*. Mrs. Cora Hazelton was a bookseller registered at Upper Prospect Place, possibly in Hythe Village, on the west bank of the Solent, accessible by ferry. W.H. Smith and Sons operated an outlet from the railway terminus. *Source*: Author.

- ● 1: Christian Knowledge Society. 6 Prt
- ○ 2: Gilbert, H.M. 26½ Abv
- ● 3: Dyer Alfred. 52 Abv ††
- ○ 4: Lyne, George Alma. 62 Abv †
- ● 5: Phillips, G. 12 HS †
- ● 6: Phillips, G. 169 HS
- ○ 7: Virtue and Co. J.S. 23 HS ††
- ● 8: Paul Brothers, 77 HS ††, †††
- ● 9: Gutch and Cox. 150 HS
- ● 10: Southampton Book Society. 178 HS
- ● 11: Rayner, John, F.180-181 HS
- ● 12: Broadbere, Kelita. 5 Pm †††
- ○ 13: Cawte, G. 5 Wst †††
- ● 14: Buxey, George. 21 Brg
- ● 15: James, Thomas and Co. 42 Bnd
- ● 16: Adams, John. 49 Oxf

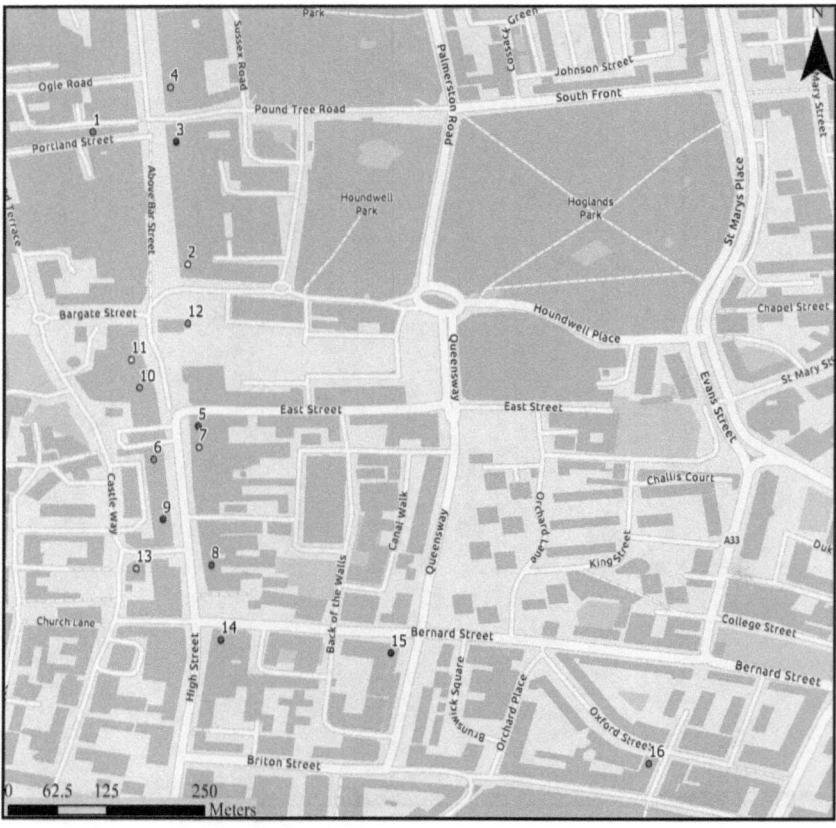

Map 7.2. Southampton bookstores, 1887. By 1887, the business of G. Phillips had become Philips and Sons. Edward Knight was manager of Southampton Book Society. Bernard Street, from where James specialized in secondhand books, connected the High Street to Oxford Street that provided access to the Terminus rail station and docks. James Beal ran a bookselling outlet from Woolston on the east bank of the River Itchen, accessible via ferry. By 1891, Chaplin, W. and Sons had a business in Waterloo Place; possibly of the same family as the Chaplin who went into partnership as Chaplin and Weeks. W.H. Smith and Sons announce their address as Railway Terminus in 1891, but not in 1897. *Source*: Author.

○ 1: Burbidge, J. Church Book Depot. 6 Prt
● 2: Gilbert, H.M. 26½ Abv
○ 3: Virtue and Co. J.S. 23 HS ††
○ 4: Paul Brothers. 77 HS †††
● 5: Cox and Sharland. 150 HS †††
○ 6: Southampton Book Society. 178 HS
● 7: Rayner, John, F.180-181 HS
● 8: Broadbere, Kelita. 11 Hnv †††
○ 9: Cawte and Sons, 5 Wst †††
● 10: Buxey, George. 21 Brg
○ 11: James, Thomas and Co. 42 Bnd
○ 12: Adams, John. 49 Oxf
○ 13: Budden and Sons. 85 StMry

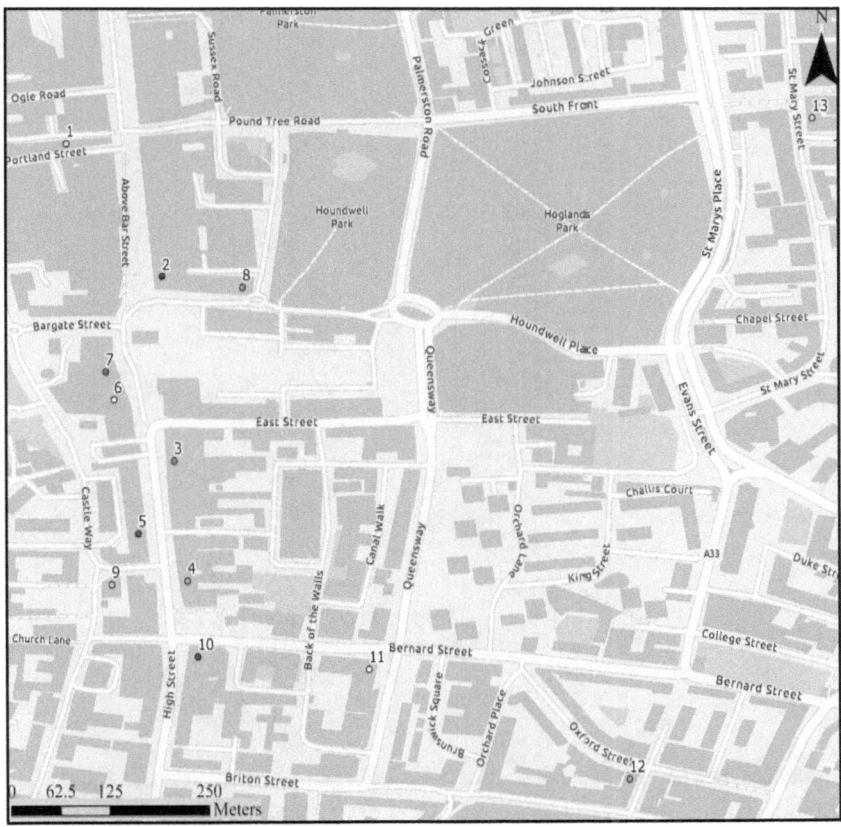

Map 7.3. Southampton bookstores, 1897. In 1891, 6 Portland Street was announced as an outlet for the Society for the Promotion of Christian Knowledge, managed by J. Stadden. The shop at 178 High Street was run by the Southampton Book Society until 1894, after which the premises were taken over briefly by Chaplin and Weeks around 1895, by William Blackball around 1897, and then occupied over a longer duration by Robert Batt. In new premises on St Mary's Street, W. Budden had become Budden and Sons by 1891, and was emphasizing †††. Mrs. Cora Hazelton was still trading in 1891, but there is no evidence of this for 1897. A secondhand bookseller, Moody and Co., was operating from 10 London Road, which lay slightly north of the High Street. Chaplin and Roberts were still operating from Waterloo Place in 1895, though the Chaplin of Chaplin and Weeks died in 1894. *Source*: Author.

Map 7.4. Southampton bookstores, 1900–1901. The evidence suggests that Blackwood La Bas and Co. may only have been in operation by 1903 but is included in this map to capture bookselling activity at this address. Moody's still operated from London Road. The general ironmongers and county suppliers Lankester and Crook appear around this period as booksellers, operating, like James Beal, from Woolston on the east bank of the River Itchen, accessible via ferry, and thereafter from other outlets around the city. John Barnaby operated as a bookselling colporteur, from Eastleigh, a railway-industry village to the north of Southampton. W.H. Smith's announced their business address as Railway Station West (not Southampton Blechynden), now Southampton Central. *Source*: Author.

Map 7.5. Southampton bookstores, 1905–1907. The Caxton Publishing Co. moved from their premises in 147½ High Street, formerly occupied by Blackwood La Bas, to 5 Portland Street, by 1907. W.H. Smith and Sons in Southampton transitioned from a railway-station-only business to the High Street around 1907 and retained their outlets at Station West and the Railway Terminus. Thomas James was registered at number 42 Bernard Street in 1905 but number 34 by 1907. Lankester and Crook operated from Woolston and several other neighboring locations. An Alfred Walters operated from 49 London Road, whose precise business is unknown. *Source*: Author.

or careerists looking to exploit local cultural and financial capital. Any Southampton-born subject to have its head raised sufficiently above the parapet of obscurity could expect to have a publishing and sales project attached to it and, indeed, one striking thing about the city's late-nineteenth-century book trade is its not making far more of the town's connections to Jane Austen, as is currently the case.[10] Trade that was less locally wedded came often in the form of the London firm's branch office, while the entire High Street has profited from the presence of traffic attracted to and passing through the docks, not least during gold-rush periods in the colonies and in the US. Gender is performed in the division of labor and between trades—the bookbinder's sewers are young women; with the arrival of typewriting technologies, general copying services are provided by business owners who are demonstrably "Miss," in contrast with the men who are agents for typewriting manufacturers. But overall, the inference to be drawn is that trade in book retail was not only in need of other lines such as stationery, bags, and fancy goods—and, as technologies developed, adding color picture-postcards, photographs, and typewriters—but that often it was integrated into a range of allied business activities such as publishing, printing, binding, and news agency, which could variously supplement or be supplemented by the trade in book retail. Furthermore, the economies that the city's bookselling networks enabled were not only financial but as importantly interpersonal, too.

The example of religious organizations as a supposedly tangential yet powerful force in the production and distribution of print comes with the business in Portland Street, which was a development of genteel residences built in the 1820s and '30s, and now Grade II listed buildings. According to the household listings, Mrs. Harle was not an independent bookseller but the agent for a Mr. Irvine Harle, who managed the book depot of the Christian Instruction Society, one of many socially minded Christian organizations, and one placed earlier in the century in opposition to the Christian Evidence Society, the former proposing that biblical scripture was intended metaphorically rather than as historic fact.[11] By 1887, the premises housed two depots—of the Christian Knowledge Society (their secretary was Rev. T. Davies) and of the National Society for Promoting the Education of the Poor—before passing to the Society for the Promotion of Christian Knowledge (SPCK) by 1891. Until 1880, the curate of nearby Christ Church in Portswood (later Highfield Church) had been Rev. Frederick Edward Wigram, son of Edward Wigram, one-time treasurer of the SPCK. Registered simply as The Church Book Depot, this Christian repository was managed by a Mr. J. Burbidge until being transposed under Burbidge's management to 68 Above Bar by 1905. The 1907 Guide gives the public face of the repository as still The Church Book Depot, but under business listings that Henry March Gilbert was now agent for the two depots, of the societies of Christian Knowledge and of Promoting Education of the Poor, at that same address. Whether the fortunes of the Christian Societies had waned and the depot had been taken over by a stalwart of the trade is unclear, but by 1912–13 the 68 Above Bar premises were occupied by a hairdresser, the superbly named Pierre Moulin, and the two Christian book depots were now housed at Gilbert's premises at number 24, this time including a depot of the Society for the Propagation of the Gospel in Foreign Parts. For Henry March Gilbert, at least, religious books were an integrated part of the retail trade.

From the map data, it can be seen that, between 1876 and 1891, a John Rayner had premises at 180 and then 180–181 High Street, Below Bar, which would become a relevant address for the business of Chaplin and Weeks. In 1876, Rayner also had premises at 25 Above Bar, close to premises occupied by Henry March Gilbert by 1887, which Henry had taken over from bookseller Thomas James at number 26 1/2. At the 180 and 180–181 addresses, John Rayner is shown continuing in business—in 1884 the shop was registered as bookseller and fancy bazaar—until the directories note a change to a Miss Rayner, in 1891, from which it may be surmised that a daughter or near relative had taken over. The maps also show a Mrs. Rayner with interests in the *Southampton Observer* at 21 Bridge Street, which later would become the long-term home for George Buxey's multiple-line book business.

According to the records, in the 1840s, Charles Smith Rayner of Southampton was known as a printer and publisher of illustrations, but was only resident in the town during that decade, and had interests in London and Shropshire. John Frederick Rayner, aged eighteen in 1841, was registered as "printer" in the town census; the 1851 census located him at 180 High Street with his brother Henry G. and sister Elizabeth, in the occupation of bookseller and newsagent; his children with his wife Esther were baptized in the church opposite the shop. John's brother Charles Woodhouse Rayner had been a business partner and, between 1847 and

1849, the brothers, then in their twenties, published timetables and other information to passengers in newspapers of varying names, including the *Post Office and Railway Chronicle*, the *Southampton Royal Mail Packet*, and the *Visitors' and Steam Packet Passengers' Guide* (in the 1840s, both P. & O. and the Royal Mail Steam Packet Company selected Southampton over Falmouth for their mail packet operations, due to access by rail not available in Falmouth). The Rayners also published a number of guides to Southampton and to the Isle of Wight, as well as the town directory for 1849, including titles such as *Rayner's Sixpenny Guide to Southampton and its Neighbourhood* (after 1865)—a narrated "walk-about" guide to the standard local sights—and *The Visitants' Guide to Southampton: Being a Condensed History of the Town . . . with a Companion to the Beautiful Ruins of Netley Abbey*. Netley Abbey, on the nearby eastern banks of the Solent, had long been a tourist destination, particularly in periods of Gothic revival, having been enthused over by Horace Walpole, and had even been deemed worthy of a painting by John Constable.[12]

The fragmentation of a business between family members and its succession by former employees can be seen as Charles Rayner left the number 180 address by 1851, to resurface as a bookseller, newsagent, and stationer in Totton—a village around eight kilometers east of the town—and in Bridge Street in the town center. Not just the men, but women of the Rayner family assumed business responsibilities. On Charles's death, his business at Bridge Street passed to his wife, Charlotte, Mrs. C.W. Rayner, from where she was noted as sole proprietress of the *Southampton Observer* and, in 1863, Mrs. C.W. Rayner can be seen operating two central premises at 51 Lower East Street and at 21 Bridge Street. After Charlotte's death on 10 April 1879, the Bridge Street business passed to her manager and her husband's foreman, George Buxey, who continued publishing the paper until 1909. It may well be that the 21 Bridge Street business had a longer history in the trade, as there is an extant engraving from the end of the eighteenth century, showing a bookseller by the name of Phillips—possibly George Phillips—at 21 Bernard Street; the discrepancy in the street name is due to Bridge Street once comprising the western end of Bernard Street (its name derived from the town ditches that it once bridged).[13] George Phillips was the proprietor of a bookselling business at 12 High Street, Below Bar, and later at numbers 12 and 169, and appears in the record as the publisher of an illustrated view of Canute Road from the docks, engraved by Newman and Co., showing the New York Hotel, built around 1850.

Exemplifying the imbrication of newspapers to bookselling, bookseller Alfred Dyer at 52 Above Bar, in 1887, was also the publisher and editor of the *Hampshire Independent* newspaper, formerly run by Southampton political activist, temperance campaigner, and son of the landlord of the Cossack Inn, Henry Pond. Several local newspapers were published from 52 and 45 Above Bar through to 1907. Southampton City's main newspaper, the *Southern Daily Echo*, and the *Football Echo* or "Sports Pink" (because of its pink sheets), were published from Dyer's former premises from 1888 until these were knocked down to make way for the West Quay shopping mall in 1997.

For records pertaining to the single map entry of George Alma Lyne of 62 Above Bar in 1887, *The London Gazette* published national lists of debtors, the 7 May 1889 edition of which included an "out of business" notice for William Robert Moreton, formerly of 65 Marland Place in Southampton, who had traded until the past six months as a bookseller and stationer with George Alma Lyne, as Lyne and Moreton.[14] It may well be coincidence, but a decade later, on 9 April 1898, the Australian newspaper *The Barrier Miner* reported police prosecution against a man named George Alma Lyne and four others for conspiracy and false pretenses in connection with fraudulent checks.[15]

On the more respectable side, James Sprent Virtue (1829–1892) was a British publisher from the dead-center of publishing that was Paternoster Row in London, who in 1855 took over his father's firm, which specialized in printed illustrations, often of artworks and landscapes by accomplished artists.[16] With numerous UK branches, James Sprent had explored business opportunities in America, where the company also had a branch, and produced highlights such as several improved editions of Charles Knight's *Shakespeare* from 1871, and *Picturesque Palestine* from 1880. The Southampton branch appears in the 1876 directory, managed by J. McLardy, at 23 High Street Below Bar, and continued at that address until the move to 71 Below Bar by 1903, remaining in operation at number 71 over 1912–13 as a Southern Counties agency, and still active in 1917. It might be supposed that the stability of the business was assisted by its status as a branch office, and by the access to capital and savings through centralizing services that would have been available to metropolitan, international organizations, and thus it represents Southampton's bookselling network dovetailing into wider global trade.

At 116 Below Bar, C. Domoney was active as a bookseller in 1876, but more correctly should be described as operating a book depot for the British and Foreign Bible Society and the Religious Tract Society—perhaps the same Charles Domoney of 64 Padwell Mount who, by 1887, had become a "waterside missionary." A report on a local meeting of the Religious Tracts Society in 1875 reveals the firepower behind Domoney's seemingly innocuous entry in the directories. Following prayers, the society's committee were pleased to announce that sales had steadily increased since the establishment of their depot at number 116 in September 1873, and could reveal that during sixteen months "there had been sold 4.193 volumes of books, 621 packets of books (averaging 30 in each packet), 736 packets of tracts and leaflets (averaging 50 in each packet), 1990 framed cards, pictures and texts, and 1032 monthly magazines."[17] Members were urged to visit the depot and help, since they still faced the spread of irreligious literature "which at the present time there was such a super abundance." Given the roughly 62,000 items of stock shifted by the societies over a year and a quarter, one wonders how much more secular stock would be needed to qualify as superabundant. In 1907, the Southampton branch of the Tract Society were still able to announce a pleasing increase in subscribers.[18]

Showing the imbrication of local prestige with local investment, Alfred Randle, of 139–140 High Street, Below Bar, was the publisher with Henry March Gilbert of *The Romance of Sir Bevis of Hamtoun, Newly Done into English Prose from the Metrical Version* (1870) by Southampton son Eustace Hinton Jones. Sir Bevis (also Beavis or Bevois) was a semi-mythical figure from a twelfth-century ballad and supposedly the Son of the Earl of Hampton. More to the point, Eustace was the son of wealthy carriage maker William Jones, with manufactory works at 40 Above Bar, described in an 1824 street directory as a coach maker to H.R.H. the Duke of Sussex. Capitalizing on the cultural value of and potential sales from a local myth, the publication may well have been favored, too, by the knowledge of family links to wealth, as a form of insurance.

Not shown on the map, but important to note, is that the booktrade premises of 147 1/2 High Street, Below Bar, by the end of the century, was also home to a business of typewriting services. Typewriting had appeared in the classified trades from at least 1895, but whereas agents for manufacturers such as Remington or the Hammond typewriter companies were male, copying services were run by women. In 1897, a Miss Hoskins was operating from 3 Canute Road, joining a Miss Stewart in the directory, who had been in operation since 1895 from Portland Terrace and who, in 1900 at 147 1/2 High Street, advertised her *Southampton Typewriting and Shorthand Office*:

General copying done in the best style at reasonable charges / skilled short hand typists (with machines if desired) sent out at shortest notice by the hour, day, or week / reference permitted to a large number of leading firms and gentlemen in Southampton.[19]

Gratifying though it is to see another woman proprietress—apart from Charlotte Rayner, women's business opportunities were often restricted to newsagencies in surrounding districts—it is also telling that Miss Stewart's typists (presumably women, too) were so impermanent a feature of business life as to be available for hire on an hourly-to-weekly basis, and furthermore that they relied on the endorsements of gentlemen.

Further down the High Street, there was Thomas Gutch, who had taken over a book business of the Fletcher family, established in the late 1700s by bookseller and printer Isaac Fletcher. He was one of a number of disaffected local Liberals who were involved in an internal party spat and who set up the short-lived *Southampton Free Press and General Advertiser*, in press from 1 December 1856 to 24 March 1857. In 1863, Thomas Gutch was registered as a bookseller, stationer, and printer at 154 High Street, Below Bar. But he also published a number of local guides, such as the possibly opportunistic *Guide to Southampton Compiled Especially for the Use of Visitors to the Bath and West of England Meeting, May and June 1869*, priced one penny, comprising an eight-page advertiser; another generic walk-about guide to local sights at nine pages (a shorter derivative of Charles Rayner's guide); and *Gutch's Pictorial Almanac, for 1875, with 'Once a Year,' a Local Miscellany*. The cover illustration to *Gutch's Pictorial Almanac* provides a perfect example of the interweaving of book-trade sectors in that it comprised an image of the town's Caxton's Steam Printing Office building at 150 High Street, showing two upper-story wall-plaques to the facade's left and right, bearing the words "Booksellers, Stationers, Bookbinders, Music" on one, and on the other "Letterpress, Lithographic Copper-Plate Printers"; and, since the term was omitted from the facade plaques, the words "Circulating Library" were provided above the illustration as a caption.[20]

By 1875, Gutch's business had morphed into the 150 High Street business of Gutch and Cox, and then by 1897 Cox and Sharland. Records show a James Charles Cox (b. 1818) who, after training in the print trade, became a bookseller, printer, and stationer in Lower St. Mary's Street in 1846, and then proprietor and editor of the *Southampton Examiner* in 1854—he also belonged to the same group of the town's disaffected

Liberals as Gutch. Cox was a town councilor and poor law guardian but, in May 1857, he was exposed as having misappropriated funds from a local Widows and Orphans Fund. He was forced to sell his trading stock in July 1857, and was confined for three months in Southampton jail. By 1858, Cox's paper, now titled the *Southampton Examiner and Free Press* resurfaced; it's title allying itself with Gutch's *Southampton Free Press* in a party-oriented news-trade altercation against the *Hampshire Advertiser* and the *Hampshire Independent* (see Alfred Dyer of 52 Above Bar). The venture was short lived and, on 26 February 1857, Cox was again arrested for insolvency and, again, spent time in Southampton jail. In 1876, by which time Gutch and Cox has come into existence, James Charles Cox had been operating as a printer at 4 Park View; in 1884, there also being a Charles Cox registered as a stationer and fancy goods warehouse at 161 High Street, Below Bar. By 1887, the fancy goods warehouse at number 161 had disappeared and, back at number 150, Gutch and Cox were registered simply as "booksellers." It is tempting to think that down-at-the-heels Cox had been taken in by his old political ally Gutch, as the former pursued a series of disastrous business ventures, and that Cox had eventually taken over Gutch's business.

Not much is known about Cox and Sharland, apart from a William Sharland who published a number of engravings around the 1850s and 1860s, at which time (1863 through to 1876) he was registered as a bookseller and stationer at 33 High Street. Beyond this date, Sharland seems to disappear. By 1897 through to 1907, the 150 High Street business of Cox and Sharland is given as a bookseller, with a specialization in book binding, although a short history of the binders Cawte's states that the only other binding business in the town was Broadbere's. In 1907, the street listing notes Cox and Sharland as printers, stationers, and sellers of maps by the ordnance survey, but the same Cox and Sharland were also the publishers of volumes of legal documents, including charters and court records from after 1906. A further Mr. W. Sharland was still registered at 33 High Street, Below Bar, as a bookseller and bookbinder in 1949.

As an example of the significance of discounting in Southampton retail trade, advertisements for the Southampton Book Society at 178 High Street appear from as early as 1867, offering cut-priced books and catalogues available from Mr. E.H. Knight. Reflecting discourse around "underselling" at the time, their advertisement in the *Hampshire Advertiser* cites a letter to *The Times* drawing attention to their righteous campaign against exorbitant trade profits on overpriced books, periodicals of all kinds, and music: "a discount of 15 to 20 per cent is always allowed off the published price of books, and this is only owing to the determined perseverance of a small minority of the trade, who identify their own interests with that of the public in small profits and quick returns."[21] The Southampton Book Society was part of The Town and Country Book Society, a chain business working on the principle of high-volume turnover at lowest retail price, which enabled the public to procure "the current literature of the day on the best terms."[22] It had two branches in London (64 King William Street and 25 Pall Mall) and three additional branches, in Brighton, Plymouth, and Southampton. More of a cut-priced retail operation than charitable cooperative, the Society nevertheless, or perhaps accordingly, presented its services as a moral activity for gentlemen, backing its business with a letter of recommendation from "a Clergyman" who recognized that the distribution of the society's catalogues was a duty to everyone interested in the advancement of literature. Orders could be sent directly to the Southampton manager and would be supplied from the London depot, carriage paid by the purchaser. The shop must have become a successful landmark, since throughout the 1880s surgeon-dentist H.C. Corke advertised his London-practiced painless dental treatment from premises found above the Southampton Book Society.

The Southampton Book Society remained at 178 Below Bar until 1894, when it was taken over by Chaplin and Weeks, whose business, after a disastrous and telling fire, was in turn taken over, briefly, by William Blackhall, who operated a circulating library by 1897, before a larger sustainable business run by Robert Batt settled into the premises by 1900. Batt advertised sales of books, stationery, newspapers, magazines, music, fancy goods, bookbinding, printing, pictures, and then photographs, and it is likely that he retailed childrens' books since, in 2017, an online secondhand book site offered an 1899 Macmillan and Co. copy of Lewis Carroll's *The Hunting of the Snark*, illustrated by Henry Holliday, with a bookseller's ticket from Robert C. Batt of Southampton fixed to the pastedown. Front and center of Batt's advertising was his circulating library with its additional special notice to non-subscribers of books lent at 2d per volume per week (see figures 7.1 and 7.2). As noted by *The Successful Bookseller*, Batt's adoption of an NBA-era circulating library was no historical anomaly, and his business must have been relatively forward thinking since he was among the early adopters of a telephone, in 1907, listed with telephone number 15, extension 1.

In 1905, an editorial piece for the *Hampshire Advertiser* provided a roundup of High Street attractions for Christmas. From shops on Market Lane could be had 5,000 turkeys, geese, and game, while from H.M.

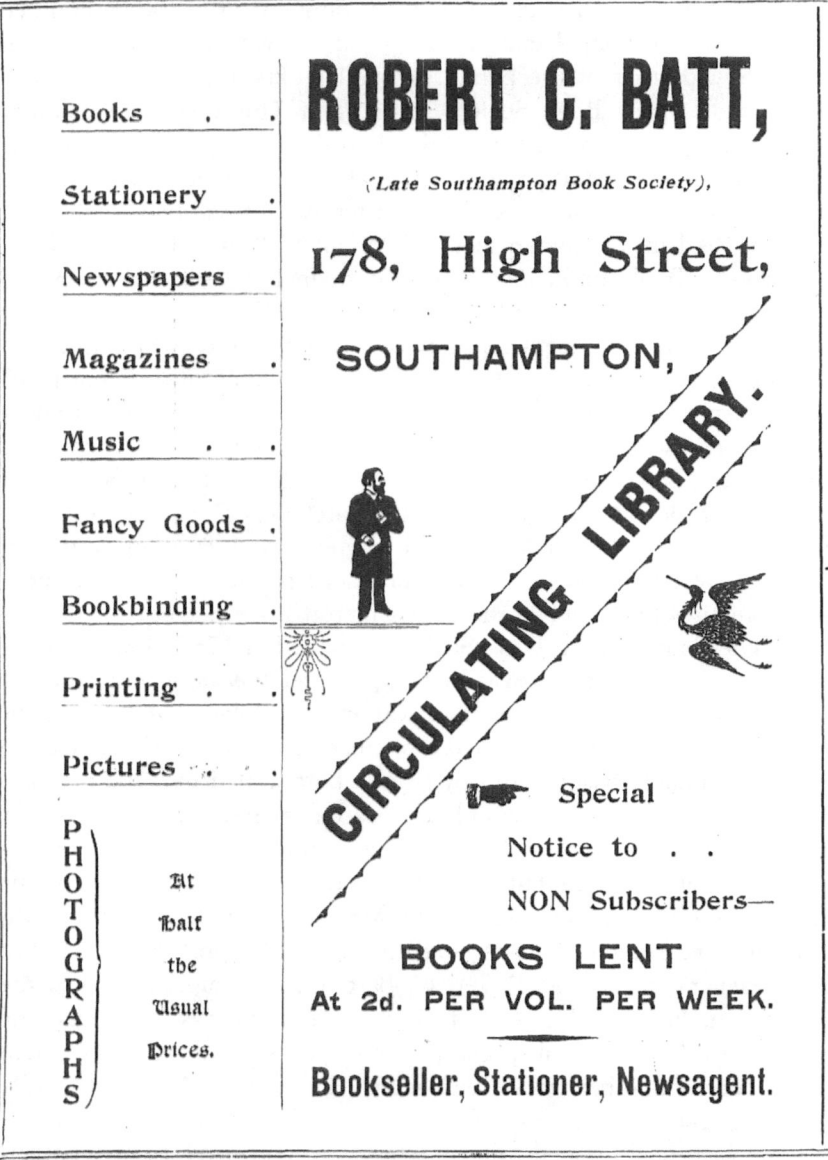

Figure 7.1. Advertisement for bookseller Robert Batt, *Southampton Annual*, 1902. Southampton: Topographical Publishing Company. *Source*: Southampton Local Studies and Maritime Library.

High Street Southampton Bookshops

Figure 7.2. Southampton High Street, Below Bar, showing on the left the bookshop of Robert Batt, after 1900. *Source*: Author's private collection.

Gilbert and Sons a wide choice in books were available, "the best of friends and companions," and the same could be said by the editorial of Messrs. Robert Batt and Co., who also specialized in Christmas greeting cards and pictorial cards, "including Mr. Frank McFadden's new etching."[23] Frank McFadden was a copperplate printer for the Ordnance Survey in Southampton but was known locally for his *Vestiges of Southampton* (1891), a collection of twelve etchings of local sites published by H.M. Gilbert (who else). Clearly tenacious, Batt made their Christmas drive in spite of also suffering fire damage earlier in the year, as Batt and Co. were advertising their thanks to customers for their sympathy over the fire and soliciting custom for the Christmas period.[24]

Broadbere's were a bookbinding business of long standing, operating out of Pembroke Square, a tiny court-like area on the east flank of the Bargate, demolished in the 1930s. Bookseller Thomas Hibberd James remembered the Square in the late 1890s as "a delightful little corner with the Herald Office, Old Broadbeer's [sic], who occasionally did some binding for us, and there was, I remember, a little bar where you could get port wine for 3d a glass."[25] Although many businesses offered binding services, Broadbere's was one of two major bookbinding businesses, the other being Cawte's. By 1900, Broadbere's had moved to adjoining Hanover Buildings and were trading by 1907 as Broadbere and Son. There is good reason to suspect that bookbinding and book retail overlapped, or rather that perceptions of supposedly "natural" market divisions may be geographically and historically conditioned. Book services often merged in the provinces, whereby, for example, the sellers of new books "invariably had an extensive second-hand trade," from which used books could be rebound, either by the shop for resale or by the customer for their private collection.[26] It should be remembered, too, that in the days before the ease of online searches and print-on-demand, books that were out of print could only be found secondhand, so that a battered secondhand copy might still be the only option for a determined buyer, and its condition would necessitate a new binding. Both Gilbert's and Batt's offered binding services and, as Thomas Hibberd remarked, "Old Broadbere" occasionally carried out work for the secondhand trade. For an international comparison of how trade departments might vary considerably from the demarcations that our presentism encourages, book binders such as the wealthy Norwegian businessman and book binder Frederick Jacobsen Brun from Oslo operated what was essentially a vast book retail business based on binding, where quires and other sheets were bought from various print markets throughout the North, and then sold either bound or still unbound to Oslo's citizens.[27]

In addition to Broadbere's, Pembroke Square was also home to the Topographical Publishing Company (see figure 7.3). This was a publishing, printing, and photo-engraving business, which published an illustrated guide to the town and local district known as the *Southampton Annual* in 1899, 1900, 1901, and 1902. They also published a weekly periodical from 1899 entitled the *Southamptonian: A Weekly Journal of Gossip, Literature, Sport and Amusement*. Though short lived, the journal serves to demonstrate how central fiction was to the trade, as well as fiction's ability to generate revenue in an imbrication of book-trade sectors. The Topographical Publishing Company was avowedly a publishing company, yet its diminutive journal chose to highlight fiction and journalistic narrative. Edited by E.H. Synge, and with an appetite to ridicule the rival *Southampton Echo*, the journal presented lighthearted descriptions of city life, a page of football notes, and serial fiction. By issue number 3, it had doubled its serial fiction, so that its sixteen pages comprised a double-page cartoon, around seven pages of gossip written as narrative, four full pages of novelistic fiction—serializations of *The Ruby Ring*, by Ida Linn Gerard, and *One of Life's Ordeals*, by R. Silverman—and the rest

Figure 7.3. Topographical Publishing Company, in Pembroke Square, 1899. *Southampton Annual*, Topographical Publishing Company. *Source*: Southampton Local Studies and Maritime Library.

comprising an assortment of letters, quizzes, and advertisements. Though a publisher, the firm was also firmly in the business of retailing fiction.

Some of the strengths and fragilities of a generational business model are indicated in the case of the bookbinders H.G. Cawte, who had operated from a number of premises in Southampton before settling into 9 St. Michael's Square in 1859. In 1883, they moved into purpose-built premises at 5 West St., nearby, becoming Cawte and Sons by 1897. The only heating in the new premises was purportedly from a coal fire used for making glue and other pastes, around which two or three employees would sit working on sewing presses, where, in the bookbinding division of labor, these tasks were assigned to young women. In 1884, they posted a "boy wanted" sign in the window—the role was not intended for a girl—that was answered by Henry Daubney Cox (b. 1869), who had moved with his mother to Southampton after his father died. The apprenticeship that Henry undertook paid a rate of 4s per week rising to 9s per week over six years, from 23 July 1884 to precisely that day in 1890, when the terms of the indenture were served out. George William Cawte (not H.G.) married and had a son, who, rather than bookbinding, preferred to open a newsagents in Commercial Street, so, in 1912, former apprentice Henry Cox took over the bookbinding business, which he managed to build up, specializing in binding minute books of the town's civic corporation, books for the town library, and libraries intended for the transatlantic liners. Work orders were received from throughout the UK and from overseas. Henry Cox and his wife Ada had three sons: Henry James, Frank, and Gordon. Henry James died of peritonitis in 1913, aged 13, and Frank began as a bookbinder but eventually joined the offices of the Ordnance Survey—the headquarters of the National Ordnance Survey had moved to Southampton from London after 1841—working in document and book restoration. Old man Henry continued working at his binder's shop through two world wars, surviving the bombing of 1940, and only stopped completely three months before his death in 1960. Gordon was the author of the article on Henry Cox in the *Southampton Local History Forum Journal*.

A few doors away from Cawte's in St. Michael's Square, at number 14, there was a Mrs. Clarke registered to Phillips's printing office for St. Michael's National Schools, in 1876, but in what way this operation may have been connected to St. Michael's School is unclear.

George Buxey, as already noted, was a foreman for Charles Woodhouse Rayner and manager for Charlotte Rayner, and took over the Rayner's Bridge Street business at number 21 after Charlotte's death in 1879. Buxey's operated nearly every department of the trade, wholesale and retail—bookselling, stationery, printing, binding and newsagents—offering the standard three pence in the shilling for cash on all books. They were known to have published religious tracts, such as Charles Gordon's *Observations on the Holy Communion: Short Notes on Reading the Scriptures* (1885), and made a sales point of their large assortment of Bibles, prayer books, and hymn books. The firm published *Buxey's Illustrated Southampton*, in 1897, priced 6d (or 8 1/2d including postage), as well as *Geo. Buxey's 6d Map of Southampton*. In 1888, they published *Charles Dibdin, One of Southampton's Sons: What He Did for the Nation, and What the Nation Has Done for Him*, and that the famous composer had only spent the first 10 years of his life in the city was clearly not an obstacle. With one eye on an opportunity drawn from the self-worth of local readers, the volume was dedicated tellingly to those who would do "honour to *themselves* by helping to perpetuate the memory of . . . a fellow townsman" (my italics).[28] The business had a telephone with the early number 8, and its ambitions are reflected in its advertisements, as Buxey's were regular advertisers in local directories and almanacs, taking half-page advertisements, which was not always the practice of many others in the trade, and they consistently had their name duplicated in the various trades listed in the directories' classified section (see figure 7.4). Buxey and Co. afterwards as Buxey Ltd., continued at Bridge Street into the early 1930s, with a change of building number to 27, and then at 10 Bernard Street. Perhaps a clue to when George finally left the business is given in the publication of *The Limerick A, B, C: A Collection of Puns by 'Dunlop,'* which was published in 1907 by S.L. Buxey of Southampton.

At 42 Bernard Street was Thomas James, who had arrived from what would become H.M. Gilbert's premises at 26 1/2 Above Bar by 1887, where he had been since at least 1863. He had moved to Southampton with his wife, Sarah Anne, from Christchurch in 1849, when he set up a secondhand bookshop, initially in The Strand, a road extending north from the Canal Walk ditches, then in the High Street, Below Bar, and then in Above Bar before settling in Bernard Street, where the shop remained until after the Blitz bombings. The Southampton Society for Mutual Education, a society that briefly existed between about 1857 and about 1865, and whose president in 1860 was the same Eustace Hinton

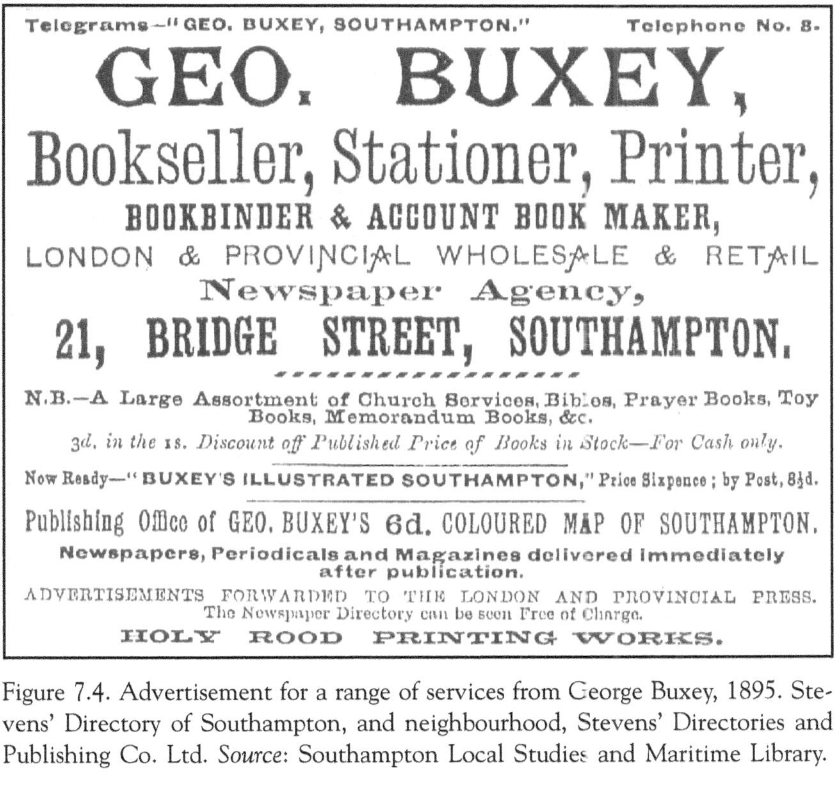

Telegrams—"GEO. BUXEY, SOUTHAMPTON." Telephone No. 8.

GEO. BUXEY,
Bookseller, Stationer, Printer,
BOOKBINDER & ACCOUNT BOOK MAKER,
LONDON & PROVINCIAL WHOLESALE & RETAIL
Newspaper Agency,
21, BRIDGE STREET, SOUTHAMPTON.

N.B.—A Large Assortment of Church Services, Bibles, Prayer Books, Toy Books, Memorandum Books, &c.

3d. in the 1s. Discount off *Published Price of Books in Stock—For Cash only.*

Now Ready—"**BUXEY'S ILLUSTRATED SOUTHAMPTON**," Price Sixpence; by Post, 8½d.

Publishing Office of GEO. BUXEY'S **6d.** COLOURED MAP OF SOUTHAMPTON.
Newspapers, Periodicals and Magazines delivered immediately after publication.
ADVERTISEMENTS FORWARDED TO THE LONDON AND PROVINCIAL PRESS.
The Newspaper Directory can be seen Free of Charge.
HOLY ROOD PRINTING WORKS.

Figure 7.4. Advertisement for a range of services from George Buxey, 1895. Stevens' Directory of Southampton, and neighbourhood, Stevens' Directories and Publishing Co. Ltd. Source: Southampton Local Studies and Maritime Library.

Jones of *The Romance of Sir Bevis*, had a record of renting rooms in the bookshop of Thomas James for its meetings. In 1891, James's traded for a period under the grand title of the South of England Book Emporium.

Thomas and Sarah Anne's son was Thomas Hibberd James, who moved to London, intending to train in medicine, but having met and married and in 1880 become a father, Thomas Hibberd moved back to Southampton with his wife, Rosina, and their child to work in the family business, which he took over in 1904 after the death of Thomas senior. Thankfully for this study, it was Thomas Hibberd who developed an interest in photography, soon after his thirtieth birthday in 1886—an interest that took him across the country, but also specifically onto the Southampton High Street, where he photographed a number of scenes, including his father's secondhand book shop in Bernard Street (see figure 7.5). The shop had a central entrance, the windows dressed with full displays of books and prints—heeding *The Successful Bookseller*'s advice with a large 6d sales notice visible from across the street—with narrow desks and shelf-displays on the street. Two photographs he also took were of the Above Bar shop of Henry March Gilbert (see figure 7.6 and figure 9.1 in chapter 9).

In his personal recollection, recorded toward the end of his life, Thomas Hibberd described the day as follows:

> Being in the booktrade of course I knew old Gilbert and I recollect that I took these two pictures as much for him as anyone else. . . . it was one of those glorious sunny evenings—it must have been about 1895—when the town was really quiet. . . . A lot of shops used to stay open in those days, and I remember the shop assistants had to work all the hours God gave them. Shopping was very different then: carriages could pull up outside any of the dozens of little shops. . . . I managed to get everyone just where I wanted for the first picture and then the man with the bowler hat came up and stood still only long enough to make a ghost. I decided then that I would take another view . . . I still got a couple of intruders though, as you can see. I remember when I developed the plate I laughed when I saw the little dog . . . I wonder if Gilbert's have still got that hand cart with their name painted on the side?[29]

Figure 7.5. Thomas James's secondhand bookshop, photographed by his son, Thomas Hibberd James, after 1886. *Source*: Southampton Museums, Cultural Services.

154   Reading, Wanting, and Broken Economics

Figure 7.6. View of Gilbert's bookshop, 26 1/2 High Street, Above Bar, photographed by T.H. James, ca. 1895. Notice "50000 volumes always in stock." The delivery handcart at the curb belongs to Gilbert's. *Source*: Southampton Museums, Cultural Services.

John Adams at 25 and then 49 Oxford Street was presented in the directories as a bookseller and stationer, claiming establishment in 1854, and verified from at least 1859. By 1876, Adams had become the letter receiving house for the Great Western Railway Co.'s office. Before the advent of the street postbox in the 1850s, some ten years after the penny post was introduced, receiving houses were designated premises for outgoing mail to be picked up by a coaching or railway company, a system which, in Adams's case, was still operative twenty-five years later. By 1887 they were noted, in addition to booksellers, as a wholesale and export stationers, and by 1898 they were advertising a host of allied services (see figure 7.7).

From 49 Oxford Street and 10 Bernard Street premises, they claimed expertise as export booksellers, stationers, heraldic die sinkers, copper-plate, lithographic, and letterpress printers, bookbinders, picture framers, and nautical booksellers and agents for shipping, forwarding,

Figure 7.7. The all-round book business of John Adams, 1899. *Historical Guide to Southampton and the Neighbourhood*, with over sixty photographic illustrations. *Source*: Southampton Local Studies and Maritime Library.

and insurance. The lineage is uncertain but it may well be that the business became F.W. Adams and Co., printers, of nearby 50 Bernard Street into the 1940s, but the record does attest to a wide integration of business sectors that made good use of the city's transport connections and the port. Trying their hand at literature publishing, they produced a beautifully embossed octavo volume of *A Selection of Plays and Poems* by Edward Carus-Wilson, in 1872[30]—printed by Alfred Dyer's *Hampshire Independent* press—and it was John Adams who published *Adams's Guide to Netley Abbey* from 1865, and in several reprints thereafter, written by the same Eustace Hinton Jones whose *Romance of Sir Bevis* was later published by Gilbert's. The firm was responsible for at least ten publications until 1910 that capitalized on local interests, including various almanacs, local historical and traveler's guides, and souvenir books: one for Southampton Docks from 1898, promising 60 half-tone illustrations of ocean liners, splendid views, and the opening ceremonies of various docks; and one for the Mary Anne Rogers memorial fountain set up through public subscription in 1901 to commemorate a stewardess who saved lives from the wreck of the Stella off the Channel islands in 1899—a wreck whose severity for locals was only eclipsed by the sinking of the Titanic thirteen years later.

Just off the city center in the St. Mary's district, where the first free public library opened, and where the city's chief football team first had its home, there was William Budden at 15 Lower St. Mary's Street. Operating as a bookbinder there from 1853, Budden's then moved to 41 St. Mary's Street, and to 85 St. Mary's Road as Budden and Sons, surviving as a stationer and bookbinder until at least 1891, to reappear as Walter Budden in Cecile Avenue in nearby Shirley by 1901. In Prospect Place, Mrs. Cora Hazelton had run a business listed under booksellers by 1865, taking over what had been a letters receiving house run by William Hazelton in 1863, and by 1887 the business was registered as a post office, stationer, and telegraph office before falling from the records after 1891.

Toward the end of the nineteenth century, as the city extended its docks and developed its industries, adjacent districts were further developed for workers' housing in areas such as Northam, New Town, Shirley, Freemantle, Millbrook, St. Deny's, and Bitterne, and small businesses serving these communities followed. Some of the contestation over cultural space from these expansions—and an example of what Graham Law calls the ability of the periphery to select its own interpretations of meaning—can be seen in the results of the second bridge across the river Itchen, built upstream from the City's Northam bridge, in 1883.[31] Cobden Bridge was built by the National Land Company, which owned housing developments on the newly opened-up east bank of the river at Bitterne Park. The company wanted to connect their new development across the river to the city by presenting the town with a new bridge. On opposite banks were two populations, of St. Deny's on the city-center side west of the river and of newly accessible Bitterne Park on the east bank, who had differing interests to protect, which included claims by Bitterne Park men that St. Deny's lads were chasing "their" local girls. Given an excuse, pitched battles ensued, with gangs of youth and men fighting on Sunday afternoons. The *Daily Echo* reported the experience of Mr. C.E. Godwin, who had been involved: "the first Sunday with two friends . . . on returning over the bridge we were set upon by about 100 lads, who knocked us about like ninepins . . . the following Sunday brought hundreds of men and lads of all ages out from the town, when a sharp fight took place with fists, boots and sticks."[32] By the following Sunday, police put an end to proceedings through an organized baton charge.

Because the space where center meets periphery could be contested, likewise the bookselling practices of the city center could not be replicated in adjoining districts. When they did emerge, it was as smaller-scale book retailing activities, and in a mode that again shifts along an axis of gender. John Bellenger pops up as a bookbinder in Lyon Street, in Newtown; but, under the listings of booksellers, Mrs. Curtis appears as a stationer in 1895 at 30 High Street, Shirley; Miss M.A. Thomas as a bookseller and stationer at 8 High Street, Shirley, between 1891 and 1895; Mrs. Wood running a post office and stationer in Portswood Road, northwest of Newtown, by 1900; Mrs. E.M. Wake in charge of a post office and stationer at 242 Derby Road in Newtown between 1891 and 1900; and a Miss Hunt appearing as a bookseller and stationer at 8 Hamilton Terrace in Commercial Road in 1891, moving to 6A Bedford Place by 1900, still advertising as a bookseller in 1907. Clearly, the periphery offered better opportunities for women than the male-dominated city High Street.

On the southeast side of the river in Woolston, Lankester and Crook appear from around this period in advertisements and listings for booksellers, from 1900 onward until after 1905 (see figures 7.8 and 7.9). This was a multiple-branch county supply store, which had previously been

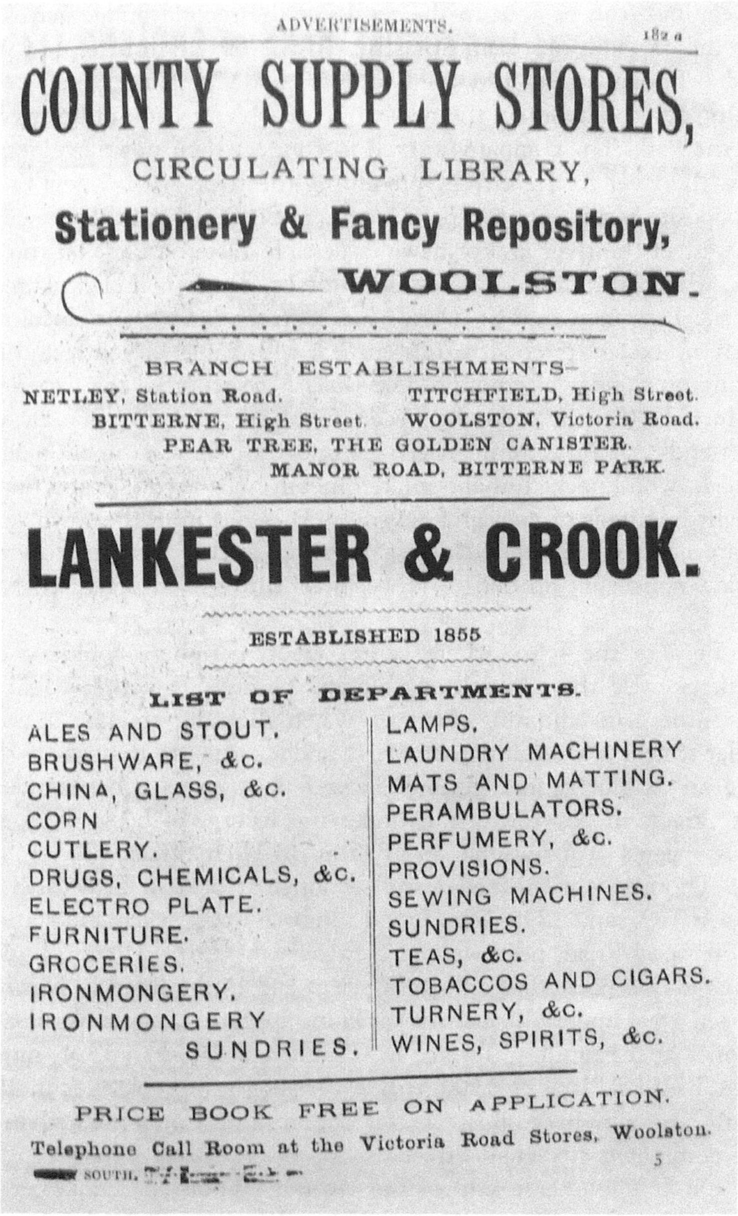

ADVERTISEMENTS. 182 a

COUNTY SUPPLY STORES,

CIRCULATING LIBRARY,

Stationery & Fancy Repository,

WOOLSTON.

BRANCH ESTABLISHMENTS—
NETLEY, Station Road.   TITCHFIELD, High Street.
BITTERNE, High Street.   WOOLSTON, Victoria Road.
PEAR TREE, THE GOLDEN CANISTER.
MANOR ROAD, BITTERNE PARK.

LANKESTER & CROOK.

ESTABLISHED 1855

LIST OF DEPARTMENTS.

ALES AND STOUT.	LAMPS.
BRUSHWARE, &c.	LAUNDRY MACHINERY
CHINA, GLASS, &c.	MATS AND MATTING.
CORN	PERAMBULATORS.
CUTLERY.	PERFUMERY, &c.
DRUGS, CHEMICALS, &c.	PROVISIONS.
ELECTRO PLATE.	SEWING MACHINES.
FURNITURE.	SUNDRIES.
GROCERIES.	TEAS, &c.
IRONMONGERY.	TOBACCOS AND CIGARS.
IRONMONGERY SUNDRIES.	TURNERY, &c.
	WINES, SPIRITS, &c.

PRICE BOOK FREE ON APPLICATION.
Telephone Call Room at the Victoria Road Stores, Woolston.
SOUTH.

5

Figure 7.8. Advertisement for Lankester and Crook, selling everything from a circulating library service to ironmongery. *Kelly's Directory of Southampton and Neighbourhood*, 1900. *Source*: Southampton Local Studies and Maritime Library.

Figure 7.9. Lankester and Crook, County Supply Stores, Obelisk Road, Woolston, ca. 1896. *Sotonopedia: A Descriptive Account of Southampton—Illustrated*. Source: Southampton Local Studies and Maritime Library.

and continued to be (until the 1980s) a grocer and provision merchant, but who now offered a circulating library service, as well as a stationery and fancy goods repository, with branches in satellite positions around the city: Netley, Titchfield, Peartree, Bitterne High Street, and Bitterne Park. Claiming establishment since 1855, they had specialized in tobaccos, teas, wines and spirits, groceries, and ironmongery, and eventually included a bakery and a post office, but were now selling fiction and other reading services as one of the service goods made available to the public.

Back in the city center, businessman Edwin Jones, an important figure for the Liberal Association who had begun life as a draper and rose to Alderman and Mayor, had opened a large department store that became increasingly larger as he bought up surrounding properties, eventually establishing one of the most impressive department stores in the region: firstly in the building Manchester House and then in the Queen's Buildings facing Hoglands Park in the city center.[33] By 1891, the store had begun advertising its book department, and it continued to feature in the booksellers listings well into the 1920s, until the department was so integrated as to no longer warrant special mention. Indeed, the Debenhams chain that traded from the Edwin Jones's buildings continued to sell books, unabated, until the store's final collapse under the 2020 pandemic.

In Southampton, the entrepreneurial book and newspaper distribution and retail firm of W.H. Smith (and Sons, after 1846) had a contract to sell newspapers in the city docks since at least 1851.[34] For the 1850s, William Henry II drew up a table of rents payable to various companies, in which rents to Southampton Docks were ranked 13th, at £10 per annum, significantly behind rents for multiple outlets payable to rail companies such as the Great Northern at £1,100 to £1,300 per annum.[35] Small though its Southampton operation was, Smith's gradually built up its presence, focusing on the more profitable terminus rail station, as its business model prescribed. The Railway Terminus outlet, which can be seen advertised from 1863, became known alternatively as the Southampton Docks branch in Terminus Road. This was joined by another outlet at Southampton West rail station by 1895, near the former Blechynden station that led out west along the coast, located a hundred or so meters from the current Southampton Central Station. The 1900 directories list Southampton West as managed by Harry Moore, then by a Mr. A.E Jordan, in 1907, who managed both the Southampton West and Terminus branches; joined in 1907, too, by a Mr. J.H. Tribe as manager of a newly opened W.H. Smith store in the High Street, advertising as newsagents, stationers, booksellers, and librarians. Smith's continue as a bookseller and newsagent today, both on the High Street and at the Central Station and airport. At their most prodigious, the company returned to their initial ships' passenger trade and opened a further outlet located inside the grounds of the Eastern Docks, in Central Road by 1931, which survived beyond 1952.

Overall, during a thirty-year period from the end of the nineteenth century to the first decade of the twentieth, book retail was mostly one feature in a print, information, library, binding, stationery, and fancy goods trade that extended beyond the limits of print culture; or, from another point of view, one operation in what advanced marketing would call a business in service goods, where the physical object merely facilitates a means of exchange for the true good, which is an intangible service. The fancy goods and souvenir and tourist guides offered pleasure and promised to satisfy aspirations. Insurance and forwarding services offered reliable care, while stationery could promise a sense of belonging. Printing services offered local entrepreneurs a chance to sell their narrative projects. Private libraries, especially after the NBA, offered readers thrift in the form of access to the latest writing more cheaply than, and without the risks of, outright purchase. Books, glassware, and fancy bindings were small leisure-time pleasures in all their simplicity and profundity. Equally important in this integrated service network were the people running its operations—their (mis)judgments determining what was available to the public—and nowhere can the importance of interpersonal relationship and personal judgment be more highlighted than in the case of Chaplin and Weeks.

The story of Chaplin and Weeks is not evidenced in directories and local histories; it needs to be teased out of court records covered in the local newspapers, concerning two High Street addresses, at 178 and 180 High Street, Below Bar, which had been in use as book-trade premises for several decades. Below the dentist Corke's, who used the bookshop beneath as a landmark for prospective clients, the Southampton Book Society at number 178 provided bulk-bought cut-price book retail, posing as a charitable cooperative, while from number 180 the Rayner family dynasty sold books, music, stationery, and fancy goods. On 12 August 1893, John Rayner announced his forthcoming retirement in a local paper, and drew notice on the business being taken over by Chaplin and Weeks, the latter claiming they had experience of both wholesale and retail and would henceforth offer the best prices in all lines, including "magazines, newspapers, periodicals, etc., carefully attended to and sent out on the day of publication."[36]

On Saturday 24 February 1894, the *Hampshire Advertiser* could report that fire had broken out at 180 High Street, entirely destroying the stock and forcing Chaplin and Weeks to decamp to 15 High Street. By Saturday 21 April that year, the same paper announced that Chaplin and Weeks had bought the Southampton Book Society at 178 High Street, and by 17 September the partners were advertising in the *Southern Echo* a "Marvellous Clearance Sale of Books, Fancy Goods and Stationary to make room for Christmas Goods," having additionally taken on the Book Society's stock, and were presumably attempting to convert their holdings into cash.[37] Advertisements for Chaplin and Weeks continued for around a further year and then vanished. But by 1902, the same *Hampshire Advertiser* could report that Mr. Frank Weeks had applied for discharge from what must have been a bankruptcy at the Southampton Court.[38]

What transpires from the court summaries in local newspapers is how important were a distinct set of combined social and financial issues for successful trade. Crucial factors were the role that personality plays in business, the large amounts of capital investment required to produce fairly small amounts of revenue, and the general precariousness of the business, which at any time might face calamity, as indeed it did, and which so often relied on chance access to investment capital through personal relations. What is also notable from the narrative is the absence of any mention of types of books, especially in relation to changes in taste, which one might expect would be the driving force behind a shop's fortunes. Nowhere is the bookseller's ability to satisfy literary tastes ever addressed, let alone that the arrival of something later called modernism might ever be germane in this high-street environment.

Frank Weeks had been made bankrupt in 1895, and in 1902 was applying to be discharged from his bankruptcy to start trading again. He and Chaplin had begun trading in August 1893, buying Rayner's bookselling and newsagents business for £800, each of the partners putting in £350, leaving £100 owing to John Rayner. For his contribution, Frank had borrowed the £350 from his father, which remained unrepaid at the time of the bankruptcy. Between Weeks and Chaplin there was no official partnership agreement, but profits were seemingly agreed to be shared equally. When the fire broke out, their stock was valued at £3000, of which only £1000 had been paid. The remaining £2000 worth of stock was owed to creditors. Unfortunately, the insurance was woefully inadequate—Frank later claiming this was Chaplin's fault, this being his side of the business—and the partners received only £700 from the Royal Insurance Office and £200 from Sun Office, out of which they repaid Rayner the outstanding £100. After moving to various premises around the city, for which they were obliged to pay high rents, the partners acquired the Book Society at number 178 for £1000. At the end of a period of some twelve months on from the purchase of Rayner's in August 1893, to the fire breaking out in February 1894, and the Book Society acquisition in April, Chaplin died in August 1894—whether his death was precipitated by the catastrophe, only his loved ones would know.

To continue the business, Frank prepared a balance sheet, valuing the business implausibly at a meager £60, which he acknowledged later must have been "incorrect," but he managed to settle with Chaplin's representatives a sum of £300, but only paying £100, leaving the remainder as debt. At this point, for this outlay of £100, Frank took possession of the remains of his and Chaplin's business, and the remnants of Rayner's business and that of the Book Society with a business value of £1000. On the down side, the £2000 of stock lost in the fire had not yet been paid, nor the £200 owing to Chaplin's representatives, nor the £350 to his father.

It was at then that Frank took on a new partner, Mr. L.J. Bywater, who was allowed to buy into the business for £800, the same sum initially paid by Frank and Chaplin to Rayner, although only £650 was paid. The business must have been deemed profitable at this point, to command such a sum, but whether or not Bywater knew about the outstanding debts is open to question. Nevertheless, for the payment, Frank Weeks and Bywater were able to draw a weekly salary of £2. Remembering Jack London and Henry Mayhew's estimations of what a factory worker could earn weekly, between eight and eleven shillings, £2 was a not luxurious but sustaining income.

A notice in the *Southern Echo* from 19 November 1895, after Bywater had joined the firm, reveals the business's precarious state. The notice reports an application for legal partnership between Bywater and Frank Weeks, since Bywater, as part of his defense in a debtor's court case, maintained he had only previously been an assistant. The backstory to the application for partnership came from a London stationary company, Jacobsen, Welch and Co., for payment on fancy stationery goods selected by and supplied to Weeks. The London stationers claimed they had previously denied Weeks credit but, when introduced to Mr. Bywater as a new wealthy partner, and thus reassured of the Southampton business's good financial health, they had extended credit to Weeks's business and supplied the relevant goods. Bywater was claiming that he was not liable since he was an assistant and not a partner, so the case under current consideration was whether Bywater should be acknowledged as a legal partner, and thus take a share of the debt. Bywater claimed ignorance that Weeks had previously been denied credit, and furthermore claimed that the sum he had paid to Weeks—£350 was the figure given by Bywater, rather than £650—was by way of a loan pending partnership.

Prior to the partnership case, Frank Weeks had already been declared bankrupt, at some time around the summer of 1895, with proven liabilities—according to evidence given on his application for discharge—of a whopping £2,964 2s 2d. From the remaining assets sold off, which were not otherwise assigned, a total of £1,276 14s 10d was raised, meaning that a dividend of 4s 2d in the pound could be repaid to creditors, thus leaving creditors with losses of approximately 80% of what they were owed.

The situation had been exacerbated, the judge concluded, not only by the woeful lack of insurance prior to the fire, and equally inadequate bookkeeping, but by the fact that Frank Weeks had begun gambling at his local club, playing solo whist and "nap" (the latter being the card game Napoleon), sustaining losses of anything up to £5 on any single occasion—although Frank steadfastly maintained his loses were always balanced out by his gains.

Since his bankruptcy, Frank Week's counsel claimed that Frank's behavior had been exemplary. Prior to his bankruptcy, Frank had also managed to get married, in April 1895, settling his furniture and an insurance policy on his life to his wife. His new father-in-law was able to testify to Frank's redeemed character, that Frank had given up gambling, and that he "was desirous of advancing his interests every way possible," to the extent that the father was now willing to advance sufficient funds so that his daughter and Mr. Weeks might commence in business again.[39] His Honour, instead, chose to stress Frank's gross carelessness, and considered postponing the discharge from bankruptcy for much longer than the further two years that he eventually did.

No further notice of Frank Weeks has come to light, so what trade he undertook following the discharge in 1904 is unclear. But it is far from certain that his case is atypical. The business of William Blackhall, who took over from Chaplin and Weeks at number 178, was short lived, too, his name remarkable in its absence from any advertising or mention in local papers. And in 1905, at the same 178 High Street address, the *Southern Daily Echo* reported—as detailed earlier in this chapter—that the bookseller and circulating library operator Robert Batt and Co. were pleased to return thanks to all their customers for messages of sympathy and regretted any inconvenience caused resulting from a recent fire. They were also pleased to announce that they now had a "complete New Stock of Books in all bindings [a matter of importance], Xmas cards, Postcards and Postcard Albums, etc. etc.: private greeting cards from 2s per dozen."[40] One assumes Batt had held adequate insurance, and that the sale was not a sign of desperation, as Chaplin and Weeks's "Marvellous Clearance Sale" had been.

We have no way of knowing how precarious were the lives of Southampton book traders, or whether what appears in the directories as a long-sustained business masks a catalog of financial near-misses. The finance capital for taking over a shop, let alone in setting one up, ran to the thousands of pounds, and there was no guarantee that the customer base secured by the previous owners would remain loyal across the transition. Given the absence of a welfare state, and the very real threat of prison and then the workhouse in cases of debt, the incentives to carry on in business must have been considerable, if only for £2 per week. This is one reason why H.M. Gilbert's business is so remarkable for its stability. Not in the least typical, Gilbert's represents the pinnacle of a trade that was genteel by today's standards yet robust in a way that many aspired to but few attained.

Chapter 8

Gilbert's

A Treetop in the Networked Forest

On page 42 of *Southampton: An Historical Guide to the Places of Interest in the Town and Neighbourhood; with 40 Specially Prepared Photographic Process Illustrations*, from 1896, there is an image of the spanking-new steam and steel floating bridge crossing the River Itchen, launched in the same year from the shipyard of Day, Summers and Co. in Northam. Horse traffic waits to leave the craft, but in a few years it would be taking motorcars—in 1901, Herbert Austin and Vickers Ltd. began car production in the UK. In 1896, too, the city corporation purchased the Electric Light and Power Company to provide the city with electricity, and provide street light by 1899. Opposite page 42, recto, as an ad insert, there is a half-page advertisement for "Ye Olde Booke Shoppe" (with faux-authentic spelling), with the words "Old and New Bookseller" reproduced in Gothic blackletter. The shop claims a sizable stock of 50,000 volumes, and in line with the recommendations of *The Successful Bookseller* issues catalogs frequently that are free on request. Old books are purchased for cash, and the business's circulating library claims connections to no less a giant than the international select library of Charles Edward Mudie (see figure 8.1).

What is fascinating about the ad is its combination of appeals. The publication is a souvenir guide making the most of its not-yet-commonly termed "photographic process illustrations," one of which of the city's latest word in industrial river crossing, at a time when the city was literally electrifying. The (jokey) inclusion of medievalism might be

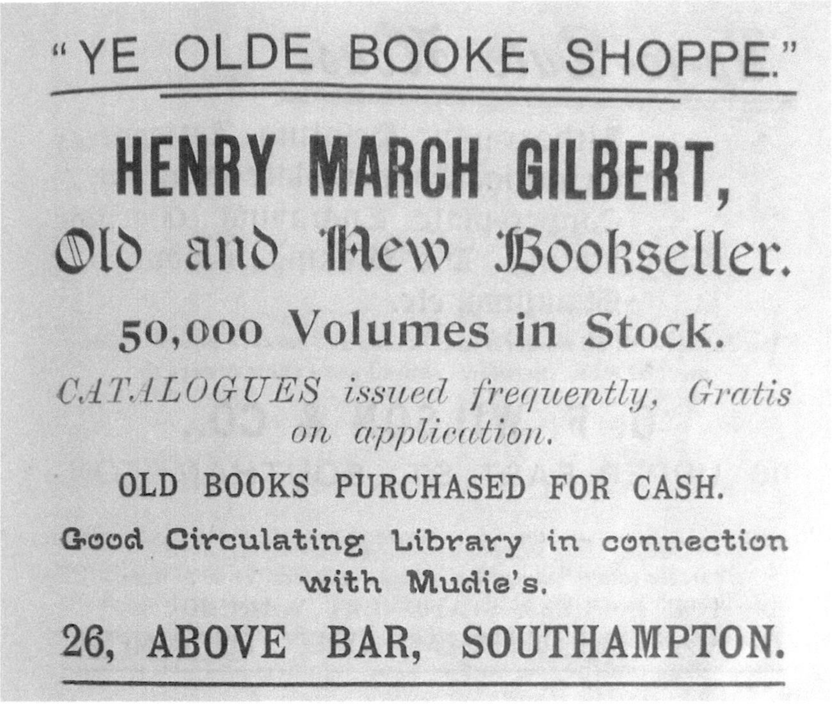

> **"YE OLDE BOOKE SHOPPE."**
>
> **HENRY MARCH GILBERT,**
> **Old and New Bookseller.**
>
> 50,000 Volumes in Stock.
>
> *CATALOGUES issued frequently, Gratis on application.*
>
> **OLD BOOKS PURCHASED FOR CASH.**
>
> Good Circulating Library in connection with Mudie's.
>
> **26, ABOVE BAR, SOUTHAMPTON.**

Figure 8.1. "Ye Olde Booke Shoppe," a carefully directed advertisement for bookseller Henry March Gilbert, 1896. *Southampton: An Historical Guide to the Places of Interest in the Town and Neighbourhood*. Source: Southampton Local Studies and Maritime Library.

regarded as anachronistic, but not necessarily. At the very least, it points to a nostalgic view of book selling that may have had currency precisely because it took place in a period of rapid modernization. The Victorian critical imperative to "match the ancients" and declare a distinctly British heritage as a superior alternative to the ancient Greco-Roman one is now a commonplace, but it was immensely popular, too, as canon authors consistently tapped this medieval British alternative. Think merely of the laureate Tennyson, who as a poet of medieval sensibilities shifted copies in bulk, and, as Kathryn Ledbetter shows, much of his popularity drew from his status as a commodity in the Victorian periodical press.[1] A short ferry ride away from Gilbert's, on nearby Isle of Wight, locals set up the Tennyson Monument in 1897 to a writer of the same *faux* medievalism.

Frequently issued catalogs meant returning business that, as shown by *The Successful Bookseller*, was the grail of the retail trade. The same guide had recommended the pleasures of browsing a catalog, which an update would reawaken even if no significant number of new titles were included. The guide went so far as to suggest that shops send out a generic wholesaler's list with a retail shop's name added.[2] As the *Southern Daily Echo* made clear, "The book-lover is often the poor man . . . but he has the second hand bookshops . . . [and] he has the catalogues to study."[3] Catalogs formed a section of the general trade but they were not merely a means by which initial steps could be encouraged until browsing turned into purchase. When thought of as an advertisement, announcing their free supply was equivalent to advertising free ads, available on request. Such a close linking of the consumer with not the product, but what the product signifies, instantiated in a piece of advertising is a cornerstone for much contemporary brand marketing strategy and, as the more *outré* theories would have it, the declared emotional goal of what are called "lovemarks."[4]

Gilbert's had operated a circulating library for many years, entirely independently, so it could not be by accident that the business connection to Mudie's only appeared in the shop's advertising at this late date. By 1896, the NBA was an agreement-in-waiting, itself a response to the increasing rapidity of the single-volume reissue that hastened the decline of the circulating libraries' three-decker, and Mudie's Select Library of London was under threat. A number of Mudie's advertisements in the local press around that time made no mention of Mudie's previous core business: "Mudie's Select Library—Cheap Books for sale . . . second-hand book list."[5] Instead of subscription, the great library focused on secondhand provision, offering cheap used goods, sent by parcel post, railway, and carrier, from what they fairly claimed was "the largest stock in the world."[6] In the same way that Gilbert's would take over the book operations of the societies of Christian Knowledge, and of Promoting Education of the Poor, perhaps by tapping into Mudie's stock, Gilbert's advertisement in the *Southampton: An Historical Guide* . . . was a sign that Henry March was taking advantage of the exertions of an ailing giant.

Overall, the 1896 ad is a careful combination of messages. In addition to its business acumen evident across differing sectors, it signifies largeness, not only in stock but in social inclusivity, including customers who might want to offload a single volume for cash, as well as those whose finances run only to catalog browsing and secondhand. But to avoid any whiff of plebeianism, the ad rolled out its tropes of Victorian nostalgia, marrying low-budget trade with respectability and thrift. Although the "Ye Olde Booke Shoppe" signifier appears to have been dropped after 1905, it is telling that in 1959 the company's letterhead still identified the business proudly as a new and secondhand bookseller, with books and libraries purchased.

The book business of Henry Gilbert (1809–1869) and afterwards of Henry March Gilbert (1845–1931) shared the practices of the Southampton trade, pursuing a mixed retail and services business, as well as publishing.[7] Established in 1859, the business was the result of Henry Gilbert leaving Halstead in Essex, where he had been a bookseller and printer but also active in religious affairs as a nonconformist and Sunday School teacher, but had become so unpopular with local Anglicans that they had supported a rival business to undermine his.[8] Henry set up at 13 Bernard Street, where his pattern of business set the template for much of the following 143 years. His announcement in the *Hampshire Chronicle, Southampton and Isle of Wight Courier* on 2 June 1860 announced that Henry respectfully informed the clergy, gentry, and public in general that he was soliciting a liberal share of their patronage and support. Prompt attention and other usual benefits were promised:

> NEW BOOKS, MAGAZINES and etc. procured to order on the shortest notice. Bibles, prayer books, church services, hymn books and etc., in a variety of sizes and bindings. Account books ruled and bound to any pattern. An assortment of SECOND HAND BOOKS, and NEW BOOKS, at second hand prices. Orders received for second hand books not in stock. Libraries and small parcels of books bought or exchanged.[9]

The business was joined by son Henry March Gilbert in 1869, after it had moved to 37 Bernard Street. After a brief period at 103 High Street, Below Bar, H.M. Gilbert's settled by 1877 into premises at 26 1/2 (later 24) Above Bar—in December 1876 advertising dual addresses at numbers 103 and 26.[10] So successful was the business under Henry March that a second shop was opened in the nearby town of Winchester in 1895, managed by Henry March's son Owen during the early years, then by a Gilbert's apprentice, Benjamin Cook, from 1908 to 1965; the Winchester shop remained in operation in various forms until 1999. The Southampton branch stayed at Above Bar under the management of Henry March and then Owen until 1939, when Owen moved the business to 2 1/2 Portland Street, which was a side road off the High Street but still in the city center. (Unfortunately, the transfer to Portland Street had not been concluded before the Blitz bombings in 1940, when the business records were lost.) Following Owen's management came Bruce Gilbert's—Bruce joining in 1946 after a period as a decorated fighter pilot in World War II, and taking over in 1953—and then Richard Gilbert took over after Bruce's passing in 1991. Richard successfully steered the business through the onset of digital retail until the full extent of online sales overtook the independent sector, and the family business was forced to close, after five generations from 1859, in 2002.

As was typically the case throughout the UK in the nineteenth century, "general-trade bookselling could differ markedly from the image of the dedicated bookstore."[11] In the early decades, Gilbert's provided secondhand, binding, stationery, magazine, and publishing services, as well as specialization in "books in many languages" and in Arts and Sciences, all of which were integrated features alongside a general trade in books. But, as the nineteenth century progressed, the advertising shows a steady development of the book buying and selling business, especially secondhand.

Before the days of print-on-demand, out-of-print titles could only be had by tracking languishing stock either in wholesale or from other retailers, or through secondhand; in the latter case, the retailer would take orders for a sought-after title that would be secured through the retailer's networks.[12] But the trade in used books in which Gilbert's specialized was also a feature of a secondhand sector that was much larger than its twenty-first-century counterpart—although its "rejuvenation" in the post-crash period may alter that. Historians of consumption Jon Stobart and Ilja van Damme explain that the narrative of linear decline in secondhand trade concurrent with the rise of increased production and more efficient commercial practices masks another picture of variation across time and space, and between different sectors, for which historically there is more evidence. As Stobart writes, "second hand remained important throughout the eighteenth and nineteenth centuries," and, in addition to staples such as clothes, there "were also vibrant markets for books, furniture, house-hold goods, carriages, artwork and even food which had previously been owned by other people."[13] Secondhand books had value for business-to-business alliances as much as business-to-end-user connections, intermediary businesses having supplied the book trade with secondhand stock since at least the seventeenth century, and the practice continuing well into the twentieth.[14] Southampton newspapers regularly carried notices from auctioneers, announcing sales of private possessions, including personal libraries, such stocks becoming available from bankruptcies, emigration, absconsion, or simply a deceased's estate. Auctioneer Mr. James Harris had been favored with the sale of superior goods and a small library in 1890,[15] while notice is given by Messrs. Lewis and Badcock, from 19 to 20 December 1894, of an auction of household effects of Mr. Peacock Esq. including 500 volumes of miscellaneous books, afternoon tea services, and Derby Spa vases.[16] These auctions provided an important link in the supply chain for the secondhand book trade. At the very least, old books could be sold on for pulp. Morely and Sons advertised in the *Bristol Magpie*, and offered to post price lists and terms for "old account books, letters, invoices and similar (for 're-manufacture only.'). Newspapers, periodicals, & old books etc. bought. Other waste materials also quoted for."[17] Alongside the sale of new titles, Gilbert's secondhand trade should be thought of not only as retailing used books to readers, but as something that extended into a wider business network.

Despite its early appeal to the clergy and gentry for patronage, Gilbert's advertising was consistently careful to aim for a wider less-resourced customer base. That Gilbert's catered to customers with small parcels of books to be sold or exchanged does not necessarily imply a segment at the "lower" end—all sorts of socioeconomic groups might want to sell small parcels—but it certainly includes that lower segment. And occasionally, local news advertising would focus deliberately on such trade: "BOOKS BOUGHT IN SMALL PARCELS, or whole libraries, for IMMEDIATE CASH, by Henry March Gilberts 'Ye Olde Booke Shoppe' Southampton."[18] A typical advertisement would use a number of paragraphs of copy each separated by a sub-line (see figure 8.2), and each headlining an attraction of the business.

An often-repeated hook would be for "Libraries Purchased—persons having libraries or LOTS OF BOOKS to SELL will find it to their advantage to apply to H.M. Gilbert."[19] The extent to which Henry March sourced his stock from private libraries is unknown, but it points to a sales strategy based not on stocking the latest publications but on competitive retail prices, and very likely the expansion of his circulating library. To make such a strategy work would require an in-store book buyer with intimate knowledge not only of what the public wanted beyond latest publications, but of the preferences of precisely that seg-

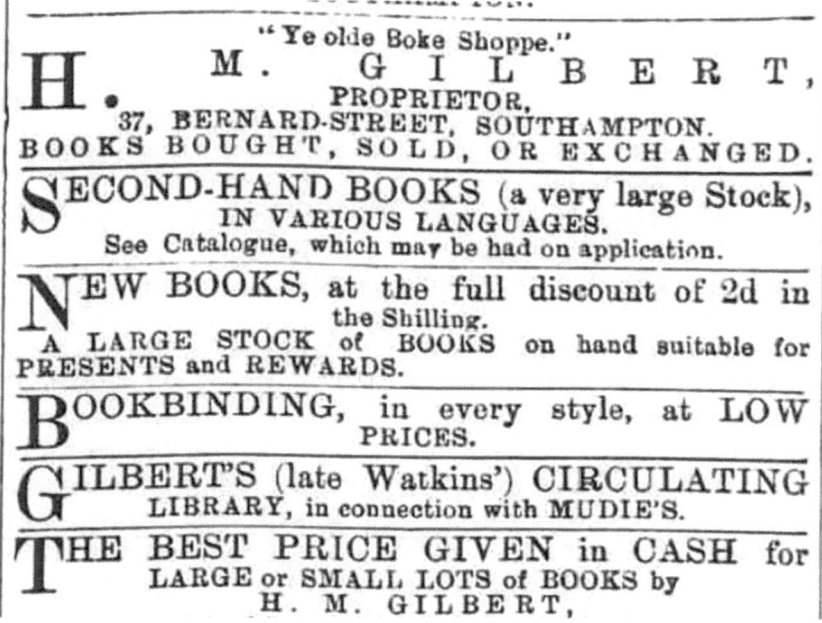

Figure 8.2. Typographic insistence: advertisement for Gilbert's, from Bernard Street days, in *Hampshire Advertiser*, 1873. Newspaper image. *Source:* © The British Library Board. All rights reserved. With thanks to the British Newspaper Archive.

ment from where most revenue was derived. By comparison, any success with new titles that the "underselling," bulk-buying Southampton Book Society might have had further down the High Street would have eaten into Gilbert's ability to compete over newly published titles on price.

For customers, the bought-for-cash trade enabled books to become a useful store of value. One occasion Ian Mitchell gives for books entering the secondhand market is when the owner wished to realize their monetary value, often as a means of paying off debts.[20] Such a trade must have also brought with it certain risks. In London issues around begging and petty crime, and around "unjustified begging," had earlier led to organizations such as the rapacious Mendicity Society, whose subscribers could hand over to beggars not cash but tickets that the receiver would present to the Society's office and be rewarded—or prosecuted, depending of the Society's view of how genuine was the receiver's case.[21] Book theft was a regular activity of prosecuted ticket holders or, as they might alternatively be called, bibliophiles: "J.C. . . . who had been seventeen times apprehended by the Society's constables and as many more by the police . . . is an old man, and his age usually excites sympathy . . . he has been convicted of stealing books, newspapers, and on one occasion an ink stand from a coffee house."[22]

At some point, J.C. may have wanted to convert his stolen books into cash. On Saturday 16 September 1876, between cases of disorderly behavior and wage claims, the Southampton Police Court heard evidence on a young man, Mr. Thomas Smith from London, who had been charged with stealing from street shelving a book valued at 2s, later found to be property of Mr. H.M. Gilbert. A Mr. George Treleven, assistant to Mr. Cotton, pawnbroker, stated that Thomas, now prisoner Smith, has offered the book in pledge on Saturday, claiming that he had bought it in London, in Oxford Street, twelve months earlier. Suspicious, the pawnbroker had called the authorities. In court, Thomas Smith persisted in his explanation of the Oxford Street purchase until a street directory was called for, which subsequently proved the assertion false. Sentencing at that time was no light matter and, for a 2s book, Thomas was given one month of imprisonment with hard labor.[23]

The experience of straightforward theft would not have been unusual for Gilbert's or any other of the city's booksellers—such were the risks of on-street displays. A theft from the Docks Terminus branch of W.H. Smith's was disturbed by a rail passenger, but when manager Thomas Palmer chased and questioned the thief, who was later arrested, he "let the prisoner go as he knew him."[24] The wider issue of theft, however, was compounded by various forms of credit and other deferred methods of payment. More inventive than Thomas Smith, a Japanese resident of Southampton, Mr. M.P. Tarro, was accused of obtaining four books from Mr. H.M. Gilbert on false pretenses.[25] In court, Henry March was shown three books, which he recognized as his property, and a presentation card, which he recognized as having been shown to him by Mr. Tarro. Owen Gilbert, Henry March's son, who had initially served Mr. Tarro, said that, on the strength of the presentation card and an assertion from Mr. Tarro that funds from a bank remittance would be available shortly, he had supplied Mr. Tarro with two books: Black's Atlas and *Voyage of the Sunbeam*—almost certainly Adam and Charles Black's *Atlas of the World* from 1856, reprinted in 1879, 1890 and beyond; and (Baroness) Annie Brassey's novel published by Longman and Co. in 1878. The card Mr.

Tarro had presented stated he was a member of the Oxford and Cambridge Club of Pall Mall, S.W. London. Two days later, Mr. Tarro returned and secured a copy of Webster's Dictionary and of *Donovan*—the latter being a three-decker novel by Edna Lyall, in which its eponymous agnostic turns to religion; it was not entirely successful, selling around only 320 copies, which suggests that its value for Tarro lay not in the currency of the prose but in the redeemable price of its three volumes.[26] Without more evidence, the chief constable asked for the prisoner to be held on remand for a week, pending further investigations. By 30 June, it was found that Mr. Tarro, an engineer by trade, had left a trail in Southampton of unpaid purchases, comprising a good deal of waterproof clothing from the London Rubber Company on the High Street worth £10 18s; cigars and a cigarette cases from the stationers G.T. Young worth £5 10s; and three weeks' unpaid rents to Ms. Emmie Hatcher in Manchester Street, who had also loaned him 7s 6d before he had disappeared. The persuasive card had been printed for Mr. Tarro by George Young, a Southampton engraver and stationer. To the reminders for payment sent to him, Mr. Tarro had faultlessly replied that "somehow my banker has delayed to answer my request," and later that "I'm sure you will think unkindly of me for not having called before now . . . but satisfactory news from town did not arrive until this morning, and my cash will be here on Thursday next, if not before."[27] During proceedings, the secretary of the Oxford and Cambridge Club was approached and could confirm that the club had no knowledge of the defendant. Tarro was later convicted, but on the day after the conviction an application for increased payment came into the Southampton Borough Bench from the secretary of the Oxford and Cambridge Club, Mr. Woodstock, for repayment of costs incurred over the court proceedings that had left him substantially out of pocket.[28] Many of those involved, it seems, lived in cash-restricted circumstances and, as court case confirms, there was a business sector at the lower end where used goods, theft, and cash were close adjuncts.

In the early 1870s, when Gilbert's were in Bernard Street under Henry March, they had operated an extensive bookbinding service "by skilled workmen"—a useful supplement when buying a tight secondhand copy but with a faulty cover—although this service gradually faded from their advertised attractions as the century progressed, perhaps outdone by specialist competitors. Cawte's, one of the city's two major binders, had moved into purpose-built premises in West Street by 1883, suggesting a growth in business. Broadbere's longstanding business thrived in the city's central Pembroke Square, while booksellers Cox and Sharland began after 1897 to advertise themselves, too, as specialists in binding. It is an obvious point, but worth repeating, that decisions taken by Henry March would not have been based solely on relations between himself and customers, but equally on interactions within and between the larger retailing network as a whole.

Around the turn of the century, Gilbert's had a range of services and goods that could be highlighted in their advertising according to the occasion. Their Christmas advertisement might remind buyers to secure Gilbert's special Christmas list of CHEAP AND WELL-BOUND BOOKS, calling out those two specific features, rather than the (invariable) 50,000 stock and circulating library.[29] Other ads would focus on sales policy and low cost, "new books at second-hand prices" with full 25% discount for cash (see table 8.1).[30]

The advertised list discounts consistently at 25%—significantly larger than the standard 10–15% discount offered for cash—and provides an indicator of how important cash flow must have been to Gilbert's business. But to display and pay for an advertisement that recalculated the 25% discount over five examples, presumably, must have been either to catch the eye or to assist those who found the calculations awkward, both explanations emphasizing equally the importance of cash flow for the customers. By contrast, this focus on trade terms was at odds with the author-and-subject advertising of other book businesses, trading on the strength of author name and topicality, while barely mentioning price. Next to Gilbert's list of discounts was an advertisement for *Blackwood's Magazine*, itself a branded commodity, but listing that month's content, and emphasizing " 'Man's Place in the Cosmos,' Prof. Huxley on nature and man; . . . 'Alexander VI and Ceasar Borgia: were they poisoned?' by

Table 8.1. Gilbert's circulating library charges.

5s	of books for	3s 9d
4s	Do.	3s 0d
3s 6d	Do.	2s 7 1/2d
. . .		
. . .		
1s 6d	Do.	1s 1 1/2d
1s	Do.	9d

Source: *Hampshire Advertiser County Newspaper*, November 29, 1893, 2.

W.W. Story; and 'Armed Europe,' how coming events cast their shadows before, by General Sir Archibald Alison."[31]

Always swinging in and out of focus, but hardly ever absent, was Gilbert's circulating library, which had been set up no later than September 1873 and run at least until 1905. The library had been acquired by Henry March from C. Watkins, who had operated a bookselling business at 25 Above Bar.[32] Much play was made of Gilbert's 50,000-volume stock: "the newest novels by notable authors . . . the principle magazines and reviews are in circulation as soon as published."[33] No budget, or class of reader, was left un-catered for—subscription payable in advance on the following terms (see table 8.2).

The price incentives were constructed in such a way as to encourage more book loans over longer periods. A subscriber could borrow one volume at a time across a period of one month for 1s 6d, but borrow one volume at a time over 6 months costing less than six times the price: 6s as opposed to 9s, representing a saving of 33% For an agreement to borrow up to six books at one time, the savings were even greater, of about 43%, when comparing one month to six. The more volumes the readers rented, the greater the saving; and the longer the reader committed to the scheme, the greater the savings. Given that volumes could be shared around a household or among trusted friends, or read aloud on those occasions when the family gathered, the potential for greater collective reading time per volume increased with increased periods of subscription, overall representing greater savings. But perhaps "saving"

Table 8.2. Gilbert's circulating library charges.

Class A	1 vol.	3 vols.	4 vols.	6 vols.
1 month	1s 6d	3s 0d	4s 6d	7s 0d
3 months	3s 6d	7s 0d	9s 6d	14s 0d
6 months	6s 0d	12s 0d	16s 0d	24s 0d
One year	10s 6d	21s 0d	28s 0d	42s 0d
Class B. for books of past seasons only				
3 months	2s 0d	3s 6d	5s 0d	7s 0d
6 months	4s 0d	6s 0d	8s 0d	12s 0d
One year	6s 0d	10s 6d	14s 0d	21s 0d

Occasional reading 2d per week.

Source: *Southern Echo*, November 11, 1905, 4.

is the wrong term. From the shop's point of view, Gilbert's price structuring accelerates the subscriber's expenditure and increases immediate revenue for the shop. More books are in circulation and that is a good thing for Henry March, because if his support for free libraries has been analyzed correctly then his belief must have been that reading encourages more reading. More importantly, the library market is not one of soft goods, where the item is used up in consumption. Any "consumption" that takes place occurs in the reading experience, making the market one comprising what marketing theory would call "experience goods" or "service goods." The means of delivery mechanism—the book—is returned to the shop with minimal deterioration. Thomas Hibberd may have wondered innocently how long Gilbert's kept using their handcart for deliveries, not knowing that the hand cart was simply a blunter instrument than the library volume.

There are occasional notices of contact with Mudie's—and evidence that the connection may have been no more than an ordering service from Mudie's in the manner of any other of Mudie's customers—but it is not until toward the end of the century that Mudie's makes a regular appearance in Gilbert's advertising material. Overall, Gilbert's prices compared favorably. A 1907 catalog from the London giant quoted one Class A book (one at a time, as often as required) at 7s on a three-month subscription, rising to 12s for 6 months, and £1 1s for 12 months.[34] For one-volume lending, this meant Gilbert's charges were 50% cheaper. For a Mudie Class A subscriber to obtain up to four books at one time, that reader would have to pay 14s for 3 months, £1 4s for 6 months and £2 2s for 12 months;, making Gilbert's 42–46% cheaper. In addition, Mudie's provincial customers were liable for full carriage costs. If local customers could be satisfied within the bounds of his 50,000-volume stock, Gilbert's could out-compete Mudie's on both price and convenience, if not on the reader's accumulation of cultural "London" capital. But for Gilbert's business model to work, again, an intimate knowledge of local tastes would be required to ensure that his limited stock met demand. In a worst-case scenario, should a reader require an unavailable title, Gilbert's could always send for it from Mudie's.

The sensitivity to local conditions can be traced throughout the extant evidence. Indeed, Henry March's engagement in civic life was prodigious. Politically active as a nonconformist and member of the Liberal Association, Henry March was among the first elected to the Southampton Borough Council after the new Secret Ballot Act in 1872, standing against conservative candidates as a liberal for the city's All Saints ward. He failed to get reelected in 1875 (see figure 8.3), but returned as an alderman in 1889, during which time he had worked closely politically with the department-store entrepreneur (and bookseller) Edwin Jones.

Figure 8.3. Henry March Gilbert, seated, left. Liberal candidates for All Saints ward, date uncertain. "Election Candidates at Southampton: Over Fifty Years Ago," newspaper title unknown, August 24, 1935, fragment. *Source*: Southampton City Archives, D/NC/5.

In 1893–94 alone, Henry March served on the Baths Committee as a deputy chairman, and as a member for the "Borough Boundaries, Free Libraries, Technical Instruction and Town Antiquities Committees."[35] His support of Southampton free libraries has been noted but, as alderman, Henry March was instrumental in supporting and appointing non-Corporation members to the council of the Hartley Institute, encouraging a democratization of the Institute and its library that might ostensibly be thought of as rival to a bookseller.[36] He appeared and spoke on the platform of an anniversary meeting of the Portland Street Baptist Chapel's Sunday School in support of the school's learning activities (Henry March ran the young men's Bible class), and he donated parcels of books for the use of those on board Southampton's lightships.[37] Indeed, the engineer Sir James Lemon, who did much to improve the sanitation of the city, had his *Reminiscences of Public Life in Southampton, 1866–1900* published by H.M. Gilbert in 1911. Overall, Henry March's book-promoting activities should be seen as integral to his conception of the public sphere, alongside his lobbying against poor-district overcrowding and his support for public hygiene in the forms of baths. For Henry March Gilbert, books performed not solely in the commercial sector but in a network of civic engagements in which the commercial bookshop was a coordinated participant.

In addition to book retail, Gilbert's book publishing should be accounted for as a final feature of the imbricated trade practices of the provincial bookshop, and of the overlap between commercial practice and the public sphere. Like other Southampton booksellers—the Rayner family, John Adams, George Buxey, and others—the Gilbert family business integrated their publishing and retail operations when opportunities appeared. Almost certainly drawing on experience with catalogs, Gilbert's took on the publication for subscribers of *Bibliotheca Hantoniensis: An Attempt at a Bibliography of Hampshire*, compiled and published by H.M. Gilbert, who, on the title page, still styled the business "Ye Olde Booke Shoppe" (1872).[38] As a dangling carrot, Henry March used much of his introduction to suggest that a full history of Hampshire might be yet compiled and that he saw a ready market for it. Sadly that project's energies were dissipated in a number of more manageable histories, and the publication instead became by 1891 *Bibliotheca Hantoniensis: A List of Books Relating to Hampshire, Including Magazine References*, compiled by Henry March Gilbert and G.N. Godwin, with an additional list of newspapers by F.E. Edwards; then, in flogging-a-dead-project manner,

Supplementary Hampshire Bibliography: Being a List of Typography Not Appearing in Bibliotheca Hantoniensis in 1897.

Gilbert's publications were neither arbitrary nor serendipitous; they were well planned, and the sales were expected. But neither were they the equivalent of a Victorian publishing firm's strategy of sourcing and shaping titles, in house, that would satisfy the house's target readerships—or of "the Gentleman's Publisher's market," which the nineteenth-century essayist Gail Hamilton less flatteringly exposed "for what it really was: a relationship [to the author] based on power, even when conducted as friendship."[39] Like any other provincial book retailer less powerfully placed than their gentleman-publisher counterparts, Gilbert's pursued a strategy of pragmatic opportunism, or of creating markets by matching local resources with potential readerships. A bookseller such as the Glasgow-based John Smith's company—established in 1751 and still in operation as a book retailer to further education—is a case in point. Along with their substantial circulating library and retail business, they published throughout the nineteenth century on two fronts: firstly, with one eye on religiously inflected civic developments, they published outputs from the city's local religious movements; and secondly, along with the rise of Glasgow's prestigious university but also its smaller vocational-education institutes, they published text- and instruction books well into the twentieth century, culminating in the iconic *Glasgow Cookery Book*, popularly known as the "purple book," in multiple editions from 1951 to 1975.[40]

Gilbert's strategy was very similar. Henry March's religious convictions brought him into contact with writers and readers who could be persuaded to produce and buy books. The pathway of the Hartley Institute from a gentleman's culture club to a semi-public educational institution that would later become the core of Southampton University was one along which Henry March was well placed, as a publisher of the Institute's proceedings. And, as for many other Southampton booksellers, the city's position as an *en route* stopover combined with its local historic interest presented a cache from which to judiciously draw. The results are evident in the bibliography of Gilbert's publications, and most readily where the three fields intersect (for a bibliography of Gilbert publications, see the appendix of this book).

Over sixty of Gilbert's publications have been discovered, and there may be more, from 1870 to 1956, most actively under Henry March. Gilbert's bibliographies, as noted, emerged from the shop's experience with catalogs and auctions; *Bibliotheca Hantoniensis* was joined by various other catalog and library lists such as *Catalogue of the Library of Rotherfield Park*, compiled and published by Henry March Gilbert (1891), *Catalogue of a Collection of Books on Naval Subjects in the Possession of T.J. Bennet*, compiled and published by Henry March Gilbert (1895), or *Catalogue of the Library at Highcliffe Castle, in the Possession of Col. the Hon. Stuart Wortley*, compiled and published by H.M. Gilbert (1902).

Gilbert's associations with the dilettante efforts of a gentleman turned into a publishing venture with the 1871 volume edition of notes, papers, and letters by Francis Sewell Cole (F.S.C., hence the pseudonym "Effessea": author of *Britain, Its Earliest History*), which were Cole's eclectic thoughts on such varied topics as ancient yachting, waterproof glue, and the castration of salmon; one brief entry was grotesque remarks on slavery.

The Hartley-oriented research publications begin in 1895 with the *Hampshire Papers: On the Natural History and Antiquities of the County, and Other Miscellanea*, volumes of which were published in Southampton and Winchester intermittently by H.M. Gilbert and Sons until at least 1956, when the *Hampshire Papers* were the last of Gilbert's publishing projects. The *Papers* were the collective efforts of the Hampshire Field Club and Archaeology Society, for the study of the county's natural history and antiquities; the club was begun in the presence of Hartley secretary Thomas William Shore, initially as the Southampton Field Club, and its papers are published still. Shore, author of many of the Hampshire papers, was responsible for organizing the club's summer outings—he referred to himself as the "Hampshire tramp"—often in the company of the Reverend George Nelson Godwin. Godwin had also had a hand in editing the 1891 *Bibliotheca Hantoniensis*, and Gilbert's published his *The Civil War in South-West Hampshire* (1886), releasing a new and revised edition in 1904, shortly before Godwin's death. One of Shore's many projects was to provide the text for Frank McFadden's sumptuously illustrated *Vestiges of Southampton*—published, again, by Gilbert's in 1891.[41]

The successor to Shore as secretary of the Field Club, William Dale, represents the crossover of Henry March's Hartley and religious interests, when Gilbert's published Dale's *The Bible Story of the Creation in Its Relation to Geological Science: An Address Delivered to a Class of Young Men* (n.d., 1880s). Presumably useful for Henry March's young men's Bible classes, this twopence publication was released alongside Unitarian and Chartist supporter Henry Shaen Solly's *Know Thyself:*

A Manual of Personal Religion for Confirmation Classes or Home Reading, also published by Gilbert's in 1886, in conjunction with the London publisher S.J. Gregg.

Book traders in the city's history had long been happy to deploy Southampton's heritage for the benefit of visitors and residents, and specifically to re-deploy John Speed's 1770 *History and Antiquity of Southampton*, then available from the city archives. Gilbert's published John Silvester Davies's *A History of Southampton, Partly from the Ms. of Dr. Speed* (1883); Cox and Sharland had another go in 1909 with Speed's *History* edited by E.R. Aubrey. Gilbert's had also published, with bookseller Alfred Randle, *The Romance of Sir Bevis of Hamtoun, Newly Done into English Prose from the Metrical Version* by Eustace Hinton Jones (1870), which Henry March followed up in the same year with *The Sir Bevis Guide to Southampton and Netley*. These publications fall in line with the very many condensed histories, six-penny guides and timetable-cum-almanac-cum-local-sight summaries produced by Buxey, Adams, and the Rayners. Slightly more ambitiously, Gilbert's reissued a section of Bernard Bolingbroke Woodward's sumptuously illustrated three-volume *A General History of Hampshire* (1861–69), which had been published by the London office of James Sprent Virtue, whose Southampton outlet arrived on the High Street around 1876. Gilbert's publication reprinted volume two of Woodward's history, complete with original pagination beginning page 131, as a single-volume *A History and Description of Southampton* (n.d., late 1870s). Similar Gilbert's projects would include Professor F.J.C. Hearnshaw's *Relics of old Southampton* (1904), as well as John Wise, *The New Forest: its History and Scenery* (1880) and Rosalie Pennell, *Account Of the Parish of Hyde* (1909), the latter published from Gilbert's Winchester operation around the time that the manager Benjamin Cook had taken over Gilbert's branch shop in 1908.

But perhaps the final word in local trade capitalizing not on public demand, but on the opportunities and obligations incurred throughout the bookselling network should go to Gilbert's publishing in 1904 of *List of the Fungi of the New Forest* by no less than fellow bookseller John Frederick Rayner, notwithstanding the Rayner family's extensive publishing interests, shortly before the author's death in 1911.

Gilbert's shop may have been outward-facing toward the public, but its business was sideways, upways, and downways locked into the local trade networks, taking in a huge range of activities from stationery to library services, from local data updates to helping the circulation of the secondhand economy. And those networks, themselves, took part in the city's civic political and cultural life, feeding as much off the advances of gas-and-water socialism as the setbacks of general strikes. Gilbert's represents the pinnacle of the city's book trade, but it is specifically a provincial trade constructed in semi-autonomy away from the metropolitan center, enabled by Southampton's role as a major port.

Robert Darnton conceived the communications circuit to describe how books came into being and reached readers in eighteenth-century Europe, and his model, with a number of adjustments, has proven remarkably durable both in modeling subsequent experiences with books in other centuries and places and in cohering the disparate studies that make up book history.[42] Alternatives have been suggested, such as Sydney Shep's model of situated knowledges (see chapter 11), and more radical updates of Darnton's circuit in Claire Squires and Padmini Ray Murray, *Book Unbound*, showing the reaggregated, disintermediated digital circuit for the twenty-first century.[43] Around 1900, the metropolitan centers of the UK *may* have been able to sustain a demarcated communications circuit most closely matched by Darnton's early model, but in Southampton in the late 1800s and early 1900s the situation depends on a large degree of reaggregation and disintermediation, more analogous with the processes described by Squires and Murray. They write of twenty-first-century digital authors pursuing self-publishing, and taking on roles of retailer and distributor; of corporate online retailers such as Amazon becoming publishers; of publishers forming direct relationships with readers and reading communities; and of readers taking on borrowing, reviewing, crowd-funding, and subscribing roles in an aggregated digital circuit, where all actants struggle to assert their power in the value chain.

Analogously, Gilbert's were as much publishers, binders, stationers, newsagents, and lenders as they were book retailers, while their library operation itself (ostensibly distribution) better represents a complication of the simplified notion of retail. Moreover, they authored books and they published them, too. They published works that had been created out of semi-public and other-trade finance, and in their pragmatic opportunism Gilbert's took advantage of those finance models to create new readers' markets. And when they bought books on the secondhand market, they shifted their position from the publisher's first buyer to a new position parallel to that of reader-end-user. Capital for Gilbert's publishing (and for sustaining his stock) was sourced directly from revenue provided by readers, if not in revenue from sales then via his printed-for-members and subscription publications that were very much crowd-sourced. Their shop was not a discrete station in a communications circuit, neither in Darnton's nor Squires and Murray's, but a networked institution that imploded book functions, on the High Street of cultural economic life.

PART THREE

Factual Fictions

Chapter 9

Five Visits to Gilbert's

The unknown reader is hopeless at following prescriptions. On the one hand, professionalized hermeneutic prescriptions for reading promise to unlock the meaning of a text, hitherto a secret, perhaps even to the author. Such close readings require significant training to embrace, but not remain trapped by, both affective and intentional fallacies that impede the disinterestedness necessary to achieve a fuller aesthetic experience. The commodity reader, however, is an efferent reader of symbolic goods.

A second unfollowed prescription is from the "rational choice" model of consumer behavior. Alongside the emergence of commodity culture in the late nineteenth century, narratives were developed from the classical economics of Adam Smith to explain market behavior, still classical in tenor but with enough refinement to warrant a prefix, becoming *neo*classical economics. Key theorists in the UK were William Stanley Jevons and Alfred Marshall (in France Léon Walras, and in Austria Carl Menger, though with important variations), and its approaches have since become the dominant institutionalized neoclassical school that explains market behavior.[1] To many, whose understanding follows the standards of popular undergraduate economics textbooks, the neo-classical variant is simply traditional "economics."[2] Jevons was instrumental in economics becoming a mathematized discipline, since economists "have to deal with quantities and complicated relations of quantities, we have to reason mathematically; we do not render the science less mathematical by avoiding the symbols of algebra."[3] It was their legacy that succeeded in having the discipline's name changed

190   Reading, Wanting, and Broken Economics

Figure 9.1. Gilbert's bookshop. The figure with the umbrella and the blurred figure wearing a bowler hat are members of the unknown public. Photographed by T.H. James, ca. 1895. *Source*: Southampton Museums, Cultural Services.

from Political Economy to Economics, to "become a pure science, shorn of political (and thus ethical) dimensions that involve subjective value judgements."[4]

Facing a bookshelf, the consumer would make her choice of goods supposedly in accordance with neoclassical prescriptions of supply and demand under conditons of scarcity: anything less means either she behaves irrationally in terms of market logic (contributing to market inefficiency) or that the model requires an overhaul. Her rational choice in this market system is her self-interest to maximize her pleasure and incur the least possible pain—Jevons referred to economics as a calculus of pleasure and pain. Higher-order pleasures might override lower order pains, and pleasurable ends justify disagreeable means, but it is this rational self-interest in tandem with adequate market knowledge that allows the market to function.[5]

With the term "market," Jevons meant a sphere of public exchange, applied to the aggregate of people who agree to meet and transact business:

By a market, I shall mean two or more persons dealing in two or more commodities, whose stock of those commodities and intentions of exchanging are known to all. It is also *essential* that the ratio of exchange between any two persons be known to all the others [italics added]. It is only so far as this community of knowledge extends that the market extends.[6]

From Jevons's definition, it should be noted how the market requires full knowledge of conditions by every participant, each acting out of self-interest: "Every individual must be considered as exchanging from a pure regard to his own requirements or private interests, and that any one will exchange with anyone else for the slightest apparent advantage."[7] In an ideal market, fewer goods mean higher prices, and more goods mean lower prices. The producer who can supply at the lowest price will satisfy the greatest demand, while the buyer pays a price derived from the goods' availability, or according to "scarcity." In the perfectly efficient market Adam Smith envisaged, the golden state of neither over- nor underpriced goods is achieved as supply equals demand, when goods or services reach an equilibrium or market price. It is a state that can only be reached "when all traders have perfect knowledge of the conditions of supply and demand," and any deviation from it must arise from "extraneous circumstances, such as defective credit of the purchasers, their imperfect knowledge of the market, and so on."[8] Economists now talk about the debilitating effects of "market power," referring back to Jevons's concern that "there be no conspiracies for absorbing and holding supplies to produce unnatural ratios of exchange," but though goods rarely achieve an equilibrium price—"the theoretical conception of a market is [only] more or less completely carried out in practice"—they are in principle always moving toward it.[9] The task for neoclassical economists and state government is to defend against Jevons's fear of "unnatural ratios of exchange," and to ensure an efficient market.

The problem is that there is nothing natural about a perfect market, despite what the invisible hand might claim. It is not a perfected organism but an ideal that is always under manual construction by imperfect people—and to a considerable degree if we consider the constructions required to prevent trends to exercise market power or development in the direction of a monopoly. Active markets are neither in a state of equilibrium nor on their way to becoming so except without regulation. That is why very many countries implement competition laws (sometimes called anti-trust laws) to guard against the "natural" drift of competitive advantage toward cartels, monopoly, and anticompetitive or collusive behavior.

Furthermore—and a point that will be developed in the next chapters—even if the market were to reach perfection, it would still believed to be determined by rational decision-making, and that rationality ought to be questioned. The vulnerability is revealed if we interrogate our capacity to make complicated decisions based on market knowledge. Certainly, in hyper-complex post-Fordist society, when even the architects of the 2008 financial crash did not fully understand the ramifications of their financial instruments, the scope for rational choice in broader markets has become truncated. Some might call it a bounded rationality that we resort to, which is a point made by Herbert Simon: that when faced with incalculable situations we simplify the phenomenon that confronts us and instead deploy a heuristic "best guess."[10] The fallibility of this best guessing, in our tendency to ignore baselines, to overreact to new information, and to under-weigh existing information is the subject of an entire branch of market-behavior science known as behavioral economics, replete with its own Nobel Memorial Prize winners.

Nowhere is this more evident than in the market of symbolic goods. The market choices described by Jevons are to be made where market conditions are in principle knowable. He described markets for corn and meat about which agreed judgments of uniform quality might be reached, and without which market equilibrium would be unachievable. Jevons called this the *law of indifference*, in that "when two objects or commodities are subject to no important difference as regards the purpose in view, they will either of them be taken . . . with perfect indifference by a purchaser."[11] Two bags of corn of apparent equal quality need to be chosen indifferently; otherwise, choice cannot then be affected through variations in price.

For retailed books, however—as for other symbolic goods—how is a symbol to be "subject to no important difference" when it is only known through the experience of reading? Rational choice may require an Archimedean starting point of indifference from which advantage can be calculated. But in the reading of symbols it is precisely this indifference that is impossible, since reading can only take place where difference is already at work. The sign, alone, is meaningless without signification achieved from valorized counter-distinctions to other signs and symbols, from a position that is itself created as a counter-distinction for readers, created from their socialization, and from cultural embeddedness.[12]

Shopping in Jevons's market and in the bookshop may both resort to, at least, some forms of rationality, but for the former it is an epistemological project to be solved through rational choice, while for the latter it is a semiotic and existential experience. Unlike the "rational choice" model, in which you might fail to think "correctly" like an economist, your reading and the way you experience a symbol cannot be incorrect. (That others may not like your experience is another matter.) With symbols and with the market for symbolic goods—is there a valid reason for not making the extension?—we enter the elastic world of interpretation, where correctness is replaced by agreement as a possibility.

A woman enters a book shop and makes a complex decision about an item whose total value is formed not merely by any quality that can be ascribed a stable price (that it is this kind of book), but moreso by the social framing of its efferent reading, which varies with who she is from time, to occasion, to place.

To understand behavior in the market of symbolic goods, new methodologies would be required that fused language studies and material semiotics with psychology and cultural studies, as both a humanities sociology and a social science. Its outlines may not yet have been drawn, but scholars of narrative literature would be well placed to advise.

As a tentative step to describing a network of readers and shops on the High Street, we might adopt an unconventional method, but one that has enjoyed over two hundred years' development, and that takes quite literally Foucault's dictum that "it is now so necessary to think through fiction."[13] Fiction does not need to betray history, since history itself is a fictional response to historical unknowability, so as a method, historically informed narrative realism could be used to describe a historical experience of the network. Admittedly, the method is not without its flaws. There are realist fictions in a purely speculative sense, where the writing is constrained only by the internal logic of language. And there is realism constrained by the (historical) consistency and coherence of the world depicted; its aim to achieve either (mere) verisimilitude, faithfully describing a so-called preexisting reality, or something deeper like revealing a world whose "reality" has been obscured by an order we have simply presumed. The synthesis of both positions lies with *homo narrans* in that meaningful reality itself is only available to us through the human practice of narrative. We have to narrate, regardless.

A narrative of the network of readers, shoppers, browsers, and book thieves in a provincial bookshop around 1900 will be an imaginative act—but so are all narrations. Its narrative, too, cannot avoid having a narrator, who in turn cannot avoid having her point of view—but so have all narrations. As Geertz says of anthropological writing, such fictions will be something made or fashioned (Latin *fictio*, as a noun, can mean equally "fiction" as well as "fashioning"), but need not be false or unfactual, and not at all "that different from constructing similar descriptions of, say, the involvements with one another of a provincial French doctor, his silly adulterous wife, and her feckless lover in nineteenth century France."[14] In the latter case of Madame Bovary, the actors and events are represented as having not existed, while in anthropological writing the representation is claimed to be actual, but in both the narrative representation remains a *fictional* construction.[15]

What I would offer, then, is something from the core of literature that is at the core of this study. The figures populating the following narratives have existed. Traces of them are extant in the historic record, but their voices are lost: a dilemma faced by historical reading studies, which databases such as the Reading Experience Database or What Middletown Read take initial steps to addressing. Since too few verifiable facts survive, it would not be right to call these narratives "creative nonfiction," at least with a level of veracity that would require an ethics checklist against giving retrospective offense. "Historical fiction" is a better term—also a realism—in that the narratives are constrained by verifiable historical facts, while not denying that their arrangement of facts is a matter of fashioning. Also fashioned is the narrator's viewpoint, itself conditioned by the cultural bias and habits of thought enacted in the author's body. The aim of these narratives is to illustrate some of the ways readers may have experienced exchange. They are not intended to be correct; their measure is plausibility.

In the photograph (see figure 9.1), two figures stand outside Gilbert's bookshop, considering making a purchase: a woman with an umbrella and a man in a bowler hat. Their faces are unseen, obscured by an umbrella and by the blur resulting from slow shutter speed. The obscurity reveals them as members of the unknown public. Their testimony was recorded by a local historian, whose narrator remarks are given in italics, and who has reconstructed their testimony from memory, remembering the occasion to be July 1903, though the photographer believed the occasion to be a few years earlier, around 1895. There is a bell hanging from a mottled brass spiral inside Gilbert's shop door. It sounds as the door is pushed . . . *Ping*.

Visit 1, Henry

On 21 November 1861, the American Civil War arrived at Southampton with the Confederate ship the Nashville.[16] In its wake was the US warship the Tuscarora, dispatched to destroy the Nashville for burning a US merchantman, the Harvey Birch, caught in the English Channel on its way north. Once the Nashville had berthed at Southampton, the men of the Harvey Birch were landed to the Sailor's Home on Canute Road, and afterwards bought return passage to New York. The Nashville made repairs, and Captain Pegram and his officers took up "sharp discussion" with the mayor and port authorities: some thought the burning of the Harvey Birch had been an affront to Britain. When the Tuscarora showed off the River Itchen, Charleston was replayed in Soton—a blockader and a blockade runner, with Captain Craven of the Tuscarora threatening to sink the Nashville in the channel whenever she left. Town feelings were mixed, but there was interest in the ships and in the war. The Lancashire cotton workers had downed tools, and suffered badly for it, when they refused to work cotton sourced from the confederate South. Others thought it was not English business. Many, such as Mr. Carlyle and Mr. Dickens, who fussed over the Governor Eyre affair, could not see why they should be disturbed about those men and women in the negro condition when England could not take care of its own. And to make any sense of taking sides awkward, a good many wanted to go to the Americas anyway, whoever paid the cost. In December, the Nashville went into dry dock, and by then the commotion died down. Wrights from Northam carried out repairs, and around this time several of the Nashville's crew jumped ship. One was caught and court-martialled, as the records show, but nothing was discovered about the remaining men, nor anything about one of them who made a life in St. Mary's. Two boys and four girls later, his youngest son sloped up in front of Gilbert's, with his eye on a bright future and 3s 10d in his pocket, intent on using it for something else than a nag: Ally Sloper, the son of a confederate deserter, on his Saturday half holiday.[17]

Ping

> What I had in mind was something like James Payn; a novel perhaps. A Beggar on Horseback had been most excellent; as was Bred in the Bone, about a son and father. It's warming the way Payn is easy with un-bred folk and has an eye for what poverty means: it also means he has good American characters

who aren't calculating and not put off by a man's position, and who might know what it was like to have roughed it out in the Great Republic. What I likes most is *The Burnt Million*, which I reckon on being Payn's best: you'd have to admire a man who could burn such a sum. There was notice of it in the *Hampshire Advertiser* when it was in serial in the *Cornhill*; but no-one where we live, at least, would afford a magazine; and I am not partial to the *Cornhill* anyway.[18] It's stuffy for a shilling monthly and thinks the world stops with England. It can't see what is slapping everyone in the face.

There was a heroine in *Burnt Million*, Grace, a rich sort that you only meet in fiction; not like St Mary's girls; unless you think on Cigarette, in Ouida's *Under Two Flags*; but she's a Frenchie, and the women down St Mary's are more unwashed than even Frenchies. Their laugh's got a leer in it, and you end up on the bank, them finding out how big's your Adam's apple. But when it's Grace in the book saying that it would be better if we all had some experience of the hard lot that falls to common people, then you know things must be changing.[19] Just like every German now has to be a common soldier, everyone should have a look at the bottom, just like Mr Payn does, and the *Cornhill* only pretends to. It's the pinch of poverty not the poverty itself, Mr Payn says, that brings a man down. We are all rich or poor by varying degrees. They say it's the poor who's got to live off 'a dinner of herbs,' but if there's not enough herbs or dinner then it pinches; so the herbs should be plenty and nicely cooked in an omelette.[20] Then life isn't half bad.

There are numbers of the *Cornhill* in the Free Public, but it is always packed and it smells rank—assuming you don't have a concession for the Hartley, which nobody does (three signatures from members of the Town Council!)—and often they haven't all the issues, so you lose part of the serial when it gets exciting. The Union is down there too, in the Kingsland Tavern, next door—firemen, carters, coal-porters, corn-runners and God knows—but it's like signing up for the army without pay.

If you make allowances, the Hants *Advertiser* can generally be trusted. Notice of an article, 'Fisticuffs in Fiction,' caught my eye, and it was pleasing to see Mr Kipling recommended again. But when the toffee *Cornhill* runs James Payn it makes you feel as we might be finally getting somewhere. Kipling is another. There are things that an empire just cannot steer. That's why Mr Kipling writes so well about ghosts in Dak Bungalows and of beasts and half dead. And Marion Crawford is another of the same—his ghosts, and his Sicilians—but it is annoying when everyone thinks the Marion you're reading is a woman: though onshore I'll read my sisters' borrows of Ouida and Corelli, who are really fine if I am honest. *Corleone* is about the best thing ever written. It is good strong stuff—man's writing—and you can tell he's American because he describes the scenes so life-like but doesn't dawdle. You can feel the crickets grating on your nerves, and for a couple of months I'd more-or-less made up my mind to join the Sicilian mafia until Uncle Stuart convinced me I could end up a steward if I kept my head down: which is a marvel because you still get to travel but stewards eat better, and pick up tips. I've been hard at it since I was fourteen, and shipped out of Southampton as a stoker's mate since seventeen, but it's hard even if you're built large.

The stewards are sharp. They know places in New York, and there are two who took me to Mulberry St. on Five Points, where I've never seen nothing like it! I'll take the Ditches any day. There's nothing that can't be bought; and the smell! Like Paul Giggs says, in Crawford's other book, *Mr Isaacs*, 'men are not everywhere born free, any more than they are everywhere in chains,' so I reckon my chains here are a little looser than they'd be in New York.[21]

On that afternoon, there was an Asian gentleman, perhaps Japanese, making hard work of a big Atlas of the World from Messrs. Adam and Black: an expensive volume. The young man waited his turn for the counter.

The really good slot would be to ship on the Hamburg-America line, or on the Hamburg-South America: some of those boats have over two thousand in steerage, alone; and me on top, picking tips from first class. What is *fantabulosa* is that they have libraries: onboard! The *Teutonic*'s got one, on the White Star line, and so has the *Campania* and *Lucania* on Cunard. They reckon the biggest are on Hamburg, on the *Amerika* and the *Kaiserin Auguste-Vic*: for third class too. Not just first: third! I've had some paper books off there; white ones not for sale here, so they're cheaper, or they get thrown away. *Cradock Nowell* goes on about Tauchnitz, and I hadn't known what it was; and I'd only read *Nowell* because it was about the New Forest and Cradock being thrown out by his father. The trouble with a deck steward is you have to be civil, in a fawning sort of way, and that'd put anyone on edge. But a 'Bibliothekssteward' on the *Amerika*! That would be a good bet. They get American volumes, cheap, and re-do them in company cloth.[22] And ship all over: to Argentina, where there's harvest work, but the risk is down to you, so that's why I've stayed a stoker.

And Hamburg lads are all bono, too. They work a good shift and don't take nonsense, and they got industry and they're going somewhere.[23] It was them who had me into reading a good deal. They've got their *pfennig* magazines and read the *General-Anzeiger* for Hamburg, for the workers. They've got a Literary Society that does people's educational evenings, where you get tickets from the social democrat party, and all run by a Jewish mush with a bookshop.[24] And what they love best is James Payn, in German! *Die Diamante der gnädigen Frau*—the Diamond of the Lady who is something—*gnädigen* is not a proper word—and they can get it from a circulating library, just like Gilbert's.[25] I, for one, cannot abide all the commotion about Germany: *Battle of Dorking* my aunt fanny. And *Riddles of the Sand*: two cakes in a boat, to save England! We should wake up to the Germans on our side, and cakes overboard. And no amount of unions amalgamating will help, either. They can amalgamate all they like when the executive comes down from London to tell us we're in the wrong! Didn't see that coming! And it left us all pretty hungry. All our family burnt their cards and granddad Burnham just cried like a tot. Anyhow—*Burnt Millions*: there's a writer who should speak out about bravery and the future.

Looks like the best going today is from the second hand box, which has a packet of old *Cornhills* for 3d, and it's got

Payn's 'A Righteous Retribution.' Once Owen's free, I'll see if he'll take a discount, which is good because Owen spends most his time these days in the new shop in Winchester. Mr Gilbert may be pious, though not so much that you'd hold his religion against him, but there's no-one who'll ever best him in a bargain. Down Tomas James's shop is another matter altogether, and I can spend all day in his second hand when I don't have enough to put on a blinker, and he's happy to have me there for the company, I reckon, which gives us both some of the best afternoons I've had.

Take care of your pennies, is the trick! Gambling isn't a problem as long as you can afford it. The *Hants Advertiser* says so in its 'Literary Gleanings,' where Mr Payn says that gambling is all misunderstandings.[26] Gambling is not just playing for money, which would mean all the adventurous speculating whereby a man may get rich, including business life. It is not just playing for high stakes, neither, because a few shillings that's nothing to a rich man is high stakes for me. No. Gambling is playing what you can't afford. That's how Stevenson has it in 'The Suicide Club,' in rich young men finding they've reached their limit.[27] That is why you must know your limit, otherwise you can't play up to it as tightly as can be. You must be, as it were, your own business: otherwise, this world won't pay you out nothing.

Now the counter's free I ask Owen for the latest by Mr Payn but he looks at me queer, like something you wouldn't wipe your boot on. He reckons there's no latest book by Mr Payn on account of him being dead for five years, which caused much of a stir among literary people. I of course explained I meant the other Mr Payn and Owen disappeared to the stacks, returning a few mo's later with some-one called G.P. Payne that was a two-volume used library edition of *Uncle Sam's Peculiarities*. I said it would do perfect and left with the bundle of Cornhills and the two volumes which all-in-all depleted me by three and six.

It is Saturday 6 June 1903. The novels columns are heated over Riddles of the Sand. *The* Southampton Echo *does not care for foreign nationals on British merchant ships, if they cannot speak English, but it flies the flag for lascar sailors whom Australia Labour were preventing from signing onto P&O mail services (the Echo writes of our "dusky sons of the empire" while noting that these sons are also highly "economic"). A man named Charles Short is severely injured in a Docks accident; the Sussex Plate (handicap) and the Laughton Plate will be run at Brighton at 3:10 and 3:45, losing the young man 3s 2d. Tonight he will only be able to buy Jenny a ginger ale when she prefers a sherry cobbler and going to Variety. Saints have just won the Southern League, again (7 points above Pompey; important to any Sotonian), and in the life of commerce, on the coming Wednesday, a life-size inflatable elephant is promised that at 200 feet will release coupons for Salmon's 2s tea, redeemable from any quality grocers.*[28] *That evening, the young man returned to his lodging earlier than expected. Jenny had been none too pleased. For comfort, he picked up his Cornhill to look for "A Righteous Retribution." His eye, straying upward, noticed that the editor of this much despised Cornhill journal is none other than James Payn.*

Visit 2, Rita

Never shy of putting a price on the need for company, a common variety of wanted ads throughout England at the time were for young "domesticated companions," often stipulating additional skills required: needlework, kitchen skills and, increasingly, cycling. A typical notice in the small ads section of the Hampshire Chronicle stated "Companion—Companion Housekeeper. Young lady seeks POST. Domesticated. Plain cooking. Good needlewoman. Musical. Cyclist—address 'Rita' Hampshire Chronicle Office, Winchester."[29]

Ping

I like Gilbert's because they have such lovely cards, and because as of last year you could get the cards with the back divided so you could leave a message, with a picture on the front. I'd had some made up of myself from a portrait done at James Parker's (or might have been Henry Brain's in the Ditches), and if you timed the delivery right—there were six a day—you could get it to the young gentleman past tea-time. 'Tonight—bring your cycle! Grand Pier at 7,' which was not in the least dreary, if you're to learn how to ride. You could angle the stamp, too, to let him know where he stood.[30] It's not that I did not like books. I have always loved books. Madam

Maes used to let us borrow from her library when I was a girl in West Gate, and sis Lorna would read aloud. Mamma could be quite forcible: 'Giv'us another chapta.' Lorna ended up stitching with Cawtes, the binders, on West St, when he built the new shop and taking a shine to Henry Cox, who'll end up running it one day—of course Lorn' should have stuck to him. Madam Maes has gone, now, and they've put up a horse trough to her on the Esplanade.[31] A horse trough! As if women didn't get a rough enough time when they was alive.

No, Yes. I love books. They let you fly, but I wish they were easier for sharing. Elsie and me get them borrowed, and next year Elsie's been promised she can get a Hartley's card, which she can on account of her being clever. We've read them all: Marie Corelli, Emily Lawless, Lucy Walford, Sarah Grand, Mrs Ward, Ellen Wood, Harriot Stowe, Josephine Butler, Charlotte Brontë, and of course Ouida but she is almost Italian, you'd think, and her *Flanders Dog* is delightful but it is also really quite silly. We went to a lecture on George Eliot and it was splendid, and Elsie said she couldn't go on as she's been doing, for she felt that half of her was being starved.

There's a tall lad going through the second-magazines. I'd noticed when he first came in—dresses too hard—wants you to think he's a steward but you don't get that whip willow from stewarding. More like a stoker. There's a toffee nose in an easy chair off on his ownsee with not the merest intension of buying anything, I warrant, while poor Owen does the fetching and carrying, and at the counter there's a foreign gentleman, looking at an Atlas. I have never seen such graceful nails on a man before, let alone for an oriental gentleman. They are slim and gentle. No doubt he is ineffably rich. *His* hands, on the other hand, are bony, which any girl will find out if she is daft enough to get caught with her back turned. It's quite disgusting. When he is away, which is often, I look through his books. Ma'am says she doesn't understand them, and if there are not dresses to be brushed or mended we read a volume of hers together. She reads all of Wilkie Collins—we've been through *Man and Wife* twice—and Hall Caine, and her Frances Trollope volumes whenever she can; most of them, I'd guess, ending up in bigamy. Or what I should say is that Ma'am reads while I dress her hair, which she likes at present smoothed with bandoline, on account of it smelling like quinces. Ma'am reads so very well, but she likes fuddy-duddy magazines that won't do her the least bit of good. I suggested she might like to read something modern: like the *Wheelwoman*! I was hoping she might take a shine to having a cycle that she'd let me lend. Ma'am said she would like-as-not break her neck, and I'd have to find another employment which wouldn't suit me at all as well as I think. She reads of her own in the evening, which is why she should let me take her out. Elsie has read the *Guidebook for Lady Cyclists*, and says that I should learn to ride because of the better positions and because in the summer next we'll be sure to borrow two cycles and take out to Lee on Solent, of a Sunday. I've never been past Woolston, which isn't quite true because I've been to Pompey to see Buffalo Bill, when Grandpa took me and I was a little girl. They had a lady sharpshooter, who could pop an apple off a wooden cowboy. Her name was Shenandoah. You can't use a word like 'Shenandoah' in Southampton.

The Master's books are all history, and travel, and Chamber's *Vestiges*, and some poetry by a Swineburne. He takes papers, too: the *Advertiser*, and the *Hampshire Telegraph* on Saturdays that does a short story—they'll have Ouida's 'Basket of Plums' in October[32]—and the *Daily Telegraph* and *Illustrated London*; besides his other mucky books second-stacked behind the front row in the bedroom bookcase. I don't look at them, and I wouldn't understand them if I did, but I did have a look at his Hector France. How could any girl resist words like *Musk, Hashish and Blood*, which was a little bit too much sensation than I'd bargained on. Ma'am should put wintergreen oil on him like auntie May does to her Raymond. I'm sure ma'am knows. She must, and Will the footman certainly does, so there's not too much secret about his *Secret Life*.[33]

Elsie has read *The Story of Mary MacLane* but she'd got it on swap, and her month's ticket ran out so she had to return it.[34] Mr Gilbert said it was not suitable for his customers so they'd sent it back and wouldn't be getting more by Miss MacLane. She was from Canada, and there had been so many men that had wanted to make love to her with writings and poems and deaths that Elsie said she must be making it up. But not the wretchedness. Elsie said she also had the same 'germ of intense life' like Miss MacLane and felt like she was already forty, too, and that happiness needs to come from more than just clean feet and fresh stockings. Elsie said it comes from the rarest times with friends.

So instead of Mary's Story, we shared *Barbara's History*, which was quite the bee's knees, because I had a month's subscription for 1s and 6d, and we had to get through its three volumes, which was a breeze.[35] He's a little more expensive by a touch, but Mr Gilbert's books are so much vivider than the other shops. Barbara in it, who turns out to be a little annoying, goes to Germany to become a painter and falls in love with Hugh, but there's an Italian woman hidden away in Broomhill Mansion, when they're married, so she runs off again to Rome. We miss the three volumes, as everything nowadays is one volume, which makes it cheaper and more handy, but there is something affluent about three volumes in your bag that makes your elbows tighten when you carry them.

We like Marie Connor Leighton, too: *Sweet Magdalen: Only a Love Story*, and *The Harvest of Sin*.[36] There was a review in the master's *St James's Gazette* of *Napoleon of the Press*, full of excruciating persons apart from a lady novelist in her first blush, who makes £5,000 in a single year.[37] What we don't like is the books of Charlotte Younge. Please, from black under-clothing; from hips that wobble as one walks; from men with fishy eyes; and from the books of Charlotte Yonge, may the Devil, please, deliver us. Elsie said we should cycle to Otterbourne and tell to her her books are dreary. Mrs Ellen Ward is another one: her and her anti-suffrage.

The books ma'am reads she just gobbles up, and I'm allowed to watch her do the gobbling. And it's not as though she gets fat on them either; just thinner and thinner, and still in want of more. Mr Gilbert sends his bill on the first of every month, which can't ever get paid because it comes back again next month, but more bulky. He says Gilbert is a scoundrel for not allowing discount on account, which he could get anywhere if he was to go to the shop in person but it was presumptuous to expect a gentleman should tie his days around a tradesman's beck and call. For Elsie and me, if we do consume anything we do it together. Whatever I get Elsie reads, or else I give it her; or we swap, and that way we don't use up our meagre pennies and we've got more than enough reading. The library selection from Gilbert's is usually fairly clean, in the margins, but you can see where some-one else has been in pencil, which is why I don't like reading in bed, though there's not much other places to read, unless its Elsie who's had the book and then I imagine her fingers on the pencil, on the pages before mine, and what she must have been thinking.

Mr Owen is very nice at serving. I buy two postcards, and a penny packet of stationery, and browse the catalogues. There is an advertisement on the board for the *Southampton Typewriting and Shorthand Office*, 147 High Street, 'all-round trained Lady typists wanted, apply to Miss Stewart: short hours only.' I'll never get trained, to be honest, only in brushing hair or frocks, and listening to ma'am being dreary. I could die sometimes and not be the tinniest bit unhappy afterwards. Elsie says we're respectable, so we should go abroad and be domestics, but what a prospect! She wouldn't tell me exactly, but she said Miss MacLane was disgusting, and that's why she really took it back and that is why we're not going to Canada. She said it was like a man-love but in a woman's-nature. The bookshop is cosy, and the sky outside has gone the colour of lead. Southampton is so dreary. I'm a desert with a clinging perfume to me that is Elsie. I'm a desert with a light on it that my soul turns to and I think one day it will rush over my soul and kill it. But the light is soft and silvery, and always it shines from Elsie.[38]

Visit 3, the Engineer

On Monday 20 July 1903, the Bournemouth Daily Echo *printed a short column entitled "A Dream of the Future" that discussed the certain and desirable removal of horses from large cities, either by taxation or legislation, which was opposed by those who believed their livelihoods were at risk, being too poor to* afford the alternative of a motor wagon.³⁹ The opinion of the Engineering Magazine was reported, which argued that this riddle of progress and poverty could be resolved by adopting a betterment on steel rails for wagons for street use that was the L-shaped rail or "plateway." Various advantages and disadvantages were discussed. A standard rail required the wagon to have a flanged wheel, thus preventing the wagon's use on flat pavement. The L-shaped plateway, on the other hand, could cup and support a standard wheel that would then be available for road use. The chief advantage, however, as the Engineering Magazine sensibly saw it, was the superior conversion of forces the plateway effected in that, "if nearly level, a man could propel as heavy a load as one horse hauls on a badly paved street." Its message to naysayers, thus, was that a ball-bearing vehicle on a plateway "will almost run itself and you yourself can propel your wagon on it!," saving "neigh-sayers" the expense of both a horse and an expensive motor replacement. Since calculating acceptable levels of back injury in a system of supply and demand was a political rather than an engineering problem, the article was able to reach the following sardonic conclusion on resistance to change: that "It is natural for a man to oppose everything that is good for him as to cry for things that hurt him."

The detail of any construction involves an immense amount of thought and labour, and I, for one, devote a great deal of time to this. Yet too often are details far from being satisfactorily settled, before those involved in consultation either stand against or fail to act on agreements. It is in this singular failing that I find the root cause of retardation to a well-functioning market. The Topographical Company, for example, are now pleased to release their *Southampton Annuals*, as Rayners used to do their *Visitants Guides* and condensed histories, but it is all romance nonsense about Sir Bevois and Netley Abbey. Adams promised 60 half-tone illustrations of ocean liners, splendid views, and the opening ceremonies of various docks, but despite several conversations at his shop to discuss how that publication might include those improvements to science and labour that are bringing us into the twentieth century, it is little more than a cheap tourist postcard.

This is the manner of my staying away from several reading establishments in the city: Chaplin and Weeks; Buxey's; Robert Batt's; although I will go when pressed. Of the various reading businesses the city can offer, Gilbert's is the most efficacious, though he, too, is forced to fill his counter with postcards and other bric-à-brac that rightly should be set to one side, in a special case. Elsewise, his is a solid endeavour with a good range of new and used titles, with much good that can be said of his library.

For novels, I've never had much time, or indeed patience, but they are an unavoidable currency that one needs to acquire and, from a survey of current literature, I would say that, despite misgivings, there can be genuine contributions to our knowledge from that quarter: the outstanding examples belonging to two gentleman only, Mr Griffith and Mr Wells, whose grasp on science and on futurity is to be much admired.

Far too much talk is spent on how certain people wish to be removed from those stations in life where we find ourselves, the lowest to be put on high, without properly acknowledging how science will already turn our lives unrecognisably in less than twenty years. Everyman, and new woman, expects to rise from their station but fails to see what is obvious to those best able to form a sound judgement; that stations, like their railway counterparts, will soon be changing to aero-stations, and take with them our expectations. Nothing will be as we presently imagine. The movement of goods by flying machines and ocean containers; communication by hand-held portable telegraphy; greater labour-saving engines supplied by petroleum and electricity; devices for cooling and preserving, for heating and making rapid; systems of advertising for the information of people; and the un-lucky hell that will be aerial warfare, all shown back to us through the new technology of the cinematic bioscope will re-draw the maps of what we pretend is the known world.

I am not speaking of science romance, which you will find from the pen of men like Mr Jules Verne, or in Mr Robert Cole's preposterous *Struggle for Empire*. I am speaking of hard facts, and of scientific truths that can be speculated upon to their conclusion, as Mr Pope suggests in his *Journey to Mars*. It is not from crude fantasy that the peaceful path to real reform will come, but from the scientific minds of men like Ebenezer Howard, who presents a keen but not insurmountable problem of how to produce engineering solutions from geometric methods, which the harmony of his Garden Cities demand. We will, for example, no longer live abutting the heat of our factories but will each day travel on specially created transports organised by manufacturers who require our labour.

It is the same manner of solution that we find in Mr Bellamy's *Looking Backward 2000* with which I have rarely indulged myself by reading twice. There is much merit in his proposal of national industry and full employment, but abroad there are far too many assumptions about what human nature ought to be and not enough research into what it is. I have not been able to discover that repetitive factory labour injures a man in any way, and if facts are that a man can better earn his keep with the aid of machinery, is it benefiting to withhold that machinery because attendance upon it may be monotonous or injurious?

Most intriguing is Mr Bellamy's notion of a card credit system that does away with money, which means increased efficiencies and reduced waste, and thus can we further concentrate on eliminating duplication. To such similar ends of general improvement, I attended a lecture on one I am told numbers amongst the greatest writers of our age. We trust our critics to know better, I am forced to assume, but having browsed Mr Tolstoy's *Resurrection* I find the man impenetrable and abandoned the volume after barely a page, and have since relied upon Mr Maude's introduction of how he wrote it, should conversation at the Hartley ever require.[40] He may well be the most famous man of Europe but one concludes that Gilbert only brought in the wretched book because of publisher friends in Christchurch who produced it. I am left with an annoying sense that Mr Tolstoy grasps the Christian benevolence of the thing but has no conception whatsoever of the material. These are estimations I expect to be verified by the performance of *Resurrection* at His Majesty's Theatre, which will doubly save me the expense of many evenings' reading.[41]

While I wait for young Owen to fetch my requests—it is uncertainty about which volume that drags me into town, rather than want of a manservant—I ponder the root causes of our country's reduced position. The unions to whose promise of betterment I can well understand the average worker turns will deliver only a road to serfdom, in toil for new lords of men whose self-interest is only surpassed by their ignorance of improved production. For all the talk of bright futures, it is the greatest irony that unionism will only lead brave but childish men backwards into feudal gloom.

The notion of a *Time Machine*, as imagined by Mr Wells, is undoubtedly a fetch too far, but his inventor expresses adequately that we must neither fear the future nor venerate the tyrannical past. One who fears the future, fears failure, and limits his activities. Failure is only the opportunity more intelligently to begin again, in which disgrace is only found by fearing to fail. And for veneration, the past is useful only as it suggests ways and means for progress. Mr Well's Morlocks are the romance of boggy men that we use to frighten children, but his inventor is right in that we must intervene in our present course!

Unfortunately, on any *solution* Mr Wells remains silent, and this is where I would be correct in saying that a majority of reasonable men consider the march to have been stolen on him by Mr Griffith in his tale of aerial warfare and the coming order. I have no doubt that there exists already such terror organisations as the good Brotherhood of which Mr Griffith writes, but they will lack effectiveness in so far as they lack an adequate knowledge of mechanical processes. Vanadian steel, for example, allows for the greatest strength with the least weight. The power of height is absolute, and he who flies highest will be so plainly victorious as to no longer warrant a shot, let alone bombs of melinite. It is precisely this insight that the War Office fails to grasp at present in the Alexander Palace ship.[42] The combination of a lighter-than-air system with a heavier-than-air fixed wing system does indeed raise capacity for suspension. But they think only of increasing motor size, ludicrously now to 600 or 800 horsepower, producing speeds of sixty miles per hour, though with Olympic indifference to the weight thereby accrued. Height not speed is the crucial thing! Mr Griffith's *Angel of the Revolution* is at heart a blessed angel, but she will not shorten the painful transition from the past without more effective engineering than the War Office currently supplies.

I observe that what Mr Griffith puts before us in the guise of his thrilling tale is a futurist manifesto: a brave call to right-thinking men of the Brotherhood, those noble members of the Terror, who can conceive from their Anglo-Saxon blood a life of unbroken tranquillity, utterly without tyranny in whatever Romanov form. I asked if Owen had enjoyed the closing scene: not a regiment of men under arms in all the civilised world and peace at last. He'd not read it yet, and cannot now when *Pearson's* serves it in parts, so will miss the guidance of other sound men in its pages like Mr Bernard Shaw.

It is undeniable that much labour has been saved by our inventions. A seamstress can now produce in one day what formerly would have taken several. A typist such as Miss Hoskins on an Underwood can produce up to sixty words per minute, with two carbon duplicates. Yet it baffles me that we are not better improved? As much ingenuity has elapsed between the Great Exhibition and now, as between George Eliot and Waterloo, yet the average man still works long hours and, without the half holiday, would still have less time for education than need for sleep. No doubt the process of improvement for working men is longer than one imagines and, as sure as the minute hand, such improvements will trickle down before long. But one cannot help but speculate on other causes.

A title that seemed to overwhelm debate in all the London papers some years ago, and around whom still quite a commotion occurs, is *Progress and Poverty*.[43] I never previously had the opportunity to read Mr Henry George's work, though of course like everyone I knew its general tenets, but only now determined to finally have it tackled. The copy Owen included for me in the improvised tower of books to my side was a Kegan Paul cloth reprint from '89, as a handy pocket duodecimo—Gilbert's are such excellent buyers. What a relief to turn from the stupefying dullness of fantasy to proper science in that Mr George outlines his problem clearly in the very first chapter. I could not concur more that the present day has been marked by a prodigious increase in wealth-producing power, with greater sub-divisions and grander scales of production. We naturally expect these labour-saving devices to lighten toil and improve the conditions of the labourer. I read on with natural pleasure at what would be the predicted outline of developments seen from a mere decade or two before. Perhaps it was a new introduction, I'm not sure, but Mr George suddenly became unclear. The issue will no doubt work itself out in the course of his book, why else would it be so regarded, but Mr George writes of crowding down wages and no prospect of pay beyond the barest living. Why then, he writes, where the conditions to which material progress everywhere are most fully realised and the machinery of production and exchange most highly developed, do we find the deepest poverty and the sharpest struggle for existence? He is mistaken, and I am surprised of his giving credence to such a claim. Our enormous increase in productive power which continues with accelerating ratio will eventually lighten the burdens of those compelled to toil. The sight of a one or two-day week is surely just within reach. Mr George should instead look to their unchecked breeding, their litters of children, and ask if they do not consume the new fruit of production too quickly!

I will confer with Mr Gilbert about George's *Progress*. This may well not be the correct edition of a book about which everyone speaks so highly, but if I am not misinformed it would seem pointless to exercise myself on further exposition. It is with some relief that I spied one of the new Net copies of Mr Jevons. There is a mathematician of economics. A man who understands that there is no place for politics in science.

Visit 4, Sylvie

Her father had excelled in little but the management of his temper, which he exerted such influence over as to reappoint it as a weapon. With that coupled to his size, few men would go the whole hog, once they'd read in his face the absence of all reticence to deploy violence. And to that end he was retained by an Argentinian gentleman, no less than the tyrant Juan Manuel de Rosas, in exile, who had taken on a farm in Swaythling: 400 acres of mixed arable and pasture, on Burgess Road overlooking Daisy Dip.[44] *Rosas believed that enemies* would reach out to England to harm him, damage his property, perhaps destroy his papers, and kill him, and for this reason he had retained her father as a "sereno" to go the rounds each night, paying four shilling a day with coal and a house, which was where she had been brought up. Like other residents in Swaythling, she'd been both enthralled and appalled by this other-worldly figure riding from his estate, among what he called the local "péons," with his poncho and bolas. She'd tasted pumpkin, and maté that Rosas implausibly claimed the locals now preferred to beer. The talk was about great commercial prospects: stockbreeding and horses from Uruguay, sheep from Spain, and a dairy, but nothing came of it and Rosas would complain to her father about local greed and about péons who had insulted him. Her father and she were turned out, eventually, accused of theft, and the Rosas estate slowly went back to being an unprofitable wet scrubland. Around '77, the former Argentine Restorer of Laws and Conqueror of the Desert was overtaken by the Hampshire damp, and died of pneumonia in, some said, considerable debt.

Sylvie had gone into packing work but had managed to progress to clerical work when her father had been better off, and her new mother had encouraged her in their joint ambition to open a newsagents. The memory of Sylvie's testimony was returned to me on reading the diaries and letters of two girls who'd been encouraged in their education, and which were made public only after the war. One letter in particular struck with some force, written just four months before the unexpected passing of one of these ladies from undetected diabetes, leaving the other isolated and in low spirits.[45] That letter conveyed the same kind of low spirits that followed Sylvie, even when she was cheerful, brought on, she believed, by memories of a fabulous estancia in Swaythling which she was no longer sure had existed.

> I do badly want a drop more sun, but I have been almost distracted these last few days. Mother is rushing all over the city looking for a news agency to take on, and has found one in Shirley High Street, just out of town, and seems very excited about it. The shop does some stationery business, and in mother's words could be 'a little gold mine.' Her plan is to do monthly magazines, London and Southampton morning and evening papers delivered promptly, and The Shirley and Freemantle Advocate and Shirley Church magazine and sundries; but mother feels too poor and harassed to consider any other point of view. It looks too quiet to me, but I expect she will have her way and take it.

I've found it well-nigh impossible to concentrate on my search for work, and can only hope I've sown seed to good purpose with heaps of societies and people I've written to, but sometimes I am tempted to lose heart. Most days I take myself to the free library and scan the papers, but there is little doubt that competition for posts is very keen.

With regard to Felix's offer, I have read his letter many times and it renews my courage but I feel I shall never leave these lanes despite what he says I can earn in the Argentine. I feel so pressed in upon by mother, and now father in St Mary's workhouse at the end of his days, that sometimes I wish I could sleep and never wake again, but that is sheer cowardice. Felix's affection gives me heart, however, and I should remember that Stevenson has said, has he not, that 'so long as we are loved we are indispensable'? But Felix's financial position becomes daily more serious I cannot see what he will do, and no-one will offer him work if he does not find a cooler disposition for his hot brain. That is why I spend time among the book shelves, here, for respite—it is such a bright little shop that to saunter its balconies is like a refreshing exploration in the country. It was on one wooded rise that I found a flutter of romance in meeting Mr Felix Portales, browsing the foreign-language section.

The last promise to myself that I've kept was not to read any more settler stories. Miss Baynton's *Bush Studies* made me feel quite sick for its lack of hope. It gave the lie to all that Noble Needlewoman tripe that any girl could see was a blatant a piece of concoction, such as the Women's Emigration society likes to print.[46] Stan went as a harvester to Argentine, and made good money, but he shakes still with sickness, and the money ran out looking to get started again when he came home. Unless you make it so big abroad that you don't need care, you must stay there, and that's why when I see *An Australian Girl* on the shelf I fear terribly for any young girl carried away by the glow of it.

I am fond of a strong man, I do admit it. 'Cause there is so much in this world that needs withstanding. Before the slums were cleared about Lock's Court, it was quite the primordial setting, as if the waters had newly retired from the face of the earth. You might catch a glimpse of life behind an opening, beneath a peaked roof, a burst of yells, a whirl of black limbs, a mass of bodies struggling under the droop of heavy motionless poverty. I sympathise keenly, but it was as though pre-historic man was cursing and welcoming you at the same time. Pop would navigate through the dark heart of it without a drop of fear, and never picking up sickness, neither. I remember him of a Saturday, if there'd been a family party playing dares, and he or Mr Andrews would draw a forfeit, and swing round and round the lamppost shouting 'my wife's had triplets'; silly devils.

Thank God there's a good map been made of the Frenchtown slums now, with a good deal of new pink brick, and now public baths, and the Lido outdoor, so there's no excuses. It needs a good hand at the wheel, and an honest one, too, because as soon as you lose your way everything that seemed to muddle along becomes overrun with greed.

Francis Crawford cuts a fine figure, too, I am sure of it. I read his *Celia: A Story of Modern Rome* last year, and there is notice of *Whoever Shall Offend* to be published next, of an Italian child in adverse circumstances. I cannot wait. His writings *do* manage to convey a wonderful lot of feeling and I am only sorry I have to strain my eyes at night to read. The characters, or the good ones, have the same abundancy of spirit that I see in women my age who were lucky to stay at school until their twenties and then begin a 'profession,' and now look smooth and fair and healthy, unlike the rest of us who started with the little we had and now plainly are a reservoir that's been sapped.

Mr Conan Doyle, as well, I've been assured, will be a fine writer one day, as pop's younger admirers have seen him play full-back for Portsmouth Association Club, not knowing he was the same famous author.[47] They say he is a little slow but has a powerful safe kick, and altogether seems reliable; and filled their heads once with detective stories on the journey back to Pompey.

In this vein, I am fond, too, of Mr Kipling's stories. It was the title of *Life's Handicap* that first attracted me: 'Stories of Mine Own People.' I picked it up second hand in this very shop, in a single volume: quite the fattest I've ever owned.⁴⁸ From the very first line, I was caught by the commitment to the thing: 'there lived three men who loved each other so greatly that neither man nor woman could come between them. They were in no sense refined . . .' And his 'Mutiny of the Mavericks' was a pure delight of devilment. There is a resilience in Mr Kipling, that does not shy away from grotesquery, but still comes back with a beaten smile and conviction. It helps me when my thoughts lack grip and coherence, so I become intent that, with a little help, once the depths have been plumbed, I shall rise again!

These bookish men, I would believe, are captains all: of a better cut than the tars and stevedores who have no chivalry among them to get what they want, but thinks they can turn everything into a 'little bit of business,' with their whiskey breath and lewd comments. I have come across such a strong writer's hand in *Blackwood's Magazine*, which can be picked up cheap almost everywhere. It is Bernard Capes, and his tale of a Colonel Lacoste who was in wild hill country somewhere attacked by wolves that the Colonel fends off valiantly until overpowered. It is quite horrific and made my arm hairs stand. Then an over-ripe priest takes the Captain's sword but cannot pull it from the scabbard, it being so caked with blood. At the moment of his demise, the priest discovers that all his piety is of no use to him and 'the utter ecstasy of horror entered into and possessed his soul.'⁴⁹ I did not think before that a horror could be an ecstasy, though, which is a bit much to digest. Next to Capes was another story on similar lines, though transposed to Africa and a Captain facing horrors, which I liked well enough, and I would read another of Mr Conrad's, but altogether found it too wordy. If nothing else is suitable today, I might take Mr Conrad's *Tales of Unrest* in hoping it might be like Mr Capes.

Felix has been asking after my father, and asking to see him, but I have made it clear to Felix what the poor house is for a place. I am confident Felix will soon give up with his requests about the Argentine Gentleman, which he makes to comfort me I am sure. He has been asking if Pop has papers from long ago when we were in Swaythling, but we have nothing from that period but memories. Felix took me strolling on the common on Sunday and when he arrived he looked distinguished and grand. Were it not for his accent, you could think he was a proper gentleman. Where the duck lake is, we cut back to Four Posts through the cemetery, which Felix was quite insistent about and went past a tall railed-off monument that didn't seem as a surprise to Felix when we found out it belonged to General Rosas. As with most things, I'd not known they'd put him there, until now. Because you never know where you are with people and things, and what you pin your hopes to, until you get to now. And you never know how now is going to turn out.

Visit 5, Milbeya

Next to its "Gossip of Men and Things," the Hampshire County Advertiser *usually gave us a column on the Southampton Police Courts as an extension, we must presume, of the gossip furnished in its previous column. Among ever-present remonstrances against dreadful noise and breaches of peace, the column reported, in "Lascars Drink too Much," of a coal porter on the P&O steamer* Victoria *who, with two others, had been found flourishing sticks outside the Southampton Yacht Club.*[50] *Through an interpreter, the charges were explained, to which the defendant replied that he had not killed any man, and was informed that the charge was not for that but flourishing his stick to the danger of the public. He was charged 5s with 5s 6d costs or seven days, for which a gentleman from the company attended and paid the penalty. Also appearing were two others who had been charged with the same offence, whom the court took to be both fellow lascars, one giving his name as Milbeya Maelbrook, a coloured seaman of the same vessel, who when asked if he understood English said "No," but that he was sorry and would go on board, with his brother, also bearing the same name, Milbeya Maelbrook. A book was found in the possession of the third man, who had otherwise remained silent, and it was questioned whether the book being in English had been stolen from any of the city's suppliers. Supt. Parker was able to confirm that none of the city's book traders had reported theft of just such a title, to which the court determined no further proceedings, turning its attentions instead to a Mr. Joseph Thomas Wren, described as an advertising agent, who was charged with stealing books from the bookstall at*

Docks Railway Station, whom the manager of Smith and Son's, Mr. Thomas Palmer had apprehended.

You ask distinctly why one of the many sons of Mundele N'dom wishes to enter a bookshop? I do not steal or kill, and I know my catechisms, and that the first people were not let down by rope from the skies but were put in Eden by God, so why would I not like your books that we call mukanda. Truth be told I am somewhat tired of books, from turning catechisms and hymns and school books from the cylinder press we set in motion at Pantops. I have skills and like all letterpress men I have a gift to travel but no press will employ a black man where there are white, or where there are boiler rooms that white men do not like to be in. So like Lukusa, who was the first, I professed my faith in Christ and the Reverend William Henry Sheppard, known to us as Mundele N'dom, the black whiteman, welcomed me into the presence of angels.[51] We were in our hundreds, more like thousands of Sunday school pupils and workers and students, and I went throughout the country on the Kasai river preaching twice a day. And afterwards I took work on the letterpress.

We loved Reverend Sheppard. His bronze skin was as dark as mine, and he was tall and powerful and always laughing, with always a wink for the ladies. He alone spoke our BaKuba, and lived in our villages. When my village had famine, he killed two Hippopotami with his rifle, which is why I came to him, and he played his banjo and rode a bicycle in Bakuba land! There is no better proof of God existing than a bicycle along the Kasai. In the beginning, our capital, Mushenge, was free of the King Leopold's *Compagnie du Kasai*. But they came and stopped us so we could hardly think, with their Français and Nederlands and English, and Reverend Sheppard tried hard against them. But Mr Dunlop's invention had to have rubber and we had rubber in the vines of our forest. There were so many vines. As the *compagnie* soldiers told us, the native does not like making rubber and must be compelled to gather it, so I left, because I liked keeping my right hand and my right hand wanted to be kept.[52] I've been to Washington and to the West Indies, and Germany and the countries around Liberia.⁵³ I have been to Belfast where Frederick Douglass had spoken, and Boston where, if they could be found, I was fond of reading the *Colored American Magazine*, or a paper like *Lux* where Celestine Edwards protests so well about Uganda.⁵⁴

My brothers from the ship are not versed in reading and are now impatient for drink. They are also nervous. They are peaceable enough but it is not unthinkable that trouble may find them despite their precautions, which is why their talk about sticks and being ready will only shorten the time for their trouble to arrive. We looked for the city's centre and a man told us to go towards the golden pineapple flying above the church of All Saints. I have been in Guiana in Georgetown where Indian and African work together, after a fashion. I know what the pineapple is for a sign, so I read it for them and they were amazed to see Southampton make such a gesture. Clearly, such a welcoming city cannot be anything but eager to meet it latest guests, so they are calmer and we have arranged to meet this evening. And I will keep faith with this arrangement. To locals of this city, we are of the same kind, whether lascar or Kubu, and they do not see our difference between Christian and Hindi. So to make the white man's life less burdensome, we are decided to be all called Milbeya by name, or sometimes 'Dick' in honour of the name they gave Lukusa, and we will be of a kind together where they can easily find us with our sticks.

What I will buy if my funds allow is a Gartenzwerge that Hamburg stokers buy for their mothers, or as English call them garden gnomes, which like the bicycles and silver sixpences they cherish will remind me of the other amulets of white men. I would like to go to variety. I would like to go to St Mary's Drill Hall and see their mad pastimes that St Mary blesses: contests, contests, contests; the grand onion eating contest, mouth organ contest, comic singing contest, and I want to see the contest for lady or gentleman making the funniest face looking through a horse collar contest. I want to see De Ora the gymnast; the climbing the pole contest; the grand smoking competition. I want to dance and I want to see all of it holding the hands of the prettiest girls in this city.

All I need for my ticket is my coin sign. The advertisement says 1d. It is the same sign on my coin and on their ticket, and the two only have to be exchanged. And woe betide the man who does not respect the sign because all of England's soldiery and God Almighty himself will come down on the man who does not respect it—we are told. I am the bearer of the coin sign and I am promised on demand one admission ticket. And I will sit next to the prettiest girls.

If you want to know about the thinness of promises, you must talk to a great poet. Canga, do ki la! Canga, li! Nearby there is a monument to your poet Tennyson, but I will not be able to get to the island. I should instead go to Winkle Street, to the offices of the Royal Mail Steam Packet Company to find hire. They contract to take mail to the West Indies and have five paddle steamers of wood that each need a good coal man, and may pay me better. They have Southampton Northam crews but crews who are not fond of yellow fever, which my brothers do not need to know until we are passed the Azores.

Canga li! If my coins cannot buy me the admission I want, then they will have to buy me what the powerful men allow me. The great Tennyson may be waiting for me in a box of second hand. I have read of him in the Frederick Douglass paper, where I read my Charles Dickens. Cannon to the right of them, canon to the left. They say he has stolen 'Canga li' from Congo Nogo to make the sound of his canon. 'Canga li!' is not from Congo Nogo.[55] But there are cannons, and bicycles and sixpences nonetheless. Tennyson said the wind on his island was so good that it was sixpence a pint. Only a poet knows you cannot sell the wind, unless another wind has been polluted. Only a poet knows how to make such a joke.[56]

In Pantops I used to give one tenth of my share to Jesus, and now that tenth will go to Mr Gilbert of this shop for his Tennyson. The poet is hiding somewhere among the shelves and boxes. And I am not the only explorer here. Like Mr Stanley whose body they carried up this High Street, I am an explorer in search of rubber among the vines—and I am not the only hunter because, at this shop's counter, there is another whose skin is not white, and he dares to have the whole world in his hands. Now that is a wonder! Adams and Black, an Atlas of the World. I have seen the book before and marvelled at it like any letterpress man. But the wonder, too, is the beautiful trim hands of this eastern man and his speaking so smooth like grasses moving, but they are not seeing in him a snake who's going to take their money and run. A letter of Introduction from the Oxford and Cambridge Club of Pall Mall! Ha! It's a promise to pay as good as any coin (depending on your skin), and I would say they fall like a cut vine.

Now if they knew how to play tricks well, Mr Gilbert would double the price he's charging and then sell the man's letter of credit to another man of business. The snake would agree to pay back to the second business man, but the paying back will never happen. Because Mr Gilbert has got twice his money for the Atlas, and then the second business man does the same as Mr Gilbert, and sells the credit letter to a third businessman for even more coin, and so on until the whole thing has gone mad, and the Atlas of the world has been sold and everybody owing everybody in the future, and the snake is laughing as well he might because he never wanted an Atlas in the first. Madness, madness; the coin contest; the great onion competition!

So I stick to my poets and look for Tennyson. And he is waiting for me, in fine green cloth but without his jacket, like a brush porcupine sleeping, trying to look like he's some sticks that I don't see him, but I see him, and I take him up and I read on the cover: *The Death of Œnone, Akbar's Dream and Other Poems*.[57] Akbar of the Vindhya mountains far away from the coast where not even my lascar brothers have been: "Love is the net of Truth, Love is the noose of God," said Abu Sa'id. Canga li! 'When creed and races shall bear false witness no more, and find their limits only as the silent alphabet of heaven in man.' I can read the signs as they stand, but they can stand for something else if we choose it to be, together. It is only an alphabet that we spend. The signs are not cast in stone.

PART FOUR

Theory, Methods, Tactics, and Politics, 2.0

Chapter 10

Reading Entertainment and the Construction of Economic Reality

Readers spend time and money on obtaining and reading books, but do they do this merely for entertainment. The correlation between consumption and reading may well draw in entertainment, but unless the observation remains shallow it is necessary to ask whether, thickly described, that entertainment might not mask something deeper. According to neoclassical economic principles, purchasers will look to maximize their gains (as suppliers will maximize theirs), so there must be strategies that readers employ to maximize gains from their entertainment and that might make its impact more than superficial. If we park for a moment the idea that a text's value resides intrinsically with its meaning, and set off instead with textual value as something created in the reading experience, it then becomes feasible to suggest that framing strategies could be one way of maximizing readerly returns. Suitably framed, the material "book" might be made to give up its treasures, and its forms made to effect a change for the reader, in a bespoke sense. But before that claim can be offered, it is necessary to follow a number of intermediate steps, including consumption, identity formation, and the social dimensions of both, alongside what this means for the book as entertainment; and, in the next chapter, how both might be thought of as an event, once we've resolved whether data on readers in commodity culture in the twenty-first century might usefully tell us something about readers in the same cultural formation in the nineteenth.

It has long been recognized that the "consumption" of intangible goods plays an important role in identity formation, a process that in commodity culture must necessarily be conducted through a trade in tangible market commodities.[1] The recognition is itself, partly, a reaction to "the totalising claims of the critical or neo-Marxist approach to consumption that has stressed the manipulative, ideological nature of consumer capitalism (for example, Horkheimer and Adorno 1944; Marcuse 1964)" and, partly, an insistence by new material culture studies and new anthropologies of consumption to keep sight of the material (purchased) object.[2] Accordingly, as economist Wilfred Dolfsma put it in *Consuming Symbolic Goods*, the link between object and identity is so emphatic that "symbolic goods may be *defined* as goods that people buy to signal their identity with" (my italics).[3]

When measuring that behavior, Dolfsma shows that consumption is fickle and, to the frustration of institutionalized economics, the role of price appears to be an important but far-from-decisive measure of the decision-making of purchasers. Other factors come into play along the borders of the individual's relationship to society; they can be grouped into the two main areas of how goods constitute identity and how they enable purchasers to communicate the commitments and identities they may have taken on. More often than not, and as the articles in *Consuming Symbolic Goods* confirm, analyses of these constitutions and commitments revolve around social, political contextualization—on how society affects and shapes the decisions of purchasers as well as on the capacity of consumers to resist that determination; and, in a reverse movement, on how their consumption affects and shapes society.

Unfortunately, far less focus is given by economists or, ironically, by the marketing research wings of business schools, to the act of consumption itself, which becomes fraught when we open up the term to its constituents of purchase and use and find an array of consumption experiences that are well fitted to neither, suggesting that the very term "consumption" may be unhelpfully structuring the debate. Following the cognitive linguistics of Lakoff and Johnson, Richard Wilk has looked at the primary metaphors governing "consumption" and found it in the "fire" and "eating" that consumes unto nothing or waste—presenting the types of engagement by which objects are used up or excreted.[4] But there are other ways of engaging with items that are objects of economic exchange, and, in a workshop led by Wilk, alternative metaphors were proposed that included consumption as sharing, or as networking, or as the sourcing of care resources.[5] This linguistic structuring has led David Graeber, under the heading of consumer culture theory, to propose that we stop thinking about consumption as a fixed analytical term and start thinking of it as something constructed by an ideological modernity.[6]

In an economy trading in symbols such as the book market, intangible goods are not exhausted by consumption in the manner of soft goods. Like service goods or experience goods, a material object or activity is required to deliver the service or experience, and thus facilitate exchange. Even when the sign is no more than a mouthful of air—to use Anthony Burgess's useful description of spoken words—it still needs its material to become a semiotic event from which decoding can then take place. But the good that the sign allows us to experience is never really "consumed." Consumption becomes, rather, a process of semiotics where the "consumer" engages with referent systems of codification, and where a decoding of a material sign is absolutely necessary. Furthermore, since the item's symbolic value is not intrinsic to the object but created by the reader, whatever "consumption" there is will vary unpredictably from purchaser to purchaser and user to user—sometimes in highly discrepant ways. For the purposes of this study, therefore, this "consumption," or decoding of a material sign for the purpose of gaining intangible goods, is called "reading." More specifically, following Deirdre McCloskey, this reading that takes away its intangible goods, and which is derived in counter-distinction to Kantian autonomous aesthetic reading, is an efferent reading (from *effero*: I take away).[7]

We must read to unpack symbolic value from our traded commodities, but it is not commodity culture that *obliges* us to do the unpacking—quite the reverse, in that the unpacking *creates* the culture. The social formation we live in might almost be defined by the semiotic processing of symbolic goods, facilitated by the commodified exchange of sign materials. As such, it is a formation that depends for its very existence on efferent readers, leaving our culture, commodity culture, not only in need of but *created by* efferent readers.

Walter R. Fisher coined the term *homo narrans* to describe a uniquely human trait of engaging in storytelling as a means to bring coherence to chaos.[8] The term was designed to address issues of human cognition, and to posit narration as a continuous meaning-making act. Through narrative and the understanding of it, people are able to meaningfully order experience, and thus the making and reading of narrative turns experienced phenomena into what we understand to be reality. But what happens when the narrated reality itself is dependent on commodity narratives, and when *the* distinguishing feature of the cultural order itself is a result of efferent reading? When the perceived "truth" of our society is that its members' identities are created through efferent reading of symbolic goods, then our society becomes doubly read: twice constructed through the reading of its social constitution and of the necessary consumption processes sustaining it. The study of the efferent reading of books, therefore, toward which this work makes a tentative start, is not merely a way of gauging the nonprofessional experience of published fiction, but is paradigmatic to the interpretation and reproduction of our culture. *Homo narrans* describes the narrative construction of reality, but when extended to describe our lives in commodity culture it becomes the more informative twin of *homo economicus*. It is *homo narrans* who constructs the reality of the symbolic economy, in a way that economic explanations based on *homo economicus* never can.

There is a point of finesse, however, in that we must be sure that reading can avail itself to social exchange, before any reading of symbols can potentially be described as an economy, rather than being merely an isolated act. One isolated reader of symbols may do something consumption-like, but unless there are grounds for believing such reading depends on and affects other people, then it would be exceptionally difficult to see how that praxis might take part in exchange or help constitute an economy. To be fully capable of engaging in exchange, and in contrast to the methodological individualism dervived from a linear self-seeking masculine *homo economicus*, we need to show that the networked intertextual feminine *homo narrans* is indeed fundamentally social, which very much needs to include her private, silent reading.

As Karin Littau has demonstrated, the body we read with is always situated.[9] The reading *space* may be private but its placement is always somewhere, part of a larger community. Edith Wharton preferred her reading in a library uncluttered by excessive furniture, free of knick-knacks and photographs, giving the reader-worker uninhibited access to the text—and on no account should there be books in a busy vestibule or domestic hall. Henry Miller, liking writers who recognised dung for dung and angels for angels, believed great works could only be truly enjoyed on the toilet—Rabelais, for example, on a plain country toilet with no push buttons, no chain, and no pink toilet paper.[10] So in addition to all the people engaged in the bookmaking professions for the benefit of Edith and Henry, both spaces also needed plumbers, builders, plasterers and glaziers, as well as institutions providing capital finance, local municipalities providing water, and bodies of people enforcing laws and maintaining the peace. Even for the most isolated reading, like that of Nelson Mandela on Robben Island, or Arthur Koestler in *Dialogue with Death*, prison reading dreams of society, and is especially defined by the society from which it is removed.[11] Even the Self constituted through memory, as Paul Ricoeur has it, is in part collective memory as it "enacts and re-enacts networks of relations among individuals and the communities to which they belong."[12]

The life story, too, the most individualistic of genres, is endlessly social. Charlotte Linde, in *Life Stories: The Creation of Coherence*, argues that life stories are a means to a sense of self, of who we are and how we came to be that way. She describes the individual's life story as discontinuous, consisting of endlessly reformulated stories in which old and new meanings are continually regenerated into coherence. These individualistic narratives, she recognizes, draw on what Theodore Sarbin describes as a narrative-saturated world, each embodying a variant cultural value and providing us with a "library of plots . . . that help us interpret our own and other people's experience."[13] It is from the collective library that we access and exchange the stories by which we create ourselves, not *into* social beings, but because we *are* social beings.[14]

The notion of reading as social exchange has a venerable history within reception studies, as Ika Willis puts it citing William Johnson, that understands reading as a complex sociocultural system "in which cognitive processes, interpretative and affective norms, bodily practices, and writing and reading technologies are bound up together in practices of reception."[15] When commodified, the process may require a visit to Gilbert's for the material books that facilitate exchange, but its economy arises not out of the price-based exchange rationalized by *homo economicus*, but out of intertextual values created by social *homo narrans*.

Science fiction writer Robert Heinlein claimed that "the process of trying to see ourselves through the eyes of others helps shape our social identities, i.e., our social selves."[16] This aspect of Self being won through other's perceptions is most succinctly modeled in Edward Higgins's self-discrepancy theory. Self-discrepancy theory, which has been covered more fully in chapter 1, works with three different categories of Self: "actual," "ideal," and "ought" (what one believes oneself to be, what one would like to be, and what one believes one should be), but which importantly are mirrored in the perception of how others see you (your imaginings about what "they" believe you are, what "they" think you'd like to be, and what "they" believe you should be). In this crowded six-point model, where social perceptions are integral, any gaps in coherency between selves means discrepancy, which in turn requires remedy. In introducing the need for remedy through gain, self-discrepancy theory suggests a way of modeling commodity culture—though never made explicit in Higgins's writings. If identity formation depends on the (consumption) reading of symbolic goods, the means to reform identity is through more reading. Reading for one's discrepant identity, therefore, would become a process that oscillates between healing and self-justification while imagining that others are watching.

As noted in chapter 1, whether turning to the postmodernism of Jean Baudrillard or the anthropology of cultural economy of Arjun Appadurai, it is agreed that material commodities "signify our lives, loves, desires, successes and failings, both to others and ourselves. . . . They derive their importance, in part at least, from their symbolic role in mediating and communicating personal, social and cultural meaning."[17] The commodity's value, in the economy of symbolic goods, is performed to ourselves and others in combination, so what the efferent reader retrieves from the signifying commodity is already saturated in society. If socialized identity drives the consumption of symbolic goods, it drives efferent reading, too—the latter being a specific mode by which goods may be "taken" from symbolic material. But importantly, that efferent reading cannot be other than social. Sustained by the services of others, and fed with their stories and desires, this praxis begins to look very much like an economy. The conventional explanation for the commodity economy offered through methodological individualism is that it is the individual equipped with self-interest who goes to market and, from an aggregate of self-interests, that the market is constructed. Its recommendation, therefore, is that we must each pursue self-interest. In the consumption of symbolic goods, however, both the Self and the values that many Selves create are already part of or a result of the market's social circulation. What, then, might be a suitable recommendation—that its society is something to be nurtured?

"Entertainment" is a term as slippery as it is value laden. An event that is merely entertaining is often considered something less than one that expands the mind, for example. Northrop Frye goes to great pains not to completely separate literature from entertainment, but he does include it in a valorized bipartite system. Reacting to the suggestion that literature must distinguish itself from entertainment, Frye responds that the separation is dangerous: "if literature ever lost its connection with entertainment then it would have 'had it' as literature."[18] The move saves entertainment, but only by trapping it as a necessary poor cousin to more enlightening processes. In Frye's optic, books that are *only* entertaining do not become literature. The point would be un-troubling—since this study does not address how literature fashions its self-distinction—were it not for a good deal of evidence that suggests entertainment is precisely the reason why people buy all sorts of books, including those by very good authors. Rather than moving to append entertainment to some greater cause, would it not be possible to remain with the term and see whether an entertainment were capable of providing symbolic goods from which the reader might, as per Dolfsma,[19] constitute identities and communicate commitments, in which case consuming entertainment would not be a superficial activity.

When entertainment is opened up to research, the often-made claim is that entertainment centers on enjoyment and that enjoyment is a matter of pleasure—or, in a more precise formulation, scholarship centers on the "satisfaction of traditional hedonic needs in research defining entertainment enjoyment."[20] Pleasure in this sense is thought of as hedonism or purely hedonic enjoyment. Unsurprisingly, as the summative material puts it,

> the notion of enjoyment as need satisfaction is not novel. Indeed, research on mood management (Zillmann & Bryant, 1985), disposition theory (Zillmann & Cantor, 1976), uses and gratifications (U&G: Katz, Blumler, & Gurevitch, 1974), and sensitivity theory (Reiss & Wiltz, 2004) has either implicitly or explicitly defined enjoyment as such. In general, these approaches define enjoyment as a pleasurable response to entertainment media.[21]

The trouble seen by Tamborini et al. is that these hedonic needs by whatever name are always treated as a positive, interchangeably called "joy," "appeal," "liking," "positive mood," or "pleasure." Consequently, in the experience of what is called "negatively valanced media," none of these terms, however generously interpreted, can quite predict why people should "enjoy" seemingly abhorrent entertainment such as tragedy and horror. Though "pleasure" may be strangely in contention, it is hard to claim that "joy" could be the precise term to cover experiencing, say, a fictionalized horrific crime. Tamborini et al. argue that the impasse is explained partly because of the limitations of the vocabulary, but more so because enjoyment is treated as serving *only* "hedonically rooted functional needs, implicating humans as mere pleasure seekers."[22] In the model Tamborini and his colleagues propose, enjoyment can involve the satisfaction of more complex higher-order needs in a viewer who is much more than a hedonistic pleasure seeker. Enjoyment of media entertainment still satisfies needs, but the suggestion is those needs are higher to an extent that pleasure and its synonyms can no longer capture. Though Tamborini does not write so, it is tempting to think of affirmation, challenge, acknowledgment, or guidance as acceptable forms of enjoyment. Like the upper ends of Maslow's hierarchy, such non-hedonic needs include the need for esteem, social belonging, and self-actualization, which in Tamborini's terms become "competence," "relatedness," and "autonomy." The enjoyment of entertainment then becomes the satisfaction of "a cluster of connected needs" from simple pleasures to the shocks of new self-conception.[23]

Peter Vorderer and Franziska Roth tackle the same problem with a slightly different solution. Rather than arguing for depth in people's responses to items that are merely entertainments, they argue for entertainment as a suitably in-depth response to literature (not that the two were ever disparate), and thus pose the title question, "How do we entertain ourselves with literary texts?" Their suspicion is that absorptive reading in which readers identify too strongly with characters and are carried away with their amusement in the narrative may not maintain the standards of an autonomous aesthetic judgement, but it may also be "what the majority of readers experience—entertainment through reading."[24] Recognizing that literary theory has moved well beyond text-centered analysis in *Rezeptionsästhetik* (think how well used is the work of Iser and Jauss in class), they are concerned nevertheless to uncover what readers "do with" their texts when the answer is to entertain themselves.

Given the political conditions of the west in the 1970s, media and culture studies understandably chose to examine their metonym for entertainment in mass media as an agent of persuasion rather than as an agent of enjoyment, and since the 1970s largely have had little to say about the mechanisms of being entertained. An "entertainment" was a designation for a particular piece of cultural production, most usually ones seeking covert political effects, rather than a mode by which an audience experiences—as it later became through theorists such as Percy Tannenbaum and Dolf Zillmann, and their colleagues Jennings Bryant and Joanne Cantor, to name early movers.[25] Similar to the position of Tamborini et al., since both emerge from the same research field, Vorderer and Roth describe how early theorization of entertainment-as-experience operated with the assumption of a positive mood as a central component, and researched how readers hedonically attempt to "create a pleasurable experiential state . . . [and thus] use various media products to achieve this goal," so that based on this pleasure principle, it seemed perverse to study "the entertaining effects of canon literature."[26] The complexity of literature's textual structures left early theorists squeamish about considering it an appropriate vehicle by which audiences could achieve hedonic pleasure.

Un-squeamishly, it is precisely the role of literature as entertainment that should be the focus of studies concerned with the nonprofessional reader, provided the term "entertainment" is not simply a pejorative but a description equitable to the experiences of people who are entertained. In Clifford Geertz's interpretive theory of culture, thick description was proposed as a means to analyze signs for their significance held by the people who used them. It meant that thick

> descriptions of Berber, Jewish, French culture must be cast in terms of the constructions we imagine Berbers, Jews, or Frenchmen to place upon what they live through, the formulae they use to define what happens to them. What it does not mean is that such descriptions are themselves Berber, Jewish, or French—that is, part of the reality they are ostensibly describing; they are anthropological—that is part of a developing system of scientific analysis.[27]

In their effort to develop a system of scientific analysis that understands entertainment gained through interaction with literary texts, Vorderer and Roth construct what in effect is a thick description. They imagine a set of effects, which they call appreciation. They set limits, define contours, and even suggest an operation of literary interpretation by which some of this appreciation is achieved. Pointing to transportation theory, they describe how, in their literary entertainments, readers may cognitively and emotionally strive to be transported to an alternate narrative world that exists only in fiction.[28] Because of this transport, readers are then able to undertake affective dispositions and satisfy whatever higher-order needs they can, including feelings of autonomy over the choice of text, competence in not being alienated by the text, and feelings of being related to other media users and characters.

Compared to pure hedonic pleasure, such an appreciative operation "involves a more deliberative, interpretative and self-reflected consideration of events presented in the narrative"—a claim they support with reference to the work of Oliver and Bartsch.[29] Their imaginings lack empirical evidence, which they suggest should be the next stage. They worry, too, about whether appreciation is an extension of enjoyment or a complement to it. For the current study, however, the requirement is not to resolve a hierarchy of needs but simply to render plausible the proposition that enjoyment of a not-merely-hedonic kind is part of a more complex entertainment experience. Because, most importantly, when read-literature is framed in the language of supply and demand, any operation beyond brute stimuli-response that comprises more deliberative, interpretative, and self-reflective consideration represents a strategy to maximize returns on entertainment investment. As Vorderer and Roth state of contending appreciation and enjoyment, and of their equal validity, "in both cases the readers use literary texts as they please, i.e., to their full advantage"; or, as Fuller and Sedo confirm, "readers engage in the various practices that are available to them and will create their own when necessary."[30] According to neoclassical economic thought, the presence of such utility maximization is a matter of course.

So what might readers be doing in their reading experiences? A number of proposals have been put forward recently in the anthology *Plotting the Reading Experience* that aim by discursive and empirical means to disclose from the experience a "heterogeneity of its functions, qualities, uses, and pleasures."[31] Initially defining the reading experience as an individual's act of sensuous cognition, in the tradition of philosophical aesthetics inaugurated with Baumgarten, the volume then explores reading as a sociocultural practice happening in time-space, where "stories shape and are shaped in the process of interactions with others."[32] Of those experiences more oriented to socialities between other media users, narrators and characters, Mariane Børsch describes a masculinist "patricidal" reading that attempts to beat the father-author, and compares that with another type of reading in which the writer and reader are alone, but intimately alone with each other, in a reading she describes as making love. This sense of a shared pleasure is given a healing twist in "More Benefit from a Well-Stocked Library than a Well-Stocked Pharmacy," in which Liz Brewster describes users' benefits from "bibliotherapy." Updating Janice Radway's seminal work on reading the romance, Cecile Naper considers the reception of a new type of bestseller social melodrama from around 2005 onward (including titles such as *The Island* [2005], *The Help* [2009], and *The Hotel on the Corner of Bitter and Sweet* [2009]). Naper shows how the target-audience's reception developed from what had previously been the domestic reassurance that truly "loving couples support each other so that both partners can live their lives as free human beings unencumbered by traditional gender roles" to become a reception in which, in these later melodramas, a more active participation is urged in gender-based struggles for freedom, equality, and justice.[33] In Mette Steenberg's study of "shared reading," texts are read aloud to a group, and then group members are encouraged to share responses and make open-ended reflections. Their shared reading for pleasure is taken "seriously and lifts personal and non-expressed responses to the literary text into a collective setting of shared reflections."[34] The socializing processes or social coordination that can occur in and, more especially, after such live *in situ* readings, enables Steenberg to call such reading a social technology. And lastly, in "Fun . . . and Other Reasons for Sharing Reading with Strangers," Danielle Fuller and DeNel Sedo examine a form of entertainment called mass reading events (MREs) to which readers are attracted by a combination of social, emotional, intellectual, and aesthetic pleasures. The events are huge public occasions but, when digital modalities open up narratives to becoming a shared social practice, they also produce "moments of intimacy, affect, and belonging for readers for whom having fun with a bunch of strangers is all part of the desire to go beyond the book."[35]

In a parallel move to ascertain readers' experiences, and working with text world theory, as well as with a stylistics and literary-linguistics strand to cognitive poetics, Sara Whiteley conducted a survey of what a small group of readers did with Kazuo Ishiguro's novel *Remains of the Day*. Whiteley's establishing thesis is that, during literary narrative discourse, "readers are thought to 'take a cognitive stance within the world of the narrative and interpret the text from that perspective.' "[36] Too crudely put here, this expresses the idea of psychological projection, where the reader of the discourse world of the book constructs their interpretation through the viewpoint(s) of a text-world character or addressee in the narrative, imaginatively taking part in the values and emotions being negotiated in the story. As an example, Whiteley cites Stockwell's work on Kipling's poem "If," which ascribes qualities such as tenacity and courage to an unspecified "you."[37] Readers responding positively to the poem tend to assume the role of "you," according to Stockwell, projecting and constructing similarities between themselves in the discourse world and the second-person addressee from the world of the text.

Whiteley asked three women readers, between twenty-four and twenty-five years of age, to discuss their readings of Ishiguro's novel. Focusing on the doomed romance between narrator Stevens and Miss Kenton, Whiteley found that their evaluations of the "truth" of the romance were derived from their projections onto either the position occupied by Stevens's narratee, or onto the figure of Miss Kenton, who functions as a frustrated focalizer (my use of the term) for the narrating protagonist Stevens. Stevens's inability to love Miss Kenton is brought to the startling fore when Stevens fails to react as Miss Kenton tells him of her plans to marry someone else. To decide which character is most afraid of being loved, the study's "participants seem collaboratively to be remembering and reconstructing the scene" in terms that are their own and not the novel's: "A: I felt . . . she wanted him to say 'marry me,' like 'here you are on a plate' and she doesn't go far enough because he won't step forward at all, then when she comes back and says 'I've accepted it' [the other man's offer of marraige] and he just says 'Oh congratulations' . . . ."[38] Their projection is made doubly fluid by the dramatic irony Ishiguro exploits in Stevens's unreliable narration, which creates uncertainty to what might be the emotional "truth" of that character's experience. Though Whiteley's target is to establish that projection can occur across multiple characters in a complexly layered literary text, the importance for the current study lies in what is being done with the text. Ishiguro's emotionally charged fictional encounter provides a service by which Whiteley's readers can reassess or confirm their own commitments to what should and should not be done for love.

David Lodge has claimed that "We read fiction, after all, not just for the story, but to enlarge our knowledge and understanding of the world."[39] But if by this he means a purely instrumental epistemological project, uncoupled from affective desires, then the evidence points elsewhere. Any systematizing of potential gains from an empirical evidence base requires a larger sample than Whiteley's three participants. Unfortunately (and ascribing a certain territorialism to academy disciplines), the idea of using empirical survey data to study literature is still relatively uncommon—the exceptions being research on reading groups, and the reception elements in many specific big-data projects from the digital humanities; in fields such as psychonarratology and some areas of cognitive poetics; and in large database projects such as, in the UK, the Reading Experience Database (with an extensive list of further resources) or, in the US, What Middletown Read—with organizational representation through societies such as SHARP (Society for the History of Authorship, Reading and Publishing) and IGEL (Internationale Gesellschaft für Empirische Literaturwissenschaft).[40]

Surveys that are relevant to the current study and that begin by canvassing the individual reader are not abundant.[41] The extensive Book Marketing Ltd. (BML) UK survey in the year 2000 questioned approximately 2000 respondents in its *Reading the Situation: Book Reading, Buying and Borrowing Habits in Britain*. This survey found that 52% of adult readers read books as a way to relax or relieve stress, and furthermore that readers found the effort of reading (for 24% of adult readers, reading was an opportunity to exercise the imagination) combined with the relaxation to form an experience distinct from the more passive absorption of watching TV or listening to music.[42] The BML study, however, was aimed at all reading (fiction and nonfiction in books but also reference and other genres in magazines and newspapers) and was driven by a pressing need to argue for the importance of libraries. It found that library lending and book buying were not competing but complementary activities, each satisfying different needs. But it is precisely the particularities of the experience of retailed fiction that is currently required.

A second survey worth noting is the Swedish, Uppsala-based Reading Fiction in the Internet Society project, in which seventy-two high-school/sixth-form college students were asked why they read fiction.[43] Overwhelmingly, they read for entertainment, or, rather, for a sense of losing oneself in fiction. Of the ten questions put to them, students firmly gravitated toward "För att få vila och avkoppling; För att uppleva verklighetsflykt; För att bli road och underhållen" (To get rest and relaxation; to experience a break from reality; to be amused and entertained) and to some extent "För att uppleva spänning och skräck" (To experience excitement and terror).

A further example comes from a relatively small-scale but rigorous survey of the outputs from reading (or "yield": *læseudbytte*), from the Nordic region. Project SKRIN, Skriftkultur og Mediebrug i Nordiske Familier (Nordic Family Reading Culture and Media Use) was a research survey of social and psychological aspects to text-media and, specifically, book use in Norway, Sweden, Denmark and, partly, Iceland, undertaken in pre-digital days from 1987 to 1989. As a joint psychology and library-science project, and concerned about the future of the book, the research attempted to assess the quality of leisure-time reading, and especially of children's reading culture, faced with a rise in audiovisual cultural products. Their opening position was to recognize the non-prescriptive differences "in people's expectations to and yield from their reading, including differences in stages of life and generational difference that can be drawn across both individual and historical developmental lines."[44] Children of eleven years old, together with both parents and at least two grandparents, were interviewed for their reading practices, including attitudes to, beliefs about (*holdninger*), and subjective gains from the books they read. Questions about their motives for reading and habitual practice, about the changes to those in their personal histories, and about memories of specific titles they had read were deemed central.

In the research's terms, both utility reading to gain knowledge and reading for pleasure produced a yield, which was gained only by a concrete reader with a concrete text. Furthermore, reader, text, and reader-experience were not considered static, but mutually constituted, thus providing a transactionist methodology, after Louise Rosenblatt's conception, in which every reading experience derived from a unique relation between reader and text producing a unique event.[45] Although the research does not use the terms, its choice of the Nordic nuclear family was a deliberate strategy to produce a normative "cis"-history, or ethnography, of sociopsychological attitudes towards books, in terms of needs and satisfactions.

In achieving its yields, the reading experience was categorized into four transactions or approaches that the reader can have with a text—"impersonal" versus "personal," and "experiential" versus "instrumental"—and which, from the interview evidence, often overlapped and occasionally revealed causal relationships. The categories of "impersonal" and "personal" attempted to capture the degree to which the reader's self-identity takes part in the reading process, and "experiential" and "instrumental" the degree to which the experience was primarily a reading for pleasure or a longer-lasting instrumental benefit. Depending on how these four points were coupled, the experience could yield the following gains (see table 10.1).[46]

Table 10.1. Four transactions and their following gains.

	Experiential	Instrumental
Personal	Personal-experiential reading: Identification	Personal-instrumental reading: Self-reflection
Impersonal	Impersonal-experiential reading: Relaxation	Impersonal-instrumental reading: Information

Source: Bernstein and Larsen, *Læsnings Former*, 19. Author's translation.

All four modes of reading experience revealed traits in reading strategy: an impersonal-experiential reading delights in plot and the actions of people (including narrators) who are seen as substantially different from the reader's perceived self, and can be read quickly as "relaxation"; the personal-experiential mode relies primarily on the reader's self-identity for interpreting the text, which in concentrated form produces "identification" and thereafter motivations for social comparison; the impersonal-instrumental reading yields informational insights that can be transferred from the reader-text relation to relations the reader may have outside the text; and the personal-instrumental mode becomes a therapeutic approach that encourages self-reflection, providing comfort or distancing from the reader's experiential reality also outside the text. None of the four yield-positions deal with what the researchers regarded as the pivotal moment of a literary critical reading that is a disinterested aesthetic reading of the text.

Much could be said of the project's methodology that, within its own terms, remains tightly structured. But if its propositional hypotheses can be accepted, the results generated are informative (see table 10.2).[47] The experiential reading was dominant, compared to the instrumental (66% compared to 34%), suggesting that people do read mostly for affective

Table 10.2. Four yeild-positions and their results.

	Experiential	Instrumental
Personal	29% Identification	4% Self-reflection
Impersonal	37% Relaxation	30% Information

Source: Bernstein and Larsen, *Læsnings Former*, 146. Author's translation.

pleasure. The impersonal reading was likewise more frequent than the personal (67% compared to 33%), suggesting that readers are twice as likely to maintain a distance between self and text, compared to a personalized self-absorptive experience. For the highest instance of both impersonal and experiential reading, the goal was relaxation, which the researchers found was best sourced from generic fiction such as crime fiction and romance.

Of the effects produced from transactions with informational texts, chief among them was support for self-confidence and the ability to conduct oneself socially, in that the experience equipped the reader with arguments to support or modify the reader's own. Yields from personal-experiential reading—most readily achieved through realist narrative, the researchers noted—were a sense of genuine contact with other people in both the identification with lives from the narratives and revealingly in text-external social interaction, often coming from conversation about the text—a process that many of those surveyed recognized as being rooted in processes of socialization. Reading as an instrumental means to yield direct self-understanding was the least significant of the results, which is telling in itself: that was not a primary gain. However, there was a suggestion that it derives *ex post facto* from the other approaches, chiefly from the intensity of the personal-experiential reading, and is a form of second-order experience. If self-understanding is a yield from reading, which this study is inclined to accept, then it happens indirectly.

In terms of age difference, there was a low degree of personal reading of both its forms among children, compared to their intense preference for impersonal reading: 86% (53% of children exhibited impersonal-experiential yields, and 33% impersonal-instrumental). The explanation proffered by the researchers was that although children would very readily exhibit affective empathy for characters, they had not yet the reflexive skills to inscribe themselves intellectually into the narrated scenes. Grandparents, by comparison, had the largest instance of personal-experiential readings, compared to children and parents (approximately 38% of all grandparents surveyed), and were masters at experiencing themselves in the place of others.

For differences between the sexes, the results showed a marked ability among women, alongside grandparents, to achieve gains from the personal-experiential reading experience, 40% of all women's readings tending to follow this approach, but only 15% of all men's readings. By contrast, men most readily followed an impersonal-experiential mode: 45% of all men surveyed, but 30% of all women. Strikingly, men overwhelmingly tended toward impersonal readings, with 82% of men preferring this mode of reading, leaving just 18% who preferred a self-absorptive personal mode. The spread between impersonal and personal readings among women, on the other hand, was fairly small: 55% to 45% respectively.

For reasons behind the men's preference for impersonal-experiential and women's preference for personal-experiential approaches, the research comes up short. The study was written before gender was widely perceived to be performative, following work by Judith Butler, and so it is unfortunately dogged by elements of biological determinism. Second-wave feminist commentary from figures such as de Beauvoir is deployed to add nuance, but what it fails to ask explicitly is whether the choice of a nuclear family as a research parameter itself may have predetermined the differences in approach. Another environment, in which masculine and feminine behavior are differently distributed between women and men, would have produced different results.

There is small chance for such a concrete survey as SKRIN to resolve the local contextualizing conditions of the study into a generally applicable model. The frame to its research was the nuclear family, so it is uncertain that its results would be applicable to readers framed by commodity culture—indeed, family life in the remotest Nordic regions still has elements of subsistence culture and barter. Conditions in Britain and elsewhere in the global north, and indeed in the late nineteenth century when commodity culture was taking hold, would have been very different. Unlike in the late nineteenth century, the opportunity costs for twenty-first-century readers in developed countries are no longer financial but temporal, and cost is now measured in time. But in considering the outputs of Nordic readers' experience, it is possible to extract useful findings around yields. It may be that the publishing industry is already supplying the gains of "support to self-confidence" from informational reading. From impersonal-experiential reading, the industry may be supplying a delight in the exploits of others, while uncoupling the reader from the stresses of the everyday; and from the identifications of personal-experiential reading, that industry might supply social understanding, or rather social creation.

Undertaken at a time when the Nordic SKRIN survey was widely unknown outside of the region, a much larger UK-wide survey was conducted in autumn 2014, building on the Swedish survey, incorporating similar wording in its questionnaire, but intending this time to capture the commercial experience.[48] Surveying fifteen towns and cities across

England and Wales, this largely quantitative survey deliberately targeted high-street bookshops as a metonymic site for reading within commodity culture; its questionnaire was directed at people leaving the bookshop to find out what they hoped to gain from the books they had just purchased. The results were simple, perhaps banal, but nonetheless informative in establishing something empirically qualified about readers' desires.

From a target of 750 purchasers over 16 years of age, the corpus comprised 559 responders—not entirely representative of UK book-buying readers as a whole, because of an element of convenience in the sample. However, given overall population figures for persons aged 15 and over (46.6 million), it was calculated that the sample brought the survey to within ±4.14% margin of error at the 95% confidence level (i.e., that there is only one chance in twenty that the survey results are more than 4.14% different from overall reality). Given the compensatory elements—of randomization in choice of venue and the definitiveness of many of the results—we can feel reasonably confident in the survey's representation of gains expected from UK high-street books.

Of the sample (54.8% female, 43.3% male, and 1.8% preferring not to say), the largest group by age were aged 16–24 (30.0%), twice the size of the group aged 25–34 (15.4%). The smallest groups were aged 65–74 (7.8 %) and 75+ (3.1 %). The multiple-choice survey of expectations was divided into three sections: first, to establish what was bought and for whom (questions 1 and 2); second, to establish what gains readers believed they would obtain from fiction (questions 3A and 3B) and then from other genres (questions 4A and 4B); and third, questions about self-perception in relation to other readers (questions 3C–E and 4C–E); following these were simple questions 5–8 on buying habits and demographics.

About two thirds of purchases were made by the intended user ("myself": 65%) rather than on behalf of other adults or children (19% and 16% respectively). Of the eleven genre options (including the option "other"), the most purchased was fiction, at 60%, with biography and autobiography in second place at a mere 6%. From this, it can be inferred that customers believed their own gains were best supplied through fiction. Furthermore, approximately a third more self-declared female respondents than male ones said they expected gains from fiction (62.5% to 37.5%).

From survey question 3A, purchasers of fiction were then asked, "What do you hope you (or the receiver) will gain most from your fiction?" and were provided with twelve options (again including "other" to create scope for individualized answers).⁴⁹ Most scught from fiction was "amusement and entertainment" (28.8%), "relaxation" (18%), and an "escape into another world" (14.9%). These three gains were categorized together as forms of "entertainment," totaling 61.7%, but were deemed less corporally intense than experiences such as "emotional involvement" and "the thrill of suspense and/or terror," which both registered surprisingly low at 7.5% and 7.1% respectively (collectively 14.6%). Compared to the Danish SKRIN survey, "entertainment" reflected well on the high levels of impersonal-experiential experience for relaxation. But the indication of low levels of affective involvement stands in tension to the SKRIN survey's findings of 30% for an intense personal-experiential experience: an aspect frustrated by the UK and SKRIN terms not being directly comparable.

What was notable from the UK survey was the dearth of gains recognized more readily from the orbit of literary studies: "better self understanding" rated merely 2%, and "an improved understanding of the world" rated 3.1%. Reading for "an intellectual challenge" rated slightly better at 6.4%, but very few said they read for an aesthetic experience, at 2.4%. That few read directly for greater self-understanding accords well with the SKRIN survey's evidence. But whereas UK purchasers were fairly impervious to fiction providing an improved understanding of the *world*, the SKRIN results were quite different. Assuming a correlation (which may not be the case) between "understanding the world" and SKRIN's impersonal-instrumental reading, two factors can explain the anomaly. First, the UK survey did not canvass children, unlike SKRIN, which found that children had a high instance of impersonal-instrumental readings. Second, the UK survey's questions 4A and 4B asked about nonfiction where, relative to fiction, there was greater expectation "of the more instrumental gains of 'more information on the subject' (16.9%), 'self-improvement' (15.3%), and 'an intellectual challenge' (12%)"— though overall results still retained a strong element of "amusement and entertainment" (20.2%) and "relaxation" (8.2%) (totaling 28.4%).⁵⁰

From a further question about fiction, 3B, the UK survey then tried to ascertain which components of fiction were hoped would be most rewarding. From the options "Characters," "Plot," "Subject or Theme," "Mind of the Author," or "Other," the survey showed that "Plot" and "Character" promised highest returns (40.4% and 23.8%, totaling 64.2%). Clearly, implications need to be contextualized by the full survey, but the finding that the interest in plot and character combines with low levels of emotional involvement and with high levels of amusement, relaxation and escape—the latter corresponding to SKRIN's impersonal-experiential mode of relaxation—may suggest that readers' expectations of plot and character are more in the manner of an enjoyably cool anthropology, rather than an intense identification. Rather than imaginatively being involved with an event, the preference is to read about, and (it is suspected) pass judgment on, what the world does to people and what they do to each other.[51] The particular subject or theme is of secondary importance (21.2%) and may only provide a fictional world frame within which characters can collide—although this is only informed speculation. What is conclusive, however, is that understanding "the mind of the author," which limped in at 12.3%, is a feature to which purchasers maintained not only affective distance but, perhaps more correctly, indifference.

The 2014 High Street survey is a crude instrument at best, and objections to it are many. The questions are questionable, and the results simplistic—but they do serve an empirical purpose in asserting that, at the time of the survey, high-street purchasers across England and Wales looked primarily for gains of relaxation, escape, and amusement—something it seems reasonable to call "entertainment." When this is coupled to research on entertainment as something more than hedonic pleasure seeking, the suggestion is that something endemic and profound is occurring.

Cautiously, a list of possible gains from efferent reading can be proposed. For extreme fans, the immediate gains are easy to spot: Nancy Baym talks of epistemophilia in a knowledge community of fans where pleasure is taken in exchanging knowledge and not just in the having of it.[52] But for less determined readers, both the experiential and instrumental pleasures and pains of reading still need to be mapped. We may, as David Lodge claims, read because we wish to enlarge our understanding of the world, but more probably we want personal encouragement, relaxation, guidance, intellectual insight, a barrier against boredom, or remedies against loneliness. Claude Pichois wrote of books that "halfway between classical theatre (where "catharsis" purged passions) and psychoanalytic clinics, they offered inexpensive cures."[53] In a development of this idea of book-as-cure, the performance artist Marie Hauge Jensen created a work called *Hvis Nogen Kunne Se Min Ensomhed* (If Someone Could See My Loneliness) in which she telephoned 2000 strangers to ask what they felt about loneliness (partly in response to her own memories of teenage years, when she had longed for someone to call her and ask her opinion). Several respondents broadcast a new conversation with Jensen on national radio, including "Hannah," who described managing loneliness by reading fiction where she could "disappear from her surroundings and create pictures in her mind, to get away."[54] Indeed, the BBC produced a guide to books that might cure loneliness; answers from its bibliotherapist, Hephzibah Anderson, included Rebecca Solnit, *A Field Guide to Getting Lost* (2005); Anna Quindlen, *Still Life With Breadcrumbs* (2014); Anne Tyler, *Back When We Were Grownups* (2001); Jean Hanff Korelitz, *You Should Have Known* (2014); but also very much George Eliot, *Middlemarch* (1871–72).[55] Under the general title of "Textual Healing," therapist Anderson went on to suggest book remedies for further conditions such as the pain of grief, the fear of commitment, homesickness, and unhappy families.

In pinning down the goods from a truly globally branded author, Katie Halsey has identified some of the appeals readers find in Jane Austen. The primary mode of Austen's writing is ironic, encouraging readers to engage between the lines with what is *not* said and, thereby, as Katherine Mansfield says, encouraging every reader to believe she "has become the secret friend of their author."[56] Halsey contends that, in addition to intimate friendship, readers also gain from finding comfort in deserving characters being rewarded with happy marriages, while at the same time overcoming the hypocrisies of wealth and rank. This combination makes us "believe in the possibility of romance, even as she [Austen] ironises it."[57] In similar vein to Halsey's remarks on Austen, Frost (2012) has tried to identify the goods available through George Eliot, from *Middlemarch*.

We may read because we think we should, or because other people do and we want to belong. We might want to read about other people, to find out how they think and why. Narratives, especially the narratives of a realist novel, are well suited to finding out about other people and provide us with opportunity to opine about those we've fictionally met. We have an opportunity to judge people at a distance, or to be enticed into their warmth. As a younger reader, I used to think "I" in the poems of Baudelaire and Rimbaud was conspicuously cool. I admired the nerve of "I" who wrote the *Tropics of Capricorn* and *Cancer*. I thought understated Marlow was unflinchingly capable. Some years on, I changed my mind and thought Marlow ought to try something difficult, like raising a family. Henry Miller needed gender-awareness training and should try holding down a job. And all those characters and authorial voices, all that "characterization"—and who can think of fiction that doesn't involve characterization in some sense—fills the market with something that readers can identify with and against. Buying fiction is a way to access differing views of ourselves from our affections and disaffection for characters, narrators, and author-figures, and to renegotiate these affections through how we imagine others see us. They provide a measure, an instrument of socialization, if you will, by which to gauge what we've become.

In an echo of Martha Nussbaum, Neil Gaiman called literature an engine of empathy.[58] It enables not just an "I" but a "We" to imaginatively engage in socialization. And, like Martha Nussbaum, it is tempting to pitch that humanities-based socializing project as a remedy to the commercial society described by economics. In contrast to the economic rationalism represented in the character of Dickens's Mr. Gradgrind, Nussbaum proposes that "Literature expresses, in its structures and its ways of speaking, a sense of life that is incompatible" with Gradgrind's vision: traffic with literature is said to shape the imagination and desires in a manner incompatible with norms described by economic science.[59] But Nussbaum's position is difficult to maintain if we admit that entertainment, including the publication of fiction, is not only part of, but itself constitutes a segment of commercial life, and thus operates *because of* a culture of gains and losses about which economics erroneously holds a discursive monopoly. What if, instead, book circulation were itself considered an example of an "economy"—just one whose central figure unexpectedly was *homo narrans*? And what might that mean for any market driven by the symbolic value of its goods, and for the discourses that presume to describe its behavior?

The struggle ought not to be for redress over the unjust ancillary position of literature, as the humanities is overwhelmed by more-demanding talk of how to pay for what we want. The aim instead should be to invent a discourse that appropriately describes the struggles of our culture. For any market of symbolic goods—and in post-Fordist times, which markets to some extent are not?—that would mean *homo narrans* taking her proper place, because without that figure economics cannot adequately explain how value is created from symbolic material. Debate about whether society can afford its fictions is misplaced. Our society is fictional, and is sustained by readings of it—and, luckily, we are in charge of how we read.

Chapter 11

Events, Frames, and History
Getting What We Want from a Book

In the book retail market in the UK, fiction is overwhelmingly purchased as entertainment, bearing in mind that the term "entertainment" needs to be thickly described, and that it designates a mode of experience rather than ontologically a set of properties. The value of book purchases, as with any other kind of symbolic goods, is constructed by individual readers seeking gains from their investment and reading labor, often as contributions to identity formation. *Homo narrars* drives this market, since it is she who construes its values, and she is effective because the system and she are part of the same social composition. This value creation and value circulation—this economy, if you will—is not accessible to explanatory models based on economic exchange values alone. The neoclassical model of economics is not well placed to describe its market, which nevertheless is still a monetized market of symbolic goods that runs on, and generates, profits measured in hard cash. To make such a model work, we need to account for how the goods within the system can be both the material book object that is necessary to facilitate exchange and a social phenomenon and networked event. What is required, therefore, is a rationale for the composite cultural and exchange values that feature in the market. Because, if those value are not intrinsic to the exchanged object alone, they must derive from relationships within the social network, for which a further account is required of the framing needed to generate overall values throughout the (book) market. Furthermore, once those values have been derived, what kinds of stability can be expected from the network that might grant those values the kinds of longevity necessary for the market to function? For these final questions, it is necessary to return to Clifford Geertz, then to actor-network theory, and then to the framing of Mieke Bal.

Approaching the book market as a cultural formation allows us to draw on insights from the fields of ethnography and cultural studies, the first of which is whether methodologically one can study the object from without or from within. Around the early 1970s, Clifford Geertz proposed a solution to the problem of how to steer between such *etic* and *emic* analysis. Etic analysis from the outside risks imposing the outside's interpretative system onto the cultural formation being studied, while emic analysis from the inside is never really attainable by anyone but a native or, eventually, to use the oxymoron, a self-ethnographer. And though the agreement among anthropologists was that culture needs to be read "*in* its own terms," requiring us to avoid any universal "psychologism" from without, it also meant, as Geertz insisted, that we should refrain from any "schematicism" by which the signs "within" are cajoled and contorted onto "our" totalizing map. Not everything makes sense, or at least makes sense as part of permanent sign system constructed hegemonically by "us," so the solution is to read culture not for fully coherent relationships between object-signs, but looking at how objects are used in an evolving pattern of life and what that might signify; "whatever, or wherever, symbol systems 'in their own terms' may be, we gain empirical access to them by inspecting *events*, not by arranging abstracted entities into unified patterns" (my italics).[1] A well-plowed field in reception studies, reading *as an event* recognizes that "the production of meaning [is] not inherent in the text, since the same text can be interpreted according to different rules of notice."[2] It is akin to Barthes's walk alongside a wadi: a reading, like a walk along a river, is an experience of all of life in the valley that creates and is created by the wadi's river.[3] From a material semiotics perspective, then, it is not the book that is important but what happens in the event of a meeting between the material book and the reader.

Following Geertz's logic, entertainment is also no longer of interest as a type of cultural object, "an entertainment." Instead, the focus is on what people do with their cultural objects, in the event of their being entertained, which is the point made by Tamborini et al. from the previous chapter. By articulating entertainment as a mode of experience, it becomes something relational, happening between reader and book in a specific time and place. Entertainment research then dovetails with material book history to allow "the book" to become an event consisting of situated readers and their bibliographic objects. In this sense, a "book" is something occurring diachronically, repeatedly—and within the parameters of this study—as a commodified entertainment. The dimensions of these events change from case to case, depending on inputs and outputs, and thus determining what kind of gains can be achieved, but what stabilizes the system, or rather what gives it the appearance of durable life, is that it is enacted in real time, from book to book and reading to reading.

In a more developed form, this conception of book as event has been articulated by Sydney Shep in "Books in Global Perspectives." Concerned with the inherent mutability and mobility of books, Shep progresses from the classic communication circuit model of book history to a model of "situated knowledges," after Donna Haraway, but with regard to books generated from the interplay between people, places, and things. Each of these three elements—people, places and things—draws in concomitant disciplinary approaches—life histories, space and place studies, and bibliographic study of the material record—in which any research might emphasize one of the three approaches but nevertheless be held in balance both by the other two elements and by crossover fields between them.[4]

> Various nodes of intersection between adjacent elements suggest rich veins of contextual research, whether the life geographies of individual actors, the object biographies of 'it-narratives' of individual books and texts, or the politics of archival space . . . the three primary elements converge in a zone of investigation termed the event horizon.[5]

In the world of bookish entertainments, the book as event does not exist prior to its readers, no longer an entertainment object as some (late) capitalist neo-liberal entrapment. As Graham Huggin wrote in 2001, "the time has surely come to set aside the myth of commodity culture as some vast imperialist conspiracy sucking in unwary victims."[6] Such a myth is replaced by analysis of regimes of value and by mapping the activities of actors operating within them. Undeniably, the entertainment system runs through its global corporate agencies, which problematically use vast resources to exploit the system and control and define terms. In this sense publishing, not as a means of disseminating material but as a gatekeeping process, becomes a contested passage through which material must pass to acquire value. The task of gatekeeping, in part, is the assignation of signs such as "bestseller" and "fastseller" that are signaling positions by which a work can be defined, or trapped—though the power to assign those terms is contested by other regimes and actors in the system, as are terms such as "good read," "page turner," and "literary classic." But among the most essential technologies belonging to that regime, along with authors and their inscriptions, is the act of purchasing, positioning any number of shoppers called 'the reader' as a primary, heterogeneous actor. It may well be true that users are often *infotained* into a stupor, or simply advertised into submission, but—ideology aside—the system continues to be recreated primarily by its readers, as well as by all the would-be "servants" of those readers, which include authors, publishers and booksellers.

If not in terms of financial capital, then in numbers and as a source of revenue, the shopping public is the primary producer of this entertainment book culture. For reading individuals, reading and gaining is simply one event made possible by the interactions between actors and elements within the entire regime, the overall constitution of which needs to be modeled firmly on material-semiotic grounds. Rather than speaking of a static reading public—let alone a preestablished "mass audience" or "society" (often the blunt measure of many sociologies of literature)—it would make more sense to speak of transient networks. A network is required that might account for high-street book buying in general and, at its most sensitive, for any given work of fiction in its various editions and for its social lifetime around the communications circuit. This type of network is not understood as a prior entity, but is created or, rather, performed in real time as a network of associations. Like public opinion, the network is not an *a priori* fact to be discovered but *a posteriori* is the effect of a particular arrangement of associations between actors and entities over a period of time. In this way it is always unstable and provisional.

The kind of network that would be suitable might be the rhizome network described by Gilles Deleuze and productively applied to the book trade at the turn of the nineteenth to twentieth century by Alison Rukavina.[7] But so well explored is the rhizome model in literary criticism that it has almost become a leitmotif of postmodernism itself, and as such would chime badly with the role needed by the current study that requires a more instrumentalist modeling. Preferable then is the actor-network described by John Law, Michel Callon, Bruno Latour, and others, revamped with Latour's *Reassembling the Social: An Introduction to Actor-Network Theory* from 2005, and summarized in a number of good introductions.[8] In *Reassembling the Social,* Latour talks of the social not as an independent domain that impacts on other forms of activity but as a result continually emerging from various associations. Society is not the already-formed realm, which Margaret Thatcher famously declared does not exist, but emerges in real time as the result of interactions between actors and entities. Private individuals, their property, transports, and mediations, and the authorities and legislations that regulate and coordinate them, together, through their network of associations, create or perform society.

Actor-network theory (ANT) conceives its network in which human and non-human agencies (known as actants) are ontologically equal, so that it is through relations that difference or distinctions emerge. The network in which books flourish as useful entertainments consists *inter alia* of writers, critics, reviewers, purchasers, readers, accountants, editors, and marketing teams, as well as all the titles, printing and photocomposition processes, shops, branded chains, credit institutions, unions (if any), operators of these technologies (and their employers), and of course hard cash. Power differences in such a network emerge because of interactions between actants and not as the result of any essential property possessed by an entity. The power of a global corporate entity, for example, is thus maintained, not because the entity is corporate, but because of its access to credit, and its ability to both enroll other actants and co-opt other network elements into adopting its terms of reference. Since the associations between entities are what produce new ways of acting, it requires study not of "essential" qualities but of the unbounded associations between actants currently constituting the network—as John Law puts it, "There is no social order. Rather, there are endless attempts at ordering."[9] This is why Latour also refers to ANT as a sociology of associations, and why that ordering is open to surprising turns.

Furthermore, unlike the terms "group" and "community," which are themselves metaphors for homogeneity, a network is oriented to heterogeneity. Indeed, the very use of group or community itself generates consensus as a central problem: the moment a group is identified is the moment that its boundaries are opened to contestation. The actor-network, on the other hand, is utterly heterogeneous.[10] It is merely a collective of variant actors and entities, human and non-human: people, their books, and the places that are their bookshops. Its actants can be human but can also be printed and distributed utterances (inscriptions, as ANT would say). What coheres the network is that each volitional actant acts on the basis of their own desires rather than from any unifying belief. In this way the network accommodates not only inner conflict but, as any cynical publisher will tell you, even self-contempt.

The purpose of the current study is not to apply wholesale the actor-network model to retailed books, or to the network that was the Southampton trade, but to an extent to adopt its network thinking. A study along comprehensive ANT lines would follow important actors in negotiations up to a conspicuous event: a book prize, say, an auspicious release, or a significant sales landmark. It would look at how the network stabilizes itself and how its elements juxtapose, and how the meanings and identities of elements are translated (or betrayed) by primary actors. The way elements are enrolled and co-opted into the network would also need to be studied, along with how its effective convergence results from power disputes between elements. An ANT study would also need to be agnostic. From the researcher's point of view, all interpretations within the network need to be unprivileged, but the model this study builds has already chosen its villains. That choice was a major impetus to the enterprise and, not so much a narrative but a counter-narrative, the study has already decided which actants should not be let off the hook.

Regenerated over time, the retail book network selling in-depth entertainment becomes a social-technical system, retrospectively giving renewed life to Pichois's poignant remark about books, the literature of consumption and compensation, being "machines for reading and dreaming."[11] The network's book-machines for reading and dreaming are socially constituted. Their wording deploys communally recognized language, the imagery relies on socialized ways of seeing. They are utterly intertextual. In a paraphrase of Daniel Maudlin and Robin Peel, to study those machines in action is to assess the value of cultural productions not through prescriptive assessment of autonomous author-outputs, but as emerging as appropriate for the various actors and users.[12] Anyone with interests in a work of fiction, along with the advertisements, reviews, book jackets, comparable titles, rival titles, and other features that are its non-human entities, together in their associations help keep the book machine in motion. Unless continually performed, the machine will break down, attested to by the ever-increasing numbers of neglected volumes: titles of which we can no longer speak.

Once an actor-network's internal system of translation and mediation is running effectively, it becomes "punctualized." The term "punctualization" refers to the point of temporary stabilization when the actor-network is seen as a single agent, and is replaced by a singularity (as an actor or token) with which other agents interact. The network becomes an object in itself, what Latour calls a black box, in which internal complexity is rendered invisible.[13] A complex of carburetor, disc brakes, motor, tires, and so on becomes a single object: a motor vehicle.[14] What hits you is not a complexity of parts but a car. Copies of a particular edition, reviews, book sales, and reading spaces become a bestselling novel. This year's prize winner roles off the production line, and whether it produces congestion or a mobile care service depends on how it is adopted into the network. The process of punctualization is reversible, too. The network can break down when we look too closely inside the black box. The car becomes a mystery of components again, and the bestselling book machine is seen to be merely the result of various international, corporate strategies.

Any published fiction can be thought of as a punctualized phenomenon, constantly (re)created so long as there are actors and entities maintaining the associations. The term "book" is homonymic, encompassing both the material book object (the book that I purchased) and a social-temporal phenomenon or, rather, event (an author's new book). And for the latter, perhaps a new coinage is required. Not a literary work, nor an art work, but a Net Work. The fiction Net Work is an "event" consisting of people, places and bibliographic objects. Take *Girl on a Train* (2015) by Paula Hawkins, for example: the collective agency of all its actors and entities, its editions, producers and end-using readers, the viewers of its film without ever reading the print version, and those who will only skim the blurb but still pass judgment, together make up the punctualized Net Work known as *Girl on a Train*. And as long as we continue to trade in, access, compare, and think about instantiations of *Girl on a Train*, it will continue to exist as a phenomenon and as an actor Net Work. Because of the Net Work, the market in exchange-objects that are its books is made possible.

Given the network is inherently unstable, what then might be its lifetime since, for a market to function, value requires some form of duration to facilitate exchange? A Net Work such as *Middlemarch* provides a case in point. It has been a bestseller since its part issue in 1871–72 (concurrent with the emergence of commodity culture) and even a popular fastseller if we consider the high sales of the significantly cheaper single-volume edition of 1874, quantities of this 7s 6d edition being so successful that Eliot declared its sales to be "wonderful beyond all whooping."[15] Punctualized since the nineteenth century, *Middlemarch* has been a staple feature of the literary-fiction market, not despite, but because of its continual reconstitution by various and at times conflicting actors within the network, each contending to define terms. In its first few decades, trade actors could capitalize on one aspect of the novel and *Middlemarch* was able to spawn a raft of spin-off eulogies on middle England and rural value: *George Eliot in Derbyshire* (1876), *Scenes from the 'George Eliot' Country* (1888), *George Eliot: Her Early Home* (1891), or travel guides such as *Pictures of Nuneaton and the George Eliot Country* (1911) and *George Eliot Country: Official Guide of the London and North Western Railway Company* (1908).[16] It was only later that its canonicity could become a value, as other trade elements were able to maximize its accrued cultural capital and status, predicted by early critics. It has since been deployed as a device to deliver twentieth-century nostalgia about the nineteenth century (not an option for nineteenth-century people); it has performed as a site of melodrama; it has comprised a feminist landmark; and it has widely been acknowledged as a sustained contemplation on the nature of love and society—a latter inscription of this Net Work appearing for Vintage Classics in 2007 as "Vintage Love," a twin-pack re-release that announced itself as the greatest books from all time with the greatest books of our time, pairing Eliot's *Middlemarch* with A.S. Byatt's *Possession*. Well adapted as an aide for teaching critical theory, it has also become a pedagogic document, a partner publication to which would be Karen Chase's *Middlemarch in the Twenty-First Century* (2006). Such long-term reconstitutions within the network have ensured *Middlemarch*'s stable currency as a punctualized Net Work.

ANT describes such a reconstitution of elements through its core concept of translation, by which the identity of an element is redefined or simply conjured through ongoing struggles to promote which of the element's identities is supposedly "authentic." Important large-scale identities, therefore, are created by, or result from, translation effects. The validity of key terms thus results from translation effects and how terms like "nature," "society," and "literature" are widely understood results from ordering struggles that involve translators, the translated, and the translation medium; translators who have the most power exert control over definitions and thereby which order prevails in a given network. In any commercially inflected network, for example, money will be an important agent of translation, allowing a greater degree of determination to those with greater access to it. Cultural and social capital, too, become media of translation for those with access. For the retail book network, translation is practiced by corporate actors, as well as by education institutions, but it is very much practiced by readers, too. In the manner of any network, the Net Work is renegotiated for as long as the act of translation serves the interests of network actors, or until the network breaks down. This feature of continuity has important repercussions for the study of a book's history and the question of how we determine what may have been the attitudes of past readers.

The actor-network model may be temporally placed but is not period specific. For example, the famous Epsom Derby event, which has consistently been performed since 1780, continues to thrive despite changes to network entities: the length of the course, the riders, the horses, and the betting regimes of the public. Despite the changes to constituent parts, it is still meaningful to talk of an Epsom Derby consistently run since 1780. Equally, the pecia system in France, which endured throughout the fourteenth century, can be thought of as an actor-network that finally broke down, in contrast to British bookshop retail in commodity culture from the late 1800s to the present, which continues to thrive. As with the horses and courses at Epsom, actors within the book actor-network are likewise subject to change. For example, in terms of commercial regulations, the Net Book Agreement allowed book shops like Gilbert's a business model built more exclusively on books, with some of its earlier diversification returning post-NBA. Or in terms of the reading experience, we might qualitatively describe changes brought about by shifts in priming and framing conditions. For Gilbert's customers in 1900, a novel by H.G. Wells could not possibly supply the neo-Victorian nostalgia it can for readers in 2016, just as current readers are denied the shock and recognition (to use Rita Felski's terms) of Wells's futurities, as they acclimatized to gas-and-water socialism and the setbacks of industrial unrest.[17] Nevertheless, many other associations maintaining the actor-network remain intact—not least the idea of readerly "gains" from entertainment fiction.

Out of a durable coincidence of leisure time, books, disposable income, and High Street shopping, a book-retail actor-network has been consistently recreated since the emergence of commodity culture in the late nineteenth century in the UK that is quite distinct from other forms of book acquisition. And if this proposition is accepted, what then is to prevent findings from the UK High Street survey, and others, being transposed to reader-shoppers at the turn of the nineteenth to twentieth centuries? Would it be contentious to say that, as with their twenty-first-century cousins, the primary goal of those networked readers around 1900 was entertainment at minimized opportunity costs, in which the concept of entertainment encompassed a range of important existential goods?

It was precisely the unknown public's appetite for entertainment that had caused Wilkie Collins so much consternation, whereas Thomas Wright showed, in chapter 3, that he need not have worried, since that public's entertainment included Collins. The artifacts that we would recognize as entertainments today, in the nineteenth century would more likely have been termed items designed "to inform and amuse," but that does not mean their relationships to readers has changed as much as the language. In defending itself against accusations of partisanship in a case of scandalous spiritualism, an editorial for the *Cornhill Magazine* stated specifically that its primary aim and that of any other magazine was "to inform and amuse the public."[18] Tellingly, the section of the *Cornhill* preceding that editorial was chapters 57 to 61 of George Eliot's *Romola* in serial, with illustrations, presumably by that same argument for the public's information and amusement.

Entertainment's informational properties were well attested, too, in examples such as Victorian societies such as the Society for the Diffusion of Useful Knowledge created for the distillation of it. And much of what we would today recognize as self-help was provided not only in the direct self-help epitomized by Samuel Smiles but more generally in what Anthony Trollope thought of as a widespread approach to novel-reading from which derives "a greater portion of the teaching of the day than any of us have yet acknowledged."[19] Similarly, in what we would recognize as bibliotherapy, were books designed to increase the prosperity of the mind, mostly obviously in gift books and prize books awarded to encourage moral and mental health. Indeed, so potent was this medicine that there were warnings against its misuse; think merely of the moral tale that is Madame Bovary.

What allowed these texts to become sites of value for individual readers was the framing of the Net Work that took place—in terms of the private frame of the reader in her social embededness, but also in terms of the approximately one-hundred-and-fifty-year master frame of widespread commodity culture that prescribed reading in terms of gains. In the late nineteenth century as well as now, readers could imagine communities of other readers, to hijack Benedict Anderson's phrase, interacting with the same material. Who the majority of those people were, the reader would never know. A few fellow readers might be ascertained, but the identity of the majority would have to be guessed—in a guessing game that can be remarkably self-confirming. If I like the title and what I gain from it, then I might suspect that others who clamor around the Net Work are equally perceptive; but if the Net Work does not please, then those same others become dupes with a weakness for poor literature, which says something about "me." As a structural feature, however, the gain that is my identity formation is sustained through the imagined community of readers.

Reading fiction offers an opportunity for membership to something unverifiable, as a strategy in the formation of a discrepant identity. It offers the chance for an imagined membership without the risk of ever having that membership disproved. I may actively enjoy the membership I have accorded to myself by "collectively" appreciating a given Net Work; I may enjoy believing I am an anarchic interloper who reads more astutely than other members; I may consider my membership a secret pleasure, which I would be embarrassed to publicly acknowledge; I may believe I know precisely who those other members are, which provides me with reasons for either liking or disliking the given fiction. But in all these cases my reading of the fiction will derive from the social network not merely in terms of the social context directly framing and making meaning from the text, but also in the social construction of the reader's (my) identity. If I have read the blurb, liked the price, and now allow the book machine to begin my dreaming, then I am ready to create a framed reading not only of the book but of myself, in that the places, people, and bibliographic objects that constitute the Net Work are part of my ongoing self-constitution. I read generously, mending faults but also malignantly and with prejudice, to paraphrase Alberto Manguel (out of context—an act he would surely appreciate): "Life happened because I turned the pages."[20] Our page turning is the translation maintaining the actor-network that is book retail, and may eventually be the exchange by which its market runs.

To paraphrase Glenn Ward's exposition of Derrida, the meanings and truth of a Net Work are never absolute or timeless, but are always framed by socially and historically specific conditions of knowledge.[21] As an analytical subject, framing and the analysis of it can be traced back to the 1970s in the dense work of Erving Goffman but, by the late 1980s, Jonathan Culler could state in *Framing the Sign* that texual phenomena are nothing but abstracted forms with socially constituted meanings, not contextualized by a static determinable set of data but always framed "by various discursive practices, institutional arrangements, systems of value, [and] semiotic mechanisms."[22] Not a heuristic process qualifying a central truth, this framing is something that constructs even to the extent of falsifying (a frame-up). Framing, as Culler insists, is something that *we* do.

Picking up on framing as an activity, Mieke Bal develops the approach in *Travelling Concepts in the Humanities* (2002). When the artwork is treated as a cultural object, it requires a reverse perspective on historical thinking, starting with the present. As a cultural object, the artwork is never not in the present, nor without its presentation, which allows Bal to treat the object as framed *mise-en-scène*: "if *mise-en-scène* is what we see, framing is what happens before the spectacle is presented."[23] Preferable to framing as context, which is primarily a noun, framing in Bal's thinking is a verb form and an activity. It creates the event for the viewer and hence is "performed by an agent who is responsible, accountable, for his or her acts," in a potentially infinite regress where "the agent of framing is framed in turn."[24] Thus, the reader frames the book object with a self that is socially framed. The text in this system then becomes what she cogently calls the "pre-text" for a framed event that is a dynamic reading exercise, rather than an immutable origin. Framing itself—of our books and ourselves—becomes a performance by which, for this study, specific values are generated and by which the retail book market is sustained. The sustaining has nothing to do with either the "truth" of books (for aesthetic essentialists) or their equilibrium price (for economists), but everything to do with participation in a networked social performance.

For an idea of the range of performances that can emerge from a pre-text, it might be helpful to turn to a few examples. The bibliographer Jim Mays has described a sea-change for Shakespeare's *Merchant of Venice* that he attributes to the actor Charles Macklin.[25] According to Mays, the character Shylock had previously been regarded as a comic character, to be played as object of ridicule. When Macklin played Shylock in 1741, he performed as an Irishman in London, in Covent Garden and, like Shylock bounded by the regime that was Venice's Jewish ghetto, he understood what it meant to be framed by unfriendly forces. Macklin spoke Shakespeare's words, as had previous actors, but changed the prosody and delivery, and performed the role as not a comedy but a tragedy. The sentences remained, but the way the pre-text was performed reframed the role into a new "truth."

Such radical but common reframing of pre-text can be seen in the British Broadcasting Company's Radio 4 series called *A Good Read*, aired over a number of years, wherein two guests are invited to discuss a book that has been important in their lives; on 4 July 2017 actor Kathy Burke discussed Patrick Hamilton's *Hangover Square* from 1941.[26] Hamilton's work on the Net Work began on Christmas Day in 1939, a few months after Britain's entrance into WWII. Its pre-text narrates a society "unable to arrest its slide into the abyss," reflected in the parallel downward slide of protagonist George Harvey Bone into alcoholism.[27] To compound Bone's (very probably schizophrenic) misery, he becomes obsessed with magnetic Netta Langdon, a bit-part actor and favorite of the drinking regulars around the seedy hotels and boarding houses of London's Earl's Court, where Hangover Square is set. Netta is a masculine-structured female seductress, defined in gender politics as the contrast to all that is gentle and caring, and if readers were in any doubt, equipped with a fetish for the fascist totems of boots and breeches, and for her sordid Blackshirt lover Peter. Bone, by contrast, is lumpen and bumbling but—when not suffering his "dead moods" in which he plots to murder Netta—is generously if not simplistically kind. Netta despises George but finds him useful, a detail of which George is painfully aware.

Kathy Burke, as one of the Net Work's readers, is a self-possessed and forceful stage and television actor and director who has described herself as a lifelong member of the non-pretty working classes. Her work is underpinned by a keen understanding of the role of female beauty in gender exploitation.[28] Therefore, her awareness of the gender forces at work in the novel can be fairly-well guaranteed. Burke had first read the novel aged fourteen. Contrary to the show's other panelist and host, who enjoyed the book for its bleak depiction of debilitating love and personal weakness, with which they believed everyone identified at some point in their lives, Burke described how she was first attracted to the book for its depiction of the lives of compulsive drinkers, which also happened to be the life of her father. As a young reader, she had wanted to know what went on in pubs. Only after years of repeated reading did her approach to the book shift from what grown-ups do when they drink, to one focused on the appalling vulnerability that can come from needing love.

At some point during the discussion, it was suggested that Netta was a vehicle for author Hamilton's misogyny, responses to which were divided to the extent that other commentators, external to the program, were referred to as witnesses for the defense and prosecution. Burke's feeling was that the novel was progressive in that it rounded out conventional two-dimensional female portraits by delving into Netta's capacity for inflicting pain, and for asking why Netta might feel compelled to do so. Along lines of gender politics, the readings of Hangover Square were refracted into a range of nuances, the extremities of which understood Netta's role in the book in entirely opposite ways—the refraction located with the readers and not the narrative. More importantly, for Burke as a young woman, the same text had already been able to perform as a book "about" paternal absence in the masculine realm of alcohol. Reconfigured in time and place, the material instantiations of the text in tandem with the physicality of what Littau calls the embodied reader's experience continually recreate the Net Work anew, performing a range of primary significations that are not only wildly variant but conflicting.[29]

Far more than merely dominant, oppositional, or negotiated, reframing can set words adrift from any referent they may have hoped to dominate, oppose, or negotiate, something that is potentially both liberating and exploitative. Debt is credit, as credit is debt, depending on your relationship to it. Liabilities are also assets, depending on who loans and who receives. Unemployment benefit or state welfare could be reframed as social investment. State investment could again become something to seed new production, rather than seen as borrowing. When reframed, corporate investment might be seen a metaphor for gaining ownership rights over the most profitable assets and either selling them for profit or charging rent for their use. The liberalization of markets can also be called deregulation for the benefit of wealthy monopolists (or, worse, "self-regulation"). Free markets purport to be free, but is the freedom for pikes the same as the freedom for minnows?[30] Talking of Alice's discovery of mad name-givers in the Looking-Glass world, Manguel recalls how "a Canadian Prime Minister tears up the railway and calls it an act of 'progress'; a Swiss businessman traffics in loot and calls it 'commerce'; an Argentinian president shelters murderers and calls it 'amnesty.'"[31] All "true" readings, Manguel claims, are against the grain. The grain, however, is not a natural condition of the wording but a question of power.

At a time when Spain was wrestling with its modernity and began to move from an economy based on agriculture to one based on industrial manufacturing, Dolores Ibárruri, better known as La Pasionaria, read several publications by and about Karl Marx that were instrumental to her adult life. She came from a poor mining family; her husband was a trade unionist, imprisoned repeatedly while Ibárruri brought up her six children, four of whom died from lack of adequate medical care and nourishment. As her political identity developed, she moved from editing radical newspapers to being elected to the central Committee of the Spanish Communist Party in 1930, delivering the famous anti-fascist speech "¡No Pasarán!" broadcast by press microphones in 1936 at the start of the Spanish Civil War. No less a figure than Frederico García Lorca promised to write a poem to her but died before he could, and in *For Whom the Bell Tolls* Ernest Hemingway described her near-saintly reputation. In "¡No Pasarán!" Ibárruri spoke inclusively of a wide community of disparate groups (communists, anarchists, socialists, republican democrats) coming together under one umbrella for a common cause. A year later Ibárruri had turned brutally against the various anarchist and republican factions she formerly supported and, by 1940, produced an apologia in praise of the "leader of peoples" and "man of the masses," Joseph Stalin, architect and head of a regime that murdered at least nine million people.[32] The shift from benevolent inclusiveness (nevertheless excluding fascists) to believing that all progressive thinking was embodied in the person of a single mass murderer took only four years. In that period, she saw no incompatibility with her readings of Marx and the overall change in her position. There are many ways to explain the incompatibility—that the writings of Marx contain an essential "evil" that only became persuasive for Ibárruri toward 1940; that she perverted the meaning inherent in Marx's work to suit her own ends; or that she eventually surrendered to the idea that the correct interpretation of Marx was a monopoly held by Stalin. Alternatively, we can think of Marx's writing as bibliographic objects that came into her life at a particular time and place, the conditions of which framed both the materials and Dolores Ibárruri in specific ways. As conditions changed, so did the framing of both her and Marx, taking with it the meaning of Ibárruri's preferred Net Work.

In a final example of translation, could a writer such as Tennyson, as resolutely imperial as Kipling, transition into the frame of radical emancipatory politics? Daniel Hack has described how Tennyson, and specifically his "Charge of the Light Brigade," had become for black readers in the 1990s a signifier of whiteness, an emblem for the canons in front of black people demanding equality.[33] But this had not always been the case. In January 1855, barely a month after its initial publication in the *London Examiner*, the poem was published by an editor and orator who had suffered enslavement—the most prominent African American activist of the antebellum period—Frederick Douglass. The *Frederick Douglass's Paper* that carried the poem was the result of a merger between Douglass's earlier self-founded paper, the *North Star*, and the *Liberty Party Paper* of white abolitionist Gerrit Smith, in 1851. By 1855 Douglass had become what Eric Gardner calls a savvy editor, employing a number of prominent black writers and political activists, including Martin Delany, James McCune Smith (also as the pseudonymous "Communipaw"), and Philip Bell ("Cosmopolite")—indeed, Bell would go on to establish black newspapers in San Francisco and be described eventually as "the Napoleon of the colored press."[34] Furthermore, 1855 was the same year that Douglass revised his successful 1845 publication, *Narrative of the Life of Frederick Douglass*, enlarging it into *My Bondage, My Freedom*, which dropped the white-author preface in favor of an introduction by McCune Smith, theorized slave power more comprehensively, and "paid much more attention to the perils of 'free' life in a racist North."[35] All those on board the *Frederick Douglass's Paper*, therefore, were astute, experienced, and acutely aware of the dangers lurking in the interface between black writers and white sympathetic voices in support of emancipation.

As Hack points out, it was not unusual for the *Paper* to print in the back four pages new British literature, as well as British periodical material, such as Dickens, alongside original work by African American writers. Of its culture and news reporting, *Paper* also offered opinions on the Crimean War, not as a distant conflict but as part of a global struggle against tyranny: "One article celebrates the fall of Sebastopol to British and French troops as a victory over 'the great autocrats of Europe' and criticizes 'the hypocritical sympathies of American Republicanism on [Russia's] behalf.'"[36] A response to "Charge of the Light Brigade" was printed in the same *Paper*, by "Communipaw" in dialogue with "Fylbel," editor Philip A. Bell. Discussing the first lines, Communipaw declared the poem's worth in terms of the Western literary tradition, its rhythms more successful than Virgil's *Quatit ungula campum* (Virgil's galloping meter often cited as a perfect example of onomatopoeia). But for the four lines beginning with "Canon to the right of them," Fylbel complains that the Tennyson has indulged in theft. The lines, or rather its sound, its anaphora, the stressed first syllable "can-," and to some extent the meter, are taken from an ancient Congo Nogo chant that is "as old as—Africa":

> Canga bafio te,
> Canga moune de le,
> Canga do ki la,
> Canga li.[37]

Fylbel's point was that the chant had traveled with enslaved people to the New World and into cosmopolitan print culture.[38] How seriously the claim was supposed to be taken, we do not know, but what it deftly achieved was an inversion of hierarchies of indebtedness that would have been daring, indeed, at the time. Communipaw and Fylbel then go onto to discuss how "Canga Li!" was used to rally rebel slaves in St. Domingo, and that it might be again used in a Black revolution in the United States.

Later commentators recommended abandoning "Charge of the Light Brigade" as a literature for black youth in favor of poems such as George Henry Boker's "The Second Louisiana" (also called "The Black Regiment"). Marcus Garvey proposed to rename a ship intended for the Black Star Line from the *Tennyson* to the *Phyllis Wheatley*, but, according to Hack, a series of references to "Charge" persisted that maintained an ambiguous relationship to Tennyson's notions of valor and blame (both the "thunder" and "blunder" of Tennyson's poem)—in poems such as James Bell's "The Day and the War" (1864), and Paul Dunbar's "The Coloured Soldiers" (1895); in Henry McNeal Turner's 1868 speech to the Georgia State legislature (the General Assembly for the State of Georgia), who were refusing to seat elected black representatives, with Turner describing his black colleagues as having "cannon to the right of them / cannon to the left of them / cannon in front of them"; and perhaps more significantly in W.E.B. Du Bois's *The Souls of Black Folk* (1903) when he discussed the failure of post–Civil War America to establish the rights of freed slaves and in particular the failures of the Freedmen's Bureau and its first commissioner, Union General Oliver Howard. Du Bois wrote that nothing was more convenient than to heap all the evils of the day upon the Freedmen's Bureau and damn it for the blunder that was made, "but it is neither sensible nor just. *Some one had blundered*, but that was long before Oliver Howard was born," the criminal "blunder" being the forced Atlantic transportation of African peoples beginning in the fifteenth century.[39] Not the whiteness of Tennyson's poem, but the *j'accuse* in the fashion of Émile Zola could be wrought when the performance of the pre-text was suitably reframed, instantly recognizable to anyone who has experienced the fist of institutional power. No wonder then that the same Net Work proved a staple among unknown readers in England, in Southampton, and elsewhere.

In its use of twenty-first-century modeling and theorization over historical data about bookselling in Southampton around 1900, this study punctualizes that long-term actor-network into a cis-narrative of High Street book retail. High Street retailers like the Rayner's family, John Adams, or the multi-line business of George Buxey represent specific chains in an actor-network. In contrast to other book-trade businesses, those three retailers were tied into publishing operations, their access to capital and to printing technologies representing an ability to enroll non-volitional actants into the network that other businesses could not match. Booksellers such as Alfred Dyer, James Sprent Virtue, or the Southampton Book Society, by contrast, had access to large institutional structures, in the form of newspaper venture capital, or to wholesale stock. They were able to draw on those resources and align the network in particular ways, to the benefit or detriment of other businesses. The Topographical Publishing Company, in its rivalry with the *Southampton Echo*, produced the *Southamptonian*, and entered the network when the success of its publication increasingly relied on serial fiction. Bookbinders like Cawte's and Broadbere's were never specifically booksellers, but their rates and practices determined what could be offered by secondhand shops such as Thomas James, and by booksellers with secondhand lines, which in effect was nearly all of them. The business of Domoney or of the Harles enlisted religious institutions into their activities, while businesses such as Gutch and Cox brought in actors and capitals from local politics. The typewriting business of Miss Hoskins and Miss Stuart and the long list of women running suburb newsagents took their places in the network because of gendered technologies and geographies, as the men on the High Street took theirs. Actors like George Lynne or the business of Chaplin and Weeks formed their chains because of their failure to favorably co-opt institutional forces such as the criminal justice system. Stationery, and the values associated with communications technologies were ubiquitous throughout the network, as were more socialized retail practices such as circulating libraries. On top of it all, plugged in most comprehensively, was the business of Henry March Gilbert and Sons, their business fingers modestly in a pie of publishing, direct retail, library circulation, binding, and catalogs of new and secondhand. But crucially, what drove the entire book-oriented network was its readers, with their efferent reading in gaining through purchasing and reading entertainments. It was driven by *homo narrans* building her identity not despite but because of other readers, while negotiating the progressive and exploitative forces of larger networks. Any temporary alignment within this network was the result of actors' abilities to narrate the disparate entities into a common history and shared space. This study is merely the latest of those narrations.

But to model that network along lines that are exclusively humanities-based or reduced to functions of economics would be to commit violence to a complex political-economic system. The book trade, like any other trade in symbolic goods, is emblematic. National agreements such as the NBA were defended on grounds of cultural value, which would be seen by free-marketers as "external" regulation and an invasion of the free market by politics. But the NBA encouraged a healthy independent trade and the robust sale of books for cultural reasons. Other regulations or deregulations will align the network in other ways, but these alignments (in any market of symbolic goods) are at no point free from the existential values created by people reading. Politics and culture are endemic features of the market, and any model that would account for the market must incorporate these dimensions. Without them, it is impossible to accurately measure and predict market behavior. What is more, without a political-cultural dimension to the model, it is also impossible to measure when outputs achieve more than increased market share or investor dividends, and in fact produce social growth and processes of socialization that we like to call democracy, which are necessary components to the life of business.

This study opened with a concern about a gap between the humanities on the one hand, and natural and social sciences that house economics on the other, a problem that if a composite term such as *Geisteswissenschaften* or *sciences humaine* were adopted would not be so acute. Most importantly, the study was concerned about how economics, which in its purely mathematized neoliberal variant prefers to think of itself not as an astrology but as a physics, too often trumps humanities discourse in the post-crash era through blunt questions of cost. The response strategy adopted here has been to ask what happens to fiction when treated as a traded commodity. The answer which is beginning to appear is that we must think of economics or, at the very least, that section of the market that comprises symbolic goods, as a political economy—but to arrive at that has required intermediate steps.

Firstly, the study has adopted the postion that the exchanged object, its wording and other material signs, does not have meaning in and of itself but that meaning, along with value *in toto*, is created in the event of the sign-objects framed—following Geertz and Bal, an idea that can be clarified by thinking of the "book" itself as a social event. Because the master frame is that regime of value known as commodity culture—initially in the UK from the last third of the nineteenth century onward, and still expanding—it means that books are treated in the network primarily for gains. For corporate publishers, the gains will be profits and dividends for shareholders; for readers, the gains will be what can be had within the general experiencing of entertainment, which includes reassurances and remedies both flippant and profound, chief among which is the ongoing building of identity. Consumption, as a term distinct from purchase, then becomes reading, whereby *homo economicus* is replaced by *homo narrans*. In the language of actor-network theory, this means the framed book event can be thought of as a meeting of people, place, and bibliographic objects, coined in the Net Work. As an ongoing process, the Net Work is sustained by print, money, technologies, readers, critics, publishers, writers, distributors, commentators, and all actants who are nominally recognized as agents of production and consumption. Both book objects and their Net Works achieve value because of the actor-network, not on grounds of intrinsic conditions to the (pre-)text, but derived from network relations. Potentially, Net Works might become constructors of politically progressive markets, not because of what they are purported to "say," but because of what people might do with them.

There is a problem, however. The actor-network with its Net Works is merely reminiscent of a "market." Institutionalized economics might recognize the value creation and circulation taking place there, but not its market constitution, and conceptually a "market" could still comprise a reified entity distinct from the network. In other words, the actor-network could still be thought of as an appendage super-glued onto the regime of financial values and the operations conducted there. It leaves the binary conception intact, albeit displaced like bubbles under the carpet. With readerly gains there is a *bridge* between progressive pleasures of the text and market-enabled values, but it is still a bridge between two separate practices: between readerly actor translations and operations in the economic regime. Reassuringly, but also slightly depressingly, it would have to be conceded that the study had done little more than add another layer to the dilemma Colin Campbell poignantly recognized in his classic, *The Romantic Ethic and the Spirit of Modern Consumerism*, when he identified a romanticized ideated reader struggling to keep a critical distance to, but at the same time feeding off and creating, the consumer market.[40] The solution, which will be proposed in the final chapter, is to find a way of conceptualizing both the book network and the regime of commodity value as part of the same heterogeneous complexity—for which we must abandon the conception of a market hypostatized in narrow economic terms in preference for a political economy.

Chapter 12

Whose Is the *Question Économique*?

In protecting its distinction, literary studies and the literature appreciation it is built upon has striven for interpretations that are more exceptional than the superficiality of everyday commentary. What is cherished by critical distinction is precisely that which is not quotidian. Leah Price wrote of a "gulf" between the interpretations of common readers described by cultural history and the "literary critic's description of his own reading of a particular text—whose interest lies in its atypicality, even its perverseness."[1] However, this literary-critical focus brings with it inattention, and at times indifference, toward the quotidian, or at worst an apathy for the sorts of retailed experience that makes up a significant part of modern living. Instead, the costs to opportunities to simply make time for everyday reading, caring, giving, and loving is explained by alternative discourses, and desire becomes an activity described through economics. And once discursive terms are established, the activity can become a fixed target. For atomic physicists, water consists of hydrogen and oxygen atoms, and one can then talk, say, of atom separation, but it would be hard to talk of wetness, let alone thirst. Left with only economic terminology, the struggle for satisfying legitimate desires has no alternative but to be in obedience to the laws of supply and demand. Though fully part of its description, water's wetness is made unspeakable, in the same way that desire cannot be spoken of by institutionalized economics other than in terms of self-interest, and where irrational behavior becomes accountable only as a market aberration. What is needed is a terminology that is built on desire's "irrationality," as well as its culture and politics, as part of retailed life.

The resistance to an economic quotidian is exemplified in a letter written in 1872 by the anarchist Mikhail Bakunin, who interrupted his comments on the extraordinary new Italian republic with a two-page tirade against political ideologues who seemed dismissive of freedom founded on simple truths about bread and material possessions. The letter was written sometime after Bakunin's break with Marxist purists who believed only a committee that understood the true movement of history could decide the best course of action for the proletariat (in effect setting up its dictatorship). In Bakunin's view, the people—whomever that may have intended—would only be further exploited by such ideologues as they would be by Giuseppe Mazzini, whose death had prompted the letter. Despite the Mazzinians' supposed devotion to the people, Bakunin believed the ideologues were more concerned with the purity of their political, poetical, and legal abstractions than daily basic needs. What occupied the minds of the masses everywhere, he suggested, was not "theological fictions" but an everyday emancipation that was "matérielle ou économique."[2] Concessions might be made by revolutionary theoreticians but only with "une sorte de condescendance dédaigneuse" (a dismissive condescension) at how the masses seemed unable to forget their bellies and devote themselves to an ideal. For Bakunin, ideals were a privilege of the privileged, and what rightly forced "eternal idealities" to fall from heaven was the daily *question économique*. Any hope for a system of fairness and humanity, therefore, had to begin with people's basic desire to purchase "stuff."

This distain for the *question économique* would seem to run through many in a cultural gatekeeping position, on both the left and the right. In *Revolution of the Ordinary*, Toril Moi identifies such a relationship to ordinary language among literary scholars (and by extension to "ordinary" thinking) as a politically charged dismissal of the everyday seen almost without exception to be ignorant or reactionary—a position attributed to figures such as Adorno, in the statement that "nothing radical could come of common sense."[3] The target of Moi's objections is found in the writings of Herbert Marcuse, who, Moi argues, celebrates his "Mandarin disdain" for the common, the familiar, the everyday, the low, and the near.

> For Marcuse, philosophy is incompatible with the ordinary. There is, he writes, an "irreducible difference . . . between the universe of everyday thinking and language on the one side, and that of philosophical thinking and language on

the other" (OM 178). The ordinary is hopelessly vague and muddled . . . to do his work, the critical philosopher must keep his distance, not submerge himself in the messiness of the ordinary: "Critical analysis must disassociate itself from that which it strives to comprehend" (193). [4]

Unfortunately, Moi also believes discussions of academic writing on the left are still "conducted almost exclusively on Marcuse's terms"—and what could be more ordinary than shopping, for both bread and books.[5]

No one undertaking literary criticism would argue for anything but a rigorous engagement with the text. The results can be breathtaking—think merely of close readings such as Paul De Man's of Wordsworth.[6] Neither does Moi in any way give up on the task of intellectual critical reading, her sense of it being that it distinguishes itself from lay readings only by the "attention, judgment, and knowledge we bring to the task."[7] But distinguished it remains, and, as the language of advertising has it, distinction is also something gorgeously "exclusive," deriving its value precisely because it excludes the non-exceptional. For engagement with the text, the ordinary must be kept at bay in what was De Man's prescription for the vigilant "self-forgetting concentration that we have been describing . . . as the proper state of mind for critical insights"—but this is not what commodity readers do.[8] Our retail book markets are too shared and too full of desire for self-forgetting, which is why inescapably our efferent readings are not "exclusive" in both senses. In the final pages of *Reception*, Ika Willis concludes her conception of the text as an "object" that has a public or collective dimension: ontologically unstable because "it is co-produced by its receiver . . . since what is 'in' a text varies from reader to reader, context to context." Thus to exert authority over a text and to claim for it a single correct interpretation necessitates ignoring "the acts of reception and systems of interpretation and signification within which those texts mean, and [acting] without an awareness that they may mean, and almost certainly have meant, something different to a different reader." Singularly exerting power over a textual object is to maintain distinction from the mass of "Other" common readings. It is to guard the sure barrier against pretenses to knowledge, as Pope had it in the *Dunciad*—at times heroic, and at others deluded (the valence depends on the social relations created)—but always phallic and not in any way a response of the belly that Bakunin would recognize in the *question économique*.

At best a miracle and at worst a bad comedy, the pursuit of exclusive readings would be fine were it not that other explanatory forces are increasingly taking over the domain of daily life. When criticism manifests itself as agnosticism to the everyday and therefore also to retailed life, Bakunin's *question économique* is instead calculated by neoliberal ideologues, who claim exchange between humans as their exclusive territory, explicable only through their brand of "theological fiction."

A parent of that neoliberal ideology is the neoclassical economic theory that developed from the nineteenth and throughout the twentieth century and that, in shorthand, has become known as "economics." Though riven with internal disputes, this field shared a common understanding of large but nevertheless limited swathes of life determined by the laws of supply and demand, in the postwar period characterized as Keynesian *contra* Friedman's free-market economics. For Keynesians, government's role was to intervene in the market to militate against social harm and thus maintain a system in which market society was socially beneficial. By contrast, the free-market monetarism championed by Milton Friedman claimed that wealth would only be generated by unhampered market operations and, subsequently, social well-being created through the "trickle-down" of greater wealth. Though followers of both had radically differing views on the role of governments and central banks—lowering interest rates and releasing central finance in times of downturn to stimulate economic activity and hence growth (but which encouraged upward inflation), *contra* raising interest rates to control inflation from which growth would ensue (but with downward pressure on the labor market and hence increasing unemployment)—both operated essentially within a neoclassical paradigm.

The latent dangers in that paradigm become obvious when it becomes colonial. As early as 1932, Lionel Robbins provided the enduring definition of neo-classical economics as "the science which studies human behaviour *as* a relationship between ends and scarce means which have alternative uses" (my italics).[9] The foreground of that definition is occupied by its methodological approach, studying human behavior *as though* it were a relationship between ends and scarce means—sometimes the case, but far from always. In the definition's background is life, the object of study over which economic rationality appears to apply its analysis. The reverse would place human behavior in the foreground and then analyze *the extent* to which that was based on rational choice or not, and *the degree* to which life consists of the deliberate calculation of maximized personal utility. (Often it does not.) Thus, in Robbins's view and that of neoclassical economics, the study is defined by its theoretical precepts and methodology, rather than being the study of specifically economic activity or, indeed, of economies: a point not lost on even the *Financial Times*, which in the post-crash era was still able to protest that economics should be "not a method but a subject—one defined by the problems it tackles and not the technique it uses. To a man with a hammer, everything looks like a nail."[10]

Unlike leftist projects in the humanities, which seldom thought it necessary to have an economic wing, neoliberalism as a right-wing political project embraced the power of economic explanation as a political tool, and commandeered "economics" into playing a major role in annexation. Professor of Economics Philip Mirowski provides a biting political account of neoliberalism in *Never Let a Serious Crisis Go to Waste* (2013), tracing its development from the Mont Pelerin Society established by Milton Friedman, Friedrich Hayek, and others, while the primary critical study of neoliberalism is David Harvey's *A Brief History of Neoliberalism* (2005).[11] But for showing how ambitious economic method thrives under neoliberalism, little more is required than the example of one-time Pelerin Society president and Nobel economist Gary Becker.

Becker's claim was that economics can explain everything and, as Ha-Joon Chang writes, by "everything," both Becker and the Chicago School he inspired really did mean everything.[12] On the brink of the Thatcher-Reagan years, the Washington Consensus, and the beginnings of neoliberalism's near-global adoption, Becker was able to write that "I have come to the position that the economic approach is a comprehensive one that is applicable *to all human behaviour*" (my italics).[13] Applying the rules of scarcity and demand to themes formerly far beyond the scope of economics, the school was able to "demonstrate" how activities such as crime, marriage, and drug addiction came under the purview of economics.

In their optic, far from being an act of altruism, parenthood turned out to be a means of investment in old age, in which families became little factories producing meals, health, skills, and children.[14] Suicide could be usefully explained not in terms of clinical depression or despair, but when "we assume that the individual kills himself when the total discounted lifetime utility remaining to him reaches zero" (remaining lifetime utility, of course, decreasing with age).[15] Marriage provides men with a supply of sexual activity, the cost of which has to be maintained against cheaper alternatives such as prostitution and pornography that "may reduce the total demand for [the partnered woman's] sexual favors, and as a result the price she can obtain will be lower."[16] Seemingly divorced from powerful human forces such as guilt, love, fear, longing, commitment, cruelty, and generosity, economics' boundless explanatory ambition was clarified in the introduction to "The Economics of Brushing Teeth" that states "Migration, maintenance of health, crime and punishment, even marriage and suicide, are all decisions which can usefully be considered from the human capital point of view. Yet economists have ignored the analysis of an important class of activities which can and should be brought within the purview of the theory": the important overlooked activity (brushing teeth), revealing how little "can and should" escape what critics have called economics imperialism.[17]

Some domains of life are supposed to have been withdrawn from market relations: religion, personal relations (identities, familial relations and friendships, bodily integrity, sexuality), the political sphere and public services, or the realm of Art, all conform or are presumed to conform to a different kind of logic than the market.[18] But so much of our lives have already been commodified. What parts of identity, sexuality, friendships, politics, public services, and the arts are not increasingly being annexed by market forces? Presumably, if boundaries between the two types of relations can be drawn on whether items are alienable or inalienable, transferable in exchange, there should be inalienable remainders that one cannot exchange (the body, trust, or faith, for example). But who owns the cell line entries gathered by human genome collection projects, for which patents can be sought? Organizations such as The Transnational Institute write of great "kidney bazaars" in which organs become alienable commodities (prices are geographically sensitive), and while a free market in human organs is currently an illegal practice, covered by the Transplantation of Human Organs Act (1994), there are proposals for state-organized trading in organs as a workable adjustment to free-market excess.[19] Even "Trust," in a recent publication by Gert Svendsen, was proposed as being the driving force behind the otherwise inexplicably successful economy of Denmark: Denmark being a country low on natural resources or large manufacturing industries, but high on cost-saving social trust.[20] In a dystopian version, one could imagine "trust" being incentivized through a system of exclusive "trust" credits.[21]

We are right to worry about where to set the line between regimes of the market and civil society, but the line has already moved so far. Books and the dreams they are machines for are already commodities, and unless we wish to operate with a model of immaterial texts of the imagination—inalienable and exempt from market forces—then we are forced to consider books under a regime of commodity value, including their meanings and the values they have for readers.

Fortunately, the annexation by economics is not foolproof. Indeed, it may have overextended itself, thus creating an opportunity for politics and culture to reengage. There are frailties in the neoclassical model based on the rational self-interested individual, in which the demands of the market economy supersede the needs of society, that were exposed during the crash of 2008, but that were papered over when that model reemerged as that crash's austerity-laden neoliberal solution.[22] Its frailties are systemic, gendered, and pervasive, but the build-up of critical studies by respected economists in exposing those frailties is approaching a tipping point.[23] David Harvey argues forcefully that neoliberal economics is part of a political program for shrinking the state and for accumulating capital, not through the expansion of labor that increases production in industry and agriculture, but as a process of taking over existing assets that he calls accumulation through dispossession.[24] In *Economyths: Ten Ways Economics Gets It Wrong* (2010), mathematician David Orrell provides a history of economic modeling and proposes why economies are neither rational nor fair.[25] Part 1 of Steven Keen's 2011 *Debunking Economics* is devoted to "Foundations: The logical flaws in the key concepts of conventional economics."[26] In *The Death of Homo Economicus* (2017), Peter Fleming details not only the flaws in the figure but the utter inadvisability of handing over the labor market to such a utility-maximizing self-interested individual.[27] Recent titles would include David Pilling, *The Growth Delusion: The Wealth and Well-Being of Nations* (2018), Nicholas Shaxson, *The Finance Curse: How Global Finance Is Making Us All Poorer* (2018), Wolfgang Streeck, *How Will Capitalism End? Essays on a Failing System* (2016), Yanis Varoufakis, *Talking to My Daughter about the Economy* (2017), Yves Smith, *ECONned: How Unenlightened Self-Interest Undermined Democracy and Corrupted Capitalism* (2010), and Guy Standing, *The Corruption of Capitalism: Why Rentiers Thrive and Work Does Not Pay* (2017). Major works by Thomas Piketty and Joseph Stiglitz are essential to this critical mass, along with Mariana Mazzucato's *The Value of Everything: Making and Taking in the Global Economy* (2018); as is the work of Ann Pettifor, who was one of the few to accurately predict the crash and who has detailed common misconceptions about the creation of money that underpin the neoliberal agenda.[28]

A comprehensive critique has been put forward by Katrine Marçal in *Who Cooked Adam Smith's Dinner* (2015).[29] Part of her objection lies in the frailty of the "efficient market" hypothesis wherein markets systemically attain a natural equilibrium, proposed in Adam Smith's "invisible hand."[30] As Marçal suggests, the hand's efficiency can obtain, but only if we ignore the emotional partisan so-called irrationality, and acts of unreasonable generosity and sacrifice traditionally gendered as "female"—along with the exploitation of them. Marçal's aim is not so much to reassess those acts of devotion into activities compatible with self-interest, but to suggest that the program of rational self-interested itself seeks to establish that measurement as the only valid criteria. Denounced as an embodiment of all that is coincidentally not feminine, the sovereign individual known as *homo economicus* must be independent of the other body from which it was born, as it remains independent from other bodies throughout its life. Otherwise, *economicus* might act "according to her bond with others. Not just out of self-interest and the denial of all context and power relationships."[31]

Behavior has as much to do with pride, senses of belonging, and power as it has with calculation, but the former, along with the labor of Adam Smith's mother, have been exorcised from the higher consciousness of the efficient market's invisible hand. Thus, the only humans who can operate within it are dispassionately male, and the only relationships they can have are based on competition. Doubtless, those following Gary Becker's "Freakonomic" innovations consider their thinking to be unflinching, but from another perspective it may appear ignorantly totalizing.

More widespread and less contentious, though no less valid than Marçal, are the observations of behavioral economics, established by Amos Tversky and Daniel Kahneman (both Nobel Memorial Prize winners). Their behavioral approach emerges from a marriage of psychology and economics in which modeling of brain information processing is mapped onto economic activity. For behavioral economics, "man" is no longer rational in the classical and neoclassical sense, but instead is predictably irrational; his capacity for rationality and selfishness instead bounded, or directed by emotion at the most immediate and pressing requirements. For example, in terms of consumption, the emotional drive for fairness can, at times, override or create constraints on rational profit-seeking and resist utilitarian surges in pricing. An example Kahneman provides is that, after a snow storm when demand is highest, the price of snow shovels should increase. This follows standard economic models for the price consequences of increased demand, but it is deemed unfair or very unfair by consumers who view the increase as a private loss and deem the exploitation of market power to impose losses unacceptable.[32] Or, for another example, a sudden windfall divided unequally by one of two unequal participants cannot approach 99:1, since the receiver of 1% of the windfall (denied the other 99%), though from standard economic prescriptions still receiving a self-interested gain, will deem the transaction unfair. Perceptions of unfairness can then typically lead to retaliation, in spite of self-interest.[33]

Since behavioralists propose that decision-making often deviates from the prescriptions of utility theory—and that rational self-interest is predictably circumscribed by affective, ethical responses—it implies that neoclassical normative theory (of what people *should* do) ought not to be deployed as a descriptive theory (of what people *do* do).[34] People display traits like loyalty and have a disposition for compromise. They fight harder to prevent losses than to achieve gains, and place more weight on past events than on predictable outcomes.[35]

We think with what Kahneman calls the brain's two-part system, "system one" of which uses heuristics (cognitive shortcuts). System one is supreme in its agility required for immediate survival, using emotive reference points (such as "fairness") for quick orientation, but it also "supresses ambiguity and spontaneously constructs stories that are as coherent as possible."[36] Consequently, we are particularly poor at predicting probabilities, often ignoring baselines and biases, and we are swayed by anchoring and framing, the latter explained in the "Asian disease problem."[37] Two hypothetical alternative health-intervention programmes are proposed to combat a deadly disease that will almost certainly kill 600 people. Program A will probably save 200 people, while in Program B there is a one-third probability that 600 will be saved and a two-thirds probability that no one will. Respondents to this deliberately complex formulation significantly chose Program A, although the outcomes of both are identical. The proposition can then be re-framed with surprising results. In Program A, 400 people will almost certainly die, but in Program B there is a one-third probability that no-one will die but a two thirds probability everyone will. Respondents voted equally enthusiastically for Program B, although the consequences of both A and B in both propositions were identical.

Behavioral economics is widely predicted to provide economists with the field's next major development, and its reconstitution of the field's "Newtonian" rationality would be welcome. However, one response has been to regret human irrationality as a "fault" and, thus, recommend a corrective policy in what is called libertarian paternalism. Current economic models are unworkable if economists are no longer able to deduce according to the structural assumption that people act out of self-interest; so—as the approach would have it—people need to be nudged back into rational shape. The idea of nudging can be expressed either progressively or regressively, depending on your politics; David Halpern's *Inside the Nudge Unit* (2015), about the Behavioural Insights Team set up by UK Tory Prime Minister David Cameron, which drew on inputs from the US Obama Administration, is an ambiguous case in point.[38] But the accent on paternalism can be extreme. Drawing on US behavioral economics studies of the labor market and unemployment insurance,[39] advisers to the Unemployment Benefit Commission established by the Danish Ministry of Employment chose to frame their nudging recommendations by pointing to the often "limited rationality and self-control" of individuals who are unemployed: "limited rationality prevents job seekers from always knowing what they want," the report explained, and "limited self-control prevents job seekers from always doing what they want."[40] For the commission's advisers, so-called irrational behavior, or rather bounded rationality, is a failure in need of correction. Who then should have sovereignty over the individual's decision-making? Our decision-making takes part in an affective system, but that does not invalidate the decision; it simply means that a desire for fairness and thus empathy is also in operation. The valance of nudging lies in the power relations it establishes, but using rationality as the sole benchmark to validate human behavior has no part in any descriptive *science humaines*.

Commodities are not inherently evil, because they are not things but things experienced in the form of a particular relationship. It is in institutionalized neoclassical economics that the social texture is erased and commodities become a class of object that we wish books were not. The social relationship necessary for any object to become a commodity is also not only evil. It all depends on how liberation and exploitation are distributed in the exchange, and as John Frow writes, "the commodity form has the potential to be enabling and productive as well as to be limiting and destructive. Historically it has almost always been both of these things at the same time."[41] To identify the commodity form as something solely to be resisted is both historically naïve and politically unwise, since so much of our living is created through this relationship. For cultural critics, Bakunin was clear about the dangers of retreating from the *question économique*, especially when those critics wrote, as Evan Brier puts it of several major postwar accounts of literature and the marketplace, "compelling accounts of the marketplace context that nonetheless view literature as something utterly apart from it."[42] More subtle are those sociological accounts, pioneered in Bourdieu's *Field of Cultural Production* (1993) and critically developed in works such as James English's *Economy of Prestige* (2005) or Lawrence Rainey's *Institutions of Modernism* (1998), which view published literary works as outputs from a network of institutions whose job is to produce and sell a concept called "literature." Other outputs may include cultural capital for readers and recognition for authors—achievements reached not in spite of but because of the institutions' exclusive position in the market economy. But even these historically precise and materially aware accounts require the counter-conception of a field of mass production and "industrial literature," against which the narrow field of serious authorship appears in contrast.[43] In the clicks-and-mortar bookshop, however, all is as industrial as it ever had been for shoppers in the early-twentieth century, and narrow "literature" is still irretrievably a part of market-mediated desire as it was when books were merely one line in a provincial shop offering stationery, bags, and "fancy."

A concern remains, however, in that no matter how much cultural criticism undertakes commentary on commodities, it still seems to lack the clarity achieved by neoclassical economics. The latter's clarity comes from adopting simple determinants, in which scarcity and self-interest can be expressed as algebraic symbols, x, y, and z, and from which complex mathematical gymnastics can be performed. The clarity is achieved by taking things that can be *more* or *less* in magnitude, but then ascribing to them the condition of being quantifiable and therefore amenable to "applying differential calculus to the familiar notions of wealth, utility, value, demand, supply, capital, interest, labour and all the other notions belonging to the daily operations of industry."[44] But it is precisely this that is its limitation. Economics achieves its clarity by adopting simple determinants. It may be insightful to gather a world of seeking pleasure and avoiding pain in the unifying term "utility," in the idea that "anything which an individual is found to desire . . . must be assumed to possess utility."[45] But is it valid to claim that any item which can be more or less, such as more or less pleasure, is indeed unambiguously quantifiable? By how much is my pleasure greater than it was yesterday: two times as great or three times? Would it be possible to use pleasure as a unit of calculation if my pleasures are conflicted? Simplicity can be a strength but, as behavioralists confirm, it also "supresses ambiguity and spontaneously constructs stories" to appear as coherent as possible. Thus Jevons is able to say with coherent certainty that pleasure and pain are inversely proportional, "that to decrease pain is to increase pleasure; to add pain is to decrease pleasure."[46] Without exploring the margins of sadomasochism, it is enough to question whether that abstracted relationship is actually valid. Cannot an experience produce increases in *both* pleasure *and* pain together, and why is the opposite of pleasure and pain not better expressed as emptiness or boredom? It may be a matter of indifference if desire is expressed as a word or as a cipher x, y, or z, as Jevons claimed, but not the use of those terms in subsequent algebras, as any linguist will confirm. Human desire may be concealed in $5x$, but if we remain only at the algebraic $5x$, we will have failed fail to read the sign. Codification is not truth but material that requires reading.

Any commodity x is in the commodity form because specific human relations make it so. If there is any "evil," it comes from claiming the relationship can only be described using a simplistic concept like self-interest. Adam Smith was right in ascribing the prime motivation to economic activity as self-interest only in so far as it has a self-regenerative aspect. Adam Smith, and the Physiocrats who preceded him, constructed a counterpoint to mercantile systems of wealth protection through legislation and external sanctions, which they achieved in their conception of a circulating economics of *l'ordre naturel*: a self-regenerating system running according to internal motivations that needed to be left alone (*laissez-faire*). But to title the self-perpetuating aspect of this system "self-interest" is to equip a motion with a moral purpose. The more neutral term is "desire." The economy (that is, book retail in Southampton) runs not on self-interest but on desire, and our desires are not only difficult to quantify but impossible to reduce to the individual's self-interest. I may desire to give up, or I may make a sacrifice in the name of fairness. My desires may even be irrational and in need of nudging. I may desire that I not be required to calculate at all, and simply be allowed to copy what everyone else does. The predictive clarity we assume to be carried by economics is the clarity available to exceptional behaviors that often have little to do with the people they claim to describe.

Cultural studies do not explain the market with the brevity achieved by economics, but perhaps that is the point. When the consumption of symbolic goods comprises the rich cultural politics of subjective reading, how can that consumption be adequately described in equations of scarcity and demand with value expressed in the component of equilibrium price? In the book market, the sign's value is not derived from inherent properties, but is instead created by the reader's framed experience of the sign, making its value subjective from moment to moment and from place to place. Thus a true theory of consumption for symbolic goods must adequately account for value far beyond that determined by production costs and the labor required to produce it, and beyond that deduced when the forces of demand supposedly reach equilibrium with those of supply. It should instead be able to take full account of intense levels of situationality.

Marxist economics treats value in its two aspects of *use-value* and *exchange-value*. The use-value of a shoe, to use Aristotle's example, is derived from a wearer wearing it, compared to the value she can get for the shoe in exchange—the latter being the value of the object when alienated in a system of equivalencies, expressible through price and, since labor is required to produce the shoe, expressible in equivalent amounts of disembodied labor. It is this alienating exchange-value that equates people (and their labor) with quantities of things. The remedy for such bad equating, for Marx, comes with the use-championing refrain "from each according to his ability, to each according to his needs."

Nevertheless, the shoe's use-value is a constant concept, regardless of who wears the shoe or how. In Marx's terms, use-value is limited to the distinct properties of an object. It coincides, he wrote, "with the physical palpable existence of the commodity. Wheat for example is a distinct use-value differing from the use-value of cotton, glass, paper etc.," and it is quantitatively measurable in measurements appropriate to the physical characteristics, "for example, a bushel of wheat, a quire of paper, a yard of linen."[47] Unlike shoes, symbols are not the same regardless of who reads or how they are read, so what measurement might gauge their ability to supply gains? Shoes are good for wearing on feet, best bought in pairs, but reading books is good for nothing tangible beyond that which the reader creates. In addition, what subjectivity there is in conventional conceptions of use-value (if it can be called that) is limited to classes of people as a whole, to all bare-footed people who need shoes. It does not adequately inscribe the subjectivity of a sign reader at a momentary imaginative junction between herself and her society.

This issue of subjectivity is tackled by neoclassical economics in the theory of marginalism that operates with a value that is not intrinsic but subjective in the sense that any fixed value derived from material production is relative to the desire for its use—goods such as a bottle of clean water may be worth little, but with scarcity the price-value increases exponentially. The approach rejects the idea of value derived from production costs and quantities of disembodied labor, instead favoring a conception of value depending on subjective utility and the relative perceptions of users and suppliers. The change is something historians of economics refer to as the shift from value based on relations between capital and labor to a market-determined subjective theory of value, which took place in the second half of the nineteenth century.[48]

To achieve a proper subjective theory, as Jevons saw it, required having "a means of measuring directly the feeling of the human heart," but he was equally clear of its impossibility, in that "a unit of pleasure or of pain is difficult to even conceive."[49] The solution Jevons and his fellow marginalists arrived at was both ingenious and perfectly suited to mathematical gymnastics, in that the answer was to measure, not utility u, but comparative *change* in the levels of u that would otherwise have been immeasurable desire. It did not matter that whatever pleasure's u signified could not be unpacked (let us imagine derived from consuming item x), because increases in pleasure gained through increases of x, written as Δx, could be expressed as the whole utility (U) derived from $x + \Delta x$ that must be $u + \Delta u$. From such insight came the development of marginalism: that U is a function of Δu relative to Δx, or $\Delta u/\Delta x$. The proposal was that wants for a unit of any commodity were relative to the amount of units available, and that the more units any individual has, the less will be the desire for further units. Put bluntly, marginalism became a general theorem of "an additional unit of":

> marginal production costs are thus the diminishing costs of producing more units of something, marginal revenue is the extra revenue that an additional unit will bring in, and marginal utility refers to the diminishing desire for additional units. I want a car, I want a second car, but my want of a third and fourth diminishes, while for the hundredth car my want will approach zero. This rate of change is not only quantifiable but comparable. My want of more units of, say, apples, socks, sheets of paper, sofas, televisions, and so on will diminish at differing rates and thereby be comparable. The inscrutability of minds, in principle, is thus revealed.[50]

However, when it comes to symbolic goods, the issue is that despite all its subjectivity marginalism still operates with a fixed unit. The value of symbolic goods may no longer be that derived from production and labor costs, but they are still derived from a conceptually stable unit. Furthermore, it is the stability of such units that enables the nominal "fixity" that is the equilibrium or market price: the price achieved when the least that the marginal supplier is willing to accept equals the most that the marginal buyer is willing to pay; that is, when forces of supply and demand meet. Such "fixity" derived from a stable unit still signifies a conception of core value from which marginal activity is calculated.

For symbolic goods, however, value is structured very differently being something not intrinsic to the object but created by the reader often as a bespoke re-signaling of social identity. Value in symbolic goods is derived, therefore, not from relations between demand and scarcity, but from how the sign socializes the individual in respect of other readers. There is no core value from which marginality can be derived. Diamonds may be rare and water plentiful (in some regions), but whether a reading is unique or commonplace cannot be preempted by the text. The reading experience is conditioned not by scarcity but by intertextuality and the socialization of both the reader and her text. "Scarcity" is a term that presupposes stable repeatable units, like so many bottles of water, so how can a reading, which itself changes both reader and intertextual relationships, be adequately accounted for in its terms? The key term is no longer "scarcity" but "socialization."

For symbolic goods that are books, Lee Erickson applied marginal thinking to reading in *The Economy of Literary Form*, but not entirely successfully, wavering between the diminishing marginal utility derived from successive rereadings (additional units of reading) and the diminishing marginal utility from buying successive copies (additional copies).[51] What Erickson suggested was that in times of relative scarcity, and expensive books, readers will tend toward books that withstand increases in rereading—meaning literary works—and that in times of cheaper literature the preference is for single readings—meaning bestsellers. The idea is appealing to those wishing to guard the barrier (and who might ignore historical data showing that a title like *Middlemarch* was the bestseller and fastseller of its day, or who find it hard to believe that people might think bestsellers are rereadable), but the chief issue is that its use of utility works with a monolithic un-subjective audience, deploying its "aggregate calculus of such individual desires [that] is then reflected in the market."[52] Erickson's is still an avowedly "classic free-market economic analysis" that calculates an idealized reader applicable "for most people, most of the time"[53]—or, as Jevons puts it, "by supposing that we are always dealing with the single average individual, the unit of which population is made up."[54] In its reliance on fixed average individuals making standardized evaluations of a stable sign, marginalism disqualifies itself from being able to judge the value of symbolic goods.

In the book market, the value of an item is utterly personalized through the framing of signs, which include its wording, its peri- and epitexts, and the sign that is its price. Those signs are intertextual and experienced culturally and politically as an event that is the Net Work, while the physical book copy and the reader's hands are merely nodes among many institutional and individual actants whose collective task is to create the network. The network does not exist *despite* the market, nor as an *inverted mirror* of the market struggling to distance itself from market-based industrial fiction. It *constitutes* the market while remaining an "irrational" aberrative power-charged network of readers and their publications. Simple perhaps, but not simplistic, the claim is that the network comprises what in effect is "the market" but—stuffed as it is with the politics of identity formation, betrayal, longing, and all other power conditions that the goods of books promise to respond to—without adhering to market rationality. The network is "the market," but in a way that economics cannot express.

The first proposition has been to conceive of works of fiction as events in an ongoing network sustained by books, readers, publishers, writers, distributors, newsagents, libraries, and bookshops. The next has been to claim that the regime of value in which the network operates, which "bestows" value, and which guarantees its long-term frame, is commodity culture, emerging in the last third of the nineteenth century in the UK and still expanding. The combination of those two propositions means that Net Works are used for gains from efferent reading, produced primarily in terms of entertainments, but not purely hedonic ones, encompassing identity formation, senses of belonging, and other satisfactions of profound desires. The problem, however, has been that the two propositions are not entirely compatible. The gluing together of these propositions still leaves a binary conception of readers' desires and market-enabled values, between economics and the humanities, *unless* we admit that these actor transactions, and these operations of desire themselves, create the conditions for gains. Their actions enable market values to exist, and thus the market becomes an effect of the network. In this sense, the market economy is simply the network in operation, and what we think of as a market is simply the network with its proper "socio-political" descriptor.

To be precise, economics, or at least the section of economics that deals with the market consumption of symbolic goods, should be thought of as a political economy. We should not surrender the market, consumption, and the commodity regime to economists. We should not leave the field to an economic discipline bereft of cultural and political study. Economics is political, and not a natural law, since it is created through social engagement. For markets of symbolic goods, the economy does not run on the recalculation of value fixed by production costs according to specific conditons of demand, but instead runs on the individual's experience of intertextuality, its values created not from scarcity but from processes of socialization. And because its most fluid operative is not *homo economicus* but *homo narrans*, she can read her gains in any number of ways beyond self-interest that can be both selfish and selfless. Untrammeled by individual greed, she can choose to read in different ways and for collective reasons.

Conclusion

If there is a standoff in the humanities between the values of art, literature, and aesthetics on the one hand and economic value on the other, then the confrontation is the result of a foolish paradox. To maintain any exclusivity or, rather, its distinction, literary critical discourse needs to articulate what the voice of the collective cannot, and give voice to something that it assumes society cannot: the objects of its research, thus tending likewise to be not commercial fabrications or formulaic entertainments but works of high literary quality by serious writers. Since literary criticism practices intense criticality and not merely reflective journalistic description, the pronouncements of criticism, in the liberational sense, have to be more than a translation of what the network that is society-in-the-making is currently saying. But in doing so, the critical distinction produces exactly a retreat from the articulation of commonplace experience, and from that which the collective is already saying. Its distinctive endeavor risks saying next to nothing about the popular traffic in literatures on the High Street from the user's point of view, or about the desires that induced what Collins called the "unknown public" to turn to those literatures and sustain them.

There are good political reasons for this maneuver, too: to guard the sure barrier against commercially induced servitude and to protect a free space for autonomous thinking. But attractive as it may be, the autonomy also withdraws itself to an imaginary space beyond the large part of our lives that are commercially determined. Because as Clover and Nealon put it, the very idea of an "alternative" value results from an erroneous "division of the political and the economic into discrete domains," the improbability of which is paralleled in incongruities such as somehow, potentially, "we are politically liberated in the sense of formal [political] freedom, while we are at the same time economically unfree."[1]

Freedom if it can only be had on evenings and weekends is not real freedom, and thus the distinction that is predicated on autonomy will never articulate leisure-time dreaming that itself emerges from the labor required to achieve it. Our dreams have the shape they do *because* we spend so much of our waking lives constrained by economic contingencies. To use an ironic mirror, the autonomy of critical arts discourse if it does not take part in the economic sphere is the autonomy of Adam Smith ignoring his mother's daily unpaid labor that sustained him.

Consolidation, or "retrenchment around disciplinary commitments to the literary,"[2] merely exposes commonplace experience to other forces. And whatever succeeds in modeling the commons will exert power over it. From the far side of the mutually constituting foolishness, neoliberalism puts itself forward as a contender. Its political iteration of economics approaches the everyday and, rather than modeling economies or economic activity within it, instead turns economics into an instrument made applicable *to all human behavior*, as Becker put it[3]—or, in Marçal's formulation, "Economists have become more and more interested in trying to apply their models to everything from racism to orgasms and less and less interested in studying how real markets work."[4] Love is no longer a practice of un-Othering, an attraction to difference and an opening up to difference and its implications, as Alain Badiou suggests, but in the neoliberal optic becomes an asset to be acquired and lost.[5] Parenthood becomes investment, trust becomes a marketing strategy, our bodies become human capital from which everyone can become "a self-exploiting worker in their own enterprise"—they can be, in part, but such economizing statements are bloated.[6] Their inflation stems from spoiled metaphors. Human life creates market exchange, money, and a promise to pay "to the bearer on demand," but it creates much else besides. In short, life is in no way adequately explained by the market model, and at the same time neither is life what is left when the market is subtracted.

Fortunately, in the common experience of the consumption of symbolic goods, it becomes apparent that there are fault lines to the economics model favored by neoliberalism. Foundational terms traceable to neoclassical economics, and further back to the discipline's eighteenth-century emergence, no longer appear fit for purpose, to the extent that the model may even begin to break. Depending on how the metaphor of consumption is understood—not all goods are soft goods to be used up—in the consumption of symbolic goods nothing is consumed that is not read. Items may be purchased and used, and, as with logo T-shirts, the value of books cannot be created without some form of semiotic engagement that we can rightly call reading. It might be imagined that a reader makes a choice in purchasing a book, calculating which will bring maximum utility—that is fairly unproblematic—but the reading consumption itself importantly both results from charged personal histories, shaped by factors of class, gender, and race, and is configured in the moment at the conjuncture between reader and the frame of her society. A reading is achieved through the practice of reading, emerging from an experience of the sign framed by specific conditions, and not as something that can be predictively calculated. Utterly intertextual in both its learning and its practice, reading is foremost a verb and process happening between the ears, and those ears are always somewhere, with a culture, politics, and a history. When commodified, the process of reading symbolic value indeed requires a material object to allow an otherwise intangible sign to participate in exchange—without a material object or service there is nothing to buy—but the values that drive its economy arise out of a different process to estimating price-value under conditions of scarcity. In unpacking or, rather, creating value from symbolic goods, consumption becomes a term that is simply not very helpful in describing market behavior. It is precisely this limitation that has been recognized in other terms by consumer culture theory, expressed in David Graeber's polemical question about why it is we automatically assume that the term "consumption" makes sense.[7]

Most alarming is that in the era of post-Fordist production, when developed economies move further toward an experience economy focused on tertiary-sector services (and where brute manufacture is farmed out to unregulated export processing zones), it is hard to imagine what sorts of market do not in some way trade in symbolic goods. What possible dimension is there to the very concept of "brand" that does not take part in an economy of symbols?

Unhelpful, too, is the figure who is said to make these buying and selling calculations, equipped as he is with full knowledge of market conditions and driven by self-interest, to use Jevons's market definition. *Homo economicus* may build up experience (*Erfahrung*) that contributes to his market knowledge, but he is badly placed in the business of experiencing (*Erlebnis*). Experiencing, or reading, has no part in calculation; indeed, if premeditated calculation in any way detracts from the process of experiencing, they may be inversely proportional. And since the consumption-that-is-reading is a mode of experiencing, in what sense would *homo economicus* be a suitable figure to take part in that process? His role might be adequate if it could be confined only to supply and purchase of the material sign but, when the material's value is conditional on its symbolic dimension, is there any stage within the entire process of production, supply, and demand when reading symbolic goods is not required? Too limited by his preconception with "full-market knowledge" (and too focused on equating value to price), *homo economicus* is a really bad reader. More importantly, he is bad in a way that *homo narrans* never can be.

Modes of reading provided by *homo narrans* may be wide-ranging, from silent recital to reading the riot act; and not everything she does is applicable to her life under commodity culture—or rather, not all her readings are ones from which commodity culture can be created. However, when she *does* read material signs for the purpose of gaining intangible goods, she creates commodity culture on her own terms and provides a progressive symbolic-market model. In following economist Deirdre McCloskey who, in her counter-distinction to Kantian autonomous reading, defined a reading that takes away gains as an efferent reading,[8] *homo narrans* can become the central figure to the market of symbolic goods at her efferent best.

Neoclassical economic modeling minimizes the social, cultural dimension to consumer choice by subordinating it into individual subjective demand. Internally, the logic of such modeling may be consistent, but externally it collides with too many cases that prove the modeling inadequate. Under other conditions, the roles can be reversed, and economics becomes subordinated into the culture that subsumes economic activity within it. When not otherwise engaged in gainful labor, Southampton's unknown public of the early twentieth century sought gains from the shops of the High Street; from the affiliations, prejudices, and predilections they read out of their leisure-sector activities: at variety theatres, at race courses, at a lido, at a skating rink, and from football at the Dell; but also among the leather and fancy goods, stationery, baskets, glassware, playing cards, and pen hospitals, the same public sought gains from its books. In seeking opportunities and accepting the associated opportunity costs, they created the life of the High Street. Their market decisions may have been forged by the prejudice and generosity of their culture, but the same forging culture created the "market" High Street.

Where social relationships are most impacted by price and scarcity in book retail, we can find evidence in direct sale, but on the historically attuned High Street more often readers gained access by subscribing to circulating libraries, through longitudinal systems of secondhand supply, by the hire-purchase of installment fiction, or via catalogs distributed to private homes creating networks of aspiration, all of which were structured by social, racial, and gender hierarchies that, in addition to ability, were also drivers of the necessary companion regime of regular employment. It was interpersonal relations, and judgments based on class and gender, that enabled the nineteenth- and early-twentieth-century system of deferred payment with different rates for different classes of reader.

Readers among what Wright called the "young lady" classes lent their purchased materials to each other, as did Sylvie and Rita, and they passed on these goods to their clerk, shopkeeper, and artisan husbands, as well as to male and female friends. Their, or rather our, recommendations cause value to accrue when drawn on friendships and diminish when deposited by those to whom we are indifferent. What drives this informal, though still market-bound system are social values of affection that outstrip any idea of consumer behavior shorn of its citizenry aspect. And with the Net Book Agreement, there is a systemized example of this desire to make the market accommodate its citizenry dimension, despite pseudo-free-market rationality, on the grounds that books are somehow "different" (and where healthcare and food security could yet be). Regardless of its relative merits, the sheer longevity of the NBA demonstrates that markets *have* functioned successfully through a fusion of political-economic value.

Value creation in such networked activity overwhelms the boundaries of what can be modeled solely through sovereign-individual calculations of self-interest and scarcity. In Southampton, not only were those values created from cultural conventions, they were maintained by social, political, and juridical forces, forever subject to default—policed through contracts, which did not always turn out to be binding, re-enforced in legislations and agreements that were systemically challenged, and backed by the criminal justice system that agents such as Gilbert's shoplifters chose to ignore. Far from a free trade, the book market of symbolic goods relied and relies on policing and the policing of cultural difference.

Book retail was regulated by intra-trade relations, too, wherein the interplay of social and cultural capitals affected price. Neoclassical economics might explain these interplaying capitals as expressions of market forces, but is the ordering justified? Gilbert's stock and its delivery needed to distinguish itself from that of George Buxey, Thomas James, and the Southampton Book Society, among others, but—as a nonconformist, Liberal, and champion of free public libraries—Gilbert's was a distinguishing that took place for reasons that were religious and political as much as purely financial, as did the men's city-center businesses in distinguishing themselves from women's news agencies in the suburbs—and all inseparable from various actors' perceptions of gender, race, religion, politics, and class. Affection and allegiance helped regulate the supply chain, too. Whenever publishing opportunities arose to turn Southampton's history into printable assets, the trade was only too keen, but what created the publication's value if not a symbolic sense of city-belonging, binding readers to retail business in an imagined civic community? Not as law of or an adjunct to civic community, this publishing market was an output of the community, open to its agents for reconfiguring.

Optimistic gas-and-water socialism drove Southampton's free public libraries that were also supported by a private-business bookseller, Henry March Gilbert, as a complement to private retail, suggesting that the development of the High Street's overall reading practice should be thought of as a private-civic partnership. In the bookshop itself, symbolic values were framed by those large politicized narratives, of optimism and despair, so that the misery of the Great Dock Strike framed readers' encounters with their bibliographic objects. The framing that was of political aspirations and betrayals determined whether specific works of fiction, by MacLane and Griffith, were perceived to offer freedom or falsehood in their promises of emigration or futuristic technocracies. But as co-determinants of price-value for each book, too, do not such narratives also suggest of that there is much about "market forces" that are reliant on the culture and politics of narrative and belief?

Unlike a statement of physics, when neoclassical economics states relative positions for politics, culture, and subjective demand, it is proposing not a verifiable statement of fact but a provisional description, which proves accurate in certain cases, but in others turns out to be merely wishful thinking. And as with any description, there are alternatives. What actor-network theory proposes is a non-essentialist notion of society comprising networks of exchange, continually recreating themselves in real time. Markets can be regarded as actor-networks, according to Michel Callon, constituted by the relations between decision-making actors and the entities that are traded and used.[9] For the market of symbolic goods such as a book trade this begins to make sense. When not hunting cribbage boards and dance cards, Southampton readers browsed their literatures and created entertainments, which itself enabled processes of identity formation, fulfilled promises of solace, and provided company, advice, or just plain recreation. More than vehicles of hedonic pleasure, the values readers were able to create from their books not only sustained readers but, in effect, created the High Street retail network. Not an add-on system that maps market price onto a regime of culture, the book retail network is one in which cultural value is the driving currency. In this respect, price becomes what actor-network theory would call a means of translation, one among many, and one useful specifically to the material dimension of the overall exchange. Rather than two values deriving from two separate regimes—a cultural use value and an exchange value expressed in price—value for book retail is singularly political-economic.

The history of Southampton's High Street is one of exchange-based culture. It would be wrong, therefore, to conceive an item of cultural production, a book, entering its leisure sector to struggle or succeed there as a cultural object *despite* the economic framing. On the High Street, culture *is* trade, and bibliographic objects there are party to producing its leisure-sector network. In contrast to an institutionalized-economic modeling, however, the vital difference is that the book-object's value is measured not by an equilibrium price alone, but in its cultural politicaleconomic value as a whole. The network description does not conceive readers' culture and politics as hangovers from another regime, important only insofar as they affect subjective estimations of value. In contrast, the social-network market is constituted by symbolic (bibliographic) objects and their efferent readers, in which price and commodity exchange are important translational features helping create the network's culture and its politics. Readers, as *homo narrans*, create the conditions for readerly gains. Motivated by ambiguous desires, predicated on their discrepant self-identities, their actions allow gains to exist, and the gains emerge as an effect of the actor-network. In this sense "economics" is simply the material dimension of the network in operation, and what we think of as market activity is instead the network with its proper socioeconomic descriptor. And rather than the maximization of self-interest under conditions of scarcity, reading, or the consumption of symbolic goods, might be better described as the ongoing creating of self-identity in a process of collective socialization.

When Kipling, Conrad, and Crawford, Ouida, Eliot, and Mary MacLane performed on the High Street alongside soft mantillas, coquettish fans, Bayerisch ales and café Suisse, they performed as events. Comprising people, places, and bibliographic objects, these events were, and in enduring cases still are, phenomena of social exchange, sustained by the hopes and desires of readers. Efferent reading and gaining is simply an outcome made possible by the collective interactions that continually re-produce the network. A work of fiction, in this sense, is a networked event, a Net Work, sustained in real time for as long as there are iterations and readerly activity. As meaning is to reception studies, value in the network is not intrinsic but created as an effect of the network, in which cultural and economic value are two components of the same heterogeneous complexity. Spilling out beyond its dock gates, this High Street network reached out into old worlds and new, to Hamburg and Buenos Aires—to wherever the contextualizing frame of commodity culture emerged, and still emerges. The High Street both online and off becomes *the* global locus of coordinating cultural and economic values; and what could possibly model it if not a political economy?

The network market of symbolic goods might provide a new testbed for modeling political-economic behavior, and the retail book trade and the work of book, language, and literature historians are well-placed to contribute to that project. In the network, key terms are not intrinsic but relative, where items such as "consumption" as construed by neoclassical economics can be seen as ideological constructions rather than universal facts. Such a relative valorization is the network's *differentia specifica*. Consumption can be to consume to destruction but also, positively, to consummate. Debt is credit and credit is debt depending on your network position. In the network, whether you are the person who loans or the loanee who borrows determines whether the sum is a liability or an asset. Investment might mean what we expect, which is a support for the welfare of something, instead of covertly meaning an invasion to capture the most profitable assets and then to charge rent for their use. Unemployment benefit does not have to be a cost but could be an investment in social stability necessary to business. Tax can become stakeholding. The freedom so cherished by free-marketeers does not have to be a freedom for pikes, and the liberalization of markets need not be brutal deregulation for the benefit of wealthy monopolists. The definitions—or, rather, the conventions—of a term's use are matters of collective choice, and of politics.

Southampton at the end of the second decade of the twenty-first century is very much contextualized as it long has been by its commodity culture. But currently, the outputs of that cultural configuration are captured in absurd metrics that, once measured, are "effectivized" and financialized in economic terms. On a scale of one to five, how happy are we with our lives—but does the challenge of reducing the "residue" have to be addressed only through private enterprise? It is still possible to follow a footpath across Cobden Bridge along the river Itchen into Chapel, St. Mary's, and up to the High Street, where people are still careful about their time and money; where over- and under-consumption provides one side of a coin, to which the other is affluence but also food banks and in-work poverty. And in the most hard-pressed sections of the city, there are still readers who accept the opportunity costs of a machine for dreaming. Like disciplinary alignments, current conditions in Southampton are not the result of a universal economic law but the effects of particular choices. If we wish, we can choose something else.

Appendix
Biblioteca: Toward a Bibliography of Works Published by H.M. Gilbert and Sons

Hampshire Field Club and Archaeological Society	*Essays in Honour of Frank Warren*, edited by W.J. Carpenter Turner	Southampton: H.M. Gilbert	1956
Hampshire Field Club and Archaeological Society	*Papers and Proceedings of the Hampshire Field Club and Archaeological Society*, vol. 18, edited by W.J. Carpenter Turner	Southampton: H.M. Gilbert	1954
Hampshire Field Club and Archaeological Society	*Papers and Proceedings of the Hampshire Field Club and Archaeological Society*, vol. 17, edited by N. Cook and [Mrs.] W.J. Carpenter Turner	Southampton: H.M. Gilbert	1952
Hampshire Field Club and Archaeological Society	*Papers and Proceedings of the Hampshire Field Club and Archaeological Society*, vol. 16, edited by W.J. Ferrar, B. Vesey-FitzGerald, N. Cook	Southampton: H.M. Gilbert	1947
Hampshire Field Club and Archaeological Society	*Papers and Proceedings of the Hampshire Field Club and Archaeological Society*, vol. 15, 1940–1943, edited by W.J. Ferrar	Southampton: H.M. Gilbert	1943
Hampshire Field Club and Archaeological Society	*Papers and Proceedings of the Hampshire Field Club and Archaeological Society*, vol. 14, 1937–1939, edited by W.J. Ferrar	Southampton: H.M. Gilbert	1940

continued on next page

Hampshire Field Club and Archaeological Society	Papers and Proceedings of the Hampshire Field Club and Archaeological Society, vol. 13, 1935–1937, edited by F.N. Davis	Southampton: H.M. Gilbert	1937
Perkins, W. Frank	A New Forest Bibliography	Lymington: King and Southampton: Gilbert	1935
Hampshire Field Club and Archaeological Society	Papers and Proceedings of the Hampshire Field Club and Archaeological Society, vol. 12, 1931–1934, edited by F.N. Davis	Southampton: H.M. Gilbert	1934
James, J.L. Beaumont	James Trevaskis: A Study in Personality [local history]	Southampton: Gilbert	1932
Hampshire Field Club and Archaeological Society	Papers and Proceedings of the Hampshire Field Club and Archaeological Society, General Index to Vols. 1–10: 1885–1932, edited by F.W.C. Pepper	n/a: Gilbert	1932
Hampshire Field Club and Archaeological Society	Papers and Proceedings of the Hampshire Field Club and Archaeological Society, vol. 10, 1926–1930, edited by F.N. Davis	Southampton: H.M. Gilbert	1931
Unsworth, Alfred Leslie	Notes on the History of Compton and Shawford, in the County of Southampton	Southampton: Gilbert	1930
Kelsall, J.E.	Bird Friends	Southampton: Gilbert	1927
Hampshire Field Club and Archaeological Society	Papers and Proceedings of the Hampshire Field Club and Archaeological Society, vol. 9, 1920–1924, edited by J. Hautenville Cope	Southampton: H.M. Gilbert	1927
Rayner, John Frederick	Standard Catalogue of English Names of Our Wild Flowers: To Which Are Added the Ferns and their Allies	Southampton: H.M. Gilbert and London: Simpkin, Marshall and Co.	1927

Sumner, Heywood	*New Forest Bibliography and List of Maps*	Southampton: Gilbert	1925
Hampshire Field Club and Archaeological Society	*Papers and Proceedings of the Hampshire Field Club and Archaeological Society*, vol. 8, 1917–1919, edited by J. Hautenville Cope	n/a: Gilbert	1920
Grundy, G.B.	*On Place Names in General and Hampshire Place Names in Particular*	Southampton: H.M. Gilbert	1922
Hampshire Field Club and Archaeological Society	*Papers and Proceedings of the Hampshire Field Club and Archaeological Society*, vol. 7, 1914–1916, edited by J. Hautenville Cope	n/a: Gilbert	1916
	Plans of Excavations of Rockbourne Down	Southampton: H.M. Gilbert and Sons	1914
Westlake, Richard	*He Yet Speaketh: A Centenary Sketch of Dr. Edward Harman Maul*	Southampton: H.M. Gilbert	1913
Lemon, James[1]	*Reminiscences of Public Life in Southampton, from 1866–1900*, vol. 2	n/a: Gilbert	1911
Lemon, James	*Reminiscences of Public Life in Southampton, from 1866–1900*, vol. 1	n/a: Gilbert	1911
Royal Yacht Squadron	*Catalogue of the Library, R.Y.S. Castle, Cowes (Isle Of Wight)*	Southampton: Gilbert	1911
Hampshire Field Club and Archaeological Society	*Papers and Proceedings of the Hampshire Field Club and Archaeological Society*, vol. 6, 1907–1910, edited by F.J.C. Hearnshaw	Southampton: H.M. Gilbert	1910
Sumner, Heywood	*The Book of Gorely: Written and illustrated by H. Sumner*	Southampton, Winchester: H.M. Gilbert	1910
Pennell, Rosalie F.	*Account of the Parish of Hyde, Winchester: Past and Present*	Winchester: Gilbert	1909

continued on next page

Gilbert, H.M.	Catalogue of the Library at Minstead Manor House, in the Possession of Henry Francis Compton, Esq.	n/a: H.M. Gilbert	1907
Hearnshaw, F.J.C., and D.M. Hearnshaw, transcribers and editors	Court Leet Records [local history], vol. 1, part 2, A.D. 1578–1602	Southampton: Gilbert	1906
Hearnshaw, F.J.C., and D.M. Hearnshaw, transcribers and editors	Court Leet records [local history], vol. 1, part 1, A.D. 1550–1577	Southampton: Gilbert	1905
Hearnshaw, Fossey, and John Cobb	Publications of the Southampton Record Society	Southampton: Gilbert	1905–
Hearnshaw, Fossey, and John Cobb, eds.	Relics of Old Southampton: Memorial Volume of the Loan Exhibition	n/a: Gilbert	1904
Godwin, George Nelson	The Civil War in Hampshire (1642–45) and the story of Basing House by G.N. Godwin, rev. ed.	Southampton: Henry March Gilbert and Son	1904
Rayner, John Frederick	List of the Fungi of the New Forest	n/a: Gilbert	1904
Hartley College	Science Teaching and Nature Study: Report of the Conference and Exhibition Held at the Hartley College, Southampton, 13–14 June 1902	Southampton: Gilbert	1902
Highcliffe Castle	Catalogue of the Library at Highcliffe Castle: In the Possession of Col. the Hon. Stuart Wortley	Southampton: H.M. Gilbert	1902
Gilbert, H.M.	Catalogue of the Library in the Possession of the Earl of Essex at Cassiobury Park	Southampton: H.M. Gilbert	1896
Cowdery	Elfin [fiction]	n/a: H.M. Gilbert	1896

Gilbert, H.M.	Catalogue of a Collection of Books on Naval Subjects in the Possession of T.J. Bennett, Oxford, compiled by Henry March Gilbert	n/a: Henry March Gilbert	1895
Whitlock, J. Aston	A Brief and Popular History of the Hospital of God's House, Southampton, with Plates	Southampton: Gilbert	1894
Gilbert, H.M.	Catalogue of the Library, Royal Yacht Squadron Cowes, compiled by Henry March Gilbert, printed for members	Southampton: H.M. Gilbert	1893
Gilbert, H.M., Sumner Wilson, and G.N. Godwin	Supplementary Hampshire Bibliography: Being a List of Typography Not Appearing in Bibliotheca Hantoniensis	n/a: Henry March Gilbert	1891
McFadden, Frank	Vestiges of Old Southampton	Southampton: H.M. Gilbert	1891
Gilbert, H.M.	Catalogue of Library at Rotherfield Park, Hampshire, compiled by Henry March Gilbert	Southampton: Gilbert	1891
Gilbert, H.M., F.E. Edwards, and G.N. Godwin	Bibliotheca Hantoniensis: A list of Books Relating to Hampshire, Including Magazine References, Compiled by Henry March Gilbert and G.N. Godwin, with an additional list of newspapers by F.E. Edwards	Southampton: Gilbert	1891
Rogers, John	A Sketch of the Life and Reminiscences of John Rogers, Nurseryman, Written by Himself	Southamption: H.M. Gilbert	1889
Solly, Henry Shaen	Know Thyself: A Manual of Personal Religion for Confirmation Classes or Home Reading	Southampton: H.M. Gilbert and London: S.J. Gregg	1886
Godwin, G.N.	The Civil War in South-West Hampshire	Southampton: Gilbert	1886
Hooper, Charles E.	A System of Numbers Without the Cipher	Southampton: H.M. Gilbert	1885

continued on next page

Hampshire Field Club and Archaeological Society[2]	*Hampshire Papers, on the Natural History and Antiquities of the County, and Other Miscellanea,* by T.W. Shore, vol. 1, edited by G.W. Mins	Southampton: H.M. Gibert and Sons	1885
Davies, John Silvester	*A History of Southampton: Partly from the Ms. of Dr Speed in the Southampton Archives*	Southampton: Gilbert	1883
Phillips, J.C.	*The New Forest Handbook*	Lyndhurst: J.G. Short, Lymington: H. Doman, and Southampton: H.M. Gilbert	1880
Wise, John R.	*The New Forest: Its History and Its Scenery,* 3rd ed.	Southampton: Gilbert	1880
Dale, William[3]	*The Bible Story of the Creation in Its Relation to Geological Science (An Address Delivered to a Class of Young Men)*	Southampton: H.M. Gilbert	n.d. (1880s?)
Angell, Arthur	*The Microscopic Structure of Certain Fruits and Roots to Be Met With in the Jams and Preserves of Commerce*	Southampton: Gilbert	1876
Gilbert, H.M.	*Bibliotheca Hantoniensis: An Attempt at a Bibliography of Hampshire*	Southampton: Gilbert's, Ye Olde Booke Shoppe	1872
Effessea [pseudonym for F.S.C.: Francis Sewell Cole]	*Oceanica* [notes sent to "The Field," collected in a single volume]	Southampton: Gilbert	1871
Gilbert, H.M., and Eustace Hinton Jones	*The Sir Bevis Guide to Southampton and Netley*	Southampton: Gilbert	1870
Jones, Eustace Hinton	*The Romance of Sir Bevis of Hamtoun, Newly Done into English Prose from the Metrical Version*	Southampton: Gilbert	1870
Woodward, Bernard Bolingbroke[4]	*A History and Description of Southampton*	n/a: H.M. Gilbert	n.d. (late 1870s?)

Notes

Introduction

1. John Frow, "Gift and Commodity," in *Time and Commodity Culture: Essays in Cultural Theory and Postmodernity* (Oxford: Clarendon Press, 1997), 138.

2. Theodor Adorno and Max Horkheimer, "The Culture Industry: Enlightenment as Mass Deception," in *Dialectic of Enlightenment: Philosophical Fragments* (Stanford, CA: Stanford University Press, 1997), 120–167.

3. Leah Price, *How to Do Things with Books in Victorian Britain* (Princeton, NJ: Princeton University Press, 2012), 260.

4. Joshua Clover and Christopher Nealon, "Literary and Economic Value," in *Oxford Research Encyclopedias*, July 2017, https://doi.org/10.1093/acrefore/9780190201098.013.123.

5. Pierre Bourdieu, "The Market of Symbolic Goods," in Pierre Bourdieu, *The Field of Cultural Production* (Cambridge: Polity Press, 1993), 115–116.

6. Ika Willis, *Reception* (London: Routledge, 2018), 15.

7. See Brean Hammond, "Guard the Sure Barrier," in *Pope: New Contexts*, ed. David Fairer (Exeter, UK: Harvester Wheatsheaf, 1990), 238.

8. Immanuel Wallerstein, "Household Structures and Labour Force Formation in the Capitalist World-Economy," in *Race, Nations, Class: Ambiguous Identities*, ed. Étienne Balibar and Immanuel Wallerstein (London: Verso, 1991), 107; cited in Frow, "Gift and Commodity," 134. See also Frow, "Gift and Commodity," 134 ff.

9. See Nancy Scheper-Huges and Loïc Wacquant, eds., *Commodifying Bodies* (London: Sage, 2002).

10. Ha-Joon Chang, *Economics: The User's Guide* (New York: Bloomsbury, 2015), 125–126.

11. Edmund Conway, *50 Economics Ideas You Really Need to Know* (London: Quercus, 2009), 195. This panacean explanation of "everything" is taken up in Steven Levitt and Stephen Dubner, *Freakonomics: A Rogue Economist Explores the Hidden Side of Everything* (London: Allen Lane, 2005).

12. Anthony Glinoer, ed., *The Literary and the Social*, Living Books About History, 2019, https://doi.org/10.13098/infoclio.ch-lb-0008.

13. See Lise Jaillant, ed., *Publishing Modernist Fiction and Poetry* (Edinburgh: Edinburgh University Press, 2019), and *Modernist Journals Project*, Brown University, University of Tulsa, and National Endowment for the Humanities, www.modjourn.org.

14. Heather Love, "Close Reading and Thin Description," *Publishing Cultures* 25, no. 3 (2013): 403n3.

15. Jonathan Jones, "Get Real: Terry Pratchett Is Not a Literary Genius," *Guardian*, 31 August 2015, www.theguardian.com/artanddesign/jonathanjonesblog/2015/aug/31/terry-pratchett-is-not-a-literary-genius.

16. Sam Jordison, "Terry Pratchett's Books Are the Opposite of 'Ordinary Potboilers,'" *Guardian*, 31 August 2015, www.theguardian.com/books/booksblog/2015/aug/31/terry-pratchett-opposite-of-ordinary-potboiler-jonathan-jones.

17. Rita Felski, *Uses of Literature* (Hoboken: John Wiley and Sons, 2009), 2.

18. Felski, *Uses*, 7.

19. Felski, *Uses*, 2.

20. Felski, *Uses*, 5.

21. Felski, *Uses*, 18.

22. Colin Campbell, *The Romantic Ethic and the Spirit of Modern Consumerism* (Oxford: Basil Blackwell, 1987), 90.

23. See Simon Frost, "Othering Ourselves: Re-reading Kipling and 'The Strange Ride of Morrowbie Jukes' (1885)," *Nordic Journal of English Studies* 16, no. 2 (2017): 12–32, http://ojs.ub.gu.se/ojs/index.php/njes/article/view/4111.

24. James Proctor and Bethan Benwell, *Reading Across Worlds: Transnational Book Groups and the Reception of Difference* (Basingstoke, UK: Palgrave Macmillan, 2015).

25. James Proctor and Bethan Benwell, "Professional and Lay Readers," in Proctor and Benwell, *Reading Across Worlds*, 9–50.

26. John Guillory, "The Ethical Practice of Modernity: the Example of Reading," in *The Turn to Ethics*, ed. Marjorie Garber, Beatrice Hanssen, and Rebecca Walkowitz (London: Routledge, 2013), 31–34.

27. Andrew Glazzard, *Conrad's Popular Fictions: Secret Histories and Sensational Novels* (Basingstoke: Palgrave Macmillan, 2016), 1–6.

28. Simon Frost, *The Business of the Novel: Economics, Aesthetics and the Case of* Middlemarch (London: Pickering and Chatto, 2012), 138. For work additional to Glazzard see Simon Frost, "Public Gains and Literary Goods: A Coeval Tale of Conrad, Kipling and Francis Marion Crawford," in *Transitions in Middlebrow Writing, 1880–1930*, ed. Kate MacDonald and Christoph Singer (Basingstoke, UK: Palgrave Macmillan, 2015), 37–56. For Joyce, see Zack Bowen, *Ulysses as a Comic Novel* (Syracuse, NY: Syracuse University Press, 1989).

29. Glazzard, *Conrad's Popular Fictions*, 4.

30. Glazzard, *Conrad's Popular Fictions*, 5.
31. Martin Lyons, *A History of Reading and Writing in the Western World* (Basingstoke, UK: Palgrave Macmillan 2010), 153.
32. Daniel Maudlin and Robin Peel, eds., *The Materials of Exchange between Britain and North East America, 1750–1900* (Farnham, UK: Ashgate, 2013), 2.
33. *The Southamptonian*, pub. E.H. Synge, Topographical Publishing Co. (4 January 1899), 8 and 9.
34. *The Southamptonian* (18 January 1899), 10–11.
35. William Stanley Jevons, *The Theory of Political Economy*, 3rd ed. (London: Macmillan, 1888), vi and 27–36.
36. David Armitage and Michael Braddick, eds., *The British Atlantic Worlds, 1500–1800* (Basingstoke, UK: Palgrave Macmillan, 2009), 23–28.

Chapter 1

1. Rosalind Williams, *Dream Worlds: Mass Consumption in Late Nineteenth-Century France* (Berkeley: University of California Press, 1991), 65.
2. See Williams, *Dream Worlds*, 5–7, citing Hannah Arendt, *The Human Condition: A Study of the Central Dilemmas Facing Modern Man* (Garden City, NY: Doubleday Anchor Books, 1959), 72–83, 108–110.
3. John Maynard Keynes, "The End of Laissez-Faire," in *Essays in Persuasion* (London: Macmillan, 1933), 312.
4. Chang, *Economics*, 139.
5. Willis, *Reception*, 1–2, citing Ursula K. Le Guin, "Where do You Get Your Ideas From?" in *Dancing at the Edge of the World: Thoughts on Words, Women, Places* (London: Paladin, 1992), 198.
6. See Jerome McGann, *Black Riders: The Visible Language of Modernism* (Princeton, NJ: Princeton University Press, 1993).
7. DeNel Rehberg Sedo, "Reading Reception in the Digital Era," in *Oxford Research Encyclopedias*, June 2017, https://doi.org/10.1093/acrefore/978019020 1098.013.285.
8. Ivor Armstrong Richards, *Principles of Literary Criticism* (London: Routledge and Kegan Paul, 1959); and Louise M. Rosenblatt, *Literature as Exploration*, rev. ed. (New York: Noble and Noble, 1968).
9. Sedo, "Reading Reception."
10. Wolfgang Iser, "The Reading Process: A Phenomenological Approach," in Jane P. Tompkins, ed., *Reader-Response Criticism: From Formalism to Post-Structuralism* (Baltimore: Johns Hopkins University Press, 1980), 50–70.
11. Jonathan D. Culler, *The Pursuit of Signs: Semiotics, Literature, Deconstruction* (Ithaca, NY: Cornell University Press, 1981). (Sedo's note.)

12. Umberto Eco, *The Role of the Reader: Explorations in the Semiotics of Texts* (Bloomington: Indiana University Press, 1979). (Sedo's note.)

13. Judith Fetterley, *The Resisting Reader: A Feminist Approach to American Fiction* (Bloomington: Indiana University Press, 1978). (Sedo's note.)

14. Sedo, "Reading Reception in the Digital Era." Examples of studies of socially embedded reading cited in Sedo include Frost, *The Business of the Novel*; Elizabeth Long, "Textual Interpretation as Collective Action," in *The Ethnography of Reading*, ed. Jonathan Boyarin (Berkeley: University of California Press, 1992), 180–212; Elizabeth Long, *Book Clubs: Women and the Uses of Reading in Everyday Life* (Chicago: University of Chicago Press, 2003); Claire Squires, *Marketing Literature: The Making of Contemporary Writing in Britain* (Basingstoke: Palgrave Macmillan, 2007); and Shafquat Towheed, Rosalind Crone, and Katie Halsey, *The History of Reading: A Reader* (New York: Routledge, 2011).

15. Marisa Bortolussi and Peter Dixon, *Psychonarratology: Foundations for the Empirical Study of Literary Response* (Cambridge: Cambridge University Press, 2003), 242–244.

16. Deirdre McCloskey, "Metaphors Economists Live By," *Social Research* 62, no. 2 (1995), 215–237. See also George Lakoff and Mark Johnson, *Metaphors We Live By* (Chicago: University of Chicago Press 1980).

17. McCloskey, "Metaphors Economists Live By," 220.

18. Louise Rosenblatt, *The Reader, the Text, and the Poem: The Transactional Theory of Literary Work* (Carbondale: Southern Illinois University Press, 1978), 25–28.

19. Anthony Giddens, *Modernity and Self-Identity* (Cambridge: Polity Press, 1991).

20. William James, *The Principles of Psychology* (New York: Henry Holt, 1890), 291–292, cited in Tim Jackson, *Motivating Sustainable Consumption: A Review of Evidence on Consumer Behaviour and Behavioural Change* (Guildford: Centre for Environmental Strategy, University of Surrey, 2005), 14.

21. Rosenblatt, *The Reader, the Text, and the Poem*, 135.

22. Jonathan Rose, *The Intellectual Life of the British Working Classes* (New Haven, CT: Yale University Press, 2001), 372.

23. Thomas Richards, *The Commodity Culture of Victorian England* (Stanford, CA: Stanford University Press, 1990), 1.

24. Mark Osteen, ed., *The Question of the Gift: Essays Across Disciplines* (Abingdon, UK: Routledge, 2002).

25. Christopher Lindner, *Fictions of Commodity Culture: From the Victorian to the Post-Modern* (Aldershot, UK: Ashgate, 2003), 3.

26. Lindner, *Fictions of Commodity Culture*, 3.

27. For the implications of free trade, see Frank Trentman, *Free Trade Nation* (Oxford: Oxford University Press, 2008). For increases in relative wealth, see W. Hamish Fraser, *The Coming of the Mass Market* (London: Macmillan, 1981).

28. Simon Patten, *The New Basis of Civilization* (New York: Macmillan, 1907), 9–11.

29. Victoria Cooper and Dave Russell, "Publishing for Leisure," in *The Cambridge History of the Book in Britain*, vol. 6, *1830–1914*, ed. David McKitterick (Cambridge: Cambridge Univerity Press, 2014), 485–491.

30. Judith Flanders, *Consuming Passions* (Hammersmith, UK: Harper Press, 2006), 152.

31. Jackson, *Motivating Sustainable Consumption*, 14; Jackson recommendingly cites Roland Barthes, *Mythologies* (London: Paladin, 1973); Mihaly Czikszentmihalyi and Eugene Rochberg-Halton, *The Meaning of Things: Domestic Symbols and the Self* (Cambridge: Cambridge University Press, 1981); Helga Dittmar, *The Social Psychology of Material Possessions: To Have Is to Be* (New York: St. Martin's Press, 1992); and Grant McCracken, *Culture and Consumption: A Theoretical Account of the Structure and Movement of the Cultural Meaning of Consumer Goods* (Bloomington: Indiana University Press, 1990)

32. Tim Jackson, "Live Better by Consuming Less?: Is There a 'Double Dividend' in Sustainable Consumption?" *Journal of Industrial Ecology* 9, no. 1–2 (2005): 30.

33. See Virginia Held, "Mothering Versus Contract," in *Beyond Self-Interest*, ed. Jane Mansbridge (Chicago: University of Chicago Press, 1990), cited in Katrine Marçal, *Who Cooked Adam Smith's Dinner?* (London: Portobello, 2017), 155.

34. Marçal, *Who Cooked Adam Smith's Dinner?* 153–156.

35. John Searle, *The Construction of Social Reality* (Harmondsworth, UK: Penguin, 1995), 23–26.

36. For the potential of Mead's work for studies of consumption, see Cele Otnes, "Mind, Self and Consumption: George Herbert Mead," in *Canonical Authors in Consumption Theory*, ed. Søren Askegaard and Benoît Heilbrunn (London: Routledge, 2010), 113–119.

37. Jackson, *Motivating Sustainable Consumption*, ix.

38. Jackson, *Motivating Sustainable Consumption*, 77–8.

39. Jackson, *Motivating Sustainable Consumption*, 77–8.

40. McCloskey, "Metaphors Economists Live By," 215–237.

Chapter 2

1. See Peter A. Hall and David Soskice, eds., *Varieties of Capitalism: The Institutional Foundations of Comparative Advantage* (Oxford: Oxford University Press, 2001); Bob Hancké, ed., *Debating Varieties of Capitalism: A Reader* (Oxford: Oxford University Press, 2009); and, for a critical reevaluation, Kathleen Thelen, *Varieties of Liberalisation and the New Politics of Social Solidarity* (Cambridge: Cambridge University Press, 2014). Within the EU regime, the arguments for

the welfare state as an economically necessary social investment are addressed in Nathalie Morel, Bruno Palier, and Joakim Palme, eds, *Towards a Social Investment Welfare State?* (Bristol: Policy Press, 2012).

2. The Post-Crash Economic Society was initiated by students of economics at the University of Manchester dissatisfied with the monopolizing neoclassical curriculum they were taught: see the website for Post-Crash Economics Society, Manchester University, www.post-crasheconomics.com, and specifically Andrew Haldane (Executive Director for Financial Stability at the Bank of England), "Introduction: The Revolution in Economics," in *Economics, Education and Unlearning*, Post-Crash Economics Society, April 2014, www.post-crasheconomics.com/economics-education-and-unlearning/. See also Cambridge Society for Economic Pluralism, www.cambridgepluralism.org/; and Positive Money: Making Money and Banking Work for Society, https://positivemoney.org/. For a soon-to-be-superseded list of titles and new-economy theorists, see chapter 12 of this study. More popularizing commentary includes titles such as John Lanchester, *How to Speak Money* (London: Faber and Faber, 2016); and George Monbiot, *How Did We Get Into This Mess?* (London: Verso, 2016). Concerns over the limitations of free-market thinking are also widespread in electronic media commentary, such as "Making Money," hosted by David Grossman, *The New Age of Capitalism*, BBC Radio 4, 14 September 2018, www.bbc.co.uk/programmes/b0bjppmr, or "Economist Kate Barker on the Free Market," *A History of Ideas*, BBC, 22 July 2015, https://www.bbc.co.uk/sounds/play/b062ktlh.

3. See ALCS (Authors' Licensing and Collecting Society), *2018 Authors' Earnings: a Survey of UK Writers*, 2018, https://wp.alcs.co.uk/app/uploads/2018/06/ALCS-Authors-earnings-2018.pdf. In 2018, the minimum wage for those over 25 was £7.83, while those few professional writers working full time (35-hour week) to bring an average annual income of £10,437 earned £5.73 per hour.

4. Jason Potts, John Hartley, Lucy Montgomery, Cameron Neylon and Ellie Rennie, "A Journal is a Club: A New Economic Model for Scholarly Publishing," *Prometheus* 35, no. 1 (2017), 75–92.

5. See Ha-Joon Chang, *23 Things They Don't Tell You About Capitalism* (London: Penguin, 2011), 1–10.

6. For more on the myth of the free market, see Ha-Joon Chang, "The Economics and Politics of Regulation," in *Globalisation, Economic Development and the Role of the State* (London: Zed Books, 2004), 177ff.; Jong-Il You and Ha-Joon Chang, "The Myth of the Free Labour Market in Korea," *Contributions to Political Economy* 12, no. 1 (1993): 29–46.

7. Hall and Soskice, *Varieties of Capitalism*, 9.

8. Laura Miller, *Reluctant Capitalists: Bookselling and the Culture of Capitalism* (Chicago: University of Chicago Press, 2007), 67–86.

9. Jacques Derrida, "Parergon," in *The Truth of Painting*, trans. Geoff Bennington and Ian McLeod (Chicago: University of Chicago Press, 1987), 54.

10. Alexis Weedon, *Victorian Publishing: The Economics and Book Production for a Mass Market, 1836–1916* (Aldershot, UK: Ashgate, 2003), 66ff. and 85ff.

11. Simon Eliot, "From Few and Expensive to Many and Cheap: The British Book Market 1800–1890," in *A Companion to the History of the Book*, ed. Simon Eliot and Jonathan Rose (Oxford: Blackwell, 2007), 298–299; and Simon Eliot, "The Three-Decker Novel and its First Cheap Reprint, 1862–94," *Library* 7 (1985): 38–53. Pre-decimal currency in Britain was counted in pounds (£), shillings (s) and pence (d). Twenty shillings made a pound and twelve pence made a shilling. The advantage of twelve units (pennies to a shilling) was that, in a deal, the shilling could be divided among both equal and unequal parties, by both 2s or 4s, as well as 3s. The guinea, worth £1 1s, was useful in trade involving some form of broker, in that the trading parties could trade in £s, leaving the broker with 1s in every £1 traded. Furthermore, for convenience, 12s 6d often would have been written 12/6; 5s might have appeared as 5/–.

12. "Notice," *Dover Express*, 1 September 1899, 5. The newspaper articles referred to in this study are available from a variety of sources. A good number are held in online archives, including the The British Newspaper Archive, British Library and Findmypast Newspaper Archive Limited, www.britishnewspaperarchive.co.uk; print editions are held at various national libraries, and in local city archives, including Southampton City Libraries and Southampton Central Library, searchable via https://southampton.spydus.co.uk/cgi-bin/spydus.exe/MSGTRN/OPAC/HOME. Occasionally, relevant cuttings from newspapers, or highly localized publications such as the *Shirley and Freemantle Gazette*, are held by the Southampton City Archives.

13. James Barnes, *Free Trade in Books: A Study of the London Book Trade since 1800* (Oxford: Clarendon Press, 1964), 56.

14. Liyan Chen, "The Most Profitable Industries in 2016," *Forbes Magazine*, 21 December 2015, www.forbes.com/sites/liyanchen/2015/12/21/the-most-profitable-industries-in-2016/; or Sean Ross, "What Profit Margin is Usual for a Company in the Retail Sector?" *Investopedia*, 4 August 2019, www.investopedia.com/ask/answers/071615/what-profit-margin-usual-company-retail-sector.asp.

15. Dorothy Davis, *A History of Shopping* (London: Routledge and Kegan Paul, 2006), 297.

16. Kentin Waits, "Cheat Sheet: Retail Markup on Common Items," *Wisebread*, 15 December 2010, www.wisebread.com/cheat-sheet-retail-markup-on-common-items.

17. Weedon, *Victorian Publishing*, 29.

18. See "Number of Titles Published per Year," data visualizations, At The Circulating Library: A Database of Victorian Fiction, 1837–1901, general editor Troy J. Bassett, Purdue University Fort Wayne, updated 9 July 2019, www.victorianresearch.org/atcl/graphs_publ.php.

19. Clive Bloom, *Bestsellers: Popular Fiction since 1900* (Basingstoke, UK: Palgrave Macmillan, 2008), 85.

20. Bloom, *Bestsellers*, 84, 150, and 97.

21. Judith Flanders describes "experience-economy" events from the 1820s at Vauxhall Gardens, in London, such as an erupting Mount Vesuvius, with twenty-four-meter-high fireworks, and a restaging of the Battle of Waterloo. Flanders, *Consuming Passions*, 278–279.

22. The phrase "books are different" become something of a slogan after its use in 1962 as part of a court ruling by Mr Justice Buckley: see Ronald Barker and George Davies, *Books Are Different. An Account of the Defence of the Net Book Agreement before the Restrictive Practices Court in 1962* (London: Macmillan, 1966).

23. David Stott, "The Decay of Bookselling," *The Nineteenth Century* 36, no. 214 (1894): 932–938.

24. Stott, "The Decay of Bookselling," 935.

25. Chang, *23 Things*, 8–9, 10.

26. Frank Arthur Mumby, *Publishing and Bookselling: A History from the Earliest Times to the Present Day* (London: Jonathan Cape, 1930); Frank Arthur Mumby and Ian Norrie, *Publishing and Bookselling. Part One: From the Earliest Times to 1870; Part Two: 1870–1970* (London: Jonathan Cape, 1974); Henry Curwen, *A History of Booksellers: the Old and the New* (London: Chatto and Windus, 1873).

27. Eileen DeMarco, *Reading and Writing: Hachette's Railroad Bookstore Network in Nineteenth-Century France* (Bethlehem, PA: Lehigh University Press, 2006); Mary Hammond, *Reading, Publishing and the Formation of Literary Taste in England 1880–1914* (Aldershot, UK: Ashgate, 2006); Stephen Colclough, "'Purifying the Sources of Amusement and Information'? The Railway Bookstalls of W.H. Smith & Son, 1855–1860," *Publishing History* 56 (2004): 27–51; Simon Frost and Stephen Hall, "John Smith's: Historical Perspectives and Historical Precedence," *Book 2.0* 5, no. 1–2 (2015): 27–37; and Giles Mandelbrote, ed., *Out of Print and Into Profit: A History of the Rare and Second-hand Book Trade in Britain in the 20th Century* (London: British Library, 2006), appendices, 331–366. See also British Book Trade Archives 1830–1939, Bedfordshire University, http://britishbookarchives.beds.ac.uk/.

28. "The Decay of the Bookseller," *The Tablet*, 22 December 1894, 963–964.

29. Cited in Mumby and Norrie, *Publishing and Bookselling*, 286. See "Obituaries," *The Bookseller*, May 1888, 465.

30. Mumby and Norrie, *Publishing and Bookselling*, 231.

31. Mumby and Norrie, *Publishing and Bookselling*, 243.

32. The following titles are cited in George Watson, *Cambridge Bibliography of English Literature*, vol. 3 (Cambridge: Cambridge University Press, 1966), 102: John W. Parker, ed., *The Opinions of Certain Authors on the Bookselling Question,*

1852; W. Pickering, "Bookseller's Monopoly: Address to the Trade and to the Public," 1832; L. Ridge, "L. Ridge's Scheme for Promoting the Interests of the Country Booksellers and Publishers," 1855.

33. Mumby and Norrie, *Publishing and Bookselling*, 231.

34. See James Bigg, "The Bookselling System: Letter to Lord Campbell respecting the late enquiry into the regulations of the Booksellers' Association . . ." (London: J. Bigg and Sons, 1852), 25, held British Library, shelfmark 11902 bb 50 (5.). Bigg later argued that the lamentable underselling would disappear by means of the invisible hand: "Let there be entire freedom in the transactions between pubishers and retial booksellers" (29).

35. See Mumby and Norrie, *Publishing and Bookselling*, 244.

36. For Macmillan's involvement see Charles Morgan, *The House of Macmillan* (London: Macmillan, 1943), 179ff., or for a view of its relation to the death of the triple-decker, see Eliot, "The Three-Decker Novel."

37. Bigg, "The Bookselling System," 29.

38. Mumby and Norrie, *Publishing and Bookselling*, 230–232, 306, and 308. The volume issued by Shaw was most likely *John Bull's Other Island and Major Barbara: Also How He Lied to Her Husband* (London: Times Book Club, 1907).

39. Percival Chubb, "The Blight of Literary Bookishness," *The English Journal* 3, no. 1 (1914): 15–16.

40. John Feather, *A History of British Publishing* (London: Routledge, 1988), 193.

41. David Wright, "Book Retail," in *The Cultural Intermediaries Reader*, ed. Jennifer Maguire and Julian Matthews (London: Sage, 2014), 186.

42. Miller, *Reluctant Capitalists*, 193.

43. Miller, *Reluctant Capitalists*, 115.

44. Miller, *Reluctant Capitalists*, 193.

45. Miller, *Reluctant Capitalists*, 70.

46. Miller, *Reluctant Capitalists*, 194–195.

47. Miller, *Reluctant Capitalists*, 227.

48. Miller, *Reluctant Capitalists*, 225.

49. A term used by Harvey in his textbook study of neoliberalism to describe the shift away from the earlier "accumulation through the expansion of labour" and of production. See David Harvey, *A Brief History of Neoliberalism* (Oxford: Oxford University Press, 2007), 178.

50. John Humphrey and Hubert Schmitz, *Governance and Global Value Chains* (Brighton: Institute of Development Studies, University of Sussex, 2006), 29, cited in Melanie DuPuis, "Civic Markets: Alternative Value Chains Governance as Civic Engagement," *Crop Management* 5, no. 1 (2006):1–12, https://doi:10.1094/CM-2006-0921-09-RV.

51. DuPuis, "Civic Markets."

Chapter 3

1. Rose, *Intellectual Life*; Paul Rooney, *Railway Reading and Late-Victorian Literary Series* (London: Routledge, 2018); Christopher Hilliard, "The Twopenny Library: The Booktrade, Working-Class Readers, and 'Middlebrow' Novels in Britain 1930–42," *Twentieth Century British History* 25, no. 2 (2014): 199–220; Frost, *Business of the Novel*; Lise Jaillant, *Modernism, Middlebrow and the Literary Canon* (London: Pickering and Chatto, 2014); James Connolly, Patrick Collier, Frank Felsenstein, Kenneth Hall, and Robert Hall, eds., *Print Culture Histories Beyond the Metropolis* (Toronto: University of Toronto Press, 2016). The database What Middletown Read (Ball State University) is available at www.bsu.edu/libraries/wmr, and its print resource is Frank Felsenstein and James Connolly, *What Middletown Read: Print Culture in an American Small City* (Amherst: University of Massachusetts Press, 2015). The prime mover to all this was Janice Radway, *Reading the Romance: Women, Patriarchy, and Popular Culture* (Chapel Hill: University of North Carolina Press, 1984). See also the four-volume *Edinburgh History of Reading*, ed. Mary Hammond and Jonathan Rose (Edinburgh: Edinburgh University Press, 2020).

2. William St. Clair, "The Political Economy of Reading," John Coffin Memorial Lecture in the History of the Book, rev. ed. (Institute of English Studies, University of London, 2012), www.ies.sas.ac.uk/sites/default/files/files/Publications/StClair_PolEcReading_2012.pdf. For science writing, a superb case study is provided by James A. Secord, *Victorian Sensation: The Extraordinary Publication, Reception, and Secret Authorship of Vestiges of the Natural History of Creation* (Chicago: University of Chicago Press, 2003).

3. James Spackman, Katie Roden, and Peter McKay, "Get Over Yourself: There Is No Such Thing as 'The Reader,'" panel, London Book Fair, 15 March 2017.

4. Gordon Haight, ed. *The George Eliot Letters*, vol. 5 (New Haven, CT: Yale University Press, 1978), 243.

5. Frost, *Business of the Novel*, 9–25.

6. The following material on Collins's article and Wright's reply draws from Simon Frost, "Reconsidering the Unknown Public: A Puzzle of Literary Gains," in *Studies in Victorian and Modern Literature: a Tribute to John Sutherland*, ed. William Baker (Lanham, MD: Fairleigh Dickinson University Press, Rowman and Littlefield Publishing Group, 2015), 3–15, referred to here by kind permission of the press; all rights reserved.

7. Wilkie Collins, "The Unknown Public," *Household Words* 18 (21 August 1858), 217–222, www.web40571.clarahost.co.uk/wilkie/etext/TheUnknownPublic.htm.

8. Thomas Wright, "Concerning the Unknown Public," *The Nineteenth Century*, 13 (February 1883), 279–296.

9. Collins, "Unknown Public."
10. Collins, "Unknown Public," passim.
11. Collins, "Unknown Public."
12. Wright "Concerning," 280.
13. Wright, "Concerning," 285–286.
14. Leslie Howsam, *Kegan Paul, a Victorian Imprint: Publishers, Books and Cultural History* (New York: Routledge, 1998), 42.
15. Several numbers of *The Nineteenth Century* are held online at the Internet Archive, https://archive.org/details/a63475790Dlonduoft.
16. Josiah Flynt, *Tramping with Tramps: Studies and Sketches* (New York: Century, 1899), and Josiah Flynt, *The World of Graft* (London: McClure, Phillips and Co, 1901).
17. "What Tramps Read," *Bournemouth Daily Echo*, Wednesday 23 January 1901, 2. See also "What Tramps Read," *St. James's Gazette*, 22 January 1901, 11. With articles typically repeating between publications, one might suspect local newspapers of, if not poaching, then a high level of informal syndication.
18. Jack London, *The People of the Abyss* (London: Macmillan, 1903). Much detail can be had from chapter 20, "Coffee Houses and Doss Houses," 232–249, and chapter 21, "The Precariousness of Life," 250–262.
19. A useful bibliography of primary and secondary sources on workhouses in the British Isles can be had from Peter Higginbotham, *The Workhouse Encyclopedia* (Stroud, UK: The History Press, 2014). A documentary re-creation of Victorian slum conditions, featuring the two-penny hangover, has been provided in *The Victorian Slum*, episodes 1–5, presented by Michael Mosley, Wall to Wall Media for BBC2, 2016, http://www.bbc.co.uk/programmes/b07zd454/episodes/guide.
20. Higginbotham, *Workhouse Encyclopedia*, 96–100.
21. Higginbotham, *Workhouse Encyclopedia*, 97.
22. London, *People*, 245–246.
23. From 1817, and improved with a rubberizing process around 1844, waterproof cloth had been available, but it was heavy and smelled. In bad weather people would often stay indoors. Aquascutum helped and was used by the army in the Crimean war, but it was not until 1870 with Burberry's waterproof gabardine that waterproof clothing became more available.
24. Fraser, *Coming of the Mass Market*, 21.
25. London, *People*, 204.
26. Figures based on findings by W.A. Mackenzie's study of 1921 cited in Fraser, *Coming of the Mass Market*, 32.
27. Maud Pember Reeves, *Round About a Pound a Week* (London: Bell and Sons, 1914), 76–77.
28. Higginbotham, *Workhouse Encyclopedia*, 340. Southampton did not acquire its city status until 1964; it was previously a town. Where appropriate,

the use of "city" is adopted to reinforce the point that this narrative is written from a twenty-first-century perspective.

29. Alfred Temple Patterson, *A History of Southampton 1700–1914*, vol. 3, *Setbacks and Recoveries, 1868–1914* (Southampton: University of Southampton, 1975), 105–112. See also Andrew Mearns, *Bitter Outcry of Outcast London* (London: James Clarke, 1883), available at https://archive.org/details/bittercryofoutca00pres.

30. For emigration and reading towards the end of the nineteenth century, see Simon Frost, "A Trade in Desires: Emigration, A.C. Gunter and the Home Publishing Company," in *The Book World: Selling and Distributing British Literature, 1900–1940*, ed. Nicola Louise Wilson (Leiden: BRILL, 2016), 31–51.

31. Jennifer Jenkins, *Provincial Modernity: Local Culture and Liberal Politics in Fin-de-Siècle Hamburg* (Ithaca, NY: Cornell University Press, 2003), 277–280.

32. Patterson, *History of Southampton*, 62–68.

33. Wright, "Concerning," 283.

34. Wright, "Concerning," 293.

35. Wright, "Concerning," 228.

36. Wright, "Concerning," 287.

37. Anon. Advertisement. "St. Georger Leihbibliothek," *Hamburg Nachrichten*, 17 February 1882, 8. A good run of German newspapers (and indeed other Continental European newspapers) is hosted by Europeana, www.europeana.eu/en/collections/topic/18-newspapers.

38. See James Payn, *Wat Hij Haar Kostte*, part 1, ser. *De Locomotief: Samarangsch handels- en advertentie-blad*, 2 November 1877, 1, www.europeana.eu/en/item/9200359/BibliographicResource_3000115811103.

39. Fraser, *Coming of the Mass Market*, 21.

40. For an idea of volume price and how changes in volume price coincided with the demise of the great circulating libraries and the introduction the Net Book Agreement of 1894, see Eliot, "The Three-Decker Novel."

41. Wright, "Concerning," 282.

42. Wright, "Concerning," 282.

43. Wright, "Concerning," 282.

44. Wright, "Concerning," 288.

45. Anon. "Drivel: Weekly 1d," *The Scots Observer*, 28 December 1889, 157, cited in Peter McDonald, *British Literary Culture and Publishing Practice 1880–1914* (Cambridge: Cambridge University Press 1997), 42.

46. GB Historical GIS/University of Portsmouth, "England through time | Population Statistics | Total Population," *A Vision of Britain through Time*, www.visionofbritain.org.uk/unit/10061325/cube/TOT_POP.

47. Edward G. Salmon, "What the Working Classes Read," *The Nineteenth Century* 20 (1886): 108–117. Other details of penny periodicals are available, yet again, from At The Circulating Library, www.victorianresearch.org/atcl/index.php.

48. Reynolds studies have now established themselves, seeing numerous publications, including Anne Humphreys and Louis James, eds., *G.W.M. Reynolds* (Aldershot, UK: Ashgate 2008), and via the bicentenary conference Remarkable Reynolds, 26 July 2014, http://remarkablereynolds.wordpress.com/.
49. Salmon, "Working Classes," 112.
50. Salmon, "Working Classes," 113.
51. Wright "Concerning," 289.
52. John Sutherland, *The Stanford Companion to Victorian Fiction* (Stanford, CA: Stanford University Press, 1989), 493–494.
53. Wright, "Concerning," 290. An unmissable study is Jane Jordan and Andrew King, eds., *Ouida and Victorian Popular Culture* (Aldershot, UK: Ashgate, 2013).
54. Salmon, "Working Classes," 114.
55. Wright, "Concerning," 286.
56. The 1888 volume edition of *Stanfield Hall* retains epigraphs including Gray's "The Bard: A Pindaric Ode" and the "Affairs of Men" speech by Brutus from Shakespeare's *Julius Caesar*; see John Frederick Smith, *Stanfield Hall: Cromwell, or the Protector's Oath*, vol. 3 (London: Bradley, 1889), 20, 69.

Chapter 4

1. See Colin Platt, *Medieval Southampton: The Port and Trading Community, AD. 1000–1600* (London: Routledge and Kegan Paul, 1973), 3–30.
2. Platt, *Medieval Southampton*, 137, 152–164.
3. Davis, *A History of Shopping*, 3–24, 20.
4. Platt, *Medieval Southampton*, 6, 42–48.
5. Cited in "High Street," Sotonopedia (Local Studies Department, Southampton Central Library), http://sotonopedia.wikidot.com. See also Henry C. Englefield, *A Walk Through Southampton*, 2nd ed. (Southampton: Baker and Fletcher, 1805), 30. Two Georgian coaching inns survive, The Dolphin and The Star Hotel, as well as the medieval Red Lion pub, all still in operation; as are a number of notable nineteenth-century buildings, having survived the High Street blitz bombings of World War II, most intensively during the latter half of 1940, including a number of banks—the National Westminster Bank building at number 129 (from 1867); a neo-baroque building at number 165–6 (1900); and the neo-Jacobean Martin's Bank building at number 171 (1900)—as well as the Oakley and Watling building at number 58 (the Oakley family had been fruit and vegetable merchants in Southampton since 1843) and the Mowatt's Fish Merchants' building at number 123–4 (from ca. 1870).
6. John Stobart, *Spend, Spend, Spend: A History of Shopping* (Stroud, UK: The History Press 2008), 22.

7. Yanis Varoufakis, *Talking to My Daughter about the Economy: A Brief History of Capitalism* (London: The Bodley Head, 2017), 37ff.

8. John Rapley, "Few Things Are as Dangerous as Economists with Physics Envy," AEON, 9 February 2018, https://aeon.co/ideas/few-things-are-as-dangerous-as-economists-with-physics-envy. See also John Rapley, *Twilight of the Money Gods: Economics as a Religion and How It All Went Wrong* (London: Simon and Schuster, 2017). Gell-Mann cited in Marçal, *Who Cooked Adam Smith's Dinner*, 74.

9. See Future High Streets Forum (Government of the UK), www.gov.uk/government/groups/future-high-streets-forum.

10. *Directory for the Town of Southampton* (Cunningham, 1811), 3–34.

11. Kelly's Directory 1900, 162a.

12. Kelly's Directory 1887, 388. Berlin Wool is a style of needlepoint.

13. See Tamara Wagner, ed., *Victorian Settler Narratives: Emigrants, Cosmopolitans and Returnees in Nineteenth-Century Literature* (London: Pickering and Chatto, 2011); and Frost, "A Trade in Desires."

14. A.G.L. Leonard, *More Stories of Southampton Streets* (Southampton: Paul Cave, 1989), 161–162; and *Hampshire Advertiser*, 15 April 1874, 3.

15. Charles Emmerson, *1913: The World before the Great War* (London: The Bodley Head, 2013), 253, 257ff.

16. "From All Quarters," *Southern Echo*, 10 February 1906, 2.

17. "Topics of the Hour," *Southern Echo*, 2 December 1902, 2.

18. Norman Gannaway, *Association Football in Hampshire Until 1914*, Hampshire Papers 9 (Winchester: Hampshire County Council, 1996), 5–6.

19. Gannaway, *Association Football*, 20.

20. *Bournemouth Evening Echo*, 6 August 1904, 3.

21. Gannaway, *Association Football*, 20–21.

22. Stephen Colclough, "Procuring Books and Consuming Texts: The Reading Experience of a Sheffield Apprentice, 1798," *Book History* 3 (2000): 21–44.

23. Q.D. [Queenie] Leavis, *Fiction and the Reading Public* (London: Chatto and Windus, 1939), 3.

24. Details of Crawford's life and works can be found from only a limited number of sources, the main being as follows: John Pilkington, *Francis Marion Crawford* (New York: Twayne Publishers, 1964); Jacob Blanck, comp., *Bibliography of American Literature*, vol. 2 (New Haven: Yale University Press, 1957), 341–363; John Pilkington, "A Crawford Bibliography," *University of Mississippi Studies in English* 4 (1963): 1–20; John Pilkington, "F. Marion Crawford: Italy in Fiction," *American Quarterly* 6 (Spring 1954): 59–65; and Jane Hanna Pease, *Romance Novels, Romantic Novelist: Francis Marion Crawford* (Bloomington, IN: Author House, 2011).

25. The following section draws on Frost, "Public Gains and Literary Goods," 37–56.

26. Francis M. Crawford, *The Novel: What It Is* (New York: Macmillan, 1893), 47.

27. Preparatory work for his theorization can be seen in three Crawford publications: "False Taste in Art," *North American Review* 135 (July 1882), 89–98; "What is a Novel?" *The Forum* 14 (January 1893), 591–599; and "Emotional Tension and the Modern Novel," *The Forum* 14 (February 1893), 735–742.

28. Crawford, *The Novel*, 8–9.

29. Crawford, *The Novel*, 9.

30. Crawford, *The Novel*, 9.

31. Crawford, *The Novel*, 105.

32. Crawford, *The Novel*, 16.

33. Crawford, *The Novel*, 107.

34. Crawford, *The Novel*, 108.

35. Crawford, *The Novel*, 106.

36. Crawford, *The Novel*, 107.

37. Pilkington, *Francis Marion Crawford*, 62.

38. "The woman who falls in love with a man for his looks alone is not of a very high type, but the best and bravest men that ever lived have fallen victims to mere beauty, often without much intelligence, faith or honour." Francis Marion Crawford, *Corleone: A Tale of Sicily* (New York: Macmillan, 1897), 80.

39. Pilkington, *Francis Marion Crawford*, 133.

40. Pilkington, *Francis Marion Crawford*, 60.

41. Pilkington, *Francis Marion Crawford*, 49, and Crawford, *The Novel*, 80.

42. Thomas J. Wise, *A Bibliography of the Writings of Joseph Conrad 1895–1920*, 2nd ed. (London: Dawsons, 1964), 14–16.

43. This is the subtitle of Kipling's story collection *Life's Handicap* (1891).

44. Kieth Carabine, Lindy Stiebel, and Tom Hubbard, eds., *Lives of Victorian Literary Figures, Part VII: Joseph Conrad, Henry Rider Haggard and Rudyard Kipling by their Contemporaries*, ser. ed. Ralph Pite (London: Pickering and Chatto, 2009), 62.

45. *The Bookman*, June (1908): 395–396.

46. See Linda Peterson, *Becoming a Woman of Letters: Myths of Authorship and Facts of the Victorian Market* (Princeton, NJ: Princeton University Press, 2009); Alexis Easely, *First-Person Anonymous: Women Writers and Victorian Print Media, 1830–1870* (Aldershot, UK: Ashgate, 2004); and of course Elaine Showalter, *A Literature of Their Own: British Women Novelists from Brontë to Lessing* (Princeton, NJ: Princeton University Press, 1997).

47. John Fiske, *Reading the Popular* (Boston: Unwin Hyman, 1989), 22, cited in Amy Koritz and Douglas Koritz. "Checkmating the Consumer: Passive Consumption and the Economic Devaluation of Culture," *Feminist Economics* 17, no. 1 (2001): 46.

48. Koritz, "Checkmating the Consumer," 46–47.
49. Pilkington, *Francis Marion Crawford*, 136.
50. Pilkington, *Francis Marion Crawford*, 151.
51. Francis Marion Crawford, *Mr. Isaacs* (New York: Macmillan, 1882), 1.
52. Blanck, *Bibliography of American Literature*, 341.
53. Pilkington, *Francis Marion Crawford*, 94.
54. Pilkington, *Francis Marion Crawford*, 94.
55. Pilkington, *Francis Marion Crawford*, 72. Although comparative currency rates are maddeningly difficult to calculate, according to databases from the Swedish Riksbank applied by a Stockholm University historical statistics project, 31,250 lira in 1886 would have been worth £1,250 in the same year (see www.historicalstatistics.org).
56. Pilkington, *Francis Marion Crawford*, 162, 161.
57. "Lovers of Books," *Tamworth Herald*, Saturday 16 July 1904, 2.
58. *Warminster and Westbury Journal*, Saturday 7 January 1905, 7.
59. *The Manchester Courier*, Friday 19 October 1906, 9.
60. Pilkington notes Crawford's talent for estimating public demand. Perceiving a popular interest in "sword and sandal" history at the end of the century, Crawford produced four related titles, including *Ave Roma Immortalis* (1898) and *Via Crucis* [Stations of the Cross] (1899), hotly on the heels of Lew Wallace's *Ben Hur* (1880) and Henry Sienkiewicz's *Quo Vadis* ([1895–96] 1898).
61. *The Bookman* [London edn] 19, no. 112 (1901), 113.
62. *Manchester Courier and Lancashire General Advertiser*, 31 December 1903, 6.
63. *The Outlook*, 4 June 1898, 560.
64. *The Outlook*, 15 April 1899, 357.
65. Crawford, *Mr. Isaacs*, 136–137.
66. Rudyard Kipling, "The Mark of the Beast," in *Life's Handicap: Being Stories of Mine Own People* (London: Macmillan, 1891), 209.
67. Tabish Khair, *The Gothic, Postcolonialism and Otherness: Ghosts from Everywhere* (Basingstoke, UK: Palgrave Macmillan, 2009), 1–17.
68. Joseph Conrad, "Karain: A Memory," *Blackwood's Magazine* 67, no. 985 (1897): 630. Many of the first editons of Conrad's periodical publications are available online; see Conrad First (Department of English, Uppsala University), http://www.conradfirst.net/conrad/home.html.
69. Francis Marion Crawford, "The Upper Berth," in *Wandering Ghosts* [*Uncanny Tales*, 1895] (New York: Macmillan, 1911), 231.
70. Crawford, "Upper Berth," 220.
71. Rudyard Kipling, "The Strange Ride of Morrowbie Jukes," in *The Man Who Would Be King: And Other Stories* (New York: Dover, 1994), 38.
72. Kipling, "Mark of the Beast," 221.
73. Kipling, "Mark of the Beast," 221.

74. Joseph Conrad, "The Lagoon," *The Cornhill Magazine* 2 (January 1897): 59.

75. Joseph Conrad, "Outpost of Progress," *Cosmopolis* [UK] 7, no. 18 (1897): 610.

76. David Finkelstein, *An Index to Blackwood's Magazine 1901–1980* (Aldershot, UK: Scholar Press 1995), xiv. See also William Atkinson, "Bound in Blackwood's: The Imperialism of the *Heart of Darkness* in its Immediate Contexts," *Twentieth-Century Literature* 50, no. 4 (2004): 368–393; Simon Frost, "The Good in a Little Fiction—Conrad, Consumer Readers and Commodity Culture," *English in Africa* 35, no. 1 (2008): 45–66, reproduced at Conrad First, www.conradfirst.net/conrad/scholarship/authors/frost.html.

77. Conrad, "Karain," 631.

78. Andreas Huyssen, "Mass Culture as Woman: Modernism's Other," in *Studies in Entertainment: Critical Approaches to Mass Culture*, ed. Tania Modleski (Bloomington: Indiana University Press, 1986), 191, cited in Willis, *Reception*, 15.

79. "Literature of the Week," *Hampshire Advertiser*, 6 August 1887, 7.

80. John Frow, *The Practice of Value: Essays on Literature in Cultural Studies* (Crawley, Australia: University of Western Australia Publishing, 2013), 12–13.

81. Frow, *The Practice of Value*, 12.

Chapter 5

1. For more on Henry George and his face-off with mathematicized neoclassical economics, see Simon Frost, "Economising in Public: Publishing History as a Challenge to Scientific Method," *Book History* 17 (2014): 365–379.

2. For later-eighteenth-century production increases, see James Raven, *The Business of Books: Booksellers and the English Book Trade* (New Haven, CT: Yale University Press, 2007), and James Raven, *Publishing Business in Eighteenth-Century England* (Woodbridge, UK: Boydell Press, 2014). For the impacts of nineteenth-century industrialization, see Lee Erikson, *The Economy of Literary Form* (Baltimore: Johns Hopkins University Press, 1996); Alexis Weedon, *Victorian Publishing: The Economics and Book Production for a Mass Market 1836–1916* (Aldershot, UK: Ashgate, 2003), and Alexis Weedon, "The Economics of Print," in *The Book: A Global History*, ed. Michael Suarez and Henry Woudhuysen (Oxford: Oxford University Press, 2013), 154–168.

3. "Popular literature—the Periodical Press," *Blackwood's Edinburgh Magazine* 85, no. 519 (1859): 98. A selection of *Blackwood's Magazine*, along with *Annual Register, Gentleman's Magazine, Notes and Queries, Philosophical Transactions of the Royal Society,* and *The Builder*, are available at The Internet Library of Early Journals: A Digital Library of 18th and 19th Century Journals (Bodleian Libraries, University of Oxford), www.bodley.ox.ac.uk/ilej/.

4. See chapter 7 of this study.

5. *Kelly's Directory of Southampton and Neighbourhood, 1930–31* (London: Kelly's Directories, 1930), 97.

6. The primary reference is F.A. Edwards, *Early Hampshire Printers* (Southampton: Hampshire Independent, 1891), reprinted extract from *Papers and Proceedings* 2, Hampshire Field Club and Archeological Society, Southampton (1889): 110–134.

7. Henry Robert Plomer, *A Dictionary of the Printers and Booksellers Who Were at Work in England, 1726–1775* (Oxford: Bibliographical Society for Oxford University Press, 1932), cited in John Oldfield, *Printers, Booksellers and Libraries in Hampshire, 1750–1800*, Hampshire Papers 3 (Portsmouth: Hampshire County Council, 1993), 1.

8. Oldfield, *Printers*.

9. Raven, *Publishing Business*, passim.

10. David Finkelstein and Alister McCleery, *Introduction to Book History* (London: Routledge, 2012), 78. An early important work on this expansion is James Raven, *Judging New Wealth* (Oxford: Oxford University Press, 1997).

11. Oldfield, *Printers*, 23.

12. The National Library of Australia catalogue registers Linden's *Hampshire Chronicle* [UK] transferring to Portsmouth in 1780 but ceasing to trade in 1786, unlike the Winchester *Hampshire Chronicle* that continues today.

13. The alternative was often the very real possibility of penury.

14. For details of Thomas Skelton and the Skelton family who operated in Southampton as printers, publishers, and booksellers, see Richard Preston, "A Precarious Business: The Skelton Family of Stationers, Printers, Publishers, Booksellers and Circulating Library Owners in Southampton and Havant c. 1781–c. 1865," *Journal of Southampton Local History Forum* 21 (2013): 3–14.

15. Michael Peachin, *The Oxford Handbook of Social Relations in the Roman World* (Oxford: Oxford University Press, 2011), 183.

16. Mark Rose, "The Author as Proprietor: Donaldson vs. Becket and the Genealogy of Modern Authorship," *Representations* no. 23 (Summer 1988): 51–85.

17. Maurizio Borghi, "Copyright and the Commodification of Authorship in 18th- and 19th-Century Europe," in *Oxford Research Encyclopedias*, March 2018, https://doi.org/10.1093/acrefore/9780190201098.013.268.

18. Thomas Richards expressly states that he will "take up the analysis where Debord leaves it off" and, citing Lukács, confirms that "the problem of commodities must not be considered in isolation or even as the central problem in economics, but as the central, structural problem of capitalist society in all its aspects." Richards, *Commodity Culture*, 14.

19. From the manifesto by Guy Debord, *Society of the Spectacle* (1967), trans. Black and Red, Guy Debord Archive, 1977, www.marxists.org/reference/archive/debord/society.htm.

20. Cited in Flanders, *Consuming Passions*, 102. An example of crystal-glass gazing long before Walter Benjamin's Arcades project.

21. Richard Altick's description runs, "Lackington, who, by cheerfully violating all the traditions of the trade, set an example of aggressive enterprise which was destined to benefit the common reader of future generations. . . . The son of a journeymen shoemaker who drank himself to death, and himself an ex-shoe-maker, random amorist and converted Methodist, Lackington started a bookshop in London in 1774. . . . [His] 'Temple of the Muses' in Finsbury Square was one of the sights of London. A large block of houses had been turned into a shop, the whole surmounted by a dome and flagpole. Over the entrance appeared the sign . . . CHEAPEST BOOKSELLERS IN THE WORLD. Reportedly the interior was so spacious that a coach-and-six could be driven clear round it . . . [and] at one side, a staircase led to the 'Lounging Rooms' and to a series of circular galleries under the dome." Richard Altick, *The English Common Reader* (Chicago: University of Chicago Press 1957), 57.

22. Flanders, *Consuming Passions*, 62–71 and 53.

23. Flanders, *Consuming Passions*, 110.

24. *Hampshire Advertiser*, Monday 25 July 1825, 3.

25. The Long Depression, sometimes known as the Great Depression, was a larger category than the Great Depression of British Agriculture, the latter compounding the crisis of the former. See Peter John, ed., *British Agriculture 1875–1914* (London: Methuen, 1973).

26. Deirdre McCloskey, "Did Victorian Britain Fail?" *Economic History Review*, new series 23, no. 3 (1970): 446–459.

27. Adrian Rance, *Southampton: An Illustrated History* (Portsmouth: Milestone, 1986), 134–135.

28. Patterson, *History of Southampton*, vol. 3, 106. See also J.F.M. Brinkman, "Social action and social crisis in late Victorian Southampton," in *Journal of Southampton Local History Forum* 12 (2007): 40–48.

29. Patterson, *History of Southampton*, vol. 3, 48–49, 112.

30. Patterson, *History of Southampton*, vol. 3, 49–50.

31. Only demolished in the 1970s, the open-air Lido was an extremely popular venue and a "must" in the summer months, as those of us who lived there at the time can attest.

32. "Demand for Free Libraries," *The Hampshire Advertiser*, 18 April, 1936, page n/a, fragment, held Southampton City Archives D/NC/5; and Richard Preston, "'Pursuit of Knowledge under Difficulties': The Audit House Library, Southampton, 1831–63, and Winchester Library and Museum, 1851–63," *Journal of the Southampton Local History Forum*, 14 (2008): 1.

33. "Demand for Free Libraries," *The Hampshire Advertiser*, 18 April, 1936, page n/a, fragment, held Southampton City Archives D/NC/5.

34. Preston, "Pursuit of Knowledge," 1.

35. "Education," *Shirley and Freemantle Gazette*, 8 December 1894, 2.

36. For a thorough history of Southampton free public libraries, on which the following section draws, see Richard Preston, "The Development of Public Libraries in Southampton, 1887–1921," *Journal of the Southampton Local History Forum* 15 (2009): 1–20.

37. *Hampshire Independent*, cited in Preston, "Development of Public Libraries," 4.

38. Preston, Richard, "Pursuit of Knowledge," 11–12.

39. See Patterson, *History of Southampton*, vol. 3, 80–94.

40. George Nelson Godwin, *Mate's Illustrated Handbook to Southampton* (Bournemouth: Mate and Sons, 1900), 1.

41. Cited in David Cairns, *Southampton Working People* (Southampton: Southampton City Museums, 1991), 16–18.

42. The antagonism is still felt today in reciprocal chants sung almost every matchday in Southampton and Portsmouth football clubs.

43. "Buffalo Billeries at Portsmouth," *Southern Echo*, Tuesday 6 October 1891, 2.

44. Cairns, *Southampton Working People*, 19.

45. For the figure of the American girl, see Lisa Rodensky, ed., *The Oxford Handbook of the Victorian Novel* (Oxford: Oxford University Press, 2013), 437–441.

46. Published in the UK as Mary MacLane, *The Story of Mary Maclane [sic], by Herself* (London: Grant Richards, 1902).

Chapter 6

1. Frederick, Bateson, *The Cambridge Bibliography of English Literature*, vol. 3, *1800–1900* (Cambridge: Cambridge University Press, 1969), 101–103.

2. *Warminster and Warbury Journal and Wilts County Advertiser*, 4 March 1899, 1.

3. William W. Corp, *Fifty Years: a Brief Account of the Booksellers of Great Britain and Ireland 1895–1945* (Oxford: Basil Blackwell, 1946), 4.

4. Stott, "The Decay of Bookselling," 934.

5. Around 2005, at the UK's Stansted Airport, the revenue from carparks exceeded the landing fees paid by the airline companies, while the money earned through the sale or lease of concessions provided Heathrow Airport were its principle source of income, again exceeding landing fees; see Brian Edwards, *The Modern Airport Terminal* (London: Spon Press, 2005), 4.

6. Audrey Laing and Jo Royle, "Examining Chain Bookshops in the Context of 'Third Place,'" *International Journal of Retail & Distribution Management* 41, no. 1 (2013): 27–44.

7. Frost and Hall, "John Smith's: Historical Perspectives," 34.

8. Eliot, "From Few and Expensive," 298. See also Feather, *History of British Publishing*, 147.

9. As noted by John Spiers, the role of wholesalers is a lacuna in book studies; their central position in the market facilitated major changes in the book world. In addition to W.H. Smith, other important actors in the network were John Menzies, Marshall (including Hamilton, Adams and Co., and Kent and Co., both taken over by Simpkin's), William Dawson and Sons, John Joseph Griffin, Hodgsons, Longman, Henry Vickers, and Eason and Son in Dublin, and Mullan in Belfast. See John Spiers, ed., *The Culture of the Publisher's Series*, vol. 2, *Nationalisms and the National Canon* (Basingstoke, UK: Palgrave Macmillan, 2011), 40n10.

10. *The Successful Bookseller: A Complete Guide to Success to All Engaged in a Retail Bookselling, Stationery, and Fancy Goods Business* (London: Successful Bookselling Company, 1906), 31.

11. Bernard Langdon-Davies, *The Practice of Bookselling* (London: Phoenix House, 1951), 92.

12. Langdon-Davies, *Practice of Bookselling*, 95.

13. *The Successful Bookseller*, 33–34.

14. The Dublin bookseller James Duffy started out as a draper in the early 1800s; see Curwen, *History of Booksellers*, 459.

15. See *Publishers' Weekly* 60, no. 466 (1901), cited in The Lucile Project, ed. Sidney F. Huttner (University of Iowa), accessed 12 December 2019, http://sdrc.lib.uiowa.edu/lucile/publishers/lovellff/Lovellff.htm; Lynn Knight, *The Button Box: Lifting the Lid on Women's Lives* (London: Chatto and Windus, 2016), 119–120.

16. Langdon-Davies, *Practice of Bookselling*, 93.

17. Langdon-Davies, *Practice of Bookselling*, 86.

18. Langdon-Davies, *Practice of Bookselling*, 86.

19. Langdon-Davies, *Practice of Bookselling*, 93. The advice chimes perfectly with twenty-first-century financial evaluations of trust; see Gert Tingaard Svendsen, *Tillid* (Aarhus: Aarhus Universitetsforlag, 2012), in English as *Trust* (2018).

20. *The Successful Bookseller*, 35.

21. *The Successful Bookseller*, 36.

22. Squires, *Marketing Literature*, 75.

23. *The Successful Bookseller*, 67.

24. *The Successful Bookseller*, 74.

25. *Bristol Magpie*, 16 February 1889, 5.

26. *The Successful Bookseller*, 43.

27. See Kimberley Reynolds, "Rewarding Reads? Giving, Receiving, and Resisting Evangelical Reward and Prize Books," in *Popular Children's Literature in Britain*, ed. Asa Briggs, Dennis Butts, and Mathew Grenby (Abingdon, UK: Routledge, 2016), 189–208; on the redefining cultural work done by reward books for women, see Barbara Korte, "The Promotion of the Heroic Woman

in Victorian and Edwardian Gift Books," in *Reading Books and Prints as Cultural Objects*, ed. Evanghelia Stead (Basingstoke, UK: Palgrave Macmillan, 2018), 159–178.

28. *The Successful Bookseller*, 39 and 67.

29. *The Successful Bookseller*, 78–79. Tabs, or the difficult class of customer, may be those who went to Cambridge.

30. Advertisement, Pollet's Advertising Agency, London 1906, in *The Successful Bookseller*, 173.

31. *The Successful Bookseller*, 113.

32. *Southern Echo*, 11 November 1905, 4.

33. *The Successful Bookseller*, 117.

34. "Closing Down," *Birmingham Daily Post*, 6 May 1964, 6.

35. *The Successful Bookseller*, 139–141.

36. For details on advertising and the book trade, and its transition from a means of giving notice to a means of creating desire, see Frost, *Business of the Novel*, 63–67 and 86–87.

37. Langdon-Davies, *Practice of Bookselling*, 150.

38. Ian Mitchell, "'Old Books—New Bound'? Selling Second Hand Books in England, c. 1680–1850," in *Modernity and the Second-Hand Trade: European Consumption Cultures and Practices 1700–1900*, ed. Jon Stobart and Ilja Van Damme (Basingstoke, UK: Palgrave Macmillan, 2010), 149.

39. Shop owner Rupert Croft-Cooke, cited in Christopher Hilliard, "The Literary Underground of 1920s London," *Social History* 33, no. 2 (2008): 169.

40. *The Successful Bookseller*, 87.

41. "Books and Catalogues," *Southampton Daily Echo*, 13 September 1905, 2.

42. Debbie Young, "A Book is a Book: in Praise of the Argos Catalogue," *Debbie Young's Writing Life*, 3 March 2017, https://authordebbieyoung.com/2017/03/03/a-book-is-a-book-in-praise-of-the-argos-catalogue-reflections-on-childrens-reading-after-world-book-day-2017.

43. Alison Clarke, "Window Shopping at Home: Classifieds, Catalogues and New Consumer Skills," in *Material Cultures: Why Some Things Matter*, ed. Daniel Miller (Chicago: University of Chicago Press, 1998), 89.

Chapter 7

1. Southampton did not acquire its city status until 1964; it was previously a town. Where appropriate, the use of "city" is adopted to reinforce the point that this narrative is written from a twenty-first-century perspective.

2. Sotonopedia is developed and maintained by the Local Studies Department, Southampton Central Library, and is available at http://sotonopedia.wikidot.com/. The Southampton Local History and Maritime Digital Archive is the home

for the Southampton section of what once was the Portcities UK website, and is available at http://www.southampton.gov.uk/arts-heritage/southampton-archives/plimsoll.aspx. Historians of local history whose work is essential for the study of books during the period are A.G.L. [Alan] Leonard and Richard Preston. For further local history information, see Gordon Cox, "Henry Daubney Cox and the Bookbinding Business at 5 West Street," *Southampton Local History Forum Journal* 11 (Winter 2003): 19–20; Rev. J. Silvester Davies, *A History of Southampton* (Exeter: Hampshire Books, 1989; facsimile of Southampton: H.M. Gilbert, 1883); A.G.L. [Alan] Leonard, *Stories of Southampton Streets* (Southampton: Paul Cave; 1984); A.G.L. [Alan] Leonard, *More Stories of Southampton Streets* (Southampton: Paul Cave, 1989); A.G.L. [Alan] Leonard, *Southampton: The Archive Photographs Series* (Stroud, UK: Chalford Publishing Co., 1997); A.G.L. [Alan] Leonard, "Gilbert's: booksellers through five generations," *Journal of the Southampton Local History Forum*, 11 (2003): 13–15; A.G.L. [Alan] Leonard, *Southampton Memorials of Care for Man and Beast* (Southampton: Bitterne Local History Society, 2005); A.G.L. [Alan] Leonard, *Southampton: The Third Collection—Images of England* (Stroud, UK: Tempus Publishing, 2006); Roger Ottewill, "Henry March Gilbert 1846–1931: 'Staunch Liberal and Nonconformist,'" *Journal of the Local Southampton History Forum* 22 (Spring 2014): 11–18; Patterson, *A History of Southampton 1700–1914*, vol. 3, *Setbacks and Recoveries, 1868–1914*; Platt, *Medieval Southampton*; Preston, "A Precarious Business"; Preston, "Pursuit of Knowledge under Difficulties"; Adrian Rance, *A Victorian Photographer in Southampton* (Southampton: Paul Cave, 1988); Adrian Rance, *Southampton: An Illustrated History* (Portsmouth: Milestone, 1986).

    3. At the end of the 1890s, between 1897 and 1900, the building numbers to Above Bar High Street were changed, which meant that, despite occupying the same building, Gilbert's changed address from 26 1/2 to 24 Above Bar. Formerly, the numbering began at an address on the street's east side, north of the Bargate, at a narrow no-longer-extant lane named Sussex Place, linking present-day Sussex Road to the Above Bar Street. Progressing South, the numbering increased until reaching the Bargate, at 34 Above Bar. The numbering then continued on the west side from 35 Above Bar, in closest proximity to the Bargate, sequencing north back up to Portland Street, Ogle Road, and beyond. After 1900, the building numbers were ordered into even numbers on the street's east side and odd numbers on the west, beginning with the lowest numbers closest to the Bargate, and progressing north. This latter sequencing is still in use. The sequencing of High Street building numbers Below Bar remained (and remains) unaltered across the period, which means it retains the practice of not dividing the east and west sides of the street into odd and even numbers. The lowest numbers begin on the east side, Below Bar, and progress south, increasing to 84 High Street and what in 1907 was the Sun Hotel, on the Town Quay. The sequencing then continues back up the west side of the street, north, to

the Bargate: in 1907, past Robert Batt's at 178, Boots the chemist at 182, and various solicitors at 185 High Street adjacent to the Bargate itself.

4. Sidney Webb and Beatrice Webb, *Industrial Democracy* (London: Longman, Green and Co. 1897), 465, cited in David Finkelstein, "The Scottish Printing Diaspora, 1840–1914," in *Oxford Research Encyclopedias*, July 2018, https://doi.org/10.1093/acrefore/9780190201098.013.264.

5. By the 1930s the Ditches came to be regarded as slums. However, from an early age I learned from older family members of the excitement of this street and nostalgia for its passing.

6. *Hampshire Advertiser*, Saturday 17 January 1846, 3.

7. See "Old Furniture," photograph, 112 mm × 85 mm, Museum of London, Collections, ID IN653, accessed 12 December 2019 https://collections.museumoflondon.org.uk/online/object/432083.html.

8. Patterson, *History of Southampton*, vol. 3, 112–115.

9. Zoe Hartland, "How Has Life Expectancy Changed over Time?" Office for National Statistics, 9 September 2015, https://visual.ons.gov.uk/how-has-life-expectancy-changed-over-time/.

10. Apart from a prior visit in 1783 when she almost died of a fever, Austen was resident in Southampton from 1806 to 1809, but only plausibly became a "Southamptonian" as she is currently claimed to be after 1917 with the unveiling of a plaque in the central library erected by the Southampton Literary and Philosophical Society. None of Austen's novels were written during her stay in the city.

11. See Robert Taylor, *Syntagma of the Evidences of the Christian Religion: Being a Vindication of the Manifesto of the Christian Evidence Society, against the Assaults of the Christian Instruction Society* (London: Dugdale, 1828).

12. Tony Grant, "Netley Abbey and the Gothic Revival," *Jane Austen's World*, 5 January 2018, https://janeaustensworld.wordpress.com/2018/01/05/netley-abbey-and-the-gothic-by-tony-grant.

13. "Bernard Street," engraving, title date 1783, Southampton Local History and Maritime Digital Archives, accessed 12 December 2019, https://southampton.spydus.co.uk/cgi-bin/spydus.exe/FULL/OPAC/BIBENQ/61782247/26109486,23?FMT=IMG.

14. "Adjudications," *London Gazette*, 7 May 1889, 2544.

15. "Alleged Conspiracy," *Barrier Miner*, 9 April 1898, 2.

16. George Clement Boase, "Virtue, James Sprent," in *Oxford Dictionary of National Biography*, accessed December 2019, https://doi.org/10.1093/ref:odnb/28332.

17. *Hampshire Advertiser County Newspaper*, 10 February 1875, 2.

18. *Hampshire Advertiser County Newspaper*, 26 October 1907, 9.

19. See Godwin, *Mate's Illustrated Handbook*, n.p. rear advertiser.

20. See *Guide to Southampton* (Southampton: Gutch and Co., 1869), which retailed at 1d, and *Gutch's Pictorial Almanac* (Southampton: Gutch and Cox, 1875).

21. "Southampton Book Society," *Hampshire Advertiser*, 14 December 1867, 5.

22. "The Town and Country Book Society," *Hampshire Advertiser*, 21 December 1867, 5.

23. "Christmas at Southampton: a Walk Around the Shops," *Hampshire Advertiser*, 16 December 1905, 12.

24. "178 High Street, Southampton," *Southampton Daily Echo*, 13 December 1905, 2.

25. Rance, *Victorian Photographer*, 12.

26. Mitchell, "'Old books—New Bound'?" 145.

27. See Harald Tveterås, *Den Norske Bokhandels Historie*, vol. 1, *Forlag og bokhandel inntil 1850* (Oslo: Norsk Bokhandler-medhjælperforening, 1950); and Lars Roede, *Byen bytter byggeskikk: Christiania 1624–1814* (Oslo: Arkitekthøgskolen, 2001).

28. Henry Thorn, *Charles Dibdin: One of Southampton's Sons* (Southampton: Buxey, 1888), cover.

29. Rance, *Victorian Photographer*, 3–7.

30. It was Edward who was grandson to William Carus Wilson, founder of the monthly journal *The Children's Friend*, and the man dismayed to find he had been the model for Mr. Brocklehurst in *Jane Eyre*, or so was the claim of Edward in letters written by Edward about a revised Brontë manuscript that had been sent to his grandfather as an atonement by the author; see Ian Herbert, "Revealed: Why Brocklehurst's Inspiration Threatened to Sue Brontë," *Independent*, 25 May 2006, http://www.independent.co.uk/news/uk/this-britain/revealed-why-brocklehursts-inspiration-threatened-to-sue-bronteuml-479611.html.

31. Graham Law, "The Serial Revolution at the Periphery," in *Moveable Type, Mobile Nations*, ed. Simon Frost and Robert Rix (Copenhagen: Museum Tusculanum Press, 2010), 87.

32. Patterson, *History of Southampton*, vol. 3, 118, and Keith Hamilton, "Battles of Cobden Bridge," *Southern Evening Echo*, 29 December 2006, www.dailyecho.co.uk/heritage/1095584.battles-of-cobden-bridge/.

33. The store traded as Edwin Jones until the 1970s, when it assumed its corporate title of Debenhams. In the 1960s, when I was growing up, Edwin Jones was by far the most prestigious department store in the city, rivaled possibly by Tyrrel and Greens. It was especially popular with children for its lavish Christmas displays, with Santa in his Christmas grotto.

34. For a general history of the business of W.H. Smith, see Charles Wilson, *First with the News: The History of W.H. Smith 1792–1972* (London:

Jonathan Cape, 1985). For Smith and their access to readerships, see Stephen Colclough, "Distribution," in *The Cambridge History of the Book in Britain*, vol. 6, *1830–1914*, ed. David McKitterick (Cambridge: Cambridge University Press, 2009), 238–280; Stephen Colclough, "'No Such Bookselling Has Ever Before Taken Place': W.H. Smith and Propaganda, 1917–1920," in *Publishing and the First World War*, ed. Mary Hammond and Shafquat Towheed (Basingstoke, UK: Palgrave, 2007), 28–45; Stephen Colclough, "'Station to Station': The LNWR and the Emergence of the Railway Bookstall, 1848–1875," in *Printing Places: Locations of Book Production and Distribution Since 1500*, ed. John Hinks and Catherine Armstrong (London: British Library and Oak Knoll Press, 2005), 169–184; and Mary Hammond, "Sensation and Sensibility: W.H. Smith and the Railway Bookstall," in Hammond, *Reading*, 51–83.

35. Wilson, *First with the News*, 99.
36. *Hampshire Advertiser*, 12 August 1893, 4.
37. *Southern Echo*, 17 September 1894, 4.
38. *Hampshire Advertiser*, 17 May 1902, 9.
39. *Hampshire Advertiser*, 17 May 1902, 9.
40. *Southern Daily Echo*, 13 December 1905, 2.

Chapter 8

1. Kathryn Ledbetter, *Tennyson and Victorian Periodicals: Commodities in Context* (Aldershot, UK: Ashgate, 2007).
2. See chapter 6 of this book for the retail use of catalogs.
3. "Books and Catalogues," *Southern Daily Echo*, 13 September 1905, 2.
4. Kevin Roberts, *Lovemarks: The Future Beyond Brands* (New York: Powerhouse, 2007): see also Saatchi-favorite Kevin Roberts's website, www.lovemarks.com.
5. *Hampshire Advertiser*, 19 January 1895, 5.
6. *Hampshire Advertiser*, 15 December 1894, 3; and *Hampshire Advertiser*, 25 January 1890, 4.
7. Two essay sketches make up the only studies of Gilbert's before this one: Leonard, "Gilbert's," and Ottewill, "Henry March Gilbert." Their invaluable yet modest outline has been fleshed out from the archival record and from other histories, and through interviews with the last family owner-manager of Gilbert's, Richard Gilbert, across 2017–19.
8. See the entry for Henry Gilbert in British Book Trade Index (Bodleian Libraries, University of Oxford), http://bbti.bodleian.ox.ac.uk/.
9. *Hampshire Chronicle, Southampton and Isle of Wight Courier*, 2 June 1860, 4.

10. In 1867, Henry March married Mary Emma Stanesby of the same age, born in Chelsea, and the marriage was registered in Westminster. Not surprisingly, her father was a stationer and bookseller. At the time of the 1871 Southampton census, Henry and Mary were recorded as living in Bernard Street in the city, but by 1881 they had moved back to the London area in Wandsworth. At some point, they must have returned to Southampton, since the 1891 census shows them as occupying a property named "Hailstede" in Archer's Road. In addition to Henry March and Mary, their household consisted of four daughters, a governess, two apprentice booksellers, who were designated "boarders," and a general domestic servant. Clearly, the household was both thriving and very much centered on bookselling.

11. Frost and Hall, "John Smith's: Historical Perspectives," 28.

12. Even in the early 1990s, it took around six months for me to track down a copy of Giovanni Papini, *The Failure* [*Un uomo finito*] (1913), which was then out of print.

13. Jon Stobart and Ilja van Damme, eds., *Modernity and the Second-Hand Trade: European Consumption Cultures and Practices 1700–1900* (Basingstoke, UK: Palgrave Macmillan 2010), 1–17, 5; see also Mitchell, "'Old Books—New Bound'?"

14. Mitchell, "'Old Books—New Bound'?" 142–144.

15. *Hampshire Advertiser*, Saturday 25 January 1890, 4.

16. *Hampshire Advertiser*, Saturday 15 December 1894, 3.

17. *Bristol Magpie*, 8 October 1896, 18. For a sustained analysis of the importance of material books as cultural objects, see Price, *How to Do Things with Books in Victorian Britain*. Her influence on the current study is obvious and gratefully acknowledged.

18. *Hampshire Advertiser*, 14 February 1891, 1. (A shorter advertisement, again from Gilbert's, appears on page 7 of the same day's edition.)

19. *Hampshire Advertiser*, 20 September 1873, 2.

20. Mitchell, "'Old Books—New Bound'?" 142–144.

21. See "The Society for the Repression of Mendicity," Bloomsbury Project, University College London, accessed 12 December 2019, www.ucl.ac.uk/bloomsbury-project/institutions/society_suppression_mendicity.htm.

22. Henry Mayhew, et al., *The London Underworld in the Victorian Period: Authentic First-Person Accounts by Beggars, Thieves and Prostitutes* (Mineola, NY: Dover Publications, 2005), 324; a reprint of Henry Mayhew, *London Labour and the London Poor: A Cyclopaedia of the Condition and Earnings of Those that Will Work, Those that Cannot Work and Those that Will Not Work*, vol. 4, *Those that Will Not Work: Comprising Prostitutes, Thieves, Swindlers, Beggars* (s.l.: Woodfall, 1862).

23. "Police Courts," *Hampshire Advertiser*, 16 September 1876, 6. For a comparison, Saturday-night drunkenness could secure seven days in prison.

24. *Hampshire Advertiser*, 12 September 1894, 3.

25. "Police Courts," *The Hampshire Advertiser and County News*, 23 June 1894, 6. See also *Southern Echo*, 21 June 1894, 3.

26. See Sutherland, *Stanford Companion*, 52. Edna Lyall (legal name Ada Ellen Bayly) published some 20 novels between 1879 and 1902, including *Donovan*, 3 vols. (London: Hurst and Blackett, 1882).

27. "Prosecution of a Japanese Engineer," *Hampshire Advertiser and County News*, Saturday 30 June 1894, 6.

28. "Southampton Borough Bench," *Southern Echo*, 20 July 1894, 3.

29. *Hampshire Advertiser*, 20 December 1893, 2.

30. *Hampshire Advertiser County Newspaper*, 29 November 1893, 2.

31. *Hampshire Advertiser County Newspaper*, 29 November 1893, 2.

32. *Hampshire Advertiser*, 27 September 1873, 3.

33. *Southern Echo*, 11 November 1905, 4.

34. "Abridged Terms of the Lending Library," in *Catalogue of the Principal English Books in Circulation at Mudie's Select Library*, Mudie's Select Library (London: Mudie's Select Library, 1907), ii.

35. Ottewill, "Henry March Gilbert," 14.

36. *Hampshire Advertiser County Newspaper*, 16 July 1892, 3. See chapter 5 of this book for Henry March's support of a free reading room.

37. *Hampshire Advertiser County Newspaper*, 19 September 1894, 4.

38. See Henry March Gilbert, *Bibliotheca Hantoniensis* (Southampton: H.M. Gilbert, 1872), https://archive.org/details/bibliothecahanto00gilbrich.

39. Susan Coultrap McQuinn supportively commenting on Gail Hamilton's [Mary Abigail Dodge] exposé of publishing, *Battle of the Books* (1870), cited in Wyn Kelly, "'Tender Kinswoman': Gail Hamilton and Gendered Justice," in *Melville and Women*, ed. Elizabeth Schultz and Haskell Springer (Kent, OH: Kent State University Press, 2006), 107.

40. See Frost and Hall, "John Smith's: Historical Perspectives," 29.

41. For McFadden's *Vestiges*, see chapter 7 of this study.

42. Robert Darnton, "'What is the History of Books?' Revisited," *Modern Intellectual History* 4, no. 3 (2007): 495–508.

43. Claire Squires and Padmini Ray Murray, "The Digital Communications Circuit," in *The Book Unbound: Disruption and Disintermediation in the Digital Age*, University of Stirling, accessed 12 December 2019, www.bookunbound.stir.ac.uk/research/infographic/.

Chapter 9

1. For a book history view on the early publication of Jevons, and to what it lay in counter-distinction, see Frost, "Economising in Public."

2. See for example Neva Goodwin and Jonathan Harris, *Principles of Economics in Context* (New York: Routledge, 2015), a higher-education textbook that discusses neoclassical economics as a historic moment but largely uncritically adopts neoclassical precepts and minor variations on those throughout, without engaging with paradigmatic alternatives such as Austrian, Schumpeterian, feminist, or behavioralist economics.

3. Jevons, *Theory of Political Economy*, 3rd ed., 6.

4. Chang, *Economics: The User's Guide*, 87. Jevons's belief was that wherever "things treated were capable of being *more or less* in magnitude, there the laws and relations must be mathematical in nature." Jevons, *Theory of Political Economy*, 3rd ed., 4. Whether existential qualities can be properly described in terms of variable quantities—"more" satisfaction, "less" loneliness—is open to question.

5. Jevons, *Theory of Political Economy*, 3rd ed., 23–27.

6. Jevons, *Theory of Political Economy*, 3rd ed., 35–86.

7. Jevons, *Theory of Political Economy*, 3rd ed., 36.

8. Jevons, *Theory of Political Economy*, 3rd ed., 36, 87, and 91.

9. Jevons, *Theory of Political Economy*, 3rd ed., 36.

10. See Herbert Simon, "Theories of Bounded Rationality," in *Decision and Organization*, ed. Charles McGuire and Roy Radner (Amsterdam: North-Holland Publishing, 1972), 161–176; and for an overview, see Kenneth Arrow, "Is Bounded Rationality Unboundedly Rational? Some Ruminations," in *Models of a Man: Essays in Memory of Herbert A. Simon*, ed. James G. March and Mie Augier (Cambridge, MA.: MIT Press, 2004), 47–56.

11. Jevons, *Theory of Political Economy*, 3rd ed., 92.

12. There is a long tradition of refusing to understand economic activity disassociated from the social, cultural formations that enable it, and to think of preferences as effects of relational, institutional, and cultural contexts, in contrast to their conception in rational choice theory; see Karl Polyani, *The Great Transformation* (New York: Rinehart, 1944).

13. Michel Foucault, "Maurice Blanchot: The Thought From Outside," in Michel Foucault and Maurice Blanchot, *Foucault: Blanchot* (New York: Zone, 1997), 12–13.

14. Clifford Geertz, *The Interpretation of Cultures: Selected Essays* (New York: Basic Books, 1973), 15.

15. A challenging use of narrative fiction as part of philosophical discourse is found in the semi-fictional anecdotes used for critical reflection in Theodore Zeldin, *An Intimate History of Humanity* (London: Minerva, 1994).

16. For a history of the American Civil War conflict in the Solent, see Michael Hughes, *Stand-off in the Solent: The American Civil War Comes to Hampshire* (Winchester: Hampshire County Council, 2002). For Carlyle and Dickens, and the Governor Eyre Controversy, see Chris R. Vanden Bossche, *Carlyle and*

the Search for Authority, Victorian Web, 26 October 2001, www.victorianweb.org/authors/carlyle/vandenbossche/6b.html; and Frost, *Business of the Novel*, 37–38.

17. For a survey of gambling in the period, see Michael Flavin, *Gambling in the Nineteenth-Century Novel: 'A Leprosy Is o'er the Land'* (Brighton: Sussex Academic Press, 2003). Flavin's central thesis is that gambling was so vilified by Victorians as it played the unwanted double to the period's ethos of chance and speculation that was at the heart of its growing economy; Flavin, *Gambling*, 1.

18. "Literary Notices: Magazines for April," *Hampshire Advertiser*, 5 April 1890, 7. See also "Cornhill," in *Dictionary of Nineteenth Century Journalism*, ed. Laurel Brake and Marysa Demoor (London: Academia Press and British Library, 2009), 145.

19. James Payn, *The Burnt Million* (London: Collins Clear Type, 1905), 178.

20. See James Payn, "The Pinch of Poverty," *The Nineteenth Century* 7 (May 1880): 864–870.

21. Crawford, *Mr. Isaacs*, 1.

22. For transatlantic on-board reading, see Frost, "A Trade in Desires."

23. Charles Emmerson's metonymic portrait of turn-of-the-century Germany in the figure of Berlin shows the city as a modernist powerhouse full of "newspaper kiosks, telephones and trams. In 1895, the city had eight times as many telephones per head of population as London." Emmerson, *1913*, 61.

24. Jenkins, *Provincial Modernity*, 127–134.

25. *Hamburg Nachrichten*, 17 February 1882, 8, had an advertisement for the St. Georger Leihbibliothek (St.Georg district Circulating Library), Steindamm 11, announcing volumes available by Mite Kremnitz, A.J. Mordtmann, Erich Lilsen, and James Payn, with subscription rates. Similarly, in the Netherlands, Payn's *Wat Hij Haar Kostte* (What He Cost Her) was run in feuilleton from 2 November 1877 to 6 May 1878 in *De Locomotief: Samarangsch handels- en advertentie-blad*; see chapter 3 of this book, notes 37 and 38.

26. *Hampshire Advertiser*, 28 March 1885, 7.

27. Robert Louis Stevenson, "The Suicide Club," in *New Arabian Nights* (New York: Henry Holt, 1882), 3–86.

28. *Southampton Echo*, 6 June 1903, 1–4.

29. *Hampshire Chronicle*, 7 September 1907, 12.

30. See Guy Atkins, *Come Home at Once: Intriguing Messages from the Golden Age of Postcards* (London: Bantam Press, 2014). James William Parker's photographic studios in Canal Walk were not open until 1910, thus Jenny's memory would be playing her false.

31. See "Maes, Hannah Winifred," in Sotonopedia, Southampton Central Library, Local Studies Department, accessed 12 December 2019, http://sotonopedia.wikidot.com/page-browse:maes-hannah-winifred.

32. *Hampshire Telegraph*, Saturday 3 October 1903, 10.

33. Anonymous, *My Secret Life* (Amsterdam: Privately printed for subscribers, 1888). Also see Steven Marcus, *The Other Victorians: A Study of Sexuality and Pornography in Mid-Nineteenth-Century England* (New York: Meridian, 1977).

34. MacLane, *Story*.

35. Amalia Blandford Edwards, *Barbara's History* (London: Hurst and Blackett, 1864).

36. Marie Connor Leighton, *Sweet Magdalen: Only a Love Story* (London: F.V. White and Co., 1887), and Marie Connor Leighton, *The Harvest of Sin* (London: James Bowden, 1896). Leighton wrote around sixty novels, including crime stories featuring a female detective: *Joan Mar, Detective* (1910) and *Lucile Dare, Detective* (1919). She had been an actress, and at 16 eloped with the editor of a volume of juvenilia to which she had submitted her poems. As an admirer of male vigour, she encouraged her son Roland to join the war in France, where he was killed, prompting Leighton's memoir *Boy of My Heart* (1916); see Sandra Kemp, Charlotte Mitchell, and David Trotter, eds., *The Oxford Companion to Edwardian Fiction* (Oxford: Oxford University Press, 2002), 238.

37. *St James's Gazette*, 20 November 1900, 5.

38. After MacLane, "Mary: March 5th," in MacLane, *Story*, 179–183.

39. "A Dream of the Future," *Bournemouth Daily Echo*, 20 July 1903, 4.

40. Almyer Maude, "How Tolstoy wrote 'Resurrection,'" in Lev Tolstoy and Aylmer Maude, trans., *Resurrection* (Christchurch Hampshire: Free Age Press, 1901), reprinted from Aylmer Maude, *Tolstoy and His Problems: Essays by Aylmer Maude* (London: Grant Richards, 1901), 128–148. See also "Gossip of the Day: Tolstoi on 'Resurrection,'" *Portsmouth Evening News*, 14 February 1900, 2; and "Gossip of the Day: Tolstoy the Pessimist," reporting on Tolstoy's dismay at not having died, *Portsmouth Evening News*, 25 January 1901, 2.

41. A performance of *Resurrection* was planned by His Majesty's Theatre Bournemouth, following the acquisition of the English rights but with a time limitation, forcing postponement of a production of *Richard II*. See *Bournemouth Daily Echo*, 28 November 1902, 2.

42. See "Airships of the Future," *Portsmouth Evening News*, 19 March 1903, 6.

43. A local manifestation of which would include an advertisement for "Sunday Meetings for the People, St James' Hall, Commercial Road—lecture next Sunday at Seven O'Clock, Walter C. Stevens. Subject 'The Bible and the Land Question': reading from Henry George's *Progress and Poverty*. N.D.L. Hymnbook. Questions. Discussion. Collection," in *Portsmouth Evening News*, 14 December 1901, 4.

44. John Lynch, *Argentine Dictator: Juan Manuel de Rosas* (Oxford: Clarendon Press, 1981), 337–358.

45. See Tierl Thompson, ed. *Dear Girl: The Diaries and Letters of Two Working Women 1897–1917* (London: The Women's Press, 1987), 282–295.

46. See Tamara Wagner, "Emigration and 19th-Century British Colonial Settler Narratives," in *Oxford Research Encyclopedias*, February 2019, https://doi.org/10.1093/acrefore/9780190201098.013.944.

47. Gannaway, *Association Football*, 10–11.

48. The volume is Rudyard Kipling, *Life's Handicap: Being Stories of Mine Own People*, ed. printed by J. Palmer, Alexandra Street, Cambridge (London: Macmillan, 1891), in blue embossed cloth, inscribed by hand on the title page with "Ed. W. Mountford, Sept, 1891."

49. Bernard Capes, "The Sword of Colonel Lacoste," *Blackwood's Magazine* 165, 1000 (1899): 385–401. On pages 193–220 of the same issue is an installment of "Heart of Darkness." For details, see Frost, "The Good in a Little Fiction."

50. "Lascars Drink Too Much," *Hampshire Advertiser*, 12 September 1894, 3.

51. William Henry Sheppard, *Presbyterian Pioneers in the Congo* (Richmond, VA: Presbyterian Committee of Publication, 1917), 76 and 149–153. Sheppard's account of his thirty extraordinary years along the Kasai river and his mission there from May 1890, arriving just a few steps ahead of Joseph Conrad and living through the worst excesses of Leopold's *État Indépendant du Congo* and its *Force Publique*, is only surpassed by the paradox of his being sent there. This was the result of a white supremacist senator from Alabama, John Tyler Morgan, who wished to dispatch black American missionaries to the African continent as a beachhead for the "repatriation" of millions of African Americans. Like many of the back-to-Africa movements, or colonization movements, in the post-emancipation era, the project was ambiguous in meeting both the segregationist desires of white enthusiasts and the wishes of black Americans to escape the humiliation of segregation at home. A copy of Sheppard's memoirs is held by The Open Library: https://archive.org/details/presbyterianpion00shep/page/n3.

52. For Sheppard and the rubber industry, see Adam Hochschild, *King Leopold's Ghost* (London: PAN, 2011), 152–166.

53. For a conception of the pan-African Atlantic, see the seminal work by Paul Gilroy, *The Black Atlantic: Modernity and Double Consciousness* (London: Verso, 1993).

54. For listings of African American Periodicals, see African American Periodicals 1825–1995, Archive of Americana Collection, Readex, www.readex.com/content/african-american-periodicals-1825-1995; and for a brief introduction to early black writing and periodicals in Britain, see Asher Hoyles and Martin Hoyles, *Caribbean Publishing in Britain* (London: Hansib, 2011).

55. See chapter 11 for the appearance of and subsequent debate about Tennyson's poem in the *Frederick Douglass's Paper*.

56. Letter from Alfred Tennyson to William Makepeace Thackeray, dated 6 November 1859: "Whenever you feel your brains as the 'remainder biscuit' or indeed whenever you will, come over to me and take a blow on these downs

where the air, as Keats said is 'worth a sixpence a pint' and bring the girls too"; see Cecil Lang and Edgar Shannon, eds., *The Letters of Alfred Lord Tennyson*, vol. 2, *1851–1870* (Cambridge, MA: Harvard University Press, 1987), 245.

57. Alfred Tennyson, *The Death of Œnone, Akbar's Dream and Other Poems* (London: Macmillan, 1892).

Chapter 10

1. For consumption and identity formation, see chapter 1 of this study.

2. Ian Woodward, *Understanding Material Culture* (London: Sage, 2007), 22ff., 24. Woodward here refers to Theodor Adorno and Max Horkheimer, "Dialectic of Enlightenment" (1944), and Herbert Marcuse, *One-Dimensional Man* (1964).

3. Wilfred Dolfsma, ed., *Consuming Symbolic Goods: Identity and Commitment, Values and Economics* (London: Routledge, 2008), 1.

4. Richard Wilk, "Morals and Metaphors: The Meaning of Consumption," in *Elusive Consumption*, eds Karin Ekström and Helene Brembeck (Oxford: Berg, 2004), 11–26. Wilk furthermore points out a pathological variant to the metaphor of consumption as eating when wealth becomes fatness and poverty becomes starvation.

5. Karin Ekström and Helene Brembeck, eds., "Elusive Consumption in Retrospect: Report from the Conference" (Göteborg: Centre for Consumer Science, Göteborg University, 2005), https://gupea.ub.gu.se/bitstream/2077/23184/1/gupea_2077_23184_1.pdf.

6. David Graeber, "Consumption," *Current Anthropology* 52, no. 4 (2011): 502. See also Søren Askegaard and Benoît Heilbrunn, *Canonical Authors in Consumption Theory* (London: Routledge, 2010), 5–6.

7. See chapter 2 of this study.

8. Walter R. Fisher, "Narration as a Human Communication Paradigm: The Case of Public Moral Argument," *Communication Monographs* 51, no. 1 (1984): 1–22; see also Walter R. Fisher, "Homo Narrans, The Narrative Paradigm: In the Beginning," *Journal of Communication* 35, no. 4 (1985): 74–89.

9. Karin Littau, *Theories of Reading: Books, Bodies and Bibliomania* (Cambridge: Polity Press, 2006)

10. Edith Wharton and Ogden Codman, *The Decoration of Houses* (New York: W.W. Norton, 1978), 150, 115, and Henry Miller, *Black Spring* (New York: Grove, 1963), 42, both cited in Ben De Brun, "Where to Do Things with Words: Circulating Books, Decorating Rooms, and Locating Modern Reading," *Orbis Litterarum* 68, no. 6 (2013): 457–472.

11. For Mandela, see Archie Dick, "Censorship and the Reading Practices of Political Prisoners in South Africa, 1960–1990," *Innovation: Journal of Appropriate Librarianship and Information Work in Southern Africa*, no. 35 (December

2007): 24–55; and Simon Frost and Robert Rix, eds., *Moveable Type, Mobile Nations* (Copenhagen: Museum Tusculanum Press, 2010), 10–11. For Koestler, see Arthur Koestler, *Dialogue with Death*, trans. Trevor Blewitt and Phyllis Blewitt (Chicago: University of Chicago Press, 2011), 184. While imprisoned in fascist Spain, Koestler notes reading a biography of Cervantes and a novel by Pio Baroja (possibly *Tree of Knowledge*).

12. David Leichter, "Collective Identity and Collective Memory in the Philosophy of Paul Ricoeur," *Paul Ricoeur Studies* 3, no. 1 (2012): 114, cited in Bronwen Thomas, "Whose Story Is It Anyway?" *Style* 51, no. 3 (2017): 368.

13. Theodore Sarbin, "The Narrative as the Root Metaphor for Contextualisation," in *Varieties of Scientific Contextualism*, ed. Linda Hayes, Steven Hayes, Hayne Reese and Theodore Sarbin (Reno, NV: Context Press, 1993), 59, cited in Edward Taylor and Patricia Cranton, *Handbook of Transformative Learning* (San Fransisco: Jossey-Bass, 2012), 426.

14. Acknowledgement to Doctor of Education Creative and Media student Edward Wright for bringing attention to these sources.

15. Willis, *Reception*, 108–109.

16. Cited in Jim Ridgway and Michele Benjamin, *PsiFi: Psychological Theories and Science Fictions* (Leicester: British Psychological Society, 1987), 113.

17. Jackson, "Live Better by Consuming Less?" 30.

18. Northrop Frye, *Interviews with Northrop Frye*, ed. Jean O'Grady (Toronto: University of Toronto Press, 2008), 172.

19. Dolfsma, *Consuming Symbolic Goods*.

20. Ron Tamborini, Nicholas David Bowman, Allison Eden, Matthew Grizzard, and Ashley Organ, "Defining Media Enjoyment as the Satisfaction of Intrinsic Needs," *Journal of Communication* 60, no. 4 (2010): 759.

21. Tamborini et al., "Defining Media Enjoyment," 759. See also Elihu Katz, Jay Blumler, and Michael Gurevitch, "Utilization of Mass Communication by the Individual," in *The Uses of Mass Communications: Current Perspectives on Gratifications Research*, ed. Jay Blumler and Elihu Katz (Beverly Hills, CA: Sage, 1974), 19–32; Stephen Reiss and James Wiltz, "Why People Watch Reality TV," *Media Psychology* 6, no. 4 (2004): 363–378; Dolf Zillmann and Jennings Bryant, "Affect, Mood, and Emotion as Determinants of Selective Exposure," in *Selective Exposure to Communication*, eds. Dolf Zillmann and Jennnings Bryant (Hillsdale, NJ: Erlbaum, 1985), 157–190; and Dolf Zillmann and Joanne Cantor, "A Disposition Theory of Humor and Mirth," in *Humor and Laughter: Theory, Research, and Applications*, eds. Anthony J. Chapman and Hugh Foot (London: Wiley, 1976), 93–115.

22. Tamborini et al., "Defining Media Enjoyment," 759.

23. Tamborini et al., "Defining Media Enjoyment," 773.

24. Peter Vorderer and Franziska S. Roth, "How Do We Entertain Ourselves with Literary Texts?" *Scientific Study of Literature* 1, no. 1 (2011): 136–143.

25. See note 21, above; see also Percy Tannenbaum and Dolf Zillmann, "Emotional Arousal in the Facilitation of Aggression through Communication," in *Advances in Experimental Social Psychology*, vol. 8, ed. Leonard Berkowitz (New York: Academic, 1975), 149–192; and Percy Tannenbaum, *The Entertainment Functions of Television* (Hillsdale, NJ: Erlbaum, 1980).

26. Vorderer and Roth, "How Do We Entertain Ourselves," 138.

27. Clifford Geertz, "Thick Description: Towards an Interpretive Theory of Culture," in *The Interpretation of Cultures* (New York: Basic Books, 2000), 15 and 17.

28. See Melanie Green, Timothy Brock, and Geoff Kaufman, "Understanding Media Enjoyment: The Role of Transportation into Narrative Worlds," *Communication Theory* 14, no. 3 (2004): 311–327.

29. Vorderer and Roth, "How Do We Entertain Ourselves," 140. See also Mary Beth Oliver and Anne Bartsch, "Appreciation as Audience Response: Exploring Entertainment Gratifications Beyond Hedonism," *Human Communication Research* 36, no. 1 (2010): 53–81.

30. Vorderer and Roth, "How Do We Entertain Ourselves," 142; and Daneille Fuller and DeNel Sedo, "Fun . . . and Other Reasons for Sharing Reading with Strangers: Mass Reading Events and the Possibilities of Pleasure," in *Plotting the Reading Experience: Theory/Practice/Politics*, ed. Lynne McKechnie et al. (Waterloo, Canada: Wilfrid Laurier University Press, 2016), 146–147.

31. McKechnie et al., *Plotting the Reading Experience*, 3.

32. For the former see Gitte Balling, "What Is a Reading Experience? The Development of a Theoretical and Empirical Understanding," in McKechnie et al., *Plotting the Reading Experience*, 37–53. For more on Baumgarten and the aesthetic framing of reading, see Frost, *Business of the Novel*, 28 and 49; and for the latter, see Gabrielle Cliff Hodges, "Reimagining Reading," in McKechnie et al., *Plotting the Reading Experience*, 69.

33. Cecilie Naper, "Experiencing the Social Melodrama in the Twenty-First Century," in McKechnie et al., *Plotting the Reading Experience*, 328–329.

34. Mette Steenberg, "Literary Reading as a Social Technology: an Exploratory Study of Shared Reading Groups," in McKechnie et al., *Plotting the Reading Experience*, 185.

35. Fuller and Sedo, "Fun . . ." 146–147.

36. Erwin Segal, "Narrative Comprehension and the Role of Deictic Shift Theory," in *Deixis in Narrative: A Cognitive Science Perspective*, ed. Judith Duchan, Gail Bruder, and Lynne Hewitt (Hillsdale, NJ: Lawrence Erlbaum, 1995), 3–17, 15, cited in Sara Whiteley, "Text World Theory, Real Readers and Emotional Responses to *The Remains of the Day*," *Language and Literature* 20, no. 1 (2011): 25–26.

37. Peter Stockwell, *Texture: A Cognitive Aesthetics of Reading* (Edinburgh: Edinburgh University Press, 2009), 144–152, cited in Whiteley, "Text World Theory," 26.

38. Whiteley, "Text World Theory," 36.
39. David Lodge, *The Art of Fiction: Illustrated from Classic and Modern Texts* (Harmondsworth, UK: Penguin, 1992), 10.
40. For an empirical historical record of reader behavior, projects would include UK RED (The Reading Experience Database) (Open University), www.open.ac.uk/Arts/reading/UK/, and What Middletown Read (Ball State University), https://lib.bsu.edu/wmr/index.php; and from the Alexander Street Press, there are a number of oral history databases from which evidence of reading practice can be culled, including British and Irish Women's letters and Diaries, North American Women' Letters and Diaries, Black Thought and Culture, and Oral History Online, see Social and Cultural History: Letters and Diaries Online (Alexander Street, ProQuest), https://alexanderstreet.com/products/social-and-cultural-history-letters-and-diaries-online-package. For reading practice in a digital age, see Researching Readers Online (Bournemouth University), www.researchingreadersonline.com/; Transliteracies Project (University of California Santa Barbara), http://transliteracies.english.ucsb.edu/; or Digital Reading Network, www.digitalreadingnetwork.com. See also DeNel Rehberg Sedo and Danielle Fuller, *Reading Beyond the Book: The Social Practices of Contemporary Literary Culture* (New York: Routledge, 2013). Large Digital Humanities projects such as the impressive FBTEE (The French Booktrade in Enlightenment Europe: http://fbtee.uws.edu.au/main/) convey astounding empirical detail about readerships and markets, but little on the behaviors of actual readers. For approaches to literature from neuroscience and health and social sciences, publications from the University of Liverpool's *Centre for Research into Reading, Literature and Society*, under the Institute of Psychology, Health and Society, would be a place to start. Useful surveys from the pre-digital era include Victor Nell, *Lost in a Book* (New Haven, CT: Yale University Press, 1988).
41. For the following section on BML, Reading Fiction in the Internet Society, and the UK Public High Street surveys, see Simon Frost, "Readers and Retailed Literature: Findings from a UK Public High Street Survey into Purchasers' Expectations from Books," *LOGOS* 28, no. 2 (2017): 27–43.
42. BML (Book Marketing Ltd.), *Reading the Situation: Book Reading, Buying and Borrowing Habits in Britain* (London: BML, 2000), 12. For other surveys see BML, *Reading the Situation*, 3.
43. See research conducted by Torsten Pettersson, "Att lara sig något av det som inte är sant: 72 gymnasister om fiktionellt och dokumentärt berättande [To learn from what is untrue: 72 senior high school students on fictional and documentary storytelling]," in *Litteraturen på undantag? Unga vuxnas fiktionsläsning i dagens Sverige*, ed. Skans Kersti Nilsson, Olle Nordberg, Torsten Pettersson, and Maria Wennerstrom Wohrne (Göteborg: Makadam Forlag, 2015), 63–79. Of the ten questions put to seventy-two senior high school students about why they read fiction, answers overwhelmingly gravitated towards "För att få vila och

avkoppling; För att uppleva verklighetsflykt; För att bli road och underhållen" (To get rest and relaxation; to experience a break from reality; to be amused and entertained) and to some extent "För att uppleva spänning och skräck" (To experience excitement and terror). My translations.

44. Dorthe Bernstein and Steen Folke Larsen, *Læsnings Former* (Aalborg: Biblioteksarbejde og Forfatterne, 1993), 8. All translations of this text are mine.

45. Bernstein and Larsen, *Læsnings Former*, 15.

46. Bernstein and Larsen, *Læsnings Former*, 19.

47. Bernstein and Larsen, *Læsnings Former*, 146ff.

48. Frost, "Readers and Retailed Literature."

49. Options were as follows: Amusement and entertainment; Relaxation; An escape into another world; Emotional involvement; The thrill of suspense and/or terror; An intellectual challenge; Opportunity to share interests with, or to discuss with others; An improved understanding of this world; An aesthetic experience; Better self-understanding; Other.

50. Frost, "Readers and Retailed Literature," 36–37.

51. Itself a feature of affective disposition theory.

52. Cited in in Henry Jenkins, *Fans, Bloggers, and Gamers* (New York: New York University Press, 2006), 139.

53. Claude Pichois, "Pour une sociologie des faits littéraires : Les cabinets de lecture à Paris durant la première moitié du XIXe siècle," *Annales : économies, sociétés, civilisations* 14, no. 3 (1959): 522, www.persee.fr/doc/ahess_0395-2649_1959_num_14_3_2847: "À mi-chemin entre le théâtre classique (où la « catharsis » effectuait la purgation des passions) et les cliniques psychanalytiques, ils offraient des possibilités de cures peu coûteuses." My translation.

54. Marie Hauge Jensen and "Hannah," *Hvis Nogen Kunne Se Min Ensomhed*, Mikrofonholder, 49:50–51:05, Radio 24syv, 28 December 2017, http://hdl.handle.net/109.3.1/uuid:c61c959c-669c-4084-9398-5ef454567794. See also Marie Hauge Jensen, A *Random Act of Kindness*, www.mariehauge.com/a-random-act-of-kindness.html.

55. Hephzibah Anderson, "Which Books Will Cure Loneliness," *BBC Culture*, 19 February 2015, www.bbc.com/culture/story/20150219-which-books-will-cure-loneliness; see also the "Textual Healing" section of *BBC Culture*, http://www.bbc.com/culture/columns/textual-healing.

56. Katherine Mansfield, *Novels and Novelists* (London: Constable, 1930), 304, cited in Katherine Halsey, "Jane Austen's Global Influence," in *Oxford Research Encyclopedias*, January 2019, https://doi.org/10.1093/acrefore/9780190201098.013.279.

57. Halsey, "Jane Austen's Global Influence."

58. Neil Gaiman, "Neil Gaiman: face the facts, we need fiction," *Guardian*, 24 October 2013, www.theguardian.com/books/2013/oct/24/neil-gaiman-face-facts-need-fiction; see also Nihal Arthanayake, "Headliners: Neil Gaiman," *BBC Radio*

5 *live*, accessed 12 January 2018, www.bbc.co.uk/programmes/p04sxlf7. Martha Nussbaum's ideas about the democratizing power of literature will be picked up in the conclusion.

59. Martha Nussbaum, *Poetic Justice* (Boston: Beacon Press, 1995), 1–2.

Chapter 11

1. Geertz, "Thick Description," 17.
2. Willis, *Reception*, 110.
3. Roland Barthes, "From Work to Text," in *The Rustle of Language*, trans. Richard Howard (1971; repr., Berkeley, CA: University of California Press, 1989), 60, cited in Willis, *Reception*, 168.
4. Sydney Shep, "Books in Global Perspectives," in *The Cambridge Companion to the History of the Book*, ed. Leslie Howsam (Cambridge: Cambridge University Press 2015), 65–67.
5. Shep, "Books in Global Perspectives," 66.
6. Graham Huggan, *The Postcolonial Exotic: Marketing the Margins* (London: Routledge, 2001), 12.
7. Alison Rukavina, "Social Networks: Modelling the Transnational Distribution and Production of Books," in Frost and Rix, *Moveable Type, Mobile Nations*, 73–83.
8. A good anthology of actor-network theory writing by its founding proponents is John Law and John Hassard, eds., *Actor Network Theory and After* (Oxford: Blackwell, 2005). See also John Law, "Actor-Network Theory and Material Semiotics," in *The New Blackwell Companion to Social Theory*, ed. Bryan Turner (Oxford: Blackwell, 2009), 141–158, or Annemarie Mol, "Actor-Network Theory: Sensitive Terms and Enduring Tensions," *Kölner Zeitschrift für Soziologie und Sozialpsychologie* 50 (2010): 253–269. A useful application of network thinking, if not of ANT itself, to narrative forms is found in Patrick Jagoda, *Network Aesthetics* (Chicago: University of Chicago Press, 2016).
9. John Law, *Organizing Modernity* (Oxford: Blackwell, 1994), 101, and Bruno Latour, *Reassembling the Social* (Oxford: Oxford University Press, 2005), 9, both cited in Martin Müller, "Assemblages and Actor-Networks: Rethinking Socio-Material Power, Politics and Space," *Geography Compass* 9, no. 1 (2015): 30. A useful take on the power of the actor network as a heterogeneous event is provided in the example of the Boston Committee of Correspondence's "instigation" of the American War of Independence and the creation of "The United States"; see William Warner, "Transmitting Liberty: The Boston Committee of Correspondence's Revolutionary Experiments in Enlightenment Mediation," in *This Is Enlightenment*, ed. William Warner and Clifford Siskin (Chicago: University of Chicago Press, 2010), 102–119.

10. Bruno Latour, *Pandora's Hope: Essays on the Reality of Science Studies* (Cambridge, MA: Harvard University Press, 1999), 113ff.

11. Pichois, "Pour une sociologie des faits littéraires," 522. "Littérature de consommation, littérature de compensation . . . ils ont été les machines à lire et à rêver des populations urbaines" (my translation).

12. Maudlin and Peel, *Materials of Exchange*, 11.

13. Latour, *Pandora's Hope*, 304.

14. See Michel Callon, "The Sociology of an Actor Network: The Case of the Electric Vehicle," in *Mapping the Dynamics of Science and Technology: Sociology of Science in the Real World*, ed. Michel Callon, John Law, and Arie Rip (Basingstoke, UK: Macmillan, 1986), 19–34.

15. George Eliot, "GE to John Blackwood," in *The George Eliot Letters*, vol. 6, ed. Gordon Haight (New Haven, CT: Yale University Press, 1978), 75, cited in Frost, *Business of the Novel*, 22–25, 23.

16. See "Rival Books and Rival Products," in Frost, *Business of the Novel*, 147–173.

17. Felski, *Uses of Literature*, 14.

18. Stephen Fitz-James, "Spiritualism," *Cornhill Magazine* 7, no. 42 (1863): 706–719, 706. German "Pfennig Magazins" had the same conception of "für Belehrung und Unterhaltung" (for instruction and entertainment).

19. Cited in Robert Colby, "'Rational Amusement': Fiction vs. Useful Knowledge in the Nineteenth Century," in *Victorian Literature and Society*, ed. James Russell Kincaid (Columbus: Ohio State University Press, 1984), 46, 48.

20. Alberto Manguel, *A History of Reading* (London: Harper Collins, 1996), 151.

21. Glenn Ward, *Postmodernism* (Chicago: McGraw-Hill, 2004), 102.

22. Jonathan Culler, *Framing the Sign: Criticism and its Institutions* (Oxford: Basil Blackwell, 1988), ix. See also Erving Goffman, *Frame Analysis: An Essay on the Organization of Experience* (Cambridge, MA: Harvard University Press, 1974).

23. Mieke Bal, "Framing," in *Travelling Concepts in the Humanities: A Rough Guide* (Toronto: University of Toronto Press, 2002), 137.

24. Bal, *Travelling Concepts*, 135. Bal talks of responsibility, noting that some scholars may become subject to what can be perceived as a form of policing and exclusion. Contrary to Kant-inspired aesthetic theory, she states, the framed experience does not require severing the work from interests and politics but is in itself a political framing strategy to produce exclusion.

25. J.C.C. Mays, *Fredson Bowers and the Irish Wolfhound* (Clonmel, Ireland: Coracle, 2002), 47.

26. Harriet Gilbert, Kathy Burke, and Tom Allen, "A Good Read: Kathy Burke and Tom Allen," produced by Beth O'Dea, *BBC Radio 4*, 4 July 2017, https://www.bbc.co.uk/programmes/b08wp59r.

27. Anthony Quinn, "Patrick Hamilton's Hangover Square and a Slide into the Abyss," *Guardian*, 6 August 2016, www.theguardian.com/books/2016/aug/06/patrick-hamilton-hangover-square-world-slide-abyss-rereading.

28. Stefanie Marsh, "Interview—Kathy Burke: 'Life-long Member of the Non-pretty Working Classes,'" *Guardian*, 29 October 2017, www.theguardian.com/culture/2017/oct/29/kathy-burke-interview-lifelong-member-of-the-non-pretty-working-classes.

29. Littau, *Theories of Reading*, 142 ff.

30. As was perfectly put elsewhere, "freedom for the pike is death for the minnows; liberty for the strong, whether their strength is physical or economic, must be restrained. We respect this principle because the other principles, justice or equality, are as basic in men as a desire for liberty." Isaiah Berlin, "Two Concepts of Liberty," The Isaiah Berlin Virtual Library, accessed 12 December 2019, http://berlin.wolf.ox.ac.uk/published_works/tcl/tcl-c.pdf, 13.

31. Alberto Manguel, *A Visit to the Dream Bookseller* (Hamburg: International Antiquarian Book Fair, 1998), 38.

32. Robert Low, *La Pasionaria: The Spanish Firebrand* (London: Hutchinson, 1992). The death toll resulting from Stalin's policies and regime is endlessly under debate, but a reliably informed discussion can be had from Timothy Snyder, *Bloodlands: Europe between Hitler and Stalin* (New York: Basic Books, 2010).

33. Daniel Hack, "The Canon in Front of Them: African American Deployments of 'The Charge of the Light Brigade,'" in *Early African American Print Culture*, ed. Lara Langer Cohen and Jordan Stein (Philadelphia: University of Pennsylvania Press, 2012), 178–191.

34. William Wells Brown, *The Rising Son; Or, the Antecedents and Advancement of the Colored Race* (Boston: A.G. Brown, 1873), 470–471, cited in Eric Gardner, "Early African American Print Culture," in *Oxford Research Encyclopedias*, February 2018, https://doi.org/10.1093/acrefore/9780190201098.013.283.

35. Gardner, "Early African American Print Culture."

36. Hack, "The Canon in Front of Them," 180–181.

37. Hack, "The Canon in Front of Them," 182.

38. The evidence Hack provides is from Gustav d'Alaux, *L'empereur Soulouque et son empire* (Paris: Michel Lévy Frères, 1856), 63–77. See also David Geggus, "Haitian Voodoo in the Eighteenth Century: Language, Culture, Resistance," *Jahrbuch für Geshicte von Staat, Wirtscahft und Gesellscahft Lateinamericas* 28 (1991): 21–51.

39. Henry Turner, "On the Eligibility of Coloured Members to Seats in the Georgia Legislature," in *Respect Black: The Writings and Speeches of Henry McNeal Turner*, ed. Henry Turner and Edwin Redkey (New York: Arno Press, 1971), 28, and W.E.B. Du Bois, *The Souls of Black Folk*, ed. Henry Gates Jr. and Terri Oliver (New York: Norton, 1999), 33, both cited in Hack, "The Canon in Front of Them," 190–191.

40. Campbell, *The Romantic Ethic*.

Chapter 12

1. Price, *How to Do Things with Books*, 260.

2. Mikhail Alexandrovich Bakunin, "Bakounine lettre à Celso Ceretti, Locarno 13–27 mars 1872," in *Oeuvres Complètes. 1–2, Michel Bakounine et l'Italie, 1871–1872. 2e partie, La Première internationale en Italie et le conflit avec Marx : écrits et matériaux* [Complete Works 1–2, Bakunin in Italy 1871–1872. Part 2, The first International in Italy and the conflict with Marx: writings and materials], ed. Arthur Lehning (Paris: Editions Champ Libre, 1974), reproduced in Wikisource, la bibliothèque libre, modified 3 April 2019, 09:39, https://fr.wikisource.org/wiki/Lettre_in%C3%A9dite_de_Bakounine_%C3%A0_Celso_Cerretti.

3. Cited in Toril Moi, *Revolution of the Ordinary: Literary Studies after Wittengstein, Austin and Cavell* (Chicago: University of Chicago Press, 2017), 167.

4. Moi, *Revolution of the Ordinary*, 152, citing Herbert Marcuse, *One-Dimensional Man: Studies in the Ideology of Advanced Industrial Society* [OM] (Boston: Beacon Press, 1964), 178 and 193.

5. Moi, *Revolution of the Ordinary*, 163.

6. Paul De Man, "Time and History in Wordsworth," *Diacritics* 17, no. 4 (1987): 4–17.

7. Moi, *Revolution of the Ordinary*, 5.

8. De Man, "Time and History in Wordsworth," 4.

9. Lionel Robbins, *An Essay on the Nature and Significance of Economic Science* (London: Macmillan, 1935), 16.

10. John Kay, "There Is No Such Thing as the 'Economic Approach,'" *Financial Times*, 14 January 2014, www.ft.com/content/6c1ca066-7c82-11e3-b514-00144feabdc0.

11. Philip Mirowski, *Never Let a Serious Crisis Go to Waste: How Neoliberalism Survived the Financial Meltdown* (London: Verso, 2013), 41–67; Harvey, *A Brief History of Neoliberalism*.

12. Chang, *Economics: The User's Guide*, 15ff.

13. Gary Becker, *The Economic Approach to Human Behaviour* (Chicago: University of Chicago Press, 1976), 8, which was dedicated to Milton Freidman. For the sake of accuracy, it should be noted that the Nobel Prize in economics is not one of the prizes set up by Alfred Nobel but one established independently by economists after a donation by the Swedish central bank in 1968, the full title of which is Sveriges Riksbank Prize in Economic Science in Memory of Alfred Nobel.

14. Gary Becker, *A Treatise on the Family* (Cambridge, MA: Harvard University Press, 1991); see also Gary Becker, "Crime and Punishment: An Economic Approach," *Journal of Political Economy* 76, no. 2 (1968): 169–217.

15. Daniel Hamermesh and Neal Soss, "An Economic Theory of Suicide," *Journal of Political Economy* 82, no. 1 (1974): 85.

16. Roy Baumeister and Kathleen Vohs, "Sexual Economics: Sex as Female Resource for Social Exchange in Heterosexual Interactions," *Personality and Social Psychology Review* 8, no. 4 (2004): 343–344. The Austin Institute of Family and Culture runs a video explaining the drop in marriage rates through a depreciation of the value of sex, in exchange for marriage, caused by the technological shocks such as the pill and now online dating: "The Economics of Sex," Austin Institute, accessed 12 December 2019, video 9:56, www.austin-institute.org/media.

17. Alan Blinder, "The Economics of Brushing Teeth," *Journal of Political Economy* 82, no. 4 (1974): 887.

18. Frow, "Gift and Commodity," 131.

19. Praful Bidwal, "The Great Kidney Bazaar," *TNI* [The Transnational Institute], 4 February 2008, www.tni.org/en/article/the-great-kidney-bazaar. See also Scheper-Huges and Wacquant, *Commodifying Bodies*, 17. For an organ trade organized at state level, which in the US might be conducted through Medicare, see Eilene Zimmerman, "Is it Ever OK to Sell (or Buy) a Kidney?" *Insights*, Stanford Business Graduate School, 13 March 2017, www.gsb.stanford.edu/insights/it-ever-ok-sell-or-buy-kidney; or Rohin Dhar, "The Price of a Human Kidney," *Priceonomics*, 21 May 2013, https://priceonomics.com/post/50996688256/the-price-of-a-human-kidney.

20. Svendsen, *Tillid*, in English as Trust (2018), and presumably capitalizing on the Chinese market as 信任 (2016).

21. Indeed, corporate business has already identified "trust," in a somewhat instrumentalist claim, as the new currency in a tech-driven world: see Philipp Kristian Diekhöner, *The Trust Economy: Building Strong Networks and Realising Exponential Value in the Digital Age* (Singapore: Marshall Cavendish Business, 2017).

22. See Mirowski, *Never Let a Serious Crisis Go to Waste*.

23. Inconsistencies in neoclassical thinking and the false dichotomy between the demands of the market and demands of society were noted way before the crash in the work of Karl Polyani, possibly the grandfather to much of today's criticism of institutionalized neoclassical economic thinking; see Polyani, *The Great Transformation*.

24. Harvey, *Brief History*, 178.

25. David Orrell, *Economyths: Ten Ways Economics Gets It Wrong* (London: Icon, 2010), updated in 2017 as *Economyths: 11 Ways Economics Gets It Wrong*.

26. Steven Keen, *Debunking Economics—Revised and Expanded Edition: The Naked Emperor Dethroned* (London: Zed, 2011). The listing of theoretical flaws is also taken up in Kate Raworth, *Doughnut Economics: Seven Ways to Think Like a 21st Century Economist* (London: Random House Business, 2017).

27. Peter Fleming, *The Death of Homo Economicus* (London: Pluto Press, 2017): a point provided in digest form by professor of economics Mieke Meurs in her TEDxAUBG talk "The End of Homo Economicus," *TEDx Talks*, 10 May 2017, YouTube video, 15:11, www.youtube.com/watch?v=uuSLmaq3eCc.

28. See Thomas Piketty, *Capital in the Twenty-First Century* (Hoboken, NJ: Wiley, 2014); Joseph Stiglitz, *The Price of Inequality* (London: Allen Lane, 2012); Ann Pettifor, *The Production of Money: How to Break the Power of the Bankers* (London: Verso, 2017). A common historical locus for such authors, in addition to Karl Polyani, includes works such as Ernst Freidrich Schumacher, *Small is Beautiful: a Study of Economics as if People Mattered* (London: Blond and Briggs, 1973). To this list of publications might be added organizations such as the Post-Crash Economics Society noted in chapter 2, and the not-for-profit research and campaign organization Positive Money, https://positivemoney.org/.

29. Katrine Marçal, *Who Cooked Adam Smith's Dinner* (London: Portobello, 2015), translated from *Det Enda Könet* (2012) and now translated into at least six languages.

30. Marçal, *Who Cooked Adam Smith's Dinner*, 29–41 and 68–79.

31. Marçal, *Who Cooked Adam Smith's Dinner*, 188.

32. See Daniel Kahneman, *Thinking, Slow and Fast* (London: Penguin, 2012), 306. See also Daniel Kahneman and Amos Tversky, "Prospect Theory: An Analysis of Decision Making Under Risk," *Econometrica* 47, no. 2 (1979): 263–291. The third authority on this development, also a Nobel winner, is Richard Thaler; for an introduction to his work see Richard Thaler, *Misbehaving: The Making of Behavioral Economics* (New York: W.W. Norton, 2015). For a general introduction to the field, see Alain Samson, ed., *The Behavioral Economics Guide 2018* (introduction by Robert Cialdini), *Behavioraleconomics.com*, accessed 12 December 2019, www.behavioraleconomics.com/the-be-guide/, and Alain Samson, "Introduction to Behavioral Economics," *Behavioraleconomics.com*, accessed 12 December 2019, www.behavioraleconomics.com/resources/introduction-behavioral-economics/.

33. For fairness in decision making, see Ernst Fehr and Simon Gächter, "Fairness and Retaliation: The Economics of Reciprocity," *Journal of Economic Perspectives* 14, no. 3 (2000): 159–181.

34. Richard Thaler, "Towards a Positive Theory of Consumer Choice," *Journal of Economic Behavior and Organization* 1, no. 1 (1980): 39.

35. Kahneman, *Thinking*, 271 and 305.

36. Kahneman, *Thinking*, 114.

37. Kahneman, *Thinking*, 368–369—though why the disease should be Asian is not explained, unless "Asian" is supposed to prime the experiment for Anglo-American readers with a disease that is "foreign" and therefore dangerous.

38. David Halpern, *Inside the Nudge Unit* (London: W.H. Allen, 2016).

39. See, for example, Linda Babcock, William J. Congdon, Lawrence F. Katz, and Sendhil Mullainathan. "Notes on Behavioral Economics and Labor Market Policy," *IZA Journal of Labor Policy* 1, no. 2 (2012): 1–14; and William J. Congdon and Sendhil Mullainathan. *Policy and Choice: Public Finance through the Lens of Behavioral Economics* (Washington DC: Brookings Institution Press, 2011).

40. Jon Kvist, "Adfærdsøkonomi og Arbejdsløshedsforsikring: Note til Dagpengekommissionen," Dagpengekommissionen 2015, 1, https://bm.dk/arbejdsomraader/kommissioner-ekspertudvalg/dagpengekommission/afrapportering/; author's translation (Begrænset rationalitet forhindre ledige i altid at vide, hvad de vil . . . Begrænset selvkontrol forhindre ledige i altid at gøre hvad de vil, hvilket giver plads for fx udskydelser af beslutninger og handlinger).

41. Frow, "Gift and Commodity," 138.

42. Evan Brier, "The Literary Marketplace," in *Oxford Research Encyclopedias*, May 2017, https://doi.org/10.1093/acrefore/9780190201098.013.113. The studies Brier refers to are William Charvat, *Literary Publishing in America 1790–1850* (Amherst: University of Massachusetts Press, 1959); James West, *American Authors and the Literary Marketplace Since 1900* (Philadelphia: University of Pennsylvannia Press, 1988); and Lewis Hyde, *The Gift: Creativity and the Artist in the Modern World* (New York: Vintage, 2007).

43. See Brier, "The Literary Marketplace."

44. Jevons, *Theory of Political Economy*, 3rd ed., 3.

45. Jevons, *Theory of Political Economy*, 3rd ed., 38.

46. Jevons, *Theory of Political Economy*, 3rd ed., 32.

47. Karl Marx, *Critique of Political Economy*, Part 1: The Commodity, Marxists.org, accessed 12 December 2019, www.marxists.org/archive/marx/works/1859/critique-pol-economy/ch01.htm#1a (first published 1859).

48. See Mariana Mazzucato, *The Value of Everything: Making and Taking in the Global Economy* (London: Allen Lane, 2018), 6–8.

49. Jevons, *Theory of Political Economy*, 3rd ed., 13–14.

50. Frost, "Economising in Public," 367.

51. Lee Erickson, *The Economy of Literary Form* (Baltimore: Johns Hopkins University Press, 2000), 9–10. Despite differences of opinion, I would here like to acknowledge my indebtedness to Erickson who, many years ago, welded the associations between economics and literature.

52. Erickson, *Economy of Literary Form*, 9.

53. Erickson, *Economy of Literary Form*, 5 and 9n10.

54. Jevons, *Theory of Political Economy*, 3rd ed., 64.

Conclusion

1. Clover and Nealon, "Literary and Economic Value."
2. Love, "Close Reading and Thin Description," 403n3.
3. Becker, *The Economic Approach to Human Behaviour*, 8; see chapter 12.
4. Marçal, *Who Cooked Adam Smith's Dinner?* 54.
5. Alain Badiou and Nicholas Truong, *In Praise of Love*, trans. Peter Bush (London: Serpent's Tail, 2012), 95–104.

6. For self-exploitation and the destruction of the entrepreneur of the self, see Han, Byung-Chul, "Why Revolution Is No Longer Possible," *Open Democracy*, 23 October 2015, www.opendemocracy.net/en/transformation/why-revolution-is-no-longer-possible/.

7. See Graeber, "Consumption." See also chapters 1 and 10 of this study, referencing Askegaard and Heilbrunn.

8. See chapter 1 of this study.

9. Michel Callon, "Actor Network Theory—the Market Test," in Law and Hassard, *Actor Network Theory and After*, 181–195.

Appendix

1. Sir James Lemon, Borough Engineer, responsible for sewer improvements/anti-cholera measures after 1866. Liberal politician and later mayor, 1891 and 1892.

2. Thomas William Shore was an eminent historian and Hartley secretary. Rev. George William Minns was editor of the Hampshire Field Club.

3. William Dale was subsequently secretary of the Hampshire Field Club after Thomas William Shore.

4. The Southampton section of the author's *A General History of Hampshire*, 3 vols. (London: James Virtue, 1861–69), 131–374.

Bibliography

Databases and Websites

African American Periodicals 1825–1995. Archive of Americana Collection, Readex. www.readex.com/content/african-american-periodicals-1825-1995

At the Circulating Library: A Database of Victorian Fiction, 1837–1901. General editor Troy J. Bassett, Purdue University Fort Wayne. www.victorianresearch.org/atcl/index.php

Bloomsbury Project. University College London. www.ucl.ac.uk/bloomsbury-project/

British Book Trade Archives 1830–1939. Bedfordshire University. http://britishbookarchives.beds.ac.uk/

British Book Trade Index. Bodleian Libraries, University of Oxford. http://bbti.bodleian.ox.ac.uk/

The British Newspaper Archive. British Library and Findmypast Newspaper Archive Limited. www.britishnewspaperarchive.co.uk

Cambridge Society for Economic Pluralism. www.cambridgepluralism.org

Conrad First: The Joseph Conrad Periodical Archive. Department of English, Uppsala University. www.conradfirst.net

Digital Reading Network. www.digitalreadingnetwork.com

Europeana. www.europeana.eu/en/collections

Future High Streets Forum. Government of the UK. www.gov.uk/government/groups/future-high-streets-forum

The Internet Library of Early Journals: A Digital Library of 18th and 19th Century Journals. Bodleian Libraries, University of Oxford. www.bodley.ox.ac.uk/ilej/

The Lucile Project. Editor Sidney F. Huttner, University of Iowa. http://sdrc.lib.uiowa.edu/lucile/

Modernist Journals Project. Brown University, University of Tulsa, and National Endowment for the Humanities. www.modjourn.org

Museum of London Collections. www.museumoflondon.org.uk/collections

Postitive Money: Making Money and Banking Work for Society. https://positive money.org/
Post-Crash Economics Society. University of Manchester. www.post-crasheconomics.com
Researching Readers Online. Bournemouth University. www.researchingreadersonline.com
Social and Cultural History: Letters and Diaries Online. Alexander Street, ProQuest. https://alexanderstreet.com/products/social-and-cultural-history-letters-and-diaries-online-package
Sotonopedia. Local Studies Department, Southampton Central Library. http://sotonopedia.wikidot.com/
Southampton Local History and Maritime Digital Archive. Southampton City Council. www.southampton.gov.uk/arts-heritage/southampton-archives/plimsoll.aspx
Transliteracies Project. University of California Santa Barbara. http://transliteracies.english.ucsb.edu/
UK RED (The Reading Experience Database). Open University. www.open.ac.uk/Arts/reading/UK/
A Vision of Britain through Time. GB Historical GIS/University of Portsmouth. www.visionofbritain.org.uk
What Middletown Read. Ball State University. https://lib.bsu.edu/wmr/

Books, Articles, and Other Sources

Adorno, Theodor, and Max Horkheimer. "The Culture Industry: Enlightenment as Mass Deception." In *Dialectic of Enlightenment: Philosophical Fragments*, 120–167. Stanford, CA: Stanford University Press, 1997.
ALCS (Authors' Licensing and Collecting Society). *2018 Authors' Earnings: a Survey of UK Writers*. 2018. https://wp.alcs.co.uk/app/uploads/2018/06/ALCS-Authors-earnings-2018.pdf.
Altick, Richard. *The English Common Reader*. Chicago: University of Chicago Press, 1957.
Anderson, Hephzibah. "Which Books Will Cure Loneliness?" *BBC Culture*, 19 February 2015. www.bbc.com/culture/story/20150219-which-books-will-cure-loneliness.
Anonymous. *My Secret Life*. Amsterdam: Privately printed for subscribers, 1888.
Arendt, Hannah. *The Human Condition: A Study of the Central Dilemmas Facing Modern Man*. Garden City, NY: Doubleday Anchor, 1959.
Armitage, David, and Michael Braddick, eds. *The British Atlantic Worlds, 1500–1800*. Basingstoke, UK: Palgrave Macmillan, 2009.

Arrow, Kenneth. "Is Bounded Rationality Unboundedly Rational? Some Ruminations." In *Models of a Man: Essays in Memory of Herbert A. Simon*, edited by James G. March and Mie Augier, 47–56. Cambridge, MA: MIT Press, 2004.
Arthanayake, Nihal. "Headliners: Neil Gaiman." *BBC Radio 5 live*, accessed 12 January 2018. www.bbc.co.uk/programmes/p04sxlf7.
Askegaard, Søren, and Benoît Heilbrunn, eds. *Canonical Authors in Consumption Theory*. London: Routledge, 2010.
Atkins, Guy. *Come Home at Once: Intriguing Messages from the Golden Age of Postcards*. London: Bantam Press, 2014.
Atkinson, William. "Bound in Blackwood's: The Imperialism of the *Heart of Darkness* in its Immediate Contexts." *Twentieth-Century Literature* 50, no. 4 (2004): 368–393.
Austin Institute for the Study of Family and Culture. "The Economics of Sex." *Austin Institute*, accessed 12 December 2019. Video, 9:56, www.austin-institute.org/media.
Babcock, Linda, William J. Congdon, Lawrence F. Katz, and Sendhil Mullainathan. "Notes on Behavioral Economics and Labor Market Policy." *IZA Journal of Labor Policy* 1, no. 2 (2012): 1–14.
Badiou, Alain, and Nicholas Truong. *In Praise of Love*. Translated by Peter Bush. London: Serpent's Tail, 2012.
Bakunin, Mikhail Alexandrovich. *Oeuvres Complètes. 1–2, Michel Bakounine et l'Italie, 1871–1872. 2e partie, La Première internationale en Italie et le conflit avec Marx : écrits et matériaux* [Complete Works 1–2, Bakunin in Italy 1871–1872. Part 2, The first International in Italy and the conflict with Marx: writings and materials]. Edited by Arthur Lehning. Paris: Editions Champ Libre, 1963.
Bal, Mieke. *Travelling Concepts in the Humanities*. Toronto: University of Toronto Press, 2002.
Balling, Gitte. "What Is a Reading Experience? The Development of a Theoretical and Empirical Understanding." In *Plotting the Reading Experience*, edited by Lynne McKechnie, Kjell Ivar Skjerdingstad, Paulette M. Rothbauer, Knut Oterholm, and Magnus Persson, 37–53. Waterloo, Canada: Wilfrid Laurier University Press, 2016.
Barker, Kate. "Economist Kate Barker on the Free Market." *A History of Ideas*, BBC, 22 July 2015, https://www.bbc.co.uk/sounds/play/b062ktlh.
Barnes, James. *Free Trade in Books: A Study of the London Book Trade since 1800*. Oxford: Clarendon Press, 1964.
Barthes, Roland. "From Work to Text." In *The Rustle of Language*, translated by Richard Howard, 56–64. Berkeley, CA: University of California Press, 1989. First published 1971.
———. *Mythologies*. London: Paladin, 1973.

Bateson, Frederick. *The Cambridge Bibliography of English Literature*, vol. 3, 1800–1900. Cambridge: Cambridge University Press, 1969.

Baumeister, Roy, and Kathleen Vohs. "Sexual Economics: Sex as Female Resource for Social Exchange in Heterosexual Interactions." *Personality and Social Psychology Review* 8, no. 4 (2004): 339–363.

Becker, Gary. "Crime and Punishment: An Economic Approach." *Journal of Political Economy* 76, no. 2 (1968): 169–217.

———. *The Economic Approach to Human Behaviour*. Chicago: University of Chicago Press, 1976.

———. *A Treatise on the Family*. Cambridge, MA: Harvard University Press, 1991.

Berlin, Isaiah. "Two Concepts of Liberty." The Isaiah Berlin Virtual Library. Accessed 12 December 2019. http://berlin.wolf.ox.ac.uk/published_works/tcl/tcl-c.pdf.

Bernstein, Dorthe, and Steen Folke Larsen. *Læsnings Former*. Aalborg: Biblioteksarbejde og Forfatterne, 1993.

Bidwal, Praful. "The Great Kidney Bazaar." *TNI* [The Transnational Institute], 4 February 2008. www.tni.org/en/article/the-great-kidney-bazaar.

Bigg, James. "The Bookselling System: Letter to Lord Campbell respecting the late enquiry into the regulations of the Booksellers' Association . . ." London: J. Bigg and Sons, 1852. Held British Library, shelfmark 11902 bb 50 (5.)

Blanck, Jacob, comp. *Bibliography of American Literature*, vol. 2. New Haven, CT: Yale University Press, 1957.

Blinder, Alan. "The Economics of Brushing Teeth." *The Journal of Political Economy* 82, no. 4 (1974): 887–891.

Bloom, Clive. *Bestsellers: Popular Fiction since 1900*. Basingstoke: Palgrave Macmillan, 2008.

BML (Book Marketing Ltd.). *Reading the Situation: Book Reading, Buying and Borrowing Habits in Britain*. London: BML, 2000.

Boase, George Clement. "Virtue, James Sprent." In *Oxford Dictionary of National Biography*, accessed December 2019. https://doi.org/10.1093/ref:odnb/28332.

Borghi, Maurizio. "Copyright and the Commodification of Authorship in 18th- and 19th-Century Europe." In *Oxford Research Encyclopedias*, March 2018. https://doi.org/10.1093/acrefore/9780190201098.013.268.

Bortolussi, Marisa, and Peter Dixon, eds. *Psychonarratology: Foundations for the Empirical Study of Literary Response*. Cambridge: Cambridge University Press, 2003.

Bourdieu, Pierre. "The Market of Symbolic Goods." In *The Field of Cultural Production*, 112–144. Cambridge: Polity Press, 1993.

Bowen, Zack. *Ulysses as a Comic Novel*. Syracuse, NY: Syracuse University Press, 1989.

Brake, Laurel, and Marysa Demoor, eds. *Dictionary of Nineteenth Century Journalism*. London: Academia Press and British Library, 2009.

Brier, Evan. "The Literary Marketplace." In *Oxford Research Encyclopedias*, May 2017. https://doi.org/10.1093/acrefore/9780190201098.013.113.

Brinkman, J.F.M. "Social Action and Social Crisis in Late Victorian Southampton." *Journal of Southampton Local History Forum* 12 (2007): 40–48.

Brown, William Wells. *The Rising Son; Or, the Antecedents and Advancement of the Colored Race*. Boston: A.G. Brown, 1873.

Cairns, David. *Southampton Working People*. Southampton: Southampton City Museums, 1991.

Callon, Michel. "Actor Network Theory—the Market Test." in *Actor Network Theory and After*, edited by John Law and John Hassard, 181–195. Oxford: Blackwell, 2005.

———. "The Sociology of an Actor Network: The Case of the Electric Vehicle." In *Mapping the Dynamics of Science and Technology: Sociology of Science in the Real World*, edited by Michel Callon, John Law, and Arie Rip, 19–34. Basingstoke, UK: Macmillan, 1986.

Campbell, Colin. *The Romantic Ethic and the Spirit of Modern Consumerism*. Oxford: Basil Blackwell, 1987.

Capes, Bernard. "The Sword of Colonel Lacoste." *Blackwood's Magazine* 165, no. 1000 (1899): 385–401.

Carabine, Kieth, Lindy Stiebel, and Tom Hubbard, eds. *Lives of Victorian Literary Figures, Part VII: Joseph Conrad, Henry Rider Haggard and Rudyard Kipling by their Contemporaries*. Series edited by Ralph Pite. London: Pickering and Chatto, 2009.

Chang, Ha-Joon. "The Economics and Politics of Regulation." In *Globalisation, Economic Development and the Role of the State*, 157–198. London: Zed Books, 2004.

———. *Economics: The User's Guide*. New York: Bloomsbury, 2015.

———. *23 Things They Don't Tell You About Capitalism*. London: Penguin, 2011.

Charvat, William. *Literary Publishing in America 1790–1850*. Amherst: University of Massachusetts Press, 1959.

Chen, Liyan. "The Most Profitable Industries in 2016." *Forbes Magazine*, 21 December 2015. www.forbes.com/sites/liyanchen/2015/12/21/the-most-profitable-industries-in-2016/.

Chubb, Percival. "The Blight of Literary Bookishness." *The English Journal* 3, no. 1 (1914): 15–27.

Clarke, Alison. "Window Shopping at Home: Classifieds, Catalogues and New Consumer Skills." In *Material Cultures: Why Some Things Matter*, edited by Daniel Miller, 73–102. Chicago: University of Chicago Press, 1998.

Clover, Joshua, and Christopher Nealon. "Literary and Economic Value." In *Oxford Research Encyclopedias*, July 2017. https://doi.org/10.1093/acrefore/9780190201098.013.123.

Colby, Robert. "'Rational Amusement': Fiction vs. Useful Knowledge in the Nineteenth Century." In *Victorian Literature and Society*, edited by James Russell Kincaid, 46–73. Columbus: Ohio State University Press, 1984.

Colclough, Stephen. "Distribution." In *The Cambridge History of the Book in Britain*, vol. 6, *1830–1914*, edited by David McKitterick, 238–280. Cambridge: Cambridge University Press, 2009.

———. "'No Such Bookselling Has Ever Before Taken Place': W.H. Smith and Propaganda, 1917–1920." In *Publishing and the First World War*, edited by Mary Hammond and Shafquat Towheed, 28–45. Basingstoke, UK: Palgrave, 2007.

———. "Procuring Books and Consuming Texts: The Reading Experience of a Sheffield Apprentice, 1798." *Book History* 3 (2000): 21–44.

———. "'Purifying the Sources of Amusement and Information'? The Railway Bookstalls of W.H. Smith & Son, 1855–1860." *Publishing History* 56 (2004): 27–51.

———. "'Station to Station': The LNWR and the Emergence of the Railway Bookstall, 1848–1875." In *Printing Places: Locations of Book Production and Distribution Since 1500*, edited by John Hinks and Catherine Armstrong, 169–184. London: British Library and Oak Knoll Press, 2005.

Collins, Wilkie. "The Unknown Public." *Household Words*, 18, 21 August 1858, 217–222. http://www.web40571.clarahost.co.uk/wilkie/etext/TheUnknownPublic.htm.

Congdon, William J., and Sendhil Mullainathan. *Policy and Choice: Public Finance through the Lens of Behavioural Economics*. Washington, DC: Brookings Institution, 2011.

Connolly, James, Patrick Collier, Frank Felsenstein, Kenneth Hall, and Robert Hall, eds. *Print Culture Histories Beyond the Metropolis*. Toronto: University of Toronto Press, 2016.

Conway, Edmund. *50 Economics Ideas You Really Need to Know*. London: Quercus, 2009.

Conrad, Joseph. "Karain: A Memory." *Blackwood's Magazine* 67, no. 985 (1897): 630–656.

———. "The Lagoon." *The Cornhill Magazine* 2 (January 1897): 59–71.

———. "Outpost of Progress." *Cosmopolis* [UK] 7, no. 18 (1897): 609–620, and *Cosmopolis* [UK] 7, no. 19 (1897): 1–15.

Cooper, Victoria, and Dave Russell. "Publishing for Leisure." In *The Cambridge History of the Book in Britain*, vol. 6, *1830–1914*, edited by David McKitterick, 474–499. Cambridge: Cambridge Univerity Press, 2014.

Corp, William W. *Fifty Years: A Brief Account of the Booksellers of Great Britain and Ireland 1895–1945*. Oxford: Basil Blackwell, 1946.

Cox, Gordon. "Henry Daubney Cox and the Bookbinding Business at 5 West Street." *Southampton Local History Forum Journal* 11 (Winter 2003): 19–20.

Crawford, Francis Marion. *Corleone: A Tale of Sicily*. New York: Macmillan, 1897.
———. "Emotional Tension and the Modern Novel." *The Forum* 14 (February 1893), 735–742.
———. "False Taste in Art." *North American Review* 135 (July 1882), 89–98.
———. *Mr. Isaacs*. New York: Macmillan, 1882.
———. *The Novel: What It Is*. New York: Macmillan, 1893.
———. "The Upper Berth," in *Wandering Ghosts* [*Uncanny Tales*, 1895], 195–233. New York: Macmillan, 1911. First published 1895 as *Uncanny Tales*.
———. "What is a Novel?" *The Forum* 14 (January 1893): 591–599.
Csikszentmihalyi, Mihaly, and Eugene Rochberg-Halton. *The Meaning of Things: Domestic Symbols and the Self*. Cambridge: Cambridge University Press, 1981.
Culler, Jonathan D. *Framing the Sign: Criticism and its Institutions*. Oxford: Basil Blackwell, 1988.
———. *The Pursuit of Signs: Semiotics, Literature, Deconstruction*. Ithaca, NY: Cornell University Press, 1981.
Curwen, Henry. *A History of Booksellers: The Old and the New*. London: Chatto and Windus, 1873.
d'Alaux, Gustav. *L'empereur Soulouque et son empire*. Paris: Michel Lévy Frères, 1856.
Darnton, Robert. "'What is the History of Books?' Revisited." *Modern Intellectual History* 4, no. 3 (2007): 495–508.
Davies, J. Silvester. *A History of Southampton*. Exeter: Hampshire Books, 1989. Facsimile of Southampton: H.M. Gilbert, 1883.
Davis, Dorothy. *A History of Shopping*. London: Routledge and Kegan Paul, 2006.
Debord, Guy. *Society of the Spectacle* (1967), trans. Black and Red. Guy Debord Archive, 1977. www.marxists.org/reference/archive/debord/society.htm.
De Brun, Ben. "Where to Do Things with Words: Circulating Books, Decorating Rooms, and Locating Modern Reading." *Orbis Litterarum* 68, no. 6 (2013): 457–472.
De Man, Paul. "Time and History in Wordsworth." *Diacritics* 17, no. 4 (1987): 4–17.
DeMarco, Eileen. *Reading and Writing: Hachette's Railroad Bookstore Network in Nineteenth-Century France*. Bethlehem, PA: Lehigh University Press, 2006.
Derrida, Jacques. "Parergon." In *The Truth of Painting*, translated by Geoff Bennington and Ian McLeod, 15–147. Chicago: University of Chicago Press, 1987.
Dhar, Rohin. "The Price of a Human Kidney." *Priceonomics*, 21 May 2013. https://priceonomics.com/post/50996688256/the-price-of-a-human-kidney.
Dick, Archie. "Censorship and the Reading Practices of Political Prisoners in South Africa, 1960–1990." *Innovation: Journal of Appropriate Librarianship and Information Work in Southern Africa*, no. 35 (December 2007): 24–55.

Diekhöner, Philipp Kristian. *The Trust Economy: Building Strong Networks and Realising Exponential Value in the Digital Age*. Singapore: Marshall Cavendish Business, 2017.

Dittmar, Helga. *The Social Psychology of Material Possessions: To Have Is to Be*. New York: St. Martin's Press, 1992.

Dolfsma, Wilfred, ed. *Consuming Symbolic Goods: Identity and Commitment, Values and Economics*. London: Routledge, 2008.

Du Bois, W.E.B. *The Souls of Black Folk*. Edited by Henry Gates Jr. and Terri Oliver. New York: Norton, 1999.

DuPuis, Melanie. "Civic Markets: Alternative Value Chains Governance as Civic Engagement." *Crop Management* 5, no. 1 (2006): 1–12. https://doi:10.1094/CM-2006-0921-09-RV.

Easely, Alexis. *First-Person Anonymous: Women Writers and Victorian Print Media, 1830–1870*. Aldershot, UK: Ashgate, 2004.

Eco, Umberto. *The Role of the Reader: Explorations in the Semiotics of Texts*. Bloomington: Indiana University Press, 1979.

Edwards, Amalia Blandford. *Barbara's History*. London: Hurst and Blackett, 1864.

Edwards, Brian. *The Modern Airport Terminal*. London: Spon Press, 2005.

Edwards, F.A. *Early Hampshire Printers*. Southampton: Hampshire Independent, 1891. Reprinted extract from *Papers and Proceedings* 2, Hampshire Field Club and Archeological Society, Southampton (1889): 110–134.

Ekström, Karin, and Helene Brembeck, eds. "Elusive Consumption in Retrospect: Report from the Conference." Göteborg: Centre for Consumer Science, Göteborg University, 2005. https://gupea.ub.gu.se/bitstream/2077/23184/1/gupea_2077_23184_1.pdf.

Eliot, George. *The George Eliot Letters*. Edited by Gordon Haight. New Haven, CT: Yale University Press, 1978.

Eliot, Simon. "From Few and Expensive to Many and Cheap: The British Book Market 1800–1890." In *A Companion to the History of the Book*, edited by Simon Eliot and Jonathan Rose, 291–302. Oxford: Blackwell, 2007.

———. "The Three-Decker Novel and its First Cheap Reprint, 1862–94." *Library* 7 (1985): 38–53.

Emmerson, Charles. *1913: The World Before the Great War*. London: The Bodley Head, 2013.

Englefield, Henry C. *A Walk Through Southampton*. 2nd ed. Southampton: Baker and Fletcher, 1805.

English, James F. *The Economy of Prestige: Prizes, Awards, and the Circulation of Cultural Value*. Cambridge, MA: Harvard University Press, 2005.

Erickson, Lee. *The Economy of Literary Form*. Baltimore: Johns Hopkins University Press, 2000.

Feather, John. *A History of British Publishing*. London: Routledge, 1988.

Fehr, Ernst and Simon Gächter. "Fairness and Retaliation: The Economics of Reciprocity." *Journal of Economic Perspectives* 14, no. 3 (2000): 159–181.

Felsenstein, Frank, and James Connolly. *What Middletown Read: Print Culture in an American Small City.* Amherst: University of Massachusetts Press, 2015.
Felski, Rita. *Uses of Literature.* Hoboken, NJ: John Wiley and Sons, 2009.
Fetterley, Judith. *The Resisting Reader: A Feminist Approach to American Fiction.* Bloomington: Indiana University Press, 1978.
Finkelstein, David. *An Index to Blackwood's Magazine 1901–1980.* Aldershot, UK: Scholar Press, 1995.
———. "The Scottish Printing Diaspora, 1840–1914." In *Oxford Research Encyclopedias*, July 2018. https://doi.org/10.1093/acrefore/9780190201098.013.264.
Finkelstein, David, and Alister McCleery. *Introduction to Book History.* London: Routledge, 2012.
Fisher, Walter R. "Homo Narrans, The Narrative Paradigm: In the Beginning." *Journal of Communication* 35, no. 4 (1985): 74–89.
———. "Narration as a Human Communication Paradigm: The Case of Public Moral Argument." *Communication Monographs* 51, no. 1 (1984): 1–22.
Fiske, John. *Reading the Popular.* Boston: Unwin Hyman, 1989.
Flanders, Judith. *Consuming Passions.* Hammersmith, UK: Harper Press, 2006.
Flavin, Michael. *Gambling in the Nineteenth-Century Novel: 'A Leprosy Is o'er the Land.'* Brighton: Sussex Academic Press, 2003.
Fleming, Peter. *The Death of Homo Economicus.* London: Pluto Press, 2017.
Flynt, Josiah. *Tramping with Tramps: Studies and Sketches.* New York: Century, 1899.
———. *The World of Graft.* London: McClure, Phillips and Co., 1901.
Foucault, Michel. "Maurice Blanchot: The Thought from Outside." In Michel Foucault and Maurice Blanchot, *Foucault: Blanchot*, 7–58. New York: Zone, 1997.
Fraser, W. Hamish. *The Coming of the Mass Market.* London: Macmillan, 1981.
Frost, Simon. *The Business of the Novel: Economics, Aesthetics and the Case of Middlemarch.* London: Pickering and Chatto, 2012.
———. "Economising in Public: Publishing History as a Challenge to Scientific Method." *Book History* 17 (2014): 365–379.
———. "The Good in a Little Fiction—Conrad, Consumer Readers and Commodity Culture." *English in Africa* 35, no. 1 (2008): 45–66. Reproduced at Conrad First, www.conradfirst.net/conrad/scholarship/authors/frost.html.
———. "Othering Ourselves: Re-reading Rudyard Kipling and 'The Strange Ride of Morrowbie Jukes' (1885)." *Nordic Journal of English Studies* 16, no. 2 (2017): 12–32. http://ojs.ub.gu.se/ojs/index.php/njes/article/view/4111.
———. "Public Gains and Literary Goods: A Coeval Tale of Conrad, Kipling and Francis Marion Crawford." In *Transitions in Middlebrow Writing, 1880–1930*, edited by Kate MacDonald and Christoph Singer, 37–56. Basingstoke, UK: Palgrave Macmillan, 2015.
———. "Readers and Retailed Literature: Findings from a UK Public High Street Survey into Purchasers' Expectations from Books." *LOGOS* 28, no. 2 (2017): 27–43.

———. "Reconsidering the Unknown Public: A Puzzle of Literary Gains." In *Studies in Victorian and Modern Literature: A Tribute to John Sutherland*, ed. William Baker, 3–15. Lanham, MD: Fairleigh Dickinson University Press, Rowman and Littlefield Publishing Group, 2015. Pre-print open-access ed. at Bournemouth University Repository, http://eprints.bournemouth.ac.uk/28361/.

———. "A Trade in Desires: Emigration, A.C. Gunter and the Home Publishing Company." In *The Book World: Selling and Distributing British Literature, 1900–1940*, edited by Nicola Wilson, 31–51. Library of the Written Word: The Industrial World 49. Leiden: BRILL, 2016.

Frost, Simon, and Robert Rix, eds. *Moveable Type, Mobile Nations*. Angles on the English Speaking World 10. Copenhagen: Museum Tusculanum Press, 2010.

Frost, Simon, and Stephen Hall. "John Smith's: Historical Perspectives and Historical Precedence." *Book 2.0* 5, no. 1–2 (2015): 27–37. Pre-print open access ed. at Bournemouth University Repository, http://eprints.bournemouth.ac.uk/28360/.

Frow, John. "Gift and Commodity." In *Time and Commodity Culture: Essays in Cultural Theory and Postmodernity*, 102–217. Oxford: Clarendon Press, 1997.

———. *The Practice of Value: Essays on Literature in Cultural Studies*. Crawley, Australia: University of Western Australia Publishing, 2013.

———. *Time and Commodity Culture: Essays in Cultural Theory and Postmodernity*. Oxford: Clarendon Press, 1997.

Frye, Northrop. *Interviews with Northrop Frye*. Edited by Jean O'Grady. Toronto: University of Toronto Press, 2008.

Fuller, Danielle, and DeNel Sedo. "Fun . . . and Other Reasons for Sharing Reading with Strangers: Mass Reading Events and the Possibilities of Pleasure." In *Plotting the Reading Experience: Theory/Practice/Politics*, edited by Lynne McKechnie, Kjell Ivar Skjerdingstad, Paulette M. Rothbauer, Knut Oterholm, and Magnus Persson, 133–148. Waterloo, Canada: Wilfrid Laurier University Press, 2016.

Gaiman, Neil. "Neil Gaiman: Face the Facts, We Need Fiction." *Guardian*, 24 October 2013. www.theguardian.com/books/2013/oct/24/neil-gaiman-face-facts-need-fiction.

Gannaway, Norman. *Association Football in Hampshire until 1914*. Hampshire Papers 9. Winchester: Hampshire County Council, 1996.

Gardner, Eric. "Early African American Print Culture." In *Oxford Research Encyclopedias*, February 2018. https://doi.org/10.1093/acrefore/9780190201098.013.283.

Geertz, Clifford. *The Interpretation of Cultures: Selected Essays*. New York: Basic Books, 1973.

———. "Thick Description: Towards an Interpretive Theory of Culture." In *The Interpretation of Cultures*, 3–32. New York: Basic Books, 2000.

Geggus, David. "Haitian Voodoo in the Eighteenth Century: Language, Culture, Resistance." *Jahrbuch für Geschichte von Staat, Wirtschaft und Gesellschaft Lateinamerikas* 28 (1991): 21–51.

Giddens, Anthony. *Modernity and Self-Identity*. Cambridge: Polity Press 1991.

Gilbert, Harriet, Kathy Burke, and Tom Allen. "A Good Read: Kathy Burke and Tom Allen." Produced by Beth O'Dea. *BBC Radio 4*, 4 July 2017. www.bbc.co.uk/programmes/b08wp59r.

Gilbert, Henry March. *Bibliotheca Hantoniensis*. Southampton: H.M. Gilbert, 1872. https://archive.org/details/bibliothecahanto00gilbrich.

Gilroy, Paul. *The Black Atlantic: Modernity and Double Consciousness*. London: Verso, 1993.

Glazzard, Andrew. *Conrad's Popular Fictions: Secret Histories and Sensational Novels*. Basingstoke, UK: Palgrave Macmillan, 2016.

Glinoer, Anthony, ed. *The Literary and the Social*. Living Books About History, 2019. https://doi.org/10.13098/infoclio.ch-lb-0008.

Godwin, George Nelson. *Mate's Illustrated Handbook to Southampton*. Bournemouth: Mate and Sons, 1900.

Goffman, Erving. *Frame Analysis: An Essay on the Organization of Experience*. Cambridge, MA: Harvard University Press, 1974.

Goodwin, Neva, and Jonathan Harris. *Principles of Economics in Context*. New York: Routledge, 2015.

Graeber, David. "Consumption." *Current Anthropology* 52, no. 4 (2011): 489–511.

Grant, Tony. "Netley Abbey and the Gothic Revival." *Jane Austen's World*, 5 January 2018. https://janeaustensworld.wordpress.com/2018/01/05/netley-abbey-and-the-gothic-by-tony-grant.

Green, Melanie, Timothy Brock, and Geoff Kaufman. "Understanding Media Enjoyment: The Role of Transportation into Narrative Worlds." *Communication Theory* 14, no. 3 (2004): 311–327.

Grossman, David, host. "Making Money." *The New Age of Capitalism*. BBC Radio 4, 14 September 2018, www.bbc.co.uk/programmes/b0bjppmr.

Guide to Southampton. Southampton: Gutch and Co., 1869.

Guillory, John. "The Ethical Practice of Modernity: the Example of Reading." In *The Turn to Ethics*, edited by Marjorie Garber, Beatrice Hanssen, and Rebecca Walkowitz, 29–46. London: Routledge, 2013.

Gutch's Pictorial Almanac. Southampton: Gutch and Cox, 1875.

Hack, Daniel. "The Canon in Front of Them: African American Deployments of 'The Charge of the Light Brigade.'" In *Early African American Print Culture*, edited by Lara Langer Cohen and Jordan Stein, 178–191. Philadelphia: University of Pennsylvania Press, 2012.

Haight, Gordon, ed. *The George Eliot Letters*. 9 vols. New Haven, CT: Yale University Press, 1978.

Haldane, Andrew. "Introduction: The Revolution in Economics." In *Economics, Education and Unlearning*, Post-Crash Economics Society, Manchester University, April 2014, http://www.post-crasheconomics.com/economics-education-and-unlearning/.
Hall, Peter A., and David Soskice, eds. *Varieties of Capitalism: the Institutional Foundations of Comparative Advantage*. Oxford: Oxford University Press, 2001.
Halpern, David. *Inside the Nudge Unit*. London: W.H. Allen, 2016.
Halsey, Katherine. "Jane Austen's Global Influence." In *Oxford Research Encyclopedias*, January 2019. https://doi.org/10.1093/acrefore/9780190201098.013.279.
Hamermesh, Daniel, and Neal Soss. "An Economic Theory of Suicide." *Journal of Political Economy* 82, no. 1 (1974): 83–98.
Hamilton, Keith. "Battles of Cobden Bridge." *Southern Evening Echo*, 29 December 2006. www.dailyecho.co.uk/heritage/1095584.battles-of-cobden-bridge/.
Hammond, Brean. "Guard the Sure Barrier." In *Pope: New Contexts*, edited by David Fairer, 225–240. Exeter, UK: Harvester Wheatsheaf, 1990.
Hammond, Mary. *Reading, Publishing and the Formation of Literary Taste in England 1880–1914*. Aldershot, UK: Ashgate, 2006.
Hammond, Mary, and Jonathan Rose, eds. *Edinburgh History of Reading*. 4 vols. Edinburgh: Edinburgh University Press, 2020.
Han, Byung-Chul. "Why Revolution Is No Longer Possible." *Open Democracy*, 23 October 2015. www.opendemocracy.net/en/transformation/why-revolution-is-no-longer-possible/.
Hancké, Bob, ed. *Debating Varieties of Capitalism: A Reader*. Oxford: Oxford University Press, 2009.
Hartland, Zoe. "How Has Life Expectancy Changed over Time?" Office for National Statistics, 9 September 2015. https://visual.ons.gov.uk/how-has-life-expectancy-changed-over-time/.
Harvey, David. *A Brief History of Neoliberalism*. Oxford: Oxford University Press, 2007.
Held, Virginia. "Mothering Versus Contract." In *Beyond Self-Interest*, ed. Jane Mansbridge, 287–304. Chicago: University of Chicago Press, 1990.
Herbert, Ian. "Revealed: Why Brocklehurst's Inspiration Threatened to Sue Brontë." *Independent*, 25 May 2006. http://www.independent.co.uk/news/uk/this-britain/revealed-why-brocklehursts-inspiration-threatened-to-sue-bronteuml-479611.html.
Higginbotham, Peter. *The Workhouse Encyclopedia*. Stroud, UK: History Press, 2014.
Hilliard, Christopher. "The Literary Underground of 1920s London," *Social History* 33, no. 2 (2008): 164–182.
———. "The Twopenny Library: The Booktrade, Working-Class Readers, and 'Middlebrow' Novels in Britain 1930–42." *Twentieth Century British History* 25, no. 2 (2014): 199–220.

Hochschild, Adam. *King Leopold's Ghost*. London: PAN, 2011.
Hodges, Gabrielle Cliff. "Reimagining Reading." In *Plotting the Reading Experience*, edited by Lynne McKechnie, Kjell Ivar Skjerdingstad, Paulette M. Rothbauer, Knut Oterholm, and Magnus Persson, 55–72. Waterloo, Canada: Wilfrid Laurier University Press, 2016.
Howsam, Leslie. *Kegan Paul, a Victorian Imprint: Publishers, Books and Cultural History*. New York: Routledge, 1998.
Hoyles, Asher, and Martin Hoyles. *Caribbean Publishing in Britain*. London: Hansib, 2011.
Huggan, Graham. *The Postcolonial Exotic: Marketing the Margins*. London: Routledge, 2001.
Hughes, Michael. *Stand-off in the Solent: The American Civil War Comes to Hampshire*. Hampshire Papers 23. Winchester: Hampshire County Council, 2002.
Humphrey, John, and Hubert Schmitz. *Governance and Global Value Chains*. Brighton: Institute of Development Studies, University of Sussex, 2006.
Humphreys, Anne, and Louis James, eds. *G.W.M. Reynolds*. Aldershot, UK: Ashgate, 2008.
Huyssen, Andreas. "Mass Culture as Woman: Modernism's Other." In *Studies in Entertainment: Critical Approaches to Mass Culture*, edited by Tania Modleski, 188–207. Bloomington: Indiana University Press, 1986.
Hyde, Lewis. *The Gift: Creativity and the Artist in the Modern World*. New York: Vintage, 2007.
Iser, Wolfgang. "The Reading Process: A Phenomenological Approach." In *Reader-Response Criticism: From Formalism to Post-Structuralism*, edited by Jane P. Tompkins, 50–70. Baltimore: Johns Hopkins University Press, 1980.
Jackson, Tim. "Live Better by Consuming Less?: Is There a 'Double Dividend' in Sustainable Consumption?" *Journal of Industrial Ecology* 9, no. 1–2 (2005): 19–36.
———. *Motivating Sustainable Consumption: A Review of Evidence on Consumer Behaviour and Behavioural Change*. Guildford: Centre for Environmental Strategy, University of Surrey, 2005.
Jagoda, Patrick. *Network Aesthetics*. Chicago: University of Chicago Press, 2016.
Jaillant, Lise. *Modernism, Middlebrow and the Literary Canon*. London: Pickering and Chatto, 2014.
———, ed. *Publishing Modernist Fiction and Poetry*. Edinburgh: Edinburgh University Press, 2019.
James, William. *The Principles of Psychology*. New York: Henry Holt, 1890.
Jenkins, Henry. *Fans, Bloggers, and Gamers*. New York: NYU Press, 2006.
Jenkins, Jennifer. *Provincial Modernity: Local Culture and Liberal Politics in Fin-de-Siècle Hamburg*. Ithaca, NY: Cornell University Press, 2003.
Jensen, Marie Hauge. *A Random Act of Kindness*. 2015. https://www.mariehauge.com/a-random-act-of-kindness.html.

Jensen, Marie Hauge, and "Hannah." *Hvis Nogen Kunne Se Min Ensomhed*, Mikrofonholder, 49:50–51:05. Radio 24syv, 28 December 2017. http://hdl.handle.net/109.3.1/uuid:c61c959c-669c-4084-9398-5ef454567794.

Jevons, William Stanley. *The Theory of Political Economy*, 3rd ed. London: Macmillan, 1888.

John, Peter, ed. *British Agriculture 1875–1914*. London: Methuen, 1973.

Jones, Jonathan. "Get Real: Terry Pratchett Is Not a Literary Genius." *Guardian*, 31 August 2015. https://www.theguardian.com/artanddesign/jonathanjonesblog/2015/aug/31/terry-pratchett-is-not-a-literary-genius.

Jordan, Jane, and Andrew King, eds. *Ouida and Victorian Popular Culture*. Aldershot, UK: Ashgate, 2013.

Jordison, Sam. "Terry Pratchett's Books Are the Opposite of 'Ordinary Potboilers.'" *Guardian*, 31 August 2015. https://www.theguardian.com/books/booksblog/2015/aug/31/terry-pratchett-opposite-of-ordinary-potboiler-jonathan-jones.

Kahneman, Daniel. *Thinking, Slow and Fast*. London: Penguin Books, 2012.

Kahneman, Daniel, and Amos Tversky. "Prospect Theory: An Analysis of Decision Under Risk." *Econometrica* 47, no. 2 (March 1979): 263–292.

Katz, Elihu, Jay Blumler, and Michael Gurevitch. "Utilization of Mass Communication by the Individual." In *The Uses of Mass Communications: Current Perspectives on Gratifications Research*, edited by Jay Blumler and Elihu Katz, 19–32. Beverly Hills, CA: Sage, 1974.

Kay, John. "There Is No Such Thing as the 'Economic Approach.'" *Financial Times*, 14 January 2014. www.ft.com/content/6c1ca066-7c82-11e3-b514-00144feabdc0.

Keen, Steven. *Debunking Economics—Revised and Expanded Edition: The Naked Emperor Dethroned*. London: Zed, 2011.

Kelly, Wyn. "'Tender Kinswoman': Gail Hamilton and Gendered Justice." In *Melville and Women*, edited by Elizabeth Schultz and Haskell Springer, 98–120. Kent, OH: Kent State University Press, 2006.

Kemp, Sandra, Charlotte Mitchell, and David Trotter, eds. *The Oxford Companion to Edwardian Fiction*. Oxford: Oxford University Press, 2002.

Keynes, John Maynard. "The End of Laissez-Faire." In *Essays in Persuasion*, 312–322. London: Macmillan, 1933.

Khair, Tabish. *The Gothic, Postcolonialism and Otherness: Ghosts from Everywhere*. Basingstoke, UK: Palgrave Macmillan, 2009.

Kipling, Rudyard. "The Mark of the Beast." In *Life's Handicap: Being Stories of Mine Own People*, 208–224. London: Macmillan, 1891.

———. "The Strange Ride of Morrowbie Jukes." In *The Man Who Would Be King: And Other Stories*, 21–40. New York: Dover, 1994. First published 1885.

Knight, Lynn. *The Button Box: Lifting the Lid on Women's Lives*. London: Chatto and Windus, 2016.

Koestler, Arthur. *Dialogue with Death*. Translated by Trevor Blewitt and Phyllis Blewitt. Chicago: University of Chicago Press, 2011.

Koritz, Amy, and Douglas Koritz. "Checkmating the Consumer: Passive Consumption and the Economic Devaluation of Culture." *Feminist Economics* 17, no. 1 (2001): 45–62.
Korte, Barbara. "The Promotion of the Heroic Woman in Victorian and Edwardian Gift Books." In *Reading Books and Prints as Cultural Objects*, edited by Evanghelia Stead, 159–178. Basingstoke, UK: Palgrave Macmillan, 2018.
Kvist, Jon. "Adfærdsøkonomi og Arbejdsløshedsforsikring: Note til Dagpengekommissionen," Dagpengekommissionen, 2015. https://bm.dk/arbejdsomraader/kommissioner-ekspertudvalg/dagpengekommission/afrapportering/.
Lakoff, George, and Mark Johnson. *Metaphors We Live By*. Chicago: University of Chicago Press, 1980.
Laing, Audrey, and Jo Royle. "Examining Chain Bookshops in the Context of 'Third Place.'" *International Journal of Retail & Distribution Management* 41, no. 1 (2013): 27–44.
Lanchester, John. *How to Speak Money*. London: Faber and Faber, 2016.
Lang, Cecil, and Edgar Shannon, eds. *The Letters of Alfred Lord Tennyson*, vol. 2, *1851–1870*. Cambridge, MA: Harvard University Press, 1987.
Langdon-Davies, Bernard. *The Practice of Bookselling*. London: Phoenix House, 1951.
Latour, Bruno. *Pandora's Hope: Essays on the Reality of Science Studies*. Cambridge, MA: Harvard University Press, 1999.
———. *Reassembling the Social*. Oxford: Oxford University Press, 2005.
Law, Graham. "The Serial Revolution at the Periphery." In *Moveable Type, Mobile Nations*, edited by Simon Frost and Robert Rix, 85–98. Angles on the English Speaking World 10. Copenhagen: Museum Tusculanum Press, 2010.
Law, John. "Actor-Network Theory and Material Semiotics." In *The New Blackwell Companion to Social Theory*, edited by Bryan Turner, 141–518. Oxford: Blackwell, 2009.
———. *Organizing Modernity*. Oxford: Blackwell, 1994.
Law, John, and John Hassard, eds. *Actor Network Theory and After*. Oxford: Blackwell, 2005.
Leavis, Q.D. [Queenie]. *Fiction and the Reading Public*. London: Chatto and Windus, 1939.
Ledbetter, Kathryn. *Tennyson and Victorian Periodicals: Commodities in Context*. Aldershot, UK: Ashgate, 2007.
Le Guin, Ursula K. "Where do You Get Your Ideas From?" In *Dancing at the Edge of the World: Thoughts on Words, Women, Places*, 192–200. London: Paladin, 1992.
Leichter, David. "Collective Identity and Collective Memory in the Philosophy of Paul Ricoeur." *Paul Ricoeur Studies* 3, no. 1 (2012): 114–131.
Leighton, Marie Connor. *The Harvest of Sin*. London: James Bowden, 1896.
———. *Sweet Magdalen: Only a Love Story*. London: F.V. White, 1887.

Leonard, A.G.L. [Alan]. "Gilbert's: Booksellers through Five Generations." *Journal of the Southampton Local History Forum* 11 (2003): 13–15.

———. *More Stories of Southampton Streets*. Southampton: Paul Cave, 1989.

———. *Southampton Memorials of Care for Man and Beast*. Southampton: Bitterne Local History Society, 2005.

———. *Southampton: The Archive Photographs Series*. Stroud, UK: Chalford, 1997.

———. *Southampton: The Third Collection—Images of England*. Stroud, UK: Tempus Publishing, 2006.

———. *Stories of Southampton Streets*. Southampton: Paul Cave, 1984.

Leonard, Garry. *Advertising and Commodity Culture in Joyce*. Gainesville: University Press of Florida, 1998.

Levitt, Steven, and Stephen Dubner. *Freakonomics: A Rogue Economist Explores the Hidden Side of Everything*. London: Allen Lane, 2005.

Lindner, Christopher. *Fictions of Commodity Culture: From the Victorian to the Post-Modern*. Aldershot, UK: Ashgate, 2003.

Littau, Karin. *Theories of Reading: Books, Bodies and Bibliomania*. Cambridge: Polity Press, 2006.

Lodge, David. *The Art of Fiction: Illustrated from Classic and Modern Texts*. Harmondsworth, UK: Penguin, 1992.

London, Jack. *The People of the Abyss*. London: Macmillan, 1903.

Long, Elizabeth. *Book Clubs: Women and the Uses of Reading in Everyday Life*. Chicago: University of Chicago Press, 2003.

———. "Textual Interpretation as Collective Action." In *The Ethnography of Reading*, edited by Jonathan Boyarin, 180–212. Berkeley: University of California Press, 1992.

Love, Heather. "Close Reading and Thin Description." *Publishing Cultures* 25, no. 3 (2013): 401–434.

Low, Robert. *La Pasionaria: The Spanish Firebrand*. London: Hutchinson, 1992.

Lynch, John. *Argentine Dictator: Juan Manuel de Rosas*. Oxford: Clarendon Press, 1981.

Lyons, Martin. *A History of Reading and Writing in the Western World*. Basingstoke, UK: Palgrave Macmillan, 2010.

MacLane, Mary. *The Story of Mary Maclane* [sic], *by Herself*. London: Grant Richards, 1902.

Mandelbrote, Giles, ed. *Out of Print and Into Profit: A History of the Rare and Secondhand Book Trade in Britain in the 20th Century*. London: British Library, 2006.

Manguel, Alberto. *A History of Reading*. London: Harper Collins, 1996.

———. *A Visit to the Dream Bookseller*. Quod Libet 5. Hamburg: International Antiquarian Book Fair, 1998.

Mansbridge, Jane, ed. *Beyond Self-Interest*. Chicago: University of Chicago Press, 1990.

Mansfield, Katherine. *Novels and Novelists*. London: Constable, 1930.
Marçal, Katrine. *Who Cooked Adam Smith's Dinner?* London: Portobello, 2017.
Marcus, Steven. *The Other Victorians: A Study of Sexuality and Pornography in Mid-Nineteenth-Century England*. New York: Meridian, 1977.
Marcuse, Herbert. *One-Dimensional Man: Studies in the Ideology of Advanced Industrial Society*. Boston: Beacon Press, 1964.
Marsh, Stefanie. "Interview—Kathy Burke: 'Life-long Member of the Non-pretty Working Classes.'" *Guardian*, 29 October 2017. www.theguardian.com/culture/2017/oct/29/kathy-burke-interview-lifelong-member-of-the-non-pretty-working-classes.
Marx, Karl. *Critique of Political Economy, Part 1: The Commodity*. Marxists.org, accessed 12 December 2019. www.marxists.org/archive/marx/works/1859/critique-pol-economy/ch01.htm. First published 1859.
Maude, Aylmer. *Tolstoy and His Problems: Essays by Aylmer Maude*, 128–148. London: Grant Richards, 1901.
Maudlin, Daniel, and Robin Peel, eds. *The Materials of Exchange between Britain and North East America, 1750–1900*. Farnham, UK: Ashgate, 2013.
Mayhew, Henry, et al. *The London Underworld in the Victorian Period: Authentic First-Person Accounts by Beggars, Thieves and Prostitutes*. Mineola, NY: Dover Publications, 2005. Reprint of *London Labour and the London Poor: A Cyclopaedia of the Condition and Earnings of Those that Will Work, Those that Cannot Work and Those that Will Not Work*, vol. 4, *Those that Will Not Work: Comprising Prostitutes, Thieves, Swindlers, Beggars* (s.l.: Woodfall, 1862).
Mays, J.C.C. *Fredson Bowers and the Irish Wolfhound*. Clonmel, Ireland: Coracle, 2002.
Mazzucato, Mariana. *The Value of Everything: Making and Taking in the Global Economy*. London: Allen Lane, 2018.
McCloskey, Deirdre. "Did Victorian Britain Fail?" *Economic History Review*, new series 23, no. 3 (1970): 446–459.
———. "Metaphors Economists Live By." *Social Research* 62, no. 2 (1995): 215–237.
McCracken, Grant. *Culture and Consumption: A Theoretical Account of the Structure and Movement of the Cultural Meaning of Consumer Goods*. Bloomington: Indiana University Press, 1990.
McDonald, Peter. *British Literary Culture and Publishing Practice 1880–1914*. Cambridge: Cambridge University Press, 1997.
McGann, Jerome. *Black Riders: The Visible Language of Modernism*. Princeton, NJ: Princeton University Press, 1993.
McKechnie, Lynne, Kjell Ivar Skjerdingstad, Paulette M. Rothbauer, Knut Oterholm, and Magnus Persson, eds. *Plotting the Reading Experience: Theory/Practice/Politics*. Waterloo, Canada: Wilfrid Laurier University Press, 2016.

Mearns, Andrew. *Bitter Outcry of Outcast London*. London: James Clarke, 1883. https://archive.org/details/bittercryofoutca00pres.
Meurs, Mieke. "The End of Homo Economicus | Mieke Meurs | TEDxAUBG." *TEDx Talks*, 10 May 2017. YouTube video, 15:11. www.youtube.com/watch?v=uuSLmaq3eCc.
Miller, Andrew. *Novels Behind Glass: Commodity Culture in Victorian Narrative*. Cambridge: Cambridge University Press, 2008.
Miller, Henry. *Black Spring*. New York: Grove, 1963.
Miller, Laura. *Reluctant Capitalists: Bookselling and the Culture of Capitalism*. Chicago: University of Chicago Press, 2007.
Mirowski, Philip. *Never Let a Serious Crisis Go to Waste: How Neoliberalism Survived the Financial Meltdown*. London: Verso, 2013.
Mitchell, Ian. "'Old Books—New Bound'? Selling Second Hand Books in England, c. 1680–1850." In *Modernity and the Second-Hand Trade: European Consumption Cultures and Practices 1700–1900*, edited by Jon Stobart and Ilja Van Damme, 139–157. Basingstoke, UK: Palgrave Macmillan, 2010.
Moi, Toril. *Revolution of the Ordinary: Literary Studies after Wittengstein, Austin and Cavell*. Chicago: University of Chicago Press, 2017.
Mol, Annemarie. "Actor-Network Theory: Sensitive Terms and Enduring Tensions." *Kölner Zeitschrift für Soziologie und Sozialpsychologie* 50 (2010): 253–269.
Monbiot, George. *How Did We Get Into This Mess?* London: Verso, 2016.
Morel, Nathalie, Bruno Palier, and Joakim Palme, eds. *Towards a Social Investment Welfare State?* Bristol, UK: Policy Press, 2012.
Morgan, Charles. *The House of Macmillan*. London: Macmillan, 1943.
Müller, Martin. "Assemblages and Actor-Networks: Rethinking Socio-Material Power, Politics and Space." *Geography Compass* 9, no. 1 (2015): 27–41.
Mumby, Frank Arthur. *Publishing and Bookselling: A History from the Earliest Times to the Present Day*. London: Jonathan Cape, 1930.
Mumby, Frank Arthur, and Ian Norrie. *Publishing and Bookselling. Part One: From the Earliest Times to 1870; Part Two: 1870–1970*. London: Jonathan Cape, 1974.
Naper, Cecilie. "Experiencing the Social Melodrama in the Twenty-First Century." In *Plotting the Reading Experience*, edited by Lynne McKechnie, Kjell Ivar Skjerdingstad, Paulette M. Rothbauer, Knut Oterholm, and Magnus Persson, 317–330. Waterloo, Canada: Wilfrid Laurier University Press, 2016.
Nell, Victor. *Lost in a Book*. New Haven, CT: Yale University Press, 1988.
Nussbaum, Martha. *Poetic Justice*. Boston: Beacon Press, 1995.
Oldfield, John. *Printers, Booksellers and Libraries in Hampshire, 1750–1800*. Hampshire Papers 3. Portsmouth: Hampshire County Council, 1993.
Oliver, Mary Beth, and Anne Bartsch. "Appreciation as Audience Response: Exploring Entertainment Gratifications Beyond Hedonism." *Human Communication Research* 36, no. 1 (2010): 53–81.

Orrell, David. *Economyths: Ten Ways Economics Gets It Wrong.* London: Icon, 2010.
Osteen, Mark, ed. *The Question of the Gift: Essays Across Disciplines.* Abingdon, UK: Routledge, 2002.
Otnes, Cele. "Mind, Self and Consumption: George Herbert Mead." In *Canonical Authors in Consumption Theory*, edited by Søren Askegaard and Benoît Heilbrunn. London: Routledge, 2010.
Ottewill, Roger. "Henry March Gilbert 1846–1931: 'Staunch Liberal and Nonconformist.'" *Journal of the Local Southampton History Forum* 22 (Spring 2014): 11–18.
Patten, Simon. *The New Basis of Civilization.* New York: Macmillan, 1907.
Patterson, A. Temple. *A History of Southampton 1700–1914*, vol. 3, *Setbacks and Recoveries, 1868–1914*. Southampton: University of Southampton, 1975.
Payn, James. *The Burnt Million.* London: Collins Clear Type, 1905.
———. "The Pinch of Poverty." *The Nineteenth Century* 7 (May 1880): 864–870.
Peachin, Michael. *The Oxford Handbook of Social Relations in the Roman World.* Oxford: Oxford University Press, 2011.
Pease, Jane Hanna. *Romance Novels, Romantic Novelist: Francis Marion Crawford.* Bloomington, IN: Author House, 2011.
Peterson, Linda. *Becoming a Woman of Letters: Myths of Authorship and Facts of the Victorian Market.* Princeton, NJ: Princeton University Press, 2009.
Pettersson, Torsten. "Att lara sig något av det som inte är sant: 72 gymnasister om fiktionellt och dokumentärt berättande [To learn from what is untrue: 72 senior high school students on fictional and documentary storytelling]." In *Litteraturen på undantag? Unga vuxnas fiktionsläsning i dagens Sverige*, edited by Skans Kersti Nilsson, Olle Nordberg, Torsten Pettersson, and Maria Wennerström Wohrne, 63–79. Göteborg: Makadam Forlag, 2015.
Pettifor, Ann. *The Production of Money: How to Break the Power of the Bankers.* London: Verso, 2017.
Pichois, Claude. "Pour une sociologie des faits littéraires : Les cabinets de lecture à Paris durant la première moitié du XIXe siècle." *Annales : économies, sociétés, civilisations* 14, no. 3 (J 1959): 521–534. www.persee.fr/doc/ahess_0395-2649_1959_num_14_3_2847.
Piketty, Thomas. *Capital in the Twenty-First Century.* Hoboken, NJ: Wiley, 2014.
Pilkington, John. "A Crawford Bibliography." *University of Mississippi Studies in English* 4 (1963): 1–20.
Pilkington, John. "F. Marion Crawford: Italy in Fiction." *American Quarterly* 6 (Spring 1954): 59–65.
———. *Francis Marion Crawford.* New York: Twayne, 1964.
Pilling, David. *The Growth Delusion: The Wealth and Well-Being of Nations.* London: Bloomsbury, 2018.
Platt, Colin. *Medieval Southampton: The Port and Trading Community, A.D. 1000–1600.* London: Routledge and Kegan Paul, 1973.

Plomer, Henry Robert. *A Dictionary of the Printers and Booksellers Who Were at Work in England, 1726–1775*. Oxford: Bibliographical Society for Oxford University Press, 1932.

Polyani, Karl. *The Great Transformation*. New York: Rinehart, 1944.

Potts, Jason, John Hartley, Lucy Montgomery, Cameron Neylon, and Ellie Rennie. "A Journal is a Club: A New Economic Model for Scholarly Publishing." *Prometheus* 35, no. 1 (2017): 75–92.

Preston, Richard. "The Development of Public Libraries in Southampton, 1887–1921." *Journal of the Southampton Local History Forum* 15 (2009): 1–20.

———. "A Precarious Business: The Skelton Family of Stationers, Printers, Publishers, Booksellers and Circulating Library Owners in Southampton and Havant c. 1781–c. 1865." *Journal of Southampton Local History Forum* 21 (2013): 3–14.

———. "'Pursuit of Knowledge under Difficulties': The Audit House Library, Southampton, 1831–63, and Winchester Library and Museum, 1851–63." *Journal of the Southampton Local History Forum*, 14 (2008): 1–22.

Price, Leah. *How to Do Things with Books in Victorian Britain*. Princeton, NJ: Princeton University Press, 2012.

Proctor, James, and Bethan Benwell. "Professional and Lay Readers." In *Reading Across Worlds: Transnational Book Groups and the Reception of Difference*, 9–50. Basingstoke, UK: Palgrave Macmillan, 2015.

———. *Reading Across Worlds: Transnational Book Groups and the Reception of Difference*. Basingstoke, UK: Palgrave Macmillan, 2015.

Quinn, Anthony. "Patrick Hamilton's Hangover Square and a Slide into the Abyss." *Guardian*, 6 August 2016. www.theguardian.com/books/2016/aug/06/patrick-hamilton-hangover-square-world-slide-abyss-rereading.

Radway, Janice. *Reading the Romance: Women, Patriarchy, and Popular Culture*. Chapel Hill: University of North Carolina Press, 1984.

Rainey, Lawrence. *Institutions of Modernism: Literary Elites and Public Culture*. Henry McBride Series in Modernism and Modernity. New Haven, CT: Yale University Press, 1998.

Rance, Adrian. *Southampton: An Illustrated History*. Portsmouth: Milestone, 1986.

———. *A Victorian Photographer in Southampton*. Southampton: Paul Cave, 1988.

Rapley, John. "Few Things Are as Dangerous as Economists with Physics Envy." AEON, 9 February 2018. https://aeon.co/ideas/few-things-are-as-dangerous-as-economists-with-physics-envy.

———. *Twilight of the Money Gods: Economics as a Religion and How It All Went Wrong*. London: Simon and Schuster, 2017.

Raven, James. *British Fiction 1750–1770: A Chronological Check List of Prose Fiction*. Newark: Delaware University Press, 1987.

———. *The Business of Books: Booksellers and the English Book Trade*. New Haven, CT: Yale University Press, 2007.

———. *Judging New Wealth*. Oxford: Oxford University Press, 1997.
———. *Publishing Business in Eighteenth-Century England*. Woodbridge, UK: Boydell Press, 2014.
Raworth, Kate. *Doughnut Economics: Seven Ways to Think Like a 21st Century Economist*. London: Random House Business, 2017.
Reeves, Maud Pember. *Round About a Pound a Week*. London: Bell and Sons, 1914.
Reiss, Stephen, and James Wiltz. "Why People Watch Reality TV." *Media Psychology* 6, no. 4 (2004): 363–378.
Reynolds, Kimberley. "Rewarding Reads? Giving, Receiving, and Resisting Evangelical Reward and Prize Books." In *Popular Children's Literature in Britain*, edited by Asa Briggs, Dennis Butts, and Mathew Grenby, 189–208. Abingdon, UK: Routledge, 2016.
Richards, Ivor Armstrong. *Principles of Literary Criticism*. International Library of Psychology, Philosophy, and Scientific Method. London: Routledge and Kegan Paul, 1959.
Richards, Thomas. *The Commodity Culture of Victorian England*. Stanford, CA: Stanford University Press, 1990.
Ridgway, Jim, and Michele Benjamin. *PsiFi: Psychological Theories and Science Fictions*. Leicester: British Psychological Society, 1987.
Robbins, Lionel. *An Essay on the Nature and Significance of Economic Science*. London: Macmillan, 1935.
Roberts, Kevin. *Lovemarks: The Future Beyond Brands*. New York: Powerhouse, 2007.
Rodensky, Lisa, ed. *The Oxford Handbook of the Victorian Novel*. Oxford: Oxford University Press, 2013.
Roede, Lars. *Byen bytter byggeskikk: Christiania 1624–1814*. Oslo: Arkitekthøgskolen, 2001.
Rooney, Paul. *Railway Reading and Late-Victorian Literary Series*. London: Routledge, 2018.
Rose, Jonathan. *The Intellectual Life of the British Working Classes*. New Haven, CT: Yale University Press, 2001.
Rose, Mark. "The Author as Proprietor: Donaldson vs. Becket and the Genealogy of Modern Authorship." *Representations* no. 23 (Summer 1988): 51–85.
Rosenblatt, Louise M. *Literature as Exploration*, rev. ed. New York: Noble and Noble, 1968.
———. *The Reader, the Text, and the Poem: The Transactional Theory of Literary Work*. Carbondale: Southern Illinois University Press, 1978.
Ross, Sean. "What Profit Margin is Usual for a Company in the Retail Sector?" *Investopedia*, 4 August 2019. http://www.investopedia.com/ask/answers/071615/what-profit-margin-usual-company-retail-sector.asp.
Rukavina, Alison. "Social Networks: Modelling the Transnational Distribution and Production of Books." In *Moveable Type, Mobile Nations*, edited by

Simon Frost and Robert Rix, 73–83. Angles on the English Speaking World 10. Copenhagen: Museum Tusculanum Press, 2010.

Salmon, Edward G. "What the Working Classes Read." *The Nineteenth Century* 20 (July 1886): 108–117.

Samson, Alain. *The Behavioral Economics Guide 2018* (introduction by Robert Cialdini). *Behavioraleconomics.com*, accessed 12 December 2019, www.behavioraleconomics.com/the-be-guide/.

———. "Introduction to Behavioral Economics." *Behavioraleconomics.com*, accessed 12 December 2019. www.behavioraleconomics.com/resources/introduction-behavioral-economics/.

Sarbin, Theodore. "The Narrative as the Root Metaphor for Contextualisation." In *Varieties of Scientific Contextualism*, edited by Linda Hayes, Steven Hayes, Hayne Reese, and Theodore Sarbin, 44–65. Reno, NV: Context Press, 1993.

Scheper-Huges, Nancy, and Loïc Wacquant, eds. *Commodifying Bodies*. London: Sage, 2002.

Schumacher, Ernst Freidrich. *Small is Beautiful: A Study of Economics as if People Mattered* London: Blond and Briggs, 1973.

Searle, John. *The Construction of Social Reality*. Harmondsworth, UK: Penguin, 1995.

Secord, James A. *Victorian Sensation: The Extraordinary Publication, Reception, and Secret Authorship of Vestiges of the Natural History of Creation*. Chicago: University of Chicago Press, 2003.

Sedo, DeNel Rehberg. "Reading Reception in the Digital Era." In *Oxford Research Encyclopedias*, June 2017. https://doi.org/10.1093/acrefore/9780190201098.013.285

Sedo, DeNel Rehberg, and Danielle Fuller. *Reading Beyond the Book: The Social Practices of Contemporary Literary Culture*. New York: Routledge, 2013.

Segal, Erwin. "Narrative Comprehension and the Role of Deictic Shift Theory." In *Deixis in Narrative: A Cognitive Science Perspective*, edited by Judith Duchan, Gail Bruder, and Lynne Hewitt, 3–17. Hillsdale, NJ: Lawrence Erlbaum, 1995.

Shaxson, Nicholas. *The Finance Curse: How Global Finance Is Making Us All Poorer*. London: The Bodley Head, 2018.

Shep, Sydney. "Books in Global Perspectives." In *The Cambridge Companion to the History of the Book*, edited by Leslie Howsam, 53–70. Cambridge: Cambridge University Press, 2015.

Sheppard, William Henry. *Presbyterian Pioneers in the Congo*. Richmond, VA: Presbyterian Committee of Publication, 1917. https://archive.org/details/presbyterianpion00shep/page/n3.

Showalter, Elaine. *A Literature of Their Own: British Women Novelists from Brontë to Lessing*. Princeton, NJ: Princeton University Press, 1997.

Simon, Herbert. "Theories of Bounded Rationality." In *Decision and Organization*, edited by Charles McGuire and Roy Radner, 161–176. Amsterdam: North-Holland Publishing, 1972.
Smith, John Frederick. *Stanfield Hall: Cromwell, or the Protector's Oath*. London: Bradley, 1889.
Smith, Yves. *ECONned: How Unenlightened Self-Interest Undermined Democracy and Corrupted Capitalism*. Basingstoke, UK: Palgrave Macmillan, 2010.
Snyder, Timothy. *Bloodlands: Europe between Hitler and Stalin*. New York: Basic Books, 2010.
Spackman, James, Katie Roden, and Peter McKay. "Get Over Yourself: There Is No Such Thing as 'The Reader.'" Panel, London Book Fair, 15 March 2017.
Spiers, John, ed. *The Culture of the Publisher's Series*, vol. 2, *Nationalisms and the National Canon*. Basingstoke, UK: Palgrave Macmillan, 2011.
Squires, Claire. *Marketing Literature: The Making of Contemporary Writing in Britain*. Basingstoke, UK: Palgrave Macmillan, 2007.
Squires, Claire, and Padmini Ray Murray. "The Digital Communications Circuit." In *The Book Unbound: Disruption and Disintermediation in the Digital Age*. University of Stirling, accessed 12 December 2019. www.bookunbound.stir.ac.uk/research/infographic/.
Standing, Guy. *The Corruption of Capitalism: Why Rentiers Thrive and Work Does Not Pay*. Hull, UK: 2017.
St. Clair, William. "The Political Economy of Reading." John Coffin Memorial Lecture in the History of the Book, rev. ed. Institute of English Studies, University of London, 2012. https://www.ies.sas.ac.uk/sites/default/files/files/Publications/StClair_PolEcReading_2012.pdf.
Steenberg, Mette. "Literary Reading as a Social Technology: An Exploratory Study of Shared Reading Groups." In *Plotting the Reading Experience*, edited by Lynne McKechnie, Kjell Ivar Skjerdingstad, Paulette M. Rothbauer, Knut Oterholm, and Magnus Persson, 183–198. Waterloo, Canada: Wilfrid Laurier University Press, 2016.
Stevenson, Robert Louis. "The Suicide Club." In *New Arabian Nights*, 3–86. New York: Henry Holt, 1882.
Stiglitz, Joseph. *The Price of Inequality*. London: Allen Lane, 2012.
Stobart, John. *Spend, Spend, Spend: A History of Shopping*. Stroud, UK: History Press, 2008.
Stobart, Jon, and Ilja van Damme, eds. *Modernity and the Second-Hand Trade: European Consumption Cultures and Practices 1700–1900*. Basingstoke, UK: Palgrave Macmillan, 2010.
Stockwell, Peter. *Texture: A Cognitive Aesthetics of Reading*. Edinburgh: Edinburgh University Press, 2009.

Stott, David. "The Decay of Bookselling." *The Nineteenth Century* 36, no. 214 (1894): 932–938.
Streeck, Wolfgang. *How Will Capitalism End? Essays on a Failing System*. London: Verso, 2016.
The Successful Bookseller: A Complete Guide to Success to All Engaged in a Retail Bookselling, Stationery, and Fancy Goods Business. London: Successful Bookselling Company, 1906.
Sutherland, John. *The Stanford Companion to Victorian Fiction*. Stanford, CA: Stanford University Press, 1989.
Svendsen, Gert Tingaard. *Tillid* [Trust]. Aarhus: Aarhus Universitetsforlag, 2012.
———. *Trust*. Aarhus: Aarhus Universitetsforlag, 2018.
Tamborini, Ron, Nicholas David Bowman, Allison Eden, Matthew Grizzard, and Ashley Organ. "Defining Media Enjoyment as the Satisfaction of Intrinsic Needs." *Journal of Communication* 60, no. 4 (2010): 758–777.
Tannenbaum, Percy. *The Entertainment Functions of Television*. Hillsdale, NJ: Erlbaum, 1980.
Tannenbaum, Percy, and Dolf Zillmann. "Emotional Arousal in the Facilitation of Aggression through Communication." In *Advances in Experimental Social Psychology*, vol. 8, ed. Leonard Berkowitz, 149–192. New York: Academic, 1975.
Taylor, Edward, and Patricia Cranton. *Handbook of Transformative Learning*. San Fransisco: Jossey-Bass, 2012.
Taylor, Robert. *Syntagma of the Evidences of the Christian Religion: Being a Vindication of the Manifesto of the Christian Evidence Society, against the Assaults of the Christian Instruction Society*. London: Dugdale, 1828.
Tennyson, Alfred. *The Death of Œnone, Akbar's Dream and Other Poems*. London: Macmillan, 1892.
Thaler, Richard. *Misbehaving: The Making of Behavioral Economics*. New York: W.W. Norton, 2015.
———. "Towards a Positive Theory of Consumer Choice." *Journal of Economic Behavior and Organization* 1, no. 1 (1980): 39–60.
Thelen, Kathleen. *Varieties of Liberalisation and the New Politics of Social Solidarity*. Cambridge: Cambridge University Press, 2014.
Thomas, Bronwen. "Whose Story Is It Anyway?" *Style* 51, no. 3 (2017): 357–373.
Thompson, Tierl, ed. *Dear Girl: The Diaries and Letters of Two Working Women 1897–1917*. London: The Women's Press, 1987.
Thorn, Henry. *Charles Dibdin: One of Southampton's Sons*. Southampton: Buxey, 1888.
Towheed, Shafquat, Rosalind Crone, and Katie Halsey, eds. *The History of Reading: A Reader*. Routledge Literature Readers. New York: Routledge, 2011.
Trentman, Frank. *Free Trade Nation*. Oxford: Oxford University Press, 2008.

Turner, Henry. *Respect Black: The Writings and Speeches of Henry McNeal Turner*. Edited by Henry Turner and Edwin Redkey. New York: Arno Press, 1971.
Tveterås, Harald. *Den Norske Bokhandels Historie*, vol. 1, *Forlag og bokhandel inntil 1850*. Oslo: Norsk Bokhandler-medhjælperforening, 1950.
Vanden Bossche, Chris R. *Carlyle and the Search for Authority*. Victorian Web, 26 October 2001. www.victorianweb.org/authors/carlyle/vandenbossche/preface.html.
Varoufakis, Yanis. *Talking to My Daughter about the Economy: A Brief History of Capitalism*. London: The Bodley Head, 2017.
The Victorian Slum. Episodes 1–5. Presented by Michael Mosley. Wall to Wall Media for BBC2, 2016. www.bbc.co.uk/programmes/b07zd454/episodes/guide.
Vorderer, Peter, and Franziska S. Roth. "How Do We Entertain Ourselves with Literary Texts?" *Scientific Study of Literature* 1, no. 1 (2011): 136–143.
Wagner, Tamara. "Emigration and 19th-Century British Colonial Settler Narratives." In *Oxford Research Encyclopedias*, February 2019. https://doi.org/10.1093/acrefore/9780190201098.013.944.
———, ed. *Victorian Settler Narratives: Emigrants, Cosmopolitans and Returnees in Nineteenth-Century Literature*. London: Pickering and Chatto, 2011.
Waits, Kentin. "Cheat Sheet: Retail Markup on Common Items." *Wisebread*, 15 December 2010. www.wisebread.com/cheat-sheet-retail-markup-on-common-items.
Wallerstein, Immanuel. "Household Structures and Labour Force Formation in the Capitalist World-Economy." In *Race, Nations, Class: Ambiguous Identities*, edited by Étienne Balibar and Immanuel Wallerstein, 2017–112. London: Verso, 1991.
Ward, Glenn. *Postmodernism*. Chicago: McGraw-Hill, 2004.
Warner, William. "Transmitting Liberty: The Boston Committee of Correspondence's Revolutionary Experiments in Enlightenment Mediation." In *This Is Enlightenment*, edited by William Warner and Clifford Siskin, 102–119. Chicago: University of Chicago Press, 2010.
Waters, Catherine. *Commodity Culture in Dickens's Household Words*. Aldershot, UK: Ashgate, 2008.
Watson, George. *Cambridge Bibliography of English Literature*, vol. 3. Cambridge: Cambridge University Press, 1966.
Webb, Sidney, and Beatrice Webb. *Industrial Democracy*. London: Longman, Green and Co. 1897.
Weedon, Alexis. "The Economics of Print." In *The Book: A Global History*, edited by Michael Suarez and Henry Woudhuysen, 154–168. Oxford: Oxford University Press, 2013.
———. *Victorian Publishing: The Economics and Book Production for a Mass Market, 1836–1916*. Aldershot, UK: Ashgate, 2003.

West, James. *American Authors and the Literary Marketplace Since 1900*. Philadelphia: University of Pennsylvannia Press, 1988.
Wharton, Edith, and Ogden Codman. *The Decoration of Houses*. New York: W.W. Norton, 1978.
Whiteley, Sara. "Text World Theory, Real Readers and Emotional Responses to *The Remains of the Day*." *Language and Literature* 20, no. 1 (2011): 23–42.
Wilk, Richard. "Morals and Metaphors: The Meaning of Consumption." In *Elusive Consumption*, edited by Karin Ekström and Helene Brembeck, 11–26. Oxford: Berg, 2004.
Williams, Rosalind. *Dream Worlds: Mass Consumption in Late Nineteenth-Century France*. Berkeley: University of California Press, 1991.
Willis, Ika, *Reception*. New Critical Idiom. London: Routledge, 2018.
Wilson, Charles. *First with the News: The History of W.H. Smith 1792–1972*. London: Jonathan Cape, 1985.
Wise, Thomas J. *A Bibliography of the Writings of Joseph Conrad 1895–1920*. 2nd ed. London: Dawsons, 1964.
Woodward, Ian. *Understanding Material Culture*. London: Sage, 2007.
Wright, David. "Book Retail." In *The Cultural Intermediaries Reader*, ed. Jennifer Maguire and Julian Matthews, 180–191. London: Sage, 2014.
Wright, Thomas. "Concerning the Unknown Public." *The Nineteenth Century* 13 (February 1883): 279–296.
You, Jong-Il, and Ha-Joon Chang. "The Myth of the Free Labour Market in Korea." *Contributions to Political Economy* 12, no. 1 (1993): 29–46. https://doi.org/10.1093/oxfordjournals.cpe.a035619.
Young, Debbie. "A Book is a Book: in Praise of the Argos Catalogue." *Debbie Young's Writing Life*, 3 March 2017. https://authordebbieyoung.com/2017/03/03/a-book-is-a-book-in-praise-of-the-argos-catalogue-reflections-on-childrens-reading-after-world-book-day-2017.
Zeldin, Theodore. *An Intimate History of Humanity*. London: Minerva, 1994.
Zillmann, Dolf, and Jennings Bryant. "Affect, Mood, and Emotion as Determinants of Selective Exposure." In *Selective Exposure to Communication*, ed. Dolf Zillmann and Jennings Bryant, 157–190. Hillsdale, NJ: Erlbaum, 1985.
Zillmann, Dolf, and Joanne Cantor, "A Disposition Theory of Humor and Mirth." In *Humor and Laughter: Theory, Research, and Applications*, ed. Anthony J. Chapman and Hugh Foot, 93–115. London: Wiley, 1976.
Zimmerman, Eilene. "Is it Ever OK to Sell (or Buy) a Kindney?" *Insights*, Stanford Business Graduate School, 13 March 2017. https://www.gsb.stanford.edu/insights/it-ever-ok-sell-or-buy-kidney.

Index

abolitionism, 260
academic publishing, 36
actor-network theory:
  overview, 249–50
  cis-narrative and, 262
  social dynamics and, 12, 22, 253, 290
  translation and, 251–52, 255, 291
  value and, 264
Adams, John, 130, 154, 156
Adorno, Theodor, 2, 268
advertising:
  gender and, 83
  Gilbert's and, 125, 167, 169–72, 176, 178
  lighting and, 119
  Mudie's and, 169–71, 178
  Successful Bookseller and, 125
  See also catalogues
airports, 320n5
alienation, 3, 272–73, 279
altruism, 4, 271
American Civil War, 195
anarchism, 108
Anderson, Benedict, 255
Anderson, Hephzibah, 243
Anne, Sarah, 151–52
anthropology, 194, 231, 246
Appadurai, Arjun, 30, 228
Arendt, Hannah, 21

Argentina, 77
Armitage, David, 11
Arnold, Matthew, 8, 45
Associated Booksellers, 49–50
Athletic News (magazine), 29
Atkinson, William, 89
auctions, 172
Audit House Library, 106
Austen, Jane, 138, 243, 324n10
Australia, 212
authenticity, 5, 81–82, 252
authority, 269
automobiles, 167

Badiou, Alain, 286
Bacon, Francis, 85
Bakunin, Mikhail, 268, 270, 276
Bal, Mieke, 256, 264
Barthes, Roland, 246
Bateson, Frederick, 111
baths, 102–3, 213
Baths Committee, 180
Batt, Robert, 145, 147
Baym, Nancy, 242
Baudrillard, Jean, 30, 228
Baumgarten, Alexander Gottlieb, 232
Becker, Gary, 4, 9, 271, 274, 286
beggars, 173
behavioral economics, 275, 278
Bell, Philip, 260

Bellamy, Edward, 207
Benwell, Bethan, 7
Berne Convention, 100
Bernhardt, Sarah, 85
bestsellers, 42, 51, 233, 248, 251–52, 281
Bevis, 142
Bibliotheca Hantoniensis, 180, 182
bibliotherapy, 242–43
bicycles, 200, 202, 216
Bigg, James, 49, 51
binding, 138, 144, 147–50, 175
Blackhall, William, 145, 164
Blackwood's (publishing firm), 58–59
Blackwood's Magazine, 89, 214
Blitz, 12, 114, 129–30, 151, 313n5
Bloom, Clive, 42, 51
Bloom, Harold, 6
Book History (journal), 46
Book Marketing Ltd (BML), 235
Book War (1905), 50
Bookseller (magazine), 50
Booksellers' Association, 49–50
Booth, Charles, 63
Borghi, Maurizio, 99
Børsch, Mariane, 232
Bortolussi, Marisa, 23–24
Bourdieu, Pierre, 31, 277
Braddon, Mary Elizabeth, 66
Brewster, Liz, 233
Brier, Evan, 277
Brinton, George, 103
Britain:
    capitalism and, 28, 75
    currency of, 307n11
    demographics of, 68–69
Broadbere's, 147–48, 175, 262
Brun, Frederick Jacobsen, 148
Budden, William, 156
Burgess, Anthony, 225
Burke, Kathy, 257–58

Butler, Judith, 239
Buxey, George, 140, 150–51
Byatt, A.S., 252
Bywater, L.J., 163

Callon, Michel, 290
Cambridge Bibliography of English Literature, 46, 49, 111
Cameron, David, 276
Campbell, Colin, 6, 265
Campbell, John, 49–51
campus bookshops, 113
Canal Walk, 131
Capes, Bernard, 214
capitalism:
    Britain and, 28, 75
    forms of, 35–36
    gender and, 83
    spectacles, of 27, 100
    See also commodity culture; economics
Carlyle, Thomas, 49
cars, 167
catalogues, 126, 144–45, 169, 182, 289
Cawte, George William, 149
Cawte, H.G., 149
Cawte's (binder), 175, 262
Caxton's Steam Printing Office, 143
Chang, Ha-Joon, 4, 37, 44, 271
Chapman, John, 49
Chase, Karen, 252
Chicago, 271
children's reading culture, 236, 238, 241
Christian Knowledge Society, 138
Chubb, Percival, 52
Church Book Depot, 139
cis-history, 11, 236
civic markets, 55
Civil War (American), 195
Clarke, Alison, 126

Clover, Joshua, 3, 285
Coates, A.H., 111
Cobden Bridge, 157
Colclough, Stephen, 46, 78
Cole, Francis Sewell, 182
Coleridge, John D., 51
collectives, 22
Collins, Wilkie, 59–61, 65–66, 254, 285
colonialism, 89
colporteurs, 42, 131, 136
commodity culture:
   overview, 27–29
   classical economics and, 189
   entertainment and, 247–48, 254
   geography of, 239
   homo narrans and, 288
   networks and, 264
   spectacle and, 100
   symbolic value and, 225
communications circuits, 184–85
Congo, 216, 261, 332n51
Conrad, John, 8
Conrad, Joseph, 8, 79–80, 82–83, 85–91
consumption, 21, 54, 223–25, 287, 292
Cook, Benjamin, 170, 183
Cooper, Fenimore, 86
copyists, 99
copyright, 44, 99
Corke, H.C., 145
Corp, William, 112
corporate bookstores, 53
Cox and Sharland (bookseller), 143–44, 176, 183
Cox, Gordon, 150
Cox, Henry Daubney, 149–50
Cox, James, Charles, 143–44
Crawford, Francis Marion, 79–82, 83–88, 91, 197, 213

credit, 123–25, 163–64, 174, 207, 258
Crimean War, 260
Crusoe, Robinson, 22
Crystal Palace, 27
Culler, Jonathan, 256
cultural capital, 31, 51, 53–54
cultural value, 42–43, 45, 52–55, 263, 289, 291
culture industry, 2
currency, 307n11
cycling, 29, 200, 202, 216

Dale, William, 182
Darnton, Robert, 184
database projects, 235
Davis, Albert H., 103
Davis, Dorothy, 39–40
Debenhams, 160, 325n33
Debord, Guy, 27, 100
debt, 124, 163, 165, 258, 292
De Man, Paul, 269
Deleuze, Gilles, 248
Dell (stadium), 78, 288
Demarco, Eileen, 46
depression, 65, 101, 192, 273, 319n25
deregulation, 258, 263, 292
Derrida, Jacques, 38, 255
Dibdin, Charles, 150
Dickens, Charles, 244
dispossession, 54, 273
Dixon, Peter, 23–24
Dolfsma, Wilfred, 224, 229
domain models, 3
Domoney, Charles, 142, 262
Donaldson *vs.* Beckett, 99
Douglass, Frederick, 217, 260
Doyle, Conan, 51, 213
Du Bois, W.E.B., 261
DuPuis, Malanie, 55

Dyer, Alfred, 141

economics:
  behavioral, 275, 278
  classical, 189
  domain model of, 3
  politics and, 17, 283, 285, 291–92
  sustainable, 45
  trickle-down, 35, 270
  See also neoclassical economics; neoliberalism; and specific topics
Education Act (1870), 103
Edwards, Celestine, 217
Edwards, F.E., 180
efferent reading, 24–27, 32–33, 71, 109, 225–26
electricity, 119, 167
Eliot, George, 8, 58–59, 83, 252, 254
Emmerson, Charles, 77
emotions, 52, 231–34, 241–42, 272, 274
empathy, 3, 238, 244
enclosures, 3
English, James, 277
English Street, 74
entertainment:
  overview, 228–32
  commodity culture and, 247–48, 254
  surveys and, 235, 241–42
  thick description and, 223, 245–46
epistemophilia, 242
Epsom Derby, 253
Erickson, Lee, 281–82
experience goods, 178

fairness, 75, 268, 274–75
Feather, John, 52
Felski, Rita, 5–7
femininity, 67–68, 83, 90–91, 226
feminism, 239, 252

Fetterley, Judith, 31
feudalism, 75
financial crash (2008), 192, 273
Financial Times, 271
financialization, 4–5
fire, 119, 145, 147, 161–64
Fisher Walter R., 225
Fleming, Peter, 273
Fletcher, Isaac, 143
Flynt, Josiah, 61
football (soccer), 10, 29, 78, 141, 156, 200, 288
Ford, Thomas, 98
Foucault, Michel, 9, 193
framing, 254–58, 282, 290–91
Frankfurt School, 8
  See also specific authors
Fraser, William Hamish, 101
free markets:
  open-access publishing and, 36
  organ trade and, 272
  regulation of, 37, 43–45, 51, 55, 263, 270
  self-interest and, 54–55
  welfare and, 35
  See also neoclassical economics; neoliberalism; regulation
Freedmen's Bureau, 261
freedom, 95, 258, 285–86, 292
  See also free markets
French Street, 74
Friedman, Milton, 270, 271
Frow, John, 2, 91, 276
Frye, Northrop, 228–29
Fuller, Daneille, 232, 233

Gaiman, Neil, 244
gambling, 164, 199, 330n17
García Lorca, Federico, 259
Garden Cities, 207
Gardner, Eric, 260
Garvey, Marcus, 261

gas-and-water socialism, 102, 109, 184, 253, 290
Geertz, Clifford, 194, 231, 246, 264
Gell-Mann, Murray, 76
gender, 83, 90, 138
  See also femininity; feminism, masculinity; women
George Buxey's (bookstore), 130
George, Henry, 96, 209–10
Gerard, Linn, 10
ghost stories, 80, 87–89, 197
Giddens, Anthony, 26
Gilbert, Bruce, 171
Gilbert, Henry, 170
Gilbert, Henry March:
  marriage of, 327n10
  politics and, 105–6, 178–80
  public libraries and, 290
  religious activities of, 170, 180–82
  See also Gilbert's
Gilbert, Owen, 170–71, 174, 199
Gilbert, Richard, 130, 171
Gilbert's (bookshop):
  advertising for, 169–70, 172, 176
  bookbinding and, 175
  library of, 169, 177–78, 198, 204
  networks and, 176, 180, 183–85
  online shopping and, 171
  publishing and, 180–85, 142
  religious books and, 139
  secondhand books and, 125, 169–73, 175, 184
  stability of, 165
  theft and, 174
Gladstone, William, 49
Glasgow Booksellers' Protection Association, 49
Glazzard, Andrew, 8
Godwin, George Nelson, 180, 182
Goffman, Erving, 256
Graeber, David, 224, 287
Gray, Peter, 113

Great Depression, 101, 319n25
Great Dock Strike (1890), 102, 106–9, 290
greed, 45
Gregg, S.J., 183
Griffith, George W., 108, 208–9, 290
guidebooks, 117, 140, 148
Guillory, John, 7
Gutch, Thomas, 143–44, 262

Hack, Daniel 259, 261
Hall, Peter A., 35–36, 37, 38
Halpern, David, 276
Halsey, Katie, 243
Hamburg, 64–65
Hamilton, Patrick, 257
Hammond, Mary, 46
Hampshire Chronicle, 97–98
Hampshire Field Club and Archeology Society, 182
Hampshire Independent, 141
Haraway, Donna, 247
Harle, Irvine, 138
Harris, James, 172
Hartley Institute, 103–6, 181, 182
Harvey, David, 271, 273
Hawkins, Paula, 251
Hayek, Friedrich, 271
Hazelton, Cora, 156
Hazelton, William, 156
hedonism, 229–32
Heinlein, Robert, 227
Hemingway, Ernest, 259
Henry II, William, 160
hermeneutics, 5, 189
Higginbotham, Peter, 62
Higgins, Edward T., 32, 227–28
High Street, 74–77, 138, 323n3
Hill, Beatrice, 123
homo economicus, 13, 22, 226–27, 274, 287–88

homo narrans, 193, 225–27, 244–45, 263, 288
Horkheimer, Max, 2
horror, 87–89, 230
horses, 167, 201, 204–5, 253
Howard, Ebenezer, 206
Howard, Oliver, 262
Huggin, Graham, 247
Huyssen, Andreas, 90

Ibárruri, Dolores
identity, 24–27, 30–31, 226, 255
    See also self-discrepancy theory
imagined communities, 255
income, 101, 106, 131–32
    See also wages
individualism, 22, 30, 226, 228
industrialization, 28, 38, 42, 51, 64–65, 96, 207
infant mortality, 132
intangible goods, 58, 121, 223, 225, 288
intellectual property, 98, 99–100
intentionality, 30–31
interpretive anthropology, 231, 246
intertextuality, 226–27, 250, 281–83, 287
investment, 41–42, 162, 165
invisible hand, 191, 274, 309n34
Irish Famine, 101
Ishiguro, Kazuo, 234
Itchen River, 157

Jackson, Tim, 29–30, 31
James, Henry, 108
James, Thomas, 106, 151–52, 199, 262
James, Thomas Hibberd, 147, 148, 152, 178
James, William, 26
Jameson, Fredric, 8

Jauss, Iser, 230
Jensen, Marie Hauge, 242–43
Jevons, William Stanley, 11, 189–93, 210, 278, 287
    See also marginalism
John Smith's (bookshop), 113, 181
Jones, Edwin, 159–60, 179
Jones, Eustace Hinton, 142, 151–52, 156, 183

Kahneman, Daniel, 274–75
Keen, Steven, 273
Kenyon, Max, 45
Keynes, John Maynard, 22, 270
Khair, Tabish, 87
King, Henry, 60
Kingsland, 103
Kingsland Tavern, 105
Kipling, Rudyard, 79–83, 85–88, 91, 197, 213–14
Knight, E.H., 144
Knight, Lynn, 115
Knowles, Sir James, 60
Koritz, Amy, 83
Kruger, Barbara, 25

Labour Party, 107
labour-saving technology, 209–10
Lackington, James, 100
Lane, Allen, 42
Langdon-Davies, Bernard, 116, 121, 125
Latour, Bruno, 249, 251
Law, Graham, 156–57
Law, John, 249
Le Guin, Ursula K., 23
Ledbetter, Kathryn, 168
leisure, 7, 28–29, 78–80
Lemon, Sir James, 180
Leopold (king of Belgium), 216, 332n51

Liberal Association, 159
libraries:
    advertising for, 125
    bookshops and, 122–23, 130, 145, 172, 235
    NBA and, 169
    private, 43, 161
    public, 35, 103–6, 156, 180
    records of, 58
    ships and, 197–98
    social relations and, 289
    See also specific libraries
Library (journal), 46
Licensing Act, 97
life stories, 227
Linde, Charlotte, 227
Linden, James, 97–98
Lindner, Christoph, 28
literary criticism, 2, 5, 16, 248, 267–69, 285
Littau, Karin, 226, 258
Livingstone, David, 77
Lodge, David, 234, 242
London Dockers' strike (1889), 107
London Bookseller's Society, 50
London Journal, 69
London, Jack, 62–64
loneliness, 242–43
Long Depression, 101, 319n25
love, 30, 80–81, 286, 315n38
Love, Heather, 4
Lovell, Frank, 115
Low, Sampson, 49
Lukács, György, 27
luxury, 79
Lyne, George Alma, 141
Lyons, Martin, 9

Macklin, Charles, 256–57
MacLane, Mary, 109, 202–3, 204, 290

Macmillan Company, 84–85
Macmillan, Frederick, 50, 85
mafia novels, 81, 197
Mandelbrote, Giles, 46
Manguel, Alberto, 255, 258
Marçal, Katrine, 274, 286
Marcuse, Herbert, 268–69
marginalism, 279–82
market governance, 55
    See also regulation
market society, 75, 83, 91
marketization, 1–2, 4
markets:
    civic, 55
    culture and, 288
    history of, 75
    knowledge and, 191–92
    networks and, 264, 282–83
    rational-choice and, 189–90, 192–93, 274
    See also specific topics
Marryat, Frederick, 86
Marshall, Alfred, 189
Martial (Marcus Valerius Martialis), 99
Marxism, 224, 259, 268, 279
masculinity, 82–83, 86, 89–91, 226, 239
Maslow, Abraham, 230
mass media, 9, 230
mass reading events, 233
materialism, 6
Maudlin, Daniel, 250
Mayhew, Henry, 63
Mays, Jim, 256
Mazzini, Giuseppe, 268
McCloskey, Deirdre, 24–25, 33, 101, 225, 288
McFadden, Frank, 147, 182
McGann, Jerome, 23
Mearne, Andrew, 64

memory, 227
Mendicity Society, 173
mercantilism, 278
metaphors, 24, 45, 224, 286
Miller, Andrew, 100
Miller, Henry, 226
Miller, Laura, 53–54
Mirowski, Philip, 271
Mitchell, Ian, 126, 173
modernization, 80, 82, 168
Moi, Toril, 268–69
Mont Pelerin Society, 4, 271
Moore, Harry, 160
Morely and Sons, 172
Moreton, William Robert, 141
Morgan, John Tyler, 332n51
Mudie, Charles Edward, 167
Mudie's (bookstore), 48, 169, 178
Mumby, Frank, 45–46
municipal socialism, 102, 109, 184, 253, 290
Murray, Padmini Ray, 184

Naper, Cecile, 233
narratives, 193–94, 290
  See also stories
Nashville (ship), 195
Nealon, Christopher, 3, 285
neoclassical economics:
  debates in, 270
  methodology of, 15, 271, 189–91, 223, 232
  pleasure and, 11, 26–27, 32
  reductionism of, 17, 276–77
  subjectivity and, 279–80, 288
  symbolic goods and, 245, 286
neoliberalism:
  dispossession and, 54, 273
  fiction and, 270
  reductionism of, 3–4
  regulation and, 44
  symbolic goods and, 286

Net Book Agreement (NBA):
  overview, 43
  challenges to, 45, 50
  cultural value and, 55, 263, 289
  libraries and, 67, 161, 169
  stability and, 111
  underselling and, 47–48, 50–51, 309n34
Net Works, 251–5, 257–9, 262, 264, 292
networks:
  benefits of, 117
  commodity culture and, 264
  credit and, 124–25
  dynamics of, 132, 248
  Gilbert's and, 176, 180, 183–85
  markets and, 282–83
  shipping, 10
  society and, 285
  value and, 127, 292
  See also actor-network theory
New Unionism, 107
newspapers, 141, 172
  See also specific publications
Nineteenth Century (journal), 60–61
Nobel Prize, 341n13
nostalgia, 252, 253
Nordic regions, 239
Norrie, Ian, 45, 46
Northam bridge, 157
Nussbaum, Martha, 244

Oldfield, John, 98
Ong, Walter, 52
online shopping, 42, 113, 171
open-access publishing, 36
oral culture, 52
organ trade, 3, 272
Orrell, David, 273
Oswald, Thomas, 101–2
Ouida (Maria Louise Ramé), 70, 196, 201

overstocking, 114, 116

Palmer, Thomas, 174
pandemic, 160
paper, 38, 120, 131
paperbacks, 42, 52
passion, 80
paternalism, 276
patriarchy, 83
Patten, Simon, 28
Payn, James, 66–67, 70, 195–99
pecia system, 253
Peel, Robin, 250
Peet, William, 46
Penguins (paperbacks), 52
Pennell, Joseph, 85
penny-journals, 60, 61, 65–71
penny post, 154
Pettifor, Ann, 273
Philips, George, 140
photography, 152
physiocrats, 278
Pichois, Claude, 242, 250
Pilkington, John, 81, 84
Pitt, Captain G.F., 103
Platt, Colin, 74
poetry, 25
political economy, 17, 283, 285, 291–92
Pollet's Advertising Agency, 121–22
pollution, 3
Pope, Alexander, 3
population, 131
populism, 8
Portland Street, 138
Portland Street Baptist Chapel, 180
Post-Crash Economic Society, 306n2
postboxes, 154
potboilers, 5
poverty, 14, 96, 106, 195–96, 210
   See also slums
power, 9, 53, 124, 249–50, 253, 258

Pratchett, Terry, 5
Preston, Richard, 103, 105
Price, Leah, 2, 267
prices:
   calculation of, 39–40
   fixing, 47–50, 75
   libraries and, 177
   narratives and, 290
   political-economy of, 291
   production and, 38
   See also Net Book Agreement
print-on-demand, 114, 148, 171
printing presses, 97
prisons, 165, 227
Proctor, James, 7
Project SKRIN, 235–39, 241–42
profits, 39–43
Public Libraries Act (1855), 103
Publishers' Association, 50
publishing, 36, 184
   See also specific publishers

quantification, 277–78

radio, 9
Radway, Janice, 57, 233
railway stations, 130
Rainey, Lawrence, 277
Randle, Alfred, 142
Rapley, John, 76
rational-choice model, 189–90, 192–93, 270, 274, 276
Raven, James, 97, 99
Rayner, Charles, 139–40, 143
Rayner, Charlotte, 140, 143, 150
Rayner, John, 139–40, 161, 162, 183
Reading Fiction in the Internet Society, 235
realism 193, 238, 243
reception theory, 22–23, 230
recession, 65, 101, 192, 273, 319n25
Reeve, Maud Pember, 64

regulation, 37–38, 43–45, 124, 270
    See also deregulation; Net Book
        Agreement
Religious Tract Society, 142
reprints, 44, 59, 67
REST (Recreation, Entertainment,
    Sports, and Tourism), 77–78
Reynolds, George W.M., 69
Richards, Thomas, 27
Ricoeur, Paul, 227
risk, 58, 162
Robbins, Lionel, 270–71
Robert Batt and Co., 164
Rogers, Mary Anne, 156
romanticism, 80
Rome, 99
Rose, Jonathan, 27
Rose, Mark, 99
Rosenblatt, Louise, 24–25, 26, 236
Roth, Franziska, 230–31, 232
Rukavina, Alison, 248
Rydill's Book Shop, 119

Saints (Southampton Football Club),
    78, 156, 200, 288
Sala, George Augustus, 71
Salmon, Edward, 69–70
sanitation, 103, 180
Saturday Night (magazine), 29
scarcity, 190–91, 277, 280–81
Schopenhauer, Johanna, 100
science, 206
Scott, Sir Walter, 66
Seamen's Union, 106
Searle, John, 30–31
secondhand books:
    binding of, 38, 148, 175, 262
    Gilbert's and, 125, 169–73, 175,
        184
    informal economy of, 131
Secret Ballot Act, 178
Sedo, DeNel Rehberg, 23, 232, 233

self-discrepancy theory, 32–33,
    227–28
self-interest, 54–55, 191, 228, 267,
    275–76, 278
self-publishing, 184
self-reflexivity, 7
semiotics, 193, 225, 246, 248, 256,
    287
Shakespeare, William, 256–57
Sharland, William, 144
Shaw, Bernard, 51
Shep, Sydney, 184, 247
Sheppard, William Henry, 216
shipbuilding, 101
shipping, 10
situated knowledges, 247
Shore, Thomas William, 182
Simon, Herbert, 192
Simpkin Marshall (wholesaler), 114
slavery, 3, 75, 260–62
slums, 64–65, 311n19
Smiles, Samuel, 254
Smith, Adam, 22, 189, 191, 274,
    278, 286
Smith, Adolphe, 131
Smith, Gerrit, 260
Smith, James, McCune (Communipaw),
    260–61
Smith, John Frederick, 71
Smith, Thomas, 174
Smith, W.H., 96
soccer, 10, 29, 78, 141, 156, 200,
    288
social identity theory, 31
socialism, 102, 109, 184, 253, 290
Society for the Promotion of
    Christian Knowledge (SPCK),
    62, 138
Society of Authors, 50
sociology, 4, 193, 248, 249, 277
Soskice, David, 35–36, 37, 38
Sotonopedia, 129

Southampton, 10–11, 64–65, 73–77, 184, 322n1
　See also specific topics
Southampton Annual, 148
Southampton Book Society, 144–45, 161, 162, 173
Southampton Borough Council, 178
Southampton City Archives, 129
Southampton Corporation, 102, 103
Southampton Football Club (The Saints), 78, 156, 200, 288
Southampton Society for Mutual Education, 151–52
Southampton University, 181
Southamptonian (journal), 10, 148, 262
Southern Daily Echo, 141, 169, 199
Spain, 259
spectacle, 27, 100
Speed, John, 183
Spencer Esq., Herbert, 51
sports, 29
Squires, Claire, 184
St. Clair, William, 57
St. Mary's library, 105–6
St. Michael's Improvements, 102
St. Petersburg, 28
Stalin, Joseph, 259
Stanesby, Mary Emma, 327n10
stationers, 129
stealing, 174
Steenberge, Mette, 233
Stella (ship), 156
Stobart, Jon, 171
Stockwell, Peter, 234
Stoneham, John Edmund, 48
Stoneham's (bookstore), 48, 50
stories, 23, 226
　See also ghost stories; narratives
Stott, David, 112
street directories, 129
strikes, 102, 106–9, 290

subjectivity, 279–81, 288
Successful Bookseller, 111–12, 114, 117–26
supply and demand, 190–91, 232, 267, 270
surveys, 39, 64, 233, 235–42
sustainable economics, 45
Sutherland, John, 70
Svendsen, Gert, 272
symbolic goods/value:
　consumption of, 224–26, 228, 278–79
　culture and, 109
　efferent reading and, 189, 193, 225–26, 228
　homo narrans and, 226, 244–45, 288
　masculinity and, 90
　mediation of, 30
　neoliberalism and, 286
　networks and, 127
　rational-choice and, 192–93, 224
　socialization and, 281
Synge, E.H., 148

Tablet (journal), 47, 48
Tamborini, Ron, 230, 246
Tarro, M.P., 174–75
telephones, 145, 330n23
Tennyson, Alfred, 60, 168, 218–19, 259–62
textbooks, 113
Thatcher, Margaret, 249
theft, 174
thick description, 223, 231, 245–46
third place, 113
Thomson, John, 131
Tiller, Ben, 107
Times Book Club, 50
Tolstoy, Leo, 207
Topographical Publishing Company, 148, 205, 262

tourism, 140
Town and Country Book Society, 145
tramps, 61–62, 131
transactional theory, 236–38
translation, 251–53, 255, 259, 291
transportation theory, 231–32
trickle-down economics, 35, 270
Trollope, Anthony, 254
trust, 117, 272, 286, 342n21
Tversky, Amos, 274
typewriters, 142
typists, 142–43

underselling, 47, 49–51, 173
unions, 108, 130–31, 207–8
unknown public, 59–61, 66–71, 95, 194, 254, 288
US National Council of Teachers, 52
utility, 271, 275, 277, 280–81, 287

vagrants, 61–62, 131
van Damme, Ilja, 171
Varoufakis, Yanis, 75
Virtue, James Sprent, 141
volatility, 95
Vorderer, Peter, 230–31, 232

W.H. Smith and Sons, 160
wages, 63–65, 67
  See also income
war, 50, 195, 260
  See also Blitz
Ward, Ellen, 203
Ward, Glenn, 255
Watkins, C., 177

Wedgewood, Josiah, 100
weekends, 28–29
Weeks, Frank, 161–64
welfare, 35, 165
Wells, H.G., 51, 115, 208, 253
Westminster All Party Parliamentary Writers Group, 36
Wharton, Edith, 226
Whiteley, Sara, 233–34
wholesalers, 114, 122, 321n9
Wigram, Edward, 139
Wigram, Rev. Frederick Edward, 139
Williams, Rosalind, 21
Willis, Ika, 3, 23, 227, 269
window displays, 118–20, 152
Wise, John, 97–98
women:
  bookbinding and, 138, 149
  copying services and, 142–43
  periphery and, 157
  representations of, 257–58
  surveys of, 238–39
  unions and, 108
  writers, 82–83
  See also femininity; feminism; gender; and specific women
Women's Emigration Society, 212
Woodward, Bernard Bolingbroke, 183
workhouses, 62–64, 165, 311n19
Wright, David, 53
Wright, Thomas, 59–61, 66–68, 70–71, 289

Yonge, Charlotte, 203
Young, Debbie, 126
Young, George, 175

www.ingramcontent.com/pod-product-compliance
Lightning Source LLC
Chambersburg PA
CBHW020217240426
43672CB00006B/341